WOLF-WOMEN

and

PHANTOM LADIES

SUNY series in Feminist Criticism and Theory

Michelle A. Massé, editor

WOLF-WOMEN
and
PHANTOM LADIES

Female Desire in 1940s US Culture

STEVEN DILLON

Published by State University of New York Press, Albany

Printed in the United States of America

For information, contact State University of New York Press, Albany, NY
www.sunypress.edu

Production, Eileen Nizer
Marketing, Anne M. Valentine

Library of Congress Cataloging-in-Publication Data

Dillon, Steven, 1960–
Wolf-Women and Phantom Ladies : Female Desire in 1940s US Culture / Steven Dillon.
pages cm. — (SUNY series in Feminist Criticism and Theory)
Includes bibliographical references and index.
ISBN 978-1-4384-5579-2 (hc : alk. paper)—978-1-4384-5580-8 (pb : alk. paper)
ISBN 978-1-4384-5581-5 (e-book)
1. American literature—20th century—History and criticism. 2. Women in literature. 3. Desire in literature. 4. Women in popular culture. 5. Women—Sexual behavior—Psychological aspects. I. Title.

PS173.W6D55 2015
810.9'352042—dc23 2014020287

10 9 8 7 6 5 4 3 2 1

To the Bangor Public Library

Contents

Acknowledgments

The digital universe has greatly aided my research. Cartoons, educational films, B-movies, and popular songs that would have been hard to track down ten years ago can often be found on YouTube. Google's archived newspapers and magazines supplied numerous key examples. A spectacularly useful source for all things 1940s, the Internet Archive (www.archive.org) helped especially with radio programs and radio magazines. J. David Goldin's RadioGoldindex (radiogoldindex.com), although necessarily incomplete, provides an extremely helpful searchable archive. My complete run of *Tiger Girl* in *Fight Comics* came from *The Digital Comic Museum* (digitalcomicmuseum.com); thanks very much!

Of course the world has not yet been completely digitized. Many of my 1940s magazines were purchased at a local antiques shop, *Little Orphan Annie's*, from Dan Poulin, who gave me a square deal each and every time. As far as source material goes, my greatest debt is to the Bangor Public Library, who sent Bates College hundreds of items from their enormous collection of 1940s popular books. No other Maine library—academic or otherwise—comes close to this collection, and I'm not sure how I would have completed this study without their willingness both to keep these books and then to send them out.

Thanks very much to the SUNY Press readers, who gave of their time to read a long manuscript and whose excellent suggestions I have incorporated. I have also benefitted from editorial advice offered by Beth Bouloukos. Over the years I have received needed encouragement from Kathy Williamson and Liz Dillon.

1

Introduction

Sexual Visibility, or, The Duel in the Sun

Red Riding Hood: What big eyes you have, Grandma.

The Wolf: All the better to see you with, my dear.

1940s culture became an increasingly visual culture, a culture more interested in pictures and less in words. Television does not make an impact until the end of the decade, but magazines, all along, point in that direction.[1] The heightened emphasis on photographs in *Life* magazine would make it one of the most popular magazines of the period. A 1943 *Harper's* article surveyed "The Picture Magazines"; what distinguished the recent magazines—*Life*, *Look*, and *Click*—from older publications such as the *Illustrated London News* was that the newer magazines ran "picture stories," where photographs did most of the work, and the text was reduced to captions.[2] Throughout the 1940s "picture stories" could be found everywhere, regardless of whether the magazine was a picture magazine. *Coronet* offered both a "picture story" and a "picture gallery," while radio magazines would summarize plots with a sequence of pictures in order to turn the radio show into a miniature movie.[3] Pictures tell the story better than words.

In the 1944 essay "Why 100,000,000 Americans Read Comics," William Moulton Marston, an academic psychologist as well as the creator of *Wonder Woman*, justified his own excursion into comic books. People just understand things better, he says, when they can look at pictures. "Eight or nine people out of ten get more emotional 'kick' out of seeing a beautiful girl on the stage, the screen, or the picture-magazine page displaying her charms in person, or via camera or artist's pen, than they derive from verbal substitutes describing her compelling charms. It's too bad for us 'literary' enthusiasts, but it's the truth nevertheless—pictures tell any story more effectively than words."[4]

Here Marston usefully links the emergence of 1940s visual culture to 1940s sexual culture.[5] The argument is not logical, but in the way that it willfully manipulates sex and the female body, the argument is characteristic of the period. In a figurative leap, Marston says that "any story" is equivalent to a "beautiful girl . . . displaying her charms." This way he can win the argument—just like the late paperback that uses its cover to seduce a purchaser—by emphasizing sexual "oompf," an "emotional kick." It is a hugely illogical argument since many stories—about the way that bats hear or the rules of canasta—will not have much "emotional kick."[6] But logic is not the point; this debate is won by frankness. The war has made everyone franker, less euphemistic. Pictures get to the heart of the matter and so does sex.

An equally characteristic example of 1940s sexual visibility occurs in a book called *The Technique of the Picture Story: A Practical Guide to the Production of Visual Articles* (1945). This purports to be a textbook for the visually oriented future of journalism; in practice, it uses examples from *Look* and *Life* in order to make those articles seem as sophisticated, educational, and artistic as possible.[7] Their textbook analysis of a photograph of Gary Cooper and Ingrid Bergman in passionate embrace runs as follows: "The impact of this picture is unquestionable. It is the age-old impact of sex, made both violent and attractive by Ingrid Bergman and Gary Cooper in Warner Brothers' *Saratoga Trunk*. No successful modern magazine ignores the reader appeal in sex, but the responsible ones avoid dealing with it objectionably and try to contribute their share of reliable, scientific, and much-needed sex information."[8]

Marston compared the "emotional kick" of any picture story to a sexy woman on display; here is a picture of sex, full of "impact," "the age-old impact of sex." The textbook authors bring sex forward as both a traditional ("age-old") and a practical concern. This is a commercial enterprise after all; they intend to sell magazines, and "no successful modern magazine ignores the reader appeal in sex." Yet even though sex comes with a bang (a kick, an impact) and is there primarily to make money, the textbook authors still imagine themselves entirely in control, on exactly the right side of morality ("the responsible ones avoid dealing with it objectionably"), while providing scientific and educational contexts. The picture textbook authors, such as Marston the comic-defending psychologist, think that they can *see* everything. Journalism, science, and commerce combine perfectly to bring us sex, right there before our eyes.

But what does this sex look like? Ingrid Bergman looks up at Gary Cooper—or she would look if her eyes were not closed. Gary Cooper grimaces, his left hand spread out over Bergman's face and throat. The caption has the right idea: "It is the age-old impact of sex, made both violent and attractive by Ingrid Bergman and Gary Cooper." In fact, the adjectives map onto Bergman and Cooper respectively; she looks "attractive" and he looks "violent." Yet the "violence" of sex does not bother the scientific, educating authors, even though they are apparently the "responsible" people who try not to treat sex "objectionably." It is understood—scientifically and realistically—that sex is both violent and attractive. In specific, male sexuality is violent, aggressive; in the language of the times, it is "wolfish." This is just a given; hence there is nothing objectionable. By contrast, female desire is more mysterious, much harder to see. Ingrid Bergman looks beautiful, but what does she want? She consents to Gary Cooper's *visible* desire.

These two examples bring us to this book's main question. In a period overwhelmed by visible examples of male sexual desire, what does female sexual desire look like? If male sexual desire is imaged as "natural," "aggressive," or "wolfish," what images are attached to female sexual desire? If men are allowed their wolfishness—and how can they help themselves—how does society view the sexually aggressive woman, the she-wolf? For if female sexual desire becomes visible, then the woman potentially becomes pathological, oversexed, a nymphomaniac. And if female sexual desire stays invisible, then the woman potentially disappears. In the patriarchal horror show that is the 1940s, therefore, female sexual desire is apparently fated to two categories: sexually aggressive monster or self-disappearing ghost, which is to say, wolf-woman or phantom lady. In forthcoming chapters we will meet both characters many times.

In *Danse Macabre*, a history of horror in popular culture, Stephen King claims that the 1940s were not amenable to horror. Following the weirdness of the Lovecraftian thirties, says King, the forties were too scientific and rational, which was good for science fiction, but bad for the fantastic.[9] The decade prides itself on its science, such that the psychological and scientific authority around sexual discourse is inescapable and almost unquestionable. But this ubiquity, indeed this tyranny of the scientific creates its own horrors. That is what Val Lewton's *Bedlam* (1946) implies when the film prefaces its cruelty and chaos with an ironic quote: "The people of the Eighteenth Century called their Period the Age of Reason." By dividing sexual behavior into the normal and the abnormal, by supporting rather than questioning society's arbitrary expectations about gender roles, 1940s psychology makes as many monsters as any Hollywood mad scientist.

My opening emphasis on 1940s visual culture means to stress not just the continued emergence of visual media, but also the deployment of the visual as a means of power. Even radio plays an important part in 1940s visual culture. Not only does radio often work as an extension of film (in radio shows made out of movies, such as *Lux Radio Theatre*), radio also follows the same patriarchal principles of visual assessment found in movies and magazines. Although radio is intimate rather than spectacular, centered on voice rather than image, it still maintains a system of gendered surveillance and appraisal. Women are not just heard on the radio, they are viewed; even if listeners cannot see them, female characters are judged by what they look like. Thus the potentially "asexual" world of radio continues quite uninterruptedly the visual focus on sex and sexuality found in magazines and movies.[10]

1940s popular culture finds male heterosexual desire everywhere, while female sexual desire is methodically obscured. Male desire is overt, expected, visible, and violent. The male gaze and male desire are the same thing, and the man is expected to look. In films, men look women up and down, appraising them. In novels, even ones that are not hard-boiled, men look as long as they like at women: "Studying her more carefully now Slade discovered, to his surprise, that the impression of fragility was an optical illusion. Actually, as he considered her in detail, she was a remarkably beautiful and well-molded girl. . . . Her body was slender but not frail, and she carried herself with a suggestion of disciplined strength. He decided quickly that she didn't wear a girdle and could get along without a bra and not sag or lump all over the place."[11] Men are, as it were, permanently aroused, and not only look with desire, but also look like they desire. In an episode of the not normally risqué *Lux Radio Theatre*, Steve (William Powell) looks at his wife, Susan (Hedy Lamarr), in their bedroom, lights off. "You shouldn't be allowed to stand in the moonlight like that," says Steve. "It ought to be against the law, like other strong drugs."[12] But this sensuously romantic moment is interrupted by a relative knocking at the door. The intruding aunt says to Steve, "You look funny; are you all right?" This remark can only imply that when Steve looked at his wife (played by Hedy Lamarr, after all), his looking changed his looks. He looks "funny" because desire is written all over his face. The intruding aunt may not get it, but everyone in the audience does, because everyone understands that male sexual desire is both acceptable and overt.

As counterpart to this army of desiring men are a chorus line of sexualized females trained to consider themselves as both models and wives. Sexualized women are everywhere in 1940s popular culture, usually with a man's eye trained on them. The female body is scrutinized and compartmentalized by every radio comedian, psychologist, marriage counselor, gossip columnist, and advertisement. This is the decade of the female pinup, which bolsters the soldier in his wartime quarters and even appears on the side of his bomber. This is the decade of the paperback novel, whose voluptuous covers stage an escalating competition for the wandering eyes of the bookstand consumer. Radio comedians such as Bob Hope, Jimmy Durante, Groucho Marx, and even Harold Peary ("The Great Gildersleeve") fill their routines with double entendres, anecdotes about women-chasing, and overt leering. Hit songs such as "Strip Polka" (1942) and "Huggin' and Chalkin'" (1947, where the male singer uses measuring tape to keep track of his immense beloved) extends female display and male surveillance into the musical realm. *Billboard* magazine, "the world's foremost amusement weekly," not only provides industrial statistics for music, movies, and burlesque shows, but it also advertises sexy novelty items such as "Peek-a-Pen" and "Scan-Teez," which both show the drooling male viewer pictures of glamorous "models."[13] Articles and advertisements in women's magazines confirm the nationwide pinup fantasy, thereby confirming in their turn this ideal of men's own making. Ads in *Ladies' Home Journal*, in addition to *Life* and *Time*, methodically devote every feminine hairstyle, lip gloss, skin cream, brassiere, and stocking to a man's appraising gaze. Forties visual culture looks like a male-centered world where men sexually desire women, and where women, accordingly, make themselves sexually desirable to men.

Such a description is no doubt all too familiar. Feminists from Betty Friedan to Laura Mulvey have focused their attention on this phallocentric culture. Feminist critics have looked not only at the eclipsing scale of masculine desire, but also at the consequent whisper of female desire. Hence when Mary Ann Doane seeks out female agency and subjectivity, she calls her book, most instructively, *The Desire to Desire: The Woman's Film of the 1940s*.[14] Likewise, Jennifer Scanlon's study, *Inarticulate Longings: The "Ladies' Home Journal," Gender, and the Promises of Consumer Culture*, suggests that in contrast to the fantastically detailed outlines of male desire, female desire will be "inarticulate," less accessible.[15] Feminist critics such as Doane and Scanlon search through an empire of signs built by masculine desire in order to discover female desires not so readily observed.

These important projects can be expanded into 1940s popular culture. Over the course of this book I look at representations of female desire in movies, radio, comic books, best-selling fiction, music, and popular magazines. An early chapter examines novels about waiting wives on the home front during World War II; how are these women allowed to express sexual desire? Later chapters survey images associated with wolves, wolf-women, and wolfishness in comic strips and animated cartoons. All these ideas have to come from somewhere, and we will see how female heterosexuality is mapped out for young women from magazines for teenagers to college marriage studies textbooks. Film visibly presides over this glamour-obsessed decade, but radio too, although invisible, supplies many instructive models of male and female sexuality. And while female same-sex desire is invisible to the point of nonexistence in 1940s culture, we will work through the representation and evaluation of female homosexuality. Turning between the explosive visible and the suppressed invisible, we examine the ways that the period conceives of the relationship between race and sexuality.

My title deliberately places this investigation in a setting of horror. Female desire has often been rendered monstrous, and 1940s popular culture turns desiring white women into wolf-women, nonwomen, and nonwhite women. As Barbara Creed writes in *The Monstrous Feminine*, such transformations "speak to us more about male fears than about female desire or feminine subjectivity."[16] Male authorities, of course, rarely see their own fears, and 1940s sexual discourse often appears in an enlightened, bantering, self-confident light, as if everything were clear. Yet at the same time, sexuality is aligned with the animal, with the primitive, with the wolf. Who will point out the contradictions? From our point of view, the male domination of the sexual universe is a horror show unto itself, and the controlling scientists and leering comedians now seem like scary clowns. But sometimes the period itself can see the sexual violence for what it is. Horror films are prepared to reveal such darkness, and *Cat People* (Tourneur, 1942) presents a perfect reading of the period's suppression of female desire. Fritz Leiber's extraordinary horror story, "The Girl with the Hungry Eyes" (1949), not only makes a rare confession of male sexual anxiety ("I know sex can be frightening"), but it also unveils the abyss at the heart of a society that centers its attentions on the beautiful pinup. "I realized that wherever she came from, whatever shaped her, she's the quintessence of the horror behind the bright billboard."[17] Since girls with hungry eyes—with intense desire—could so easily turn into panthers or vampires or worse, rendering these women blind or invisible was often easier.

Sometimes the truth comes out, then, but far more often 1940s culture makes certain to render female desire invisible. This book concludes with examples from two brilliant lady phantoms, Ruth Herschberger and

Elizabeth Hawes, both of whom saw how popular culture represented and repressed female sexual desire. Their work is clear, logical, energetic, and often funny, yet contemporary readers had almost no idea what they were doing. Feminist projects were controversial, but identifiable, yet Herschberger's and Hawes's powerful descriptions of female sexual desire went virtually unnoticed because male heterosexual desire provided the dominant focus of sexual discourse. As we will note more than once, psychologists' and philosophers' liberating recognition of human sexual desire always applied to men, not women.

As a representative example of this universalizing tendency, a contemporary summary of the first Kinsey report in 1948 stated: "The picture of man's sexuality, as it emerges from the Kinsey data, confirms Freud's concept of the libido. The universal urge for sex expression cannot be ignored or wished away. It is a force society must recognize."[18] The book from which this quote is taken is "dedicated to the scientists whose studies in human behavior have contributed to the happiness of men," and this is liberating postwar rhetoric. Yet the 1948 Kinsey report studied only men, not women, and everything the commentary has said so far about a "universal urge for sex expression" has also treated men only. The 1940s universe has almost no interest in whether women possess the "urge for sex expression." Hence our retrospective interest in those haunting moments when the lady phantoms speak.

Much excellent work has been published on the sexual desires and behavior of women during the 1940s. John Costello's *Virtue under Fire: How World War II Changed Our Social and Sexual Attitudes* (1986) is one of the earliest discussions of the way that war transformed sexual behavior and morality.[19] Later, more specifically focused studies include Leisa D. Meyer, *Creating GI Jane: Sexuality and Power in the Women's Army Corps during World War II* (1996); Jane Mersky Leder, *Thanks for the Memories: Love, Sex, and World War II* (2006); Marilyn E. Hegarty, *Victory Girls, Khaki-Wackies, and Patriotutes: The Regulation of Female Sexuality during World War II* (2008); and Meghan K. Winchell, *Good Girls, Good Food, Good Fun: The Story of USO Hostesses during World War II* (2008). The period's concern with the sexuality of young women is treated superbly in Susan K. Cahn's *Sexual Reckonings: Southern Girls in a Troubling Age* (2007).[20] All of these splendidly researched books show the factual and experiential contours of female sexual desire within a culture that did its best to obliterate it.

By contrast, my book focuses on the obliterating culture itself. Whereas the historians just mentioned conducted countless interviews in order to find out what people actually did and thought, I interpret selections from movies, radio shows, comics, newspapers, and novels in order to trace the shape and structures of sexual representation. Just as so many readers were struck by the large gap between idealized prescriptions for sexuality and Alfred Kinsey's more graphic descriptions in *Sexual Behavior in the Human Male*, so too is there a large distance between the reality of female desire as brought to light by historical research and the representations of female desire found in various regions of popular culture. Instead of studying the lived actuality that existed behind the fantasy, this book interprets the ideological dynamics of the cultural fantasy.

Although 1940s culture is in some respects well-travelled terrain, not much academic work moves through the various media simultaneously. Radio scholars tend to study radio, film scholars mostly stick to film, and literary critics tend to write about books, not magazines or newspapers. There are myriad good reasons for these divisions given the many thousands of radio programs, movies, books, magazines, and comic books. The gaps and flaws in my approach will be quite apparent, no doubt, but I pursue my theme across all the major media. Without claiming to have read every book or every magazine, or to have listened to every radio program, cultural analysts of those days thought very comparatively—across the media—and we can do the same thing.

Why study popular culture? Nowadays we can agree that popular culture is as fruitful a field as any for intellectual analysis. But it is worthwhile, nonetheless, to say a few words about why we find ourselves here. In the first place, popular culture serves as a mirror by which we can reflect on our psychological and social identities. Perhaps it should not be this way since we know that a capitalist enterprise is trying to enrich itself by seducing us with dreams and by telling us what our desires are and should be. Yet even knowing this, the thoughtful viewer can sort through the flood of images, not only condemning certain elements, but also finding other aspects useful or energizing. Lisa Ben, creator of the first lesbian magazine, *Vice Versa* (1947–1948), shaped her project around an evaluation of lesbian images in popular culture. As all-around reviewer of everything, she not only discussed high culture novels such as Radclyffe Hall's *The Well of Loneliness* (1928), but she also looked at relevant contemporary plays, movies, and novels. She evaluated the representation of homosexuality in these works, and recommended to her readers those movies and novels that gave lesbian characters dignity and humanity. In a cultural landscape that hid away lesbian desire ("The Sisterhood may have no badge, its members are unknown"), Lisa Ben was anxious to direct her readers to those rare examples of lesbian visibility where women could see themselves in a positive light.[21] Likewise, my study seeks not only to critique dehumanizing representations, but also to celebrate characters and ideas that break through the oppressive weight of conventional discourse.

In the 1940s, when methodical studies of popular culture begin to emerge, cultural analysis was often underlined with a sense of ethical condemnation; that is, the investigator of popular culture did not omit a feeling that popular culture remains low culture or superficial culture. Adorno and Horkheimer's "The Culture Industry: Enlightenment as Mass Deception" (1944) paints a savage picture of repetition, standardization, and meaninglessness distributed throughout culture in the name of entertainment.[22] Adorno's mode of analysis was not typical for a 1940s American sociologist, but his work was known in the United States and was published alongside other work in the burgeoning discipline of communications. Toward the end of the decade, in the essay "Mass Communications, Popular Taste, and Organized Social Action," Paul Lazarsfeld and Robert Merton make a mild form of Adorno's point, arguing that the sheer repetition of popular culture does not assist progressive political action.[23] The next chapter discusses a range of 1940s popular culture critics in order to see how they handle problems of aesthetic and cultural significance. In contrast to figures such as Edmund Wilson and Lionel Trilling, who have little patience for "commercial" literature, Diana Trilling maintains a moral perspective without the patronizing condescension of most of her learned contemporaries. She is open to the possibility that ideas and truths can appear in popular literature, and her book reviews display this openness with exemplary consistency.

The most energetic and lively critical analysis of 1940s popular culture from the period itself is Marshall McLuhan's *The Mechanical Bride: Folklore of Industrial Man* (1951).[24] Built out of wide-ranging, theoretically self-aware two-page chapters, *The Mechanical Bride* looks positively futuristic and points ahead not only to Roland Barthes's *Mythologies* (1957), but also to American cultural studies today. McLuhan turns his interpretive eye toward—above all—advertisements, but also to pop culture icons (Charlie McCarthy, Tarzan, Walter Winchell, Emily Post), comics, corporate ideology, self-help books, all manner of magazines, and paperback novels. Like the present book, *The Mechanical Bride* insists that we study relationships between apparently disparate parts of culture. Thus the passive radio listener is akin to the passive *Vogue* reader; the statistical authority of sexologist Kinsey is related to that of the pollster Gallup; *Time* magazine, comic books, and book clubs produce similar combinations of sex and violence. When McLuhan jumps from a Book-of-the-Month Club newsletter to the movie magazine, *Modern Screen*, he authorizes his leap thus: "It is important to grasp the interlocking character of the mechanisms employed in these seemingly separate spheres of writing" (28). As an analytical method for the study of popular culture that last sentence cannot be improved.

The Mechanical Bride looks like it should be fun—at least as fun as a modernist artwork by Duchamp—and McLuhan plays with the idea of the book, with what words, pictures, and captions are for. Looking ahead to the way that Jean-Luc Godard denaturalizes the relationship between word and image in his criticism and films, McLuhan underlines the overwhelming visuality of 1940s culture by reproducing numerous images from ads and comic strips, many of which occupy an entire page. Chapters begin with strange surrealist questions ("How Dry I Am?"), which are neither epigraphs for the text nor captions for the pictures, and thus do not emerge from any identifiable point of view. These detachable words show that McLuhan is performing a species of critical modernism inspired not only by sociologists such as David Riesman and anthropologists such as Margaret Mead, but also by modernists such as Mallarmé and Joyce. As McLuhan says: "[Joyce] was very high-brow, very middle-brow, and especially very low-brow. To write his epic of the modern Ulysses he studied all his life the ads, the comics, the pulps, and popular speech" (59). McLuhan likes *Li'l Abner* ("Capp's vitality suggests that perhaps the obsequies of our popular culture have been prematurely sung" [64]), and with his oddball jokes, colloquial banter, and punchy visual design, he shows himself to be completely at home in the language and look of popular culture.

Yet the whole point of organizing the chaos of popular culture is for McLuhan to defend himself against it. Whereas Joyce made a life-long study of popular culture, 1940s culture simply rains down on man, on "the drowned man" (88). One needs, says McLuhan, to be a "second Ulysses" to survive the "siren onslaught" of the "visceral riot" of popular culture (97). Thus McLuhan urges us to reflect on mass culture in a detached, thoughtful way or be swept away by hallucinatory dreams. "Without the mirror of the mind, nobody can live a human life in the face of our present mechanized dreams" (97). This mass culture home is a "trance world," an unreal dream, a narcotic, an artificial, tyrannical machine. Although McLuhan is about to invent postmodernism, and although some of his modernist predecessors liked both machines (the futurists) and dreams (the surrealists), he is still just as snobby as any 1950s humanist snob since he is for the natural over the mechanical, for reality over unreality, and for the mind over the body.

In McLuhan's view, one of the main ways that popular culture drowns man is by sex and sexuality. Modern industrial society is seen as suffering from a "barrage" of sex imagery, where "sex weariness and sex sluggishness are, in measure at least, both the cause and increasingly the outcome of these campaigns" (99). Many of his contemporaries noticed the sexualized storm around them; McLuhan's twist is to emphasize the mechanical nature of sex in an industrial age. The "Mechanical Bride" is produced on the "Love-Goddess Assembly line," and is thus made out of interchangeable body parts—breasts, hips, legs (93). McLuhan wonders how this must feel to an actual woman: "The switch-over from competitive display to personal affection is not easy for the girl" (99). But for the most part McLuhan's point of view is a man's point of view, where he wonders how a man can survive the "siren onslaught." Although some of his observations support a feminist critique of cultural iconography, his goal is not to empathize with women, but to resist deathly machines and numbing dreams through intense and individual thinking. The thoughtful individual must cultivate his "inner resources" in order to "resist the mechanism of mass delirium and collective irrationalism" (144).

McLuhan thus critiques the deluge of commercialized images from the perspective of high culture individualism. His heroes—Sigfried Giedion, James Joyce, Al Capp, Parker Tyler—are chosen eclectically rather than methodologically. McLuhan regularly satirizes the representation of high culture and education by popular culture so that his innovative critique is grounded in the thoughtfulness to which high culture gives rise. But although this high culture thought can see how pernicious ads, bestsellers, and magazines are for both women and men, he is not willing to express his resistance in the form of a collective.

Thus while his analyses of 1940s masculinity and femininity are masterful and complex, McLuhan is still stuck with some very traditional notions about gender. He offers the compelling idea that the war made men threateningly macho ("early in the war we heard the cry, 'All men are wolves!' "), but that figures like Dagwood and Frank Sinatra provided an antimacho antidote. McLuhan convincingly views the 1940s as offering a variety of male ideals, yet he himself tends to equate masculine with "active" and feminine with "passive." He calls society a "kept woman" because of its passivity and says that, like an intelligent girl on a date, it must hide its intelligence. Since the whole point of his "active," "vital" thinking is to overcome the deadly, mechanical trance state, the tendency is to equate thought with the masculine and absence of thought with the feminine. It is the monstrous Medusa of the Mechanical Bride who obstructs the clear thinking of the high-cultured male. McLuhan's dreamworld is a sexual nightmare, but his individual horror is that he cannot think straight.

In this book I trade McLuhan's cultural snobbery for political snobbery. This is meant to entail a more empathic and collective response. I also perceive a sexual nightmare, but my emphasis is not on the man's bad dream ("I can't think properly"), but on woman's ("I can't exist"). I survey the same artifacts as McLuhan—ads, magazines, radio shows, movie stars, popular books—but I evaluate them according to feminist priorities. In this evaluation of culture, the "high" and "low" have to do with better portraits of women and worse. Just as we need to keep reminding ourselves of how we hurt one another or how we harm the earth, we need to continually remember and reflect on the shape and reach of patriarchal power, even though the general outline may not, at this late date, surprise.

But there are still plenty of surprises. The patriarchal regime is all-encompassing, yet still peopled with incisive pockets of resistance. It surprised me to find not only Herschberger and Hawes, but also numerous other female (and some male) writers who both see and critique the masculinist flood of sexualized culture. The critiques are there already in the 1940s. Some writers need our interpretation to draw out the politics, but some critiques are as clear as any we would make today.

Crossing sometimes rapidly between different media, this book focuses on both the horror and the heroines. I detail how male figures sequester and regulate the female body, but I also collect writers—mostly women—who challenge conventional representations. In early chapters we meet heroines such as Diana Trilling, who is throughout her book reviews interested in underrepresented sexuality, and Hannah Lees, who bravely and realistically shows a war wife whose sexuality cannot be constrained by clichés. Nancy Wilson Ross writes impassioned feminism into her novels and histories, while Jane Rice and C. L. Moore use horror and science fiction to comment on contemporary gender roles. In 1946 Jo Sinclair publishes a best-selling novel that describes a lesbian character who is three-dimensionally human rather than a stereotyped disaster. Geoffrey Gorer, whose work with Margaret Mead helped him to see outside the standard confines of "male" and "female," talks more openly about the place of homosexuality in American culture than most other commentators.

What does it mean to study and interpret female desire in popular culture? Ideally, it means finding places where women speak for themselves, where they become subjects rather than objects. Cynically, it means finding places where the patriarchal fantasy allows women to speak, but only within patriarchal guidelines. Novels written by women sometimes critique conventions around sexuality and sexual expression, and the effect can feel politically liberating. But one realizes as well that a socially constrained marketplace has to a degree determined what kinds of things can be said, and, of course, to say things does not mean anyone will hear. One can interpret the expression of sexual desire in a literal way, as limited to a relatively cordoned-off section of a single person's psyche. But one can also interpret the expression of sexuality as standing for a major political statement, where to express desire amounts to a political voice and where the absence of such expression amounts to the harshest political silencing. In this book, my interpretations will navigate among most of these positions, as I sometimes will indeed find liberating breakthroughs in sexual expression, while at other times—or even at the same time—I will find that patriarchal ideology has itself generated all the terms in a given arena.

This book usually assumes that female sexual expression is a right akin to a fundamental political right. However it also assumes that there is almost no way out of the sexual apparatus that the patriarchy has built for its own convenience. Freud argued for a subterranean sexuality that decisively organizes our lives. By contrast, 1940s popular culture sexualizes everything quite openly. Radio—although without images—and movies—although overseen by the Hays Code—are still uninterrupted purveyors of the period's overt sexual regime. So when women express sexual desire into this social space, what sexuality means and can mean has already been largely determined. Hence we find so often that when women characters express sexual desire, it comes out sounding like a man, like a "wolfish" man in a system whose terms have already been defined by men. What is easy to hope for, but hard to see, is a female voice or consciousness that has an understanding of sexuality that is more clearly separated from thoughts already provided by men.

The openly visible structure of 1940s sexuality is evidenced in a film such as *Duel in the Sun* (King Vidor, 1946). Producer David Selznick spent two years shooting and reshooting a western epic whose scale and ambition was on a par with Selznick's earlier success, *Gone with the Wind* (1939). But when the film was finally released, it ran into endless trouble with moral arbiters such as the National Legion of Decency and numerous women's organizations.[25] Even after Selznick's additions and subtractions, the film still seemed too focused on sexual themes. And even if it did not offend at the level of sex, it seemed aesthetically incomprehensible. For it appeared that Selznick had shot for two years, on an epic scale—with a huge cast of stars and thousands of extras, in spectacularly gorgeous color— all in order to tell a story about sensuousness and lust. As Bosley Crowther wrote in the *New York Times*, despite "some eye-dazzling scenes of wide-open ranching and frontiering, all in color of the very best," what the movie came down to was a "juvenile slobbering over sex."[26] What was the connection between the historical vision—the trains, herds, hundreds of men, the desert, and the town—and the erotic drama between "bad son" Lewt McCanles (Gregory Peck) and "half-breed" Pearl Chavez (Jennifer Jones)? As an integrated aesthetic object that has some idea of what it wants to be, *Duel in the Sun* made not much sense then and makes not much sense now.

But as a cultural reading of the period's overtly visible sexuality, *Duel in the Sun* provides a spectacular interpretation. 1940s sexuality is open and everywhere, "in the sun," not hidden in the night, and epic in itself, not limited to any private, walled-off space. Male sexual desire is not sublimated or displaced, but open. The film begins with Pearl dancing in a circle of gazing men, and even when she is not performing most men claim the right to stare at her. When Lewt first sees her, he leers and openly looks her up and down. If we read the film conventionally and morally, Lewt's overt expressions of lust immediately signal his badness, in contrast to good brother Jesse (Joseph Cotten) and good suitor Sam (Charles Bickford). But if we read Lewt as the powerful, appraising man who displays sexual desire as an uninterrupted norm, then he becomes emblematic of the 1940s patriarchy, which looks out over all cultural space with a measuring and coercive gaze.

The leering eyes and grin of Lewt make him and men like him present before us like ancient Greek dramatic players, who wore erect penises as part of their costumes. Male sexual desire has always been easier to read and confirm than female desire because of the penis, because of the erection. The male erection is visible proof of sexual desire. Lewt and 1940s men, in essence, have erections all the time. Their looks and looking, the way they organize social space, the way they speak, all embody this visibly confirmable desire. Lewt, the armed, leering cowboy, is not a brutal bad man in an otherwise mostly civilized culture; he is instead 1940s masculinity itself. He is not a marginal, dark figure who will eventually be overcome by civilization; instead he is at the center of what matters most for 1940s American culture.

Read in this way, *Duel in the Sun* emblematizes not only overt masculine desire, but female desire as well. The period demands visible readability. Female bodies are read for sexual desirability and availability by the male gaze. Men decide whether women are attractive, and they infer from women's costumes whether they are available. Female desire does not exist if men cannot see it. How, then, to represent female desire? In *Duel in the Sun*, female sexual desire is represented with the same literal-minded approach that attends the male erection. As the "half-breed" daughter of a sensuously dancing mother and a cultivated but derelict father (Herbert

Marshall), Jennifer Jones plays Pearl Chavez in tawny brownface throughout. In a culture where female sexual desire *others* white women into monsters, her brown face *means* sexual desire. Even though Lewt almost rapes her to begin his courtship, Pearl cannot keep herself from wanting him. Her desire to be a proper, well-behaved good girl is always conquered by her "primitive" Indian self. Again and again her sexual desire returns as we always knew it would; we could see it in her face.

When female sexual desire becomes as visible as a man's, it often starts to look like a man's desire and is organized on those terms. If desiring women do not turn into actual monsters, they might turn into men, which can be monstrous enough. Brownfaced Pearl can match leering Lewt in terms of passion, lust, and cruelty. In part, this is because she is as much a man as he is. She rides horses without any feminine delicacy, and she shoots a rifle as accurately as a man. In popular songs like "Pistol Packin' Mama" (1943) and musicals like *Annie Get Your Gun* (1946), 1940s culture registered gender anxiety through women such as these. In the famous final sequence of *Duel in the Sun*, Pearl trails Lewt up into desert rocks and shoots him from hundreds of yards away. When Pearl aims a rifle at her cruel gunslinger lover, she has become every bit the man that he is. As they crawl in the dust at the end—each having mortally wounded the other—the movie executes the couple for their wayward sexual desire with an operatic conclusion that also satisfies the Hays Code. But *Duel in the Sun* has also provided the basic terms of male and female sexual desire in the 1940s. It has shown the overt, coercive nature of male sexual desire, and it has demonstrated that if female sexual desire is visible, it will tend to look like a man's.[27]

Most of the material for this book is drawn from the years 1940 to 1950; this decade is thus eleven years long. I do not claim that abrupt boundary lines fall through the years 1940 and 1950; in terms of sexual ideology, a *Life* magazine from 1937 does not look radically different from one in 1943, and a film noir from 1949 may feel more or less the same as one from 1953. Some cultural historians would want to emphasize more strongly the division between the war years of the decade's first half and the postwar recovery of the second half. In what follows, however, I treat the decade as possessing a relatively coherent system of sexual representation and evaluation. I tend to emphasize similarities across media, rather than differences. Although I pay a good deal of attention to the role of race and ethnicity in these cultural representations, most of my examples are drawn from the white mainstream media, from the magazines, radio shows, and movies consumed by the populations of sociologically average Middletown or Elmtown, U.S.A.[28]

What allows us to treat the decade's mainstream sexual culture as a relatively coherent unit? World War II is obviously the major contributor to the presentation of sexuality in the 1940s. Although women do men's jobs in the factories, sexual roles in popular media are not necessarily confused. On the contrary, one could argue that Hollywood films aim to resolve societal confusion by restaging and exaggerating the same plot in which a desiring male gazes upon a female model. Precode Hollywood films treat sexual themes more openly and more fluidly, no doubt, but the 1940s sexual "system" is more systematic precisely because the Hays Code has regularized what is possible. The authentic threat and horror of the war gives rise to greater sexual candor in discourse around sex education and adolescent desire. And whereas businesses have always aimed to sell magazines, movies, and cars with the faces and flesh of pretty girls, the wartime model becomes a kind of angel, a culturally ubiquitous figure of hope and consolation to young men risking their lives. The war gives men the right as never before to openly express sexual desire, and it obliges women like never before to fashion themselves as the glamorous answer to such need.[29]

Chapters that follow will work through more historical specifics. "Spicy" magazines—which look mostly the same from the 1930s to the early 1940s—are put out of business by U.S. postal laws in 1943. Men's magazines such as *Esquire*, *True*, and *Argosy* needed to reinvent themselves to stay within new regulations. The most sexually graphic comics do not fold until the 1950s; we will look at an exemplary jungle comic—*Tiger Girl*—which found a perfect home in the 1940s. Wartime sexual candor made stripping popular again and even respectable; in 1942 a slew of stripping plays hit Broadway.[30] Kathleen Winsor's best-selling novel, *Forever Amber* (1944), changed the sexual range and possibilities of the historical romance. In the same year, *Seventeen* magazine confirmed the invention of the teenage girl. Paperback books are a wartime innovation; as the decade goes on their covers—and sometimes their contents—become more sexually explicit. Popular forms of psychoanalysis reached an authoritative peak during the decade; everyone wondered whether they were sexually "adjusted" or "normal." Marriage—and especially the role of sex in marriage—seems to have fallen into crisis; college courses on marriage reach their statistical height during the 1940s.

Radio, films, and magazines promote a sexual plot in which aggressive men openly pursue glamorous women. This story is the average, everyday story, and it is not just accepted but encouraged. Yet change the outline of this familiar story just a little, and it becomes a tale of monstrosity and horror. Comics and pulp fiction exaggerate characteristics of the plot, but it is really the same plot. Thus when parents complain about the bloodthirstiness and sensuality of comic books, they think that comics have crossed a line. In protest they put up this sign in the Milwaukee Public Library:

Who are your children's pals?
Werewolves?
Sex maniacs?
Murdering perverts?
Bloodthirsty bums?[31]

The parents are outraged by gory comics, and the comics are indeed outrageous. But there is a clear continuity between this wolfish, monstrous sexuality and the decade's promoted model for heterosexuality. The gory monster comics have not transgressed boundaries, so much as they have brought forward the violent truth at the heart of the manufactured fantasy of heterosexual desire.

2

Diana Trilling, Female Desire, and the Study of Popular Culture

In the 1940s people began to think more methodically and more appreciatively about popular culture. In some quarters it was hard not to think that popular movies and radio shows were not just a silly waste of time, but sophisticated critics appeared who took seriously some Hollywood films and radio programs. Gilbert Seldes wrote a regular column on popular culture for that spectacular combination of highbrow and lowbrow culture, *Esquire*. Intelligent critics such as Seldes, James Agee, and Manny Farber could find interesting and moving things in highly commercial Hollywood movies. But even for them, appreciating the surface, shiny glamour side of movies, the sexiness of movie stars, and the ribaldry of radio humor was difficult. A smart critic could not simply turn into a press agent, a press agent who talks up celebrity good looks and sex. A thoughtful critic of popular culture thus needed to navigate his position carefully, as he took an open-minded, nonelitist approach to mass culture, while maintaining a discriminating judgment with respect to sensual pleasures. As we shall see, the treatment of sexuality is often an awkward sticking point with these critics.

What does the study of popular culture look like in the 1940s? More to our point, what does gender look like in the study of popular culture in the 1940s? Since everyone thought in terms of "masculinity" and "femininity," gender played a role in many discussions of culture. But who would take the side of women, and who would speak on behalf of female desire? The first two sections of this chapter survey a range of critics and scholars who can be seen as early students of popular culture. In these necessarily brief descriptions, I focus primarily on the treatment of gender and sexuality. I then provide a more detailed reading of the work of Diana Trilling, who, although she would not have characterized her 1940s reviews as feminist, turns out to have a methodical interest in female sexual desire. I compare Trilling's 1940s criticism to other strands of popular culture study in that decade. Like the work of Elizabeth Hawes and Ruth Herschberger, whom we will meet later on, Trilling's forgotten criticism needs to be remembered for what it says about underrepresented forms of human sexuality.

Adolescent Sex and the Adult Male Film Critics

Perhaps the most prominent and systematic critic of popular culture during the 1940s was Gilbert Seldes. A 1943 *Esquire* editorial claimed that his 1923 book, *The Seven Lively Arts*, had removed the divide between elite and mass culture.

> It was nothing less than an Emancipation of the Intellectuals. It broke down the unbreachable high wall separating the Classical from the Popular in a dozen branches of American culture. It broke the Brahmin Back Bay stranglehold on the arts, and opened the way to such latter-day phenomena as the recognition of popular song-writers like Irving Berlin and George Gershwin as authentic and legitimate composers.[1]

Esquire published a monthly column by Seldes from 1933 to 1946; hence one would expect only praise and loyalty on its part. But Michael Kammen, who has written a scrupulous and critical overview of Seldes's career, agrees, arguing likewise that Seldes not only took part in the critical movement to support a democratization of culture, but he also "did much to make it happen."[2] In his regular column for *Esquire*, "The Lively Arts," Seldes discussed many more arts than just the seven of the *Seven Lively Arts*.[3] His topics during the 1940s included ballet, Abbott and Costello on Broadway, Chaplin's *The Great Dictator*, slang, parades, vaudeville, Superman, realism in war films, Jimmy Durante, Bing Crosby, night clubs, Ingrid Bergman, and the prospects for television.[4] Seldes broke down the walls between high and low culture by consistently adopting a middlebrow approach.[5] For example, a typical foray into elite culture has Seldes wondering why poetry cannot be written more clearly.[6]

That the most important critic of popular culture in the 1940s writes for *Esquire*, "the magazine for men," does not portend a nuanced interest in female psychology. The magazine puts women on pictorial display everywhere, while the article writers and humorists are eager to generalize about women as drivers, dancers, or partners in bed. The prestigious commentators—Seldes on popular culture, George Jean Nathan on Broadway theater, William Lyon Phelps on books—do not by any means follow the magazine's main emphasis on girls, girls, girls. On the contrary, their columns seem, for the most part, disconnected from the more obvious aspects of *Esquire*'s masculinist ideology. Even so, the male critics sound like men talking to men at a club. Their discourse is not risqué or ribald—although a Broadway play will sometimes cause Nathan to reflect on female pulchritude—but a woman's perspective is consistently absent. The magazine occasionally extends its democratic sympathies to African Americans, and through the early 1940s *Esquire* publishes several pieces by Chester Himes and Langston Hughes. But if Seldes and *Esquire* seek to promote a "democratization of culture," it is not a democracy that includes women.

Like other critics of his time, Seldes puts women into a separate category for aesthetic evaluation, while betraying a good deal of sexual anxiety in the process. *Esquire*'s misogyny is characterized by, on the one hand, male writers who drool over female models, and on the other hand, men who blame women for life's various catastrophes. This combination of attraction and anger results in the stupid, but buxom women who inhabit nearly all the cartoons. Seldes takes the man's side in this battle of the sexes in his June 1942 column, "What Every Woman Hater Knows," where he attacks *Woman of the Year* (Stevens, 1942) and other films for their bashings of men.[7] Less typical of *Esquire*, and more typical of Seldes—who much prefers praise to critique—is his nostalgic homage to the Gibson Girl in 1943. "In this harsh day of women in uniform, her trailing skirts, her ivory-towered beauty has a quaint and special charm."[8] His April 1944 column, "Guaranteed Innocent Praise," assembles praiseworthy women, from Agnes de Mille and Lucille Ball to Grace Hartman and Hazel Scott. Other column writers organize their material similarly around women; Phelps evaluates women writers, while Nathan reflects on women from the previous year's theater ("Herewith, in chronological order, a reviewer's memoirs of various ladies who graced the stage during the last season").[9] Unlike most of *Esquire*'s other contributors, Seldes tries to put feminine "oompf" in a dignified manner: "that stoppage of the earth's motion, reduced to the private terms of being for a second breathless, is Hedy Lamarr's unique power."[10]

This quotation is from Seldes's column on the glamour industry, which he criticized throughout the 1940s. While Seldes makes certain to report his male attraction to women—he admires Lucille Ball's "really remarkably well-fitting dresses" and grows ecstatic about Hedy Lamarr—he also congratulates Veronica Lake for looking like her Hollywood self in actual reality; that is, "I have passed within two feet of some of Hollywood's best glamour-creatures and haven't recognized them because the glamour is so synthetic."[11]

This resistance to industrialized beauty recurs in several articles. In an article on faces, Seldes argues that unless Hollywood learns to work with women's makeup more discretely, "the great American face will remain male."[12] The entire article performs a critique of women's makeup; "women are also undergoing amazing experiences today," the essay concludes, "and it's hardly worth while to conceal them." These sentiments are repeated in his October 1944 column, "Oh, Rare Miss Bergman," in which Ingrid Bergman is celebrated as an actress devoid of acting "tricks," and even devoid of makeup; "Bergman doesn't believe in make-up and shows her own face, bless her, to the camera."[13] The stance against makeup in particular and glamour more generally calls for more nature and more truth. Seldes positions himself as a man who cannot be manipulated by industrial-scale painters. Although millions may buy into this ideal of glamorous beauty, he heroically sees through it.

But what looks like hard-minded heroism might be an anxious shield flung up against female sexuality. To promote Hollywood film as the great democratizer, but then campaign against women's makeup is too contradictory. It is too late in the day to stand in Hollywood's dream factory—which *is* seductive and *is* fantastic—and say, everything's swell, but let's scrape the paint off the ladies. As time goes on, this desire for less artifice and more realism leads to a full-blown impatience with the movies. In his 1950 book, *The Great Audience*, Seldes writes that Hollywood films "are made primarily for an audience of children and adolescents."[14] According to this system of aesthetic evaluation, "maturity" counts the most.[15] Here Seldes joins fellow adult critics James Agee and Manny Farber in thinking that Hollywood's sex is too immature and too unrealistic. As I argue in a moment, however, it is the height of critical unrealism to watch a Hollywood movie while dreaming about sexual realism.

Otis Ferguson was a critic for the *New Republic* who worked in the capacious mode of Seldes, and wrote about film, music, radio, and books. Had he not died in action in 1943, his writings would probably be just as well known. As a film critic, Ferguson reveals a similar awkwardness about female sexuality. He treats women more methodically and more strangely than Seldes. The way Ferguson defends himself from the female body is to continually split the female voice away from the image. Hence Ann Sheridan—whom he repeatedly harasses—"has a voice like wagon wheels," while "there is also Hedy Lamarr to look at—and unfortunately listen to as well."[16] Ferguson wrote extensively about music, and he nearly always has interesting things to say about the quality of the sound, the role of the music, and the relationship of images to sounds in film.[17] But his treatment of women seems to evidence a more political or cultural element. That is, he wants to think about a popular form such as the cinema, but not in the usual way, which apparently means, not in a vulgar way. At bottom, he does not want to celebrate films for their collection of pretty women. So he tends to sabotage the visual pleasure women offer by referring to their voices. Hence: "Miss [Irene] Dunne has apparently become *very* interested in acting and what may be achieved with the Human Voice."[18] Ferguson laments the presence of Mary Martin ("alas!"), and says that she "wiggles" both "her voice and figure" in the movie.[19] He will not be persuaded by sexiness. But Ferguson likes Katherine Hepburn, who "wouldn't win a screen-test for pretties," so that her "metallic and even mannered voice finds its special beauty."[20] Whereas one might celebrate Marlene Dietrich's sultry good looks, Ferguson says that she "is still something to see, though her best friend is still her singing voice—a fair voice, with personality and feeling in song—for her acting presence here carries the insistent hint that she knows where the camera is."[21] Ferguson's criticism is never prudish or conventionally moralistic, yet he is methodically insistent about showing that his interest never dwells on the mere sexiness of pretty women.

James Agee, film reviewer for the *Nation*, also reveals some anxiousness about female sexuality in the movies. As most would agree, Agee was a beautifully eloquent proponent of what was good in American films. In terms of critical distinction, Agee often preferred silent films, European films, or documentaries to Hollywood's latest product. But, like Pauline Kael later on, he could celebrate the good parts of bad American movies. Like Kael, he knew that Hollywood films had little to do with art, yet he could still admire, on the one hand, a crisp, competent intelligence, or on the other, unpretentious "crude energy." When Agee found a film wanting, instead of rolling out the vicious, castigating wit of an Edmund Wilson, he worked up hilarious comic set-pieces that also presented real insights into the functioning of mass culture.

> Lack of space, libel laws, and a fondness for entertainers, all prevent any detail on the subject; but we can safely remember that every piece of entertainment, like every political speech or swatch of advertising copy, has nightmarish accuracy as a triple distilled image of a collective dream, habit, or desire.[22]

Agee's serious, fantastically articulate fun with the movies did not give the impression of an elite outsider spying self-righteously or condescendingly on the dull benighted. His comic energy created a character who loved the possibility of the movies and who therefore praised what worked well and called for reform in what failed. Agee performed a very personable humanity at every turn.

What Agee's brainy, but amateurish moviegoer lacks, however, is a straightforward way of talking about sex. Like Seldes, he refuses to be seduced by commercialized glamour. But in the process, Agee consistently oversophisticates his response to sexuality. At the heart of this evasiveness is his reasonable sense that the "suffocating genteelism" of Hollywood does not itself ever talk about sex.[23] For example, Agee concludes his review of *For Whom the Bell Tolls* (1943) by writing, amusingly, "Mr. Hemingway's sleeping bag, by the way, is so discreetly used that you can never at any moment be sure who is in or out nuendo" (49). Anyone who knows something about Hemingway will associate his work with sex, but as usual, Agee implies, the Hollywood film blocks anything approaching actual sex. By contrast, Agee mentions in a throwaway aside that he has seen a couple of films in an adults-only theater (145), while he also says that "the essence of Madame Bovary" is "masturbation, literal as often as figurative" (120). In these ways, Agee creates a film-watching persona who is neither Hays Code prude nor screen magazine smirker. Yet this more mature, realistic adult comes across, nonetheless, with his own set of evasions.

Agee's smart, amateur reviewer takes pleasure in all the ordinary ways, except for the sexual. His reviewer is constantly "moved" by this or that, by camera technique, narrative structure, acting, landscape, language. His reviews perform a fine sense of what it is like for a smart, literate person to watch films in a critical, but also generous and even enthusiastic, way. He can "like" practically anything that anyone else can with the quietly felt proviso that he is not sanctioning the film as art. "*Thank Your Lucky Stars* is the loudest and most vulgar of the current musicals. It is also the most fun, if you are amused when show people kid their own idiom, and if you find a cruel-compassionate sort of interest in watching amateurs like Bette Davis do what they can with a song" (55).

That is a splendidly fine-tuned analysis of his own process of liking, and one that occurs everywhere in Agee except around sex. With a rare full-bloodedness, he says, "Mae West is mainly as good as ever, which is still plenty good enough for me" (64), but most often the "girls" are not so much liked as they are rolled away into brilliant prose. He says that "*Cover Girl* would be worth seeing if only for Rita Hayworth at her prettiest (at certain other moments she looks as if she were daring you to stick your head in her mouth [88])." The parentheses assure us, once again, that Agee will not process pretty girls in an ordinary way. Or take this sequence from a review of *To Have and Have Not*: "The best of the picture has no plot at all, but is a leisurely series of mating duels between Humphrey Bogart at his most proficient and the very entertaining, nervy, adolescent new blonde, Lauren Bacall. Whether or not you like the film will depend I believe almost entirely on whether you like Miss Bacall. I am no judge. I can hardly look at her, much less listen to her—she has a voice like a chorus by Kid Ory—without getting caught in a dilemma between a low whistle and a bellylaugh" (121).

Agee again presents a finely-tuned analysis of his own likes, while also disqualifying himself in this instance ("I am no judge"). In fact, oversophisticated as it is, this is one of the better descriptions of what an erotic screen offers to a grown-up heterosexual man. For the most part, however, Agee's reviews do not focus much on the obvious presence of cinematic sexuality. So although Agee provides a wonderful example of how to appreciate and critique popular cultural forms, a hierarchical, restrained impulse still comes in to cordon off too much attention to issues of sexuality.

To complete this brief survey of male critics, I turn to Manny Farber, film critic for the *New Republic* throughout most of the 1940s. Farber's aesthetics are close to Agee's; he wants to find intelligence, humanity, and something like realism in a film. In his reviews, Farber repeatedly laments film censorship and the Hays Code, especially with regard to the representation of sex. He consistently argues that most Hollywood sex is either deceitful or juvenile, whereas it should be treated candidly, in an adult manner. The sex in *The Postman Always Rings Twice* (1946) is so adolescent that Farber thinks the film has been "made by a crew of bobby-sox characters."[24] Because of Hollywood censorship, *To Have and Have Not* (1944) can only "throw the audience some speck-sized erotic thrills" (196). Hays office censorship obtrudes on sex in *For Whom the Bell Tolls* (1943 [89]), *Heaven Can Wait* (1943 [99]), and *Phantom Lady* (1944 [149]). The badness of *The Great Gildersleeve* (1943) is not caused by Hollywood's "workers," but instead by censorship; "the movie code decrees that the showing of actual love is indecent" (48). These distortions of sexual representation lead to stupidity if not disaster, as in *Stage Door Canteen* (1943):

> What happens is that the movie, with lots of boys and girls, unable to be free and easy sexually and still wanting sex to be its theme, falls way over on the most unpleasant side of sex—the tongue hanging out, straining after, grasping for the kind of love which never reaches its goal. If this technique were used for a theme that was actually concerned with sexual teasing it would be perfect, but here it leads to such distorted idiocies as the boy writing the girl who gave him one very small kiss, "You made a man out of me." (92)

On a very few occasions Farber praises a Hollywood film for its treatment of sex. Minnelli's *The Clock* (1945) is "unusually good in its treatment of love, sex, or both" (237). A good treatment of sex is realistic, "emotionally accurate," and "the breakfast scene after the wedding night swims in a feeling of consummation" (237). Nearly the entire review of *The Very Thought of You* (1944) is given over to the film's admirable treatment of sex ("this picture is surprisingly cognizant of sex" [209]). Since it is about young lovers, the picture is "continually concerned, as it should be, with sex," and it often handles the subject with intelligent realism. Farber likes the fact that Eleanor Parker "gives this girl a credible lust at times"; instead of the typically desexualized good girl, "its nice-girl heroine is shown being moderately aroused during the love scenes" (209). The attention to female sexual desire is unusual in a film review, although once he gets there Farber works over the topic in rather obsessive detail. In a related example, he praises the treatment of female sexual desire in *Margie* (1946), even though here the young woman is only sixteen.

> The direction (Henry King) is sensitive to young girlisms; it tries in a candid and erotic way to express Margie's girlish sensuality by deliberate, youthfully idealized photography of her romantic posturings; her decorous walk is an effective caricature of the ladylike walk of a girl who has been raised too idealistically, and she is constantly wriggling as though her clothes hampered her. (295)

Farber's uncensored approach lingers almost too readily over the teenage girl's "wriggling." The film's "candid" approach is praiseworthy on Farber's terms, but the film's "erotic" elements are left confusingly placed between the heroine's adolescent sexuality and the male viewer's critical gaze.

All in all, Farber is more focused on sex and less anxious about sex than either Ferguson or Agee. But Seldes, Agee, and Farber all take the position that there is no sex in movies, either because the Hays Code has censored it or because it is so juvenile, blatant, and phony that no adult can count it as sex. By thinking instead of ogling, these male critics attempt to step outside of the male gaze/female object structure of the 1940s Hollywood film. That they refuse to buy into a commercialized and euphemized version of sexuality makes them more objective, credible critics. But it also puts them at odds with the vast majority of viewers who do see films and their stars—Hays Code or no—as swamped in sex and sexuality. Presumably many of those viewers know that Hollywood sex is not real sex, but they need their glamorous sexual fantasies. Is this need simply a "juvenile" need that the strong-minded can look down on? By pining for an adult sexual realism that they know Hollywood will never produce, these male critics opt for a utopian fantasy of their own, a fantasy that has no more foundation in reality than an adolescent crush on a movie star. Part of their fantasy depends on a narrative in which adult sexuality is more objective than adolescent sexuality; a more substantial part of this fantasy situates these critics as superior to everyone else's idea of sexual desire. But these men have desexualized the Hollywood film in their own way, by using an intellectual code in place of the Hays Code. Instead of recognizing and analyzing the contours of sexual desire in Hollywood film, these critics tend to deflate and dismiss the sexual.

Manny Farber may possibly be "the greatest by far of all American film critics" (Jonathan Rosenbaum), but his practice does not point a way forward.[25] Sex and sexuality need to be accounted for in Hollywood film, not dismissed. To apply the category of realism to Hollywood films makes a category mistake, since one should not expect realism in 1940s Hollywood. To dismiss nonrealistic sexuality is to stop thinking even while claiming to promote thoughtfulness. Farber's brief looks at female desire makes an interesting and (with *Margie*) awkward start.[26] But what is important to him, once again, is the realism, not the women. In the next sections anthropologists and then Diana Trilling provide more instructive and permanent ways to *think* about sexuality in popular culture.

Margaret Mead and Cultural Patterns

While male critics were writing film columns from individualized points of view, institutional studies of popular culture appeared throughout academia. Studies of popular culture often appeared under the rubric of "communications," such as *Communications in Modern Society: Fifteen Studies of the Mass Media Prepared for the University of Illinois Institute of Communications Research* (1948).[27] Wartime communication studies were interested in topics such as government control of the media and audience response to propaganda. Well-known studies in this vein include Hadley Cantril's *The Invasion from Mars* (1940), a report on the panic caused by Orson Welles's "War of the Worlds" broadcast in 1938, and *Mass Persuasion: The Social Psychology of a War Bond Drive* (1946), which looked at the response to a bond drive by Kate Smith.[28] In the early 1940s, Paul Lazarsfeld organized wide-ranging studies of radio; authors in these collections include Theodor Adorno and Rudolf Arnheim.[29] A later volume, *Communications Research 1948–1949*, includes studies of comics, radio, newspapers, and magazine reading.[30] The political biases of an Adorno is a rarity in these studies; most have a statistical emphasis with the goal of trying to report the objective facts about who reads what magazines, who listens to what radio programs and how often, and what impact these magazines and radio programs have on the average person. Moral qualms about the intellectual quality of the offerings are rarely expressed.[31]

The thesis of David Riesman's *The Lonely Crowd* (1950) gives immense formative power to the mass media. Riesman traces a historical shift in the United States from "inner-directed" character to "outer-directed," where people now seek cues outside themselves to guide their lives. The mass media plays a large role in contemporary character formation, since not only do children learn about the world from comics and movies, but parents also learn how to raise their children by reading books and magazines.[32] Methodologically *The Lonely Crowd* is far less data-driven than work associated with Lazarsfeld; instead Riesman's comments resemble the interpretive, panoramic style Margaret Mead and her followers adopted. In the 1950s Riesman would continue to provide readings of popular culture, and his practice would inspire further academic interpretation (such as Gene Balsley, "The Hot Rod Culture" in *American Quarterly* [1950]).[33]

The discipline of anthropology provided the institutional framework most likely to investigate the role of sexuality in popular culture. Sociologists kept careful track of male and female roles, of course, and social psychologists paid careful attention to sexual development and expression. But the role of sex and sexuality in culture became a foundational issue for anthropology, especially under the guidance of Margaret Mead. The Columbia University Research in Contemporary Cultures project, which Margaret Mead and Ruth Benedict created in 1948, would inspire numerous readings of sex and sexuality in American and European culture. Geoffrey Gorer's *The American People: A Study in National Character* (1948) was written as a follow-up to Margaret Mead's *And Keep Your Powder Dry: An Anthropologist Looks At America* (1943) and within the framework of the Columbia research project. *Movies: A Psychological Study* (1950) by Martha Wolfenstein and Nathan Leites is another product of this setting. Whereas Seldes and Agee might become defensive around sexual imagery, it was a main goal for Mead and her fellow researchers to analyze the role of sexuality in a given culture. Mead made a name for herself with a trio of works, *Coming of Age in Samoa* (1928), *Growing Up in New Guinea* (1930), and *Sex and Temperament in Three Primitive Societies* (1935). She then transferred her anthropological focus on sexuality to American culture in *Male and Female: A Study of the Sexes in a Changing World* (1949). These books by Mead,

Wolfenstein and Leites, and Gorer provide the best indications of what a critical thinker can do with sexuality and culture during the 1940s.

Gorer's *The American People* was uniformly knocked down in the academic press because of its lack of quantitative data. And this charge is valid. The book takes an anthropological approach to American activities such as dating and radio listening, but supplies little empirical support. Yet viewed from our perspective, the book can be seen as joining work by phantom women such as Ruth Herschberger, who wrote on subjects that were nearly incomprehensible at the time. Herschberger criticized society's representations of female desire and she was either mocked or ignored. Gorer criticized society's representation of masculinity, and while his book was widely reviewed, his most original emphases were often ignored.

A main stretch of Gorer's book argues that American masculinity is structured as a flight from homosexuality. This anxiety shapes every aspect of the parent-child relationship: "It is the overriding fear of all American parents that their child will turn into a sissy."[34] And Gorer continues this description into adult relationships between male friends. Because of the fundamental fear that men will discover or reveal a feminine inner self, male friendships must be conducted in a low-key manner. "It is considered essential that the warmer the relationship is between friends, the more ardently they shall pursue women together, because of the American panic fear of homosexuality. Among the generality of Americans homosexuality is regarded not with distaste, disgust, or abhorrence, but with panic; it is seen as an immediate and personal threat."[35]

That masculinity is built on a foundation of homophobia is today a completely familiar idea.[36] But it is a sexual understanding that made little sense at the time. Academic reviews focused on Gorer's psychocultural readings of fathers and mothers in American culture. Only Hortense Powdermaker, herself an anthropologist with an interest in American popular culture, recognized that "panic fear [of one's own] homosexuality" was one of Gorer's "major themes."[37] But she dismisses his claim. In answer to Gorer's argument that the War Department provided female entertainers and pictures of pinup girls in order to shore up the fragile masculinity of soldiers, Powdermaker says "we think it is quite normal to provide female companionship for heterosexual men who were necessarily deprived of it in camp and at the front."[38] Other than Powdermaker, no other reviewer of Gorer's book cites anything beyond a brief mention that Americans worry about potentially "sissy" sons.[39] Male heterosexual desire is generally so clear, and male homosexual desire so unimaginable, that 1940s readers found little purchase in Gorer's extraordinarily perceptive descriptions of American masculinity.

The title of *Movies: A Psychological Study* by Wolfenstein and Leites is deceptive since it follows Mead much more than Freud. The book's opening "note" of acknowledgment says "we owe very much to the work of Margaret Mead, to our collaboration with her in the Columbia University Research in Contemporary Cultures"; the authors also express their intellectual debts to both Geoffrey Gorer and David Riesman.[40] Like Mead and Gorer, the authors seek patterns in American culture. While Mead and Gorer discuss American social rituals, Wolfenstein and Leites propose to study America's "day-dreams" in the form of recent Hollywood films. Farber wanted more reality and less fantasy, and often refused to admit that Hollywood sex was sex. But Wolfenstein and Leites see sex everywhere in Hollywood daydreams.[41]

The opening chapter, "The Good–Bad Girl," describes what may be the central image of female sexuality in the 1940s. This character is not only sexually stimulating to men, but also possesses sisterly or motherly qualities. "American films thus provide an eat-your-cake-and-have-it-solution to the old conflict between sacred and profane love. The exciting qualities of the bad woman and the comradely loyalty of the good one are all wrapped up in one prize package, which we have called the good–bad girl."[42] Farber might account for her presence by the Hays Code; the "good–bad girl" is a sexually attractive woman who appears in films where nothing sexual can take place. But Wolfenstein and Leites never mention the Hays Code since this multifaceted figure appears throughout 1940s culture. Indeed, Wolfenstein and Leites propose that "the good–bad girl is perhaps a melodramatic reflection of the American popular girl," who reflects the fact that "American courtship patterns are based on a series of breaks between looking and going to bed."[43] All American teenagers know the rules: "it is possible to look and go no further, to kiss and go no further, to pet and go no further."[44] If the main female protagonist of 1940s films derives from the courtship rituals of "the American popular girl," then Seldes and Farber are right, and Hollywood emphasizes adolescent and not adult sex. But the male critics complain about Hays and sexual prudery and stop there. Instead one can work out the psychological reasons that support the masculine need to create this new female figure, this woman who is both loyal and sexy, neither virgin nor vamp.

Wolfenstein and Leites identify another version of this contradictory feminine type, in which the contradiction works to resolve sexual anxieties felt by men. Film critics in the 1940s agreed that the seductive 1920s female vamp had disappeared, or was now played only for laughs. According to Wolfenstein and Leites, the less frightening vamp now appears as the "masculine woman," who "admits without euphemism that she is interested in sex." But "unlike the vamp, she does not carry an unrelieved aura of it."[45] The vamp was frightening because "of her insistence on a passion-dominated and woman-centered existence," but the "masculine-feminine woman" views sex in male terms, as "fun" but "without the emotional hazards."[46] If *Movies: A Psychological Study* actually belonged to the discipline of psychology, the "masculine woman" would have set off alarms. No 1940s psychologist wants to see the boundaries between masculinity and femininity blur. But instead of worrying about whether this figure is feminine enough or abnormal, Wolfenstein and Leites read this film image as a fantasy solution to a major threat to male sexuality.[47] If female desire is too all-encompassing, the woman becomes monstrous, an erratic, soul-destroying vampire. By contrast, the "masculine–feminine" woman represents—from a man's point of view—just the right amount of female desire.

The reason that Gorer, Wolfenstein, Leites, and even Powdermaker can see past the rigidity of 1940s gender roles is that they have gone to school in the research of Margaret Mead and Ruth Benedict. Mead argued that the "wider range of sexual practices" in Samoan society resolved the common sex problems of American women, including frigidity and marital unhappiness.[48] Ruth Benedict's 1934 essay, "Anthropology and the Abnormal," argued in favor of cultural relativism and, more subtly, against heteronormativity.[49] Due to their close affiliation with Mead and Benedict, Gorer, Wolfenstein, and Leites were able to think more flexibly about sexual categories. Hortense Powdermaker, who alone could see the "major theme" of homosexual panic in Gorer's book, began her anthropological career conducting fieldwork in Papua New Guinea. Together, their cross-cultural understanding of sexuality allowed them to realize that sexual behavior was culturally constructed and evaluated.

Margaret Mead's *Male and Female* (1949) became her major statement on the relationship between biological sex and gendered behavior. It began by reviewing her anthropological work in the South Seas, and ended with an interpretation of contemporary American sex and sexuality. Mead had criticized the Kinsey report for its deluge of sexual statistics that omitted real thinking about sex.[50] *Male and Female*, by contrast, is short on statistics, but rich with thought and ideas. Mead interrogates the ideals of masculinity and femininity that circulate through American society. "Current practice, the scientifically supported dicta of pediatrician, dietician, physical therapist, and health-educator, the styles set by current fiction and movies and radio, the underlying assumptions and innuendoes of the advertisements—these coalesce to form an imaginary past for the pictured ideal, the imaginary future."[51] Mead criticizes the cultural models radio and magazines offered by arguing that their limited conceptions of sex role deprive both men and women of a "fullness of humanity."[52]

Whether Mead sufficiently detached herself from contemporary gender ideals when she critiqued the inflexibility of American conventions remains an open question. Betty Friedan found Mead's critique disappointing precisely because Mead had access to all those "abnormal" versions of sexuality. According to Friedan, Mead's South Seas work had allowed her "a vision of the infinite variety of sexual pattern and the enormous plasticity of human nature."[53] So that Mead "might have passed on to the popular culture a truly revolutionary vision of women finally free to realize their full capabilities in a society which replaced arbitrary sexual definitions with a recognition of genuine individual gifts as they occur in either sex."[54] Hence Friedan argues that Mead still buys into the archetypal associations of the feminine (mothering, nurturing), such that "*Male and Female* became the cornerstone of the feminine mystique."[55] From the perspective of an emerging feminism in 1963, it is quite possible to argue that Mead does not take her critique of gender norms nearly far enough. But how far can one take gendered critique in 1950?

We can address this question by looking at Diana Trilling's essay-length review of Mead's *Male and Female*. Trilling's article, "Men, Women, and Sex," summarizes and debates Mead's book more thoroughly than any other contemporary review. The feminist energy and clarity Friedan claimed are not available to Trilling or to Mead, as Trilling makes apparent: "Anyone who would wish to make a program for the sexes today must settle this major conflict of women, between feminism and 'female-ism.' To come out unequivocally for either the one side or the other in the struggle is, however, to be either ahead of or behind the time, for uncertainty is the very essence of this stage in our development."[56] As in her book reviews, and unlike nearly everyone else, Trilling pays careful attention to Mead's descriptions of homosexuality. Trilling does not treat queer topics in a twenty-first-century academic manner, but that she treats them so often and so thoughtfully distinguishes her from most of her contemporaries. Trilling's book reviews inform her that homosexuality is on the increase, and in order to rebut Mead's explanation of homosexuality, she provides an explanation of her own. "We may not know with any certainty that there is more sexual competition and strain between a feminist mother and her husband than between a 'female' mother and her husband. But the homosexual story of this century at least seems to suggest a connection between the increase in women's rights and an increase in inversion."[57] From our probably liberal point of view, this excerpt offers an inaccurate description and an absurd explanation. But compared to the rampant misogyny and homophobia everywhere else, Trilling's attempt to tell a "homosexual story" at least makes a start. The norm for sexual analysis in the 1940s is Farnham and Lundberg's *Modern Woman: The Lost Sex* (1947); as Trilling notes, Mead's *Male and Female* exposes the "dull meanness of spirit" in that work.[58] Farnham and Lundberg provide the misogyny that the decade expects; writers such as Mead and Trilling give a sense of the revolutionary possible; writers such as Elizabeth Hawes and Ruth Herschberger manage somehow to write the revolutionary impossible.

Diana Trilling saves her signature critique for last. Invoking her favorite scholar of sex, D. H. Lawrence, she undermines Mead's very notion of sexuality. "Lawrence knew what we scarcely guess from Dr. Mead's book, that sex is life itself. And he knew that life must be lived, not solved; that sex is a primary experience and not merely a means to an end. He knew that life is destroyed by program-making."[59] Trilling criticizes the abstraction of Mead's text, the "non-physical emphasis of *Male and Female*." She also implies that the scientific approach—even one as impressionistic as Mead's—cannot, in the end, know as much about sexuality as the experiential art of fiction. But she fundamentally disagrees with the idea that sexuality is entirely explicable as a social function. "How are we to prize our specific sexuality except in its exercise? And how are we to exercise our maleness and femaleness in a world such as Dr. Mead's book describes, in which the whole of our sexual motive would seem to be social motive?" Hence Trilling argues that Mead's sexuality has no sex in it. "The sexuality of *Male and Female*," she writes, "is the sexuality of ego, never of libido." What Trilling wants to see, in other words, and what she often finds in her reading, is a representation of sexual desire. What does desire look like?

Diana Trilling in the 1940s and Beyond

Diana Trilling reviewed novels for the *Nation* from 1941 to 1949. Many of these reviews were reprinted in 1978 as *Reviewing the Forties*.[60] One year earlier, Trilling had published *We Must March My Darlings: A Critical Decade* (1977), which collects essays on the mid-1960s and early-1970s.[61] Following on these expressly political reflections, *Reviewing the Forties* could have appeared as a kind of sequel, which now takes the 1940s as a "critical decade." Or *Reviewing the Forties* could have been framed as rediscovered feminism, like Ruth Herschberger's *Adam's Rib*, which was ignored in 1948, but found plenty of feminist readers when finally republished in 1970. Instead, *Reviewing the Forties* came with a preface not by Trilling, but by Paul Fussell, most well-known at the time for *The Great War and Modern Memory* (1975). Fussell rightly sees that Trilling's essays are about "the culture of the nineteen-forties, and not just 'culture' in the high-minded sense."[62] Hence Fussell summons up the songs, trains, ads, and magazines of 1940s culture to put readers in the proper frame of mind. While this context is helpful, Trilling's emphasis in these reviews is more methodical than Fussell lets on. As Fussell suggests, Diana Trilling is much less interested in high culture for its own sake than critics such as Edmund Wilson or, indeed, her husband Lionel Trilling. But she maintains a focus on sexual themes that sets her apart from almost every other critic of the period. In this respect, Diana Trilling's 1940s look directly ahead to her work in the 1960s and 1970s.

In this section I look at Trilling's reviews of fiction during the 1940s, while also following the arc of her career into the 1970s and beyond. This narrative will help us see what it was possible to do with gender and culture in the 1940s. By the 1970s Diana Trilling was invited onto major panels about women's issues and she was published in major anthologies on popular culture. With the clarity of hindsight, we can see that her 1940s reviews are aimed in that direction. But at the time, the study of sexuality in relationship to popular culture does not have a clear method. The anthropologists noted previously are probably the closest analogy, but Trilling makes her own path.

Trilling's reviews in the *Nation* touch again and again not just on sexuality, but on underrepresented sexuality. The overt politics of her reviews are "liberal," but also "anti-communist," in contrast to the communist bias of the front part of the magazine.[63] Just as the *Nation*'s film reviewer James Agee developed an aesthetics of realism in his evaluation of popular films, Trilling often focuses on sexual elements in fiction. Book reviewers in the *New Yorker* or the *Saturday Review of Literature* would, of course, tell—or warn—readers about the sexual content of novels, but Trilling shows a special interest in fiction that represents in unconventional ways female sexuality and homosexuality.

Diana Trilling had been nominated for the post of *Nation* book reviewer by her already well-known husband, Lionel Trilling. Diana Trilling's *Nation* reviews sometimes overlap in large-scale ideology with essays that Lionel Trilling wrote at the same time, and which would be collected in his surprisingly popular *The Liberal Imagination* (1950). But Diana Trilling's approach to culture makes a sharp contrast with that of her husband. Lionel Trilling—famously, academically—stocks his essays about great men (Wordsworth, Twain, James, Kipling, Freud) with cartloads of quotations from even more great men.[64] In her search for aesthetic nourishment and moral enlightenment, however, Diana Trilling purposefully wades into much less elitist waters. Instead of Lionel's ivory tower allusions, Diana's criticism often makes reference to Hollywood plots or women's magazine writing. And in her evaluations, if the subject is interesting to her, she is quite willing to forgo art or literariness. She is still a tough reviewer who does not forgive the shallow, the conventional, or the boring. Yet she is willing to work through a much wider cultural spectrum than her husband. And she would pursue this impulse throughout her career. In the 1950s, against the advice of Edmund Wilson, she began to contribute to women's magazines and popular magazines—*Vogue*, *Look*, *McCall's*, *Mademoiselle*.[65] In *The Beginning of the Journey*, the memoir of her marriage, she supposes that she was the first contributor to the *Partisan Review* who had also written for *Glamour*.[66]

To solidify this description of Diana Trilling's approach, a brief comparison with Edmund Wilson is instructive. As a weekly book reviewer for the *New Yorker* from January 1944 on, Wilson's job overlapped exactly with Diana Trilling's. However, his approach to literature was entirely different. "Like most serious intellectuals, Wilson was an intellectual snob," writes Trilling.[67] Wilson's way of dividing up the world comes through even in his title—*Classics and Commercials: A Literary Chronicle of the Forties* (1950). As often as not, Wilson reviews deceased authors instead of living ones, "classics" like Samuel Johnson, Peacock, Thackeray, Wilde, and Shaw, with two articles on George Saintsbury. "Commercials" do not usually fare very well, as exemplified by a characteristic attack on the mystery genre, "Who Cares Who Killed Roger Ackroyd?"[68] The attack metaphor takes center stage in "Ambushing a Best-Seller," where Wilson tries to steer readers away from Anya Seton's *The Turquoise* (1946) before the book can top the charts. In his assault, Wilson provides an elaborately detailed plot summary, which in itself makes the book look foolish, then crushes what remains into trashy atoms. "The whole thing is as synthetic, as arbitrary, as basically cold and dead, as a scenario for a film. And now the question presents itself: Will real men and women, in large numbers, as the publishers obviously hope, really buy and read this arid rubbish, which has not even the rankness of the juicier trash?"[69] By comparing the novel to a film script, Wilson recalls that Seton's previous novel, *Dragonwyck* (1944) had been made into a film (1946). In so doing, he links the mass culture corruption of Hollywood to the antiliterary goal of writing a bestseller. As author of the censored *Memoirs of Hecate County* (1946), Wilson makes clear he is no prude since he could frankly use more "juice." But what Wilson more often wanted was material that other readers would find dry as dust: "what are really most needed now are reprints of Saintsbury's important works."[70]

In contrast to Wilson, Diana Trilling reads less "classical" material with much more patience. Like James Agee watching a Hollywood film, Trilling does not necessarily look for high art in fiction. Intelligence and sincerity will often do. But from our perspective, Trilling takes a progressive step past Agee in her emphasis on underrepresented sexuality. Trilling treats homosexuality and female heterosexuality more methodically and more sympathetically than most other reviewers, and often more sympathetically than the novelists themselves. Like many reviewers, Trilling admires the powerful depiction of racial miscegenation in Lillian Smith's *Strange Fruit* (1944). Like few other reviewers, she sees much in Hannah Lees's depiction of sexual loneliness in *Till the Boys Come Home* (1944). Although she teases the authors for their glibness about sex, Trilling takes Rose Franken's *Another Claudia* (1943) and Ilka Chase's *In Bed We Cry* (1943) much more seriously than a serious reviewer ought because there is the attempt to represent female desire with a bit of realism. Rose Franken's hugely popular Claudia appeared in a radio program, a play, and in a series of novels; nonetheless—despite its mass appeal—Trilling finds pleasure here: "I nevertheless enjoyed reading *Another Claudia* much more than I've enjoyed reading what passes for serious fiction. The writing is simple and adequate. If there isn't much action, there's a good substitute: the sense of every page filled with the detail of day-to-day living. And after all, so few writers have anything to add to life, it is rather a relief to read someone who makes no pretense to doing more than mirror our suburban make-believe" (38–39). By refusing to reinforce the standard hierarchy of serious over popular, Trilling avoids, as she says, "by-passing modest novels that have their own validity" (115).

Trilling spends a good deal of time working out the sexual validity of individual works. She rejects the "major implication" of Anaïs Nin's *This Hunger* (1946) for what it says about men and women, just as she attacks the social determinism of sexuality implied by Truman Capote's *Other Voices, Other Rooms* (1948). She agrees with Philip Wylie in *Opus 21* (1949) that a "faulty attitude toward man's biological nature creates the horrors of modern society," but she attacks his version of Freudian theory as "foolish" and even "dangerous" (262). Trilling calls Hubert Creekmore's *The Welcome* (1948) "the most disturbing statement of the damage done to and by society by our refusal to recognize how widespread is the homosexual preference," but repeatedly describes the novel's attitude toward homosexuality as "muddled" (244). She critiques the supposedly "pornographic" scenes in Edmund Wilson's *Memoirs of Hecate County* (1946), "not because they are daring but because of the breach they make between sensation and emotion" (153). In a comparison of the first version of *Lady Chatterley's Lover* with the last, Trilling calls Lawrence's novel, "a great failure, as a thesis novel is likely to be, even at its best" (94). Even though Trilling praises Christina Stead's *For Love Alone* (1944) for its unconventional look at women's sexuality ("Miss Stead shows Teresa to be quite frenzied with sexual desire—and this seems to me to be a healthy defiance of the present-day convention which permits sexuality to married women (or children) but not to very young women" [111]), she nonetheless begins the review by saying that the best novels about "female love are still written by men" (110). In its attention to the supposed nonproblem of male virginity, Robert Gibbons's *The Patchwork Time* (1948) is a "small act of cultural revolution" (236), even though its experimental style adds up only to a "sterile mechanical purpose" (235). Passing beneath her gaze basically unscathed are Christopher Isherwood's *Prater Violet* (1945) and *The Christmas Tree* (1949) by Isabel Bolton, whom Trilling calls the "best woman writer of fiction in this country today." Like few other authors, Bolton asks the question—"what is there in our society that accounts for the alarming increase in male homosexuality?" (254). Trilling disagrees with the ways that writers such as Capote and Creekmore worked out that question, yet she has only praise for Bolton's "objective universe," which shows the problem without teetering into didacticism.

Whereas Lionel Trilling's work has its scholarly roots in the cultural criticism of Matthew Arnold, Diana Trilling's emphases emerge at least in part from the fiction and criticism of D. H. Lawrence. Before becoming book reviewer for the *Nation*, Diana Trilling had written practically nothing. Her claim to critical acuity stemmed chiefly from her editing of her husband's dissertation and first book. As she writes in *The Beginning of the Journey*: "I never doubted my competence to judge their [other writers'] work. I had no hesitation in reshaping Lionel's prose; in draft after draft of his *Matthew Arnold*, I removed, added to, or otherwise altered what he had written. What I was trying to bring to his writing was a greater directness and a greater fluidity."[71] Whereas Matthew Arnold lamented the provincial English mind cut off from continental Europe, Lawrence lamented the insularity of a mind cut off from the body. In his fiction, Lawrence was a major critic of culture, just like Arnold, except that Lawrence found truth in sexuality instead of literature. As Diana Trilling says in her introduction to Viking's *Portable D. H. Lawrence* (1947), "There have been few writers in any era, and certainly none in ours, who have combined as Lawrence did the gifts of the creative heart and the penetrations of the critical intellect."[72] Lawrence, who "lived in the years which gave birth to so many of our present-day social and political confusions, . . . hits so directly at our weaknesses that we rush to the attack upon *his* weaknesses, manifest or imagined, and try to dismiss him as reactionary, as fascist, as death-worshipping, as sexually abnormal."[73] Trilling's "Introduction" is a powerfully eloquent defense of this major but misunderstood writer. "No aspect of Lawrence's thought," she says, "has been more over-responded to, or more misrepresented[,] than his sexual ideas."[74]

Like Lawrence, Diana Trilling understands sexuality as a central element of culture, and her writing is remarkably consistent in this regard. In *The Beginning of the Journey*, she says that publishers during the forties kept asking her to write a book about women, and she considered Jane Welsh Carlyle and Freud's "friend and pupil Lou Andreas-Salomé." But she ended up writing about Lawrence. "While I was still working for the *Nation* I edited the volume on D. H. Lawrence for the Viking Portable Library; I also published a selection of Lawrence's letters. In 1950 I was awarded a Guggenheim Fellowship for a book in which I proposed to study the interplay between my family culture and the general culture of the time in which I grew up. The book was never written except as there may now be a reminiscence of it in this volume."[75] It is striking that out of all the Viking Portable Library authors, Diana Trilling was matched to D. H. Lawrence. But her *Nation* reviews had already made her interests clear. Her desire to work back and forth between private and public, between the intimate and the social, is further evidenced by her Guggenheim Fellowship award. Published many years later, *The Beginning of the Journey: The Marriage of Diana and Lionel Trilling* may only distantly recall the terms of the Guggenheim proposal and its research, but it follows through on the general tendency of her thought, which is to study the relationship of sexuality to culture.

In her reviews of the 1940s, Trilling maintains a carefully worked out structure of aesthetic evaluation. She wants the subjective world connected to an objective one. Throughout the decade, she critiques writers—especially women writers—for their "narcissistic," "claustrophobic" novels of "sensibility." In Trilling's jargon, "sensibility" is the opposite of "objective" ("Yet a faint perfume of sensibility does linger around Miss Porter's short stories, despite their vigorous objectivity" [106]). Trilling identifies the novel that turns inward without connecting itself to society as a truly dismal transformation; "I often think that the chief path being followed to the destruction of the modern novel is that of an excessive sensibility"

(127). Trilling's aesthetic demands dialectics; interiorized fiction that does not link itself to a larger cultural reality necessarily fails. When she argued that Margaret Mead's *Male and Female* talked about culture without libido, Trilling imposed her dialectic in reverse. But this dialectic is not just an abstract diagram; it is gendered and culturally concrete. For Trilling imposes it again and again on women.

Using several remarkable analogies, Trilling makes clear that she is especially concerned about the internalized, "narcissistic" novel as it appears in the hands of women. In her view, culture's deluge of glamorous advertisements leads to female self-absorption, and she does not want novels to replicate this effect. Thus she equates the "sexual narcissism" of Helen Haberman's *How about Tomorrow Morning?* (1945) with advertisements in women's magazines that carry the message, "You have never been so pretty" (130). Haberman's book is a trifle, and few other serious reviewers would bother with it. But a main goal of Trilling's reviews is to redefine what serious reviewers do and what they talk about, and she has a serious point. She wants to link the commercialized portraits of women in magazines to depictions of femininity in various kinds of fiction. Haberman's naive fiction is an easy target, but Trilling uses the same critique when she writes about Elizabeth Hardwick and Eudora Welty. Her review of Welty's *The Wide Net* (1943) builds to an enormous metaphor that compares "the chic modern department store and much of modern fiction." What the department store does is create "a myth of modern femininity" and, in Trilling's view, Welty's myth-making works along the same lines. The "self-loving dream" of the department store, of the women's magazine advertisement, is not so different from "the narcissism, the mythologizing of female selfhood, which finds so strong a support in current female writing, including Miss Welty's" (59).

Trilling's approach to popular culture is therefore both traditionally elitist and innovatively comparative. Almost all examples from the mass media are deployed as objects of scorn; magazine fiction is silly (Martha Foley is "still flogging the dead horse of the popular-magazine story" in her selections for *The Best American Short Stories*, 1943 [62]), radio is a waste of time, and novels that sound like Hollywood films are useless ("it is a tedious romance aimed at the movies" [238]). Nor is she too enthusiastic about genre fiction since a review of four thrillers is a rarity (19), and she cannot manage to read science fiction ("I am sadly without taste for fiction about life anywhere except on earth" [67]). On the other hand, Trilling also consistently upends what counts for "literature" by attacking the "pretentious" and the "self-absorbed." After her analyses, there is no more hierarchy from the serious great to the superficially popular. When she shows that

Eudora Welty and Helen Haberman are working with the same models of femininity, Trilling shows a thematic continuity between the prestigious and the commercial. And, as we have seen throughout, Trilling finds energy and truth in various kinds of work.

Trilling's clearest provocation in *Reviewing the Forties* is her championing of Isabel Bolton. Bolton's *Do I Wake or Sleep* (1946) is "quite the best novel that has come my way in the four years I have been reviewing new fiction for this magazine" (196), and Bolton's *The Christmas Tree* (1949) establishes her "as the best woman writer of fiction in this country today" (253). As Trilling notes in her review, Edmund Wilson fulsomely praised Bolton's *Do I Wake or Sleep* in the *New Yorker*. But otherwise Trilling is basically alone in her exalted opinion of these works. Her choice ranks Bolton's earlier work higher than novels by Jean Stafford, Saul Bellow, Christina Stead, William Maxwell, Elizabeth Hardwick, Christopher Isherwood, Evelyn Waugh, Lillian Smith, and Carson McCullers (just to name authors she reviewed). But her disruptive choice is entirely consistent with her aesthetic emphases. What Trilling especially admires in Bolton is what, she says, is lacking in Elizabeth Bowen, who "has never been able to relate the forces that move the individual with the forces that animate a whole society" (197). *Do I Wake or Sleep* circulates between flowing layers of interiority and precise descriptions of New York City, such that the novel "demonstrates the human outcome of cultural fact." Trilling finds in Bolton an ideal marriage of subjective and objective, of psychological desire set into a cultural network. "Our modern dilemma," according to the novel, is that the world is "thrust with such violence into one's breast," and the statement is proved when a main character watches a wartime newsreel filled with noise and nightmare from every corner of the globe.[76] The novel resolves these threats and assaults at the end, when the same character's thoughts are joined to the natural world: "She did not know. Her thoughts had become merged with the flux, the flow—with wind and leaf and bud and blossom."[77]

Both of Bolton's novels—descendants of James and Proust as Trilling observes—make a virtue of fluidity, both psychological and sexual. Just as interior states of mind are linked to various descriptions and evaluations of cultural elements, which gives the books a layered, circulating sense, sex is treated unconventionally. In reply to a wit at a party, who proposes "to give his characters symbolic names—Lydia Libido—Ida Id—Prysilla Psyche," Bridget argues that, in contrast to the Restoration, today's people no longer "hew to a formal pattern, where sex [is] harnessed to rules as formal as figures in a dance."[78] The appearance of the homosexual son in *The Christmas Tree* confirms this conceptually flowing, fragmented world, where "we have no worldly identity whatever; we are without sex, androgynous, anonymous, anybody, everybody, nobody."[79] The most conventional aspect of *The Christmas Tree* is its conclusion, in which the male homosexual is taken away by the police on a murder charge. Both Diana Trilling and the son's mother see homosexuality as a problem, and the novel cannot manage to conclude without a sensational crisis. But before the novel's end, the homosexual character is not sensationalized or exploited; instead he takes his part in fluid descriptions of the relationship between desire and society. The interrelationship of things is at the heart of Bolton's books, as Trilling observes: "In her universe as in the theology of St. Paul we are all part of one another, and if the world goes down, we all go down with it together" (256). In a sexual culture which so emphasized the boundary between male and female, and so often portrayed sexual desire as either wolfish or absent, Bolton's methodical depictions of more open possibilities serve indeed as a rehabilitating tonic.

Diana Trilling's collection of essays from the late 1960s and early 1970s, *We Must March My Darlings* (1977), makes a wide sweep across American culture, and one similarly centered on sexuality. She writes about homosexuality ("Our Uncomplaining Homosexuals"), women's liberation ("Female Biology in a Male Culture"), and once again, Lawrence ("Lawrence and the Movements of Modern Culture"). She replays her involvement in the feminist bashing of Norman Mailer's *Prisoner of Sex*, which was filmed by D. A. Pennebaker as *Town Bloody Hall* (1979). Whereas Lionel Trilling was embarrassed by movies, Diana Trilling writes a completely convincing essay on *Easy Rider*, which not only interprets its political radicalism, but also questions its mostly too-friendly reception by the media.[80] This essay had already appeared in *Mass Culture Revisited* (1971) as one of only two essays on film. What this latter collection "revisits" is one of the earliest anthologies of popular culture criticism, *Mass Culture: The Popular Arts in America* (1957). By including Diana Trilling in the 1971 version, editors Rosenberg and White recognize her for what she is: an important and unique cultural critic.

Trilling's critical emphases are allowed their most vigorous display in her 1981 book on the murder of Dr. Tarnower, *Mrs. Harris: The Death of the Scarsdale Diet Doctor*. Like her articles for women's magazines, Trilling's book takes a populist approach, and Hollywood even bought the movie rights for $1 million. The body of the book consists of an in-the-moment eyewitness description of the trial testimony; this is no doubt what the movie producers bought. But the first and last third of the book offer terrifically detailed psychological and sociological contexts for the characters in the murder. Trilling takes her part not only as a regular in court, but as a person whose social class, ethnicity, and geography put her in relationship to the main characters of the crime. She draws connections outward from these characters, so that Christopher Lehmann-Haupt could write in the *New York Times*: "What impressed this reader most about Mrs. Trilling's multi-shaded treatment of the case is the degree to which she makes it seem significant to American culture."[81] And what makes it seem most significant is Trilling's extraordinarily scrupulous attention to the machinations of sexuality and sexual desire. Her description of Mrs. Harris takes the narrative back to 1945 when she graduated from Smith College. "A major effort of public relations was mounted to prepare women for demobilization and the return to female submission. Psychoanalysis, which was now at the height of its influence in America, contributed to this impulse to emotional re-education and supplied some of its vocabulary along with its basic doctrine: Freud not only refused women cultural equality with men but also gave a strong charge of condescension to the analytical emphasis on female 'passivity.' So far as I know, this phenomenon of the forties hasn't been studied by cultural historians."[82] In passages like this, Mrs. Harris lives a version of Betty Friedan's allegorical life, coming of age in the 1940s amidst a culturally produced sense of "sexual inferiority," and then awakening with deadly contradiction to the sexual freedom practiced by the Scarsdale Diet Doctor.

Trilling's identity as a leading feminist critic is recognized most clearly with her inclusion in the anti-Mailer bash of 1971, a meeting filmed by D. A. Pennebaker and Chris Hegedus as *Town Bloody Hall* (1979). Here four eminent women confront Norman Mailer and his recently published *The Prisoner of Sex*. The four women panelists are Jacqueline Ceballos, president of the New York chapter of the National Organization of Women (NOW); Jill Johnston, columnist for the *Village Voice* and soon-to-be-author of *Lesbian Nation: The Feminist Solution* (1974); Germaine Greer, whose *The Female Eunuch* (1971) had just appeared; and Diana Trilling. Since the roast is for Norman Mailer, it makes sense to have at least one literary critic, but Trilling does more than token duty. She is not as programmatic as Ceballos, as revolutionary as Greer, nor as agitprop as Johnston (who ends her speech by rolling off the stage embraced with two women and then declining to return). Trilling looks like a Columbia academic, but she can talk some inspirational talk about female sexuality.

> And among those efforts of the women's liberationists which I find most impoverishing, most absolutist, is the doctrine now being promulgated on the female orgasm. I find it remarkable

> that the same people who properly criticize our society for its hard treatment of homosexuals have no hesitation in dictating to women—and it *is* dictation, make no mistake about that, especially when it is directed to the young—where they are to find their presumably single path to sexual pleasure. I am talking, of course, about the campaign now being mounted to persuade women that there is no such thing as a vaginal orgasm, and that they therefore might just as well dispense with men even in bed.[83]

On this panel, and before an audience packed with dignitaries—Betty Friedan and Cynthia Ozick ask Mailer questions, while Susan Sontag asks Trilling if she is offended by Mailer's patronizing address—Diana Trilling looks perfectly in place. Mailer and Greer are more flamboyant, talk in obscenities, flirt with one another (in fact), and draw most of the crowd's hostility and affection. But Trilling's more composed, mediated feminism does not look like it belongs in a classroom or at home; her sensibility lends the whole affair a reasonableness it would otherwise surely lack.

Beside her on the dais, talking in a far more revolutionary way than Trilling ever would, is Germaine Greer. Greer's *The Female Eunuch* takes as its titular center the image of a woman deprived of her sexual desires by family, education, and wider culture. "We must reject femininity as meaning *without libido*," writes Greer.[84] In 1950 Trilling criticized Margaret Mead's *Male and Female* for leaving out libido, and her book reviews quietly and unusually kept track of female desire. But now that Greer had addressed herself to female sexuality with uncompromising clarity, Trilling critiques this clarity through dialectic. When Greer throws off family, psychology, and even biology and culture, she, according to Trilling, ends up with an impossibly isolated libido. "For Miss Greer sex is not sex unless it is *only* sex, a triumphant refusal of any other of the forms in which libido may present itself."[85] As she has throughout her career, Trilling insists on the interplay between private and public, sexuality and culture. When, in the town hall meeting, Greer says that she does not resemble her mother, Trilling says: "If women are not to grow by identifications with their mothers, what are they to grow by?"

And this gets to the heart of the matter. What does female desire look like? Where will it find its model? In her memoir *When Men Were the Only Models We Had: My Teachers Barzun, Fadiman, Trilling*, Carolyn Heilbrun says that while Lionel Trilling's influence was formative for her, a respect for Diana Trilling came only very late. As she read through Diana Trilling's works, "I found myself surprised by the positive impressions of her I was gaining. Stunned by the responses of those to whom I mentioned my new and still grudging admiration for her, I became troubled by how wildly disliked or disdained she seemed to have been, and how little appreciation of her was to be found in published materials about the Trillings' circle."[86] If Diana Trilling's work needs critical rehabilitation, then this chapter seeks to support that project. She worked at a time when "men were the only models women had," and out of that work emerged a dialectical, antielitist kind of feminism with a focus on female sexuality.

What does female sexuality look like at a time when women are supposed to look like models, but men provide all the real models? Or to put it differently, what can an emerging female desire look like when male desire is all that culture represents? In *The Female Eunuch*, Greer quotes Freud's description of a libido that is only masculine, whether possessed by men or women. "Indeed, if we were able to give a more definite connotation to the concept of 'masculine' and 'feminine,' it would also be possible to maintain that libido is invariably and necessarily of a masculine nature, whether it occurs in men or women, and irrespectively of whether its object is a man or a woman."[87] Germaine Greer pares away cultural context from her newly emergent female desire, in order to emphasize autonomy and reinvention. In her turn, Diana Trilling underlines the relationship between biological impulse, active personal choice, and cultural restraint. She reminds Greer of the importance of mothers, although probably the daughter does not learn about female desire from her mother.

By surveying writers from Gilbert Seldes and Margaret Mead to Diana Trilling, we can outline the limits of what it was possible to say about sexuality in popular culture during the 1940s. Diana Trilling's own career allows us to see how her critical emphases during the forties needed decades to develop into full-scale readings. When the present book develops the implications of 1940s examples into full-scale contemporary readings, my aim is to both honor and recapitulate Trilling's career. Even though Diana Trilling's work remains mostly invisible, she still offers a useable model of cultural criticism that is well worth our second look. The next chapter starts with a detailed study of one of Trilling's real discoveries, Hannah Lees, before turning to the least invisible author of the decade, Kathleen Winsor.

3

The Waiting Room

Female Desire in Women's Wartime Fiction

According to the sexual morality codes of the 1940s, women are supposed to wait. First, women are supposed to wait to be asked for a date. Then, women are supposed to wait until marriage for sexual intercourse. Now wartime separation asks wives to wait once again. Wives are supposed to wait—chastely—for their husbands to return from the war.

This conservative morality code could be found openly expressed in women's magazines, pulp romances, newspaper advice columns, popular songs, and films.[1] In a February 1945 column for *Ladies' Home Journal*, Dorothy Thompson equates wives' fidelity with civilization itself; "she must live for what her man is fighting for, and not betray him, his cause, her country, and herself."[2] In various sorts of narrative, straying wives are scolded and ruthlessly punished. In a syndicated newspaper "story from real life," Kathleen Norris predicts doom for the unfaithful wife—"Life has a way of catching up with such women."[3] In a 1945 "true confessions" story, "Playgirl Wife," the barely straying wife is found an unfit mother and has her children taken away from her by a judge.[4] And in *Tender Comrade* (1943) the wife who goes out on dates—against strong household advice—is also the one who later finds out that her husband is dead.

Before the war, the sexual double standard was simply a cultural given. Both men and women were told to restrain themselves sexually, but only women's failings were scrutinized. In an article that complained about the hypocritical nature of contemporary courting, the advice-columnist Dorothy Dix wrote, "Just why this unequal state of affairs always has existed, nobody knows."[5] A mother from Detroit said that she "always rejected the 'double standard,'" in the face of numerous male claims to the contrary. She always tried to teach chastity to both men and women. Yet one young man told her "bluntly": "More boys would be inclined to remain virgin if they felt people expected it of them or showed confidence that they could."[6] Fathers wink at their sons, but lock up their daughters.

The war allowed the sexual double standard a newfound rationale of national security. Instead of saying, "that's just how it is," one could say with much more conviction, "your husband is fighting a war, and so must you." The argument for wifely chastity was no longer vaguely traditional, but now attached to a concrete, patriotic fight for civilization. Moreover, the argument was strengthened by comparison. However you suffer, lonely wife, it can be nothing compared with what the man suffers. In *So Your Husband's Gone to War!* (1942), Ethel Gorham encourages women to accept the sexual double standard as one of the costs of war. "Well, let your blood run cold but don't imagine he remains pure as the driven snow to match your own temperature. Men aren't made that way, but they certainly expect women to be."[7] If a wife reflects sullenly on what she is missing, Gorham chides, "have you remembered what he is giving up? Only his life, you know."[8]

An article in the October 1944 issue of *Ladies' Home Journal* makes the case for the double standard with clarity. Written by an anonymous male soldier, the article judges the wives, but excuses the husbands: "It is the rare soldier who can honestly say that he has never, even in any degree, strayed from the straight and narrow path. . . . Were it not for these occasional flings, his life would be more difficult. Through these forbidden adventures, he preserves the remnant of a private life and gains an outlet for repressed urges and a new patience to go out again."[9] A female reader might wish to argue with these overt rationalizations, but the soldier holds all the trumps. "After all," he writes, "he had the excuse of a soldier's life, while you had none." No need to wink at the sexual double standard any more when you can present the argument so candidly and with almost military force.

Although every source agrees that waiting for a husband's return is difficult, a wife's waiting is rarely taken as seriously as a husband's soldiering. In one of these rare examples, *The Very Thought of You* (1944) makes its case with romantic bravado. A young woman's home is populated with all the character-types of the day: an angry, humiliated 4–F brother, a teenage sister readily wowed by uniforms, and another sister who dates seriously while her husband is away. The young woman, Janet (Eleanor Parker), meets a soldier while he is on a short leave. They fall in love, and soon enough she is a war bride who waits for her husband to come back from overseas. Early on in the movie, soldier Dave (Dennis Morgan) shames the "bad" sister, Molly, by telling the family about wives who break up with their husbands while they are gone. One soldier, he says, got a "Dear John" letter and promptly "ran right into the Jap guns," not because he was a hero, but because he did not want to live. "I know it's tough on the women," says Dave, "to wait and be lonely, but if they knew how much tougher it was on their guys, I don't think they'd write 'Dear John.'" This is the conventional, comparative argument, where a woman's home-front troubles cannot possibly equal a Nazi-fighting man's.

Since Dave is the romantic hero, however, the movie later allows him to express a more generous, less self-concerned sentiment. When he is about to leave his wife after their "second honeymoon," she complains that she does not have the "gizzard"—the guts—to be a soldier's wife. But Dave consoles her: "It takes more gizzard to be a soldier's wife than it does to fight. You've got to be braver than I'll ever be." Romantic fantasy that he is, Dave claims that the woman who waits is braver than the man who fights. This is a splendidly chivalric gesture on Dave's part, and one rarely made in wartime. Indeed, the movie goes back to the other camp toward the end, when Molly's husband, Fred, returns stateside. Eventually the two of them reconcile, but first he needs to make sure that she understands his troubles as a soldier. "I can't blame you, Molly, but I wish you had a better idea about war is really like. 'Cause it isn't all fighting, it's waiting, days and nights of it." She has told him about her dates, about how she let a man kiss her, about how she almost wrote Fred a "Dear John" letter. Fred takes the usual approach, which is that to reflect on men's struggles in war should restrain women's desires at home. "I wish you had a better idea about what war is really like." Fred puts the conventional argument in gentle, forgiving terms, but he also manages, nonetheless, to expand the scope of those terms. Whereas the argument usually sets the fighting man over against the waiting woman, Fred's version says that a man both fights *and* waits. As Fred takes the disgraced woman back into his arms, therefore, he deprives women of any answer whatsoever.

In magazines, books, and films, the soldier's sexual desires are taken as a given, but rarely judged too harshly, whereas a wife's sexual desire is acknowledged only to be restrained. The male sexual escapades of Frederic Wakeman's *Shore Leave* (1944) have no parallel in the representation of wives waiting at home. Any loose sexual energy on the home front comes from "wolves," not wives, and that is what wives need to watch out for. In David Selznick's home-front epic, *Since You Went Away* (1944), family friend Tony Willett (Joseph Cotten) makes passes at Anne Hilton (Claudette Colbert), but she deflects them gracefully. In *Swing Shift Maisie* (1943), knowing but proper Maisie (Ann Sothern) spends the middle part of the movie helping bad girl Iris (Jean Rogers) escape from the local wolves.

The notion of the Hollywood "good–bad girl"—put forth by Wolfenstein and Leites—does not apply to this more vigorously policed terrain. Wolfenstein and Leites describe a film heroine who is at once both good (morally chaste) and bad (sexually desirable and sometimes with an appetite of her own). But the wartime morality around wifely waiting is closer to daytime serials than Hollywood; here there are no paradoxes—only good women or bad. In soaps there are still perfectly "good" women, such as Mary Noble of *Backstage Wife*, who must defend her husband from hordes of sexually aggressive "bad" women. Time and narrative can allow "bad" woman back into the social fold, but this is a different plot from the one where the "good–bad" woman is discovered never to have fallen in the first place. In these moralized stories of waiting women, wives are divided into good girls who ward off wolves, while showing little sexual desire themselves, and bad girls who give into wolves and who are then punished for their weakness.

This chapter focuses on two home-front novels that do a great deal more to represent the sexual desires of lonely wives during the war. In *Till the Boys Come Home* (1944), Hannah Lees presents a wife who, in fact, does not wait for her husband to come home. Because the wife is not judged according to the moralizing stereotypes of "good girl–bad girl," her book was received with some controversy. In *Star Money* (1950), Kathleen Winsor looks back over the war years of another soldier's wife, although now through the lens of a best-selling novelist. While Hannah Lees's sexual candor makes a useful contribution to the discourse of mental hygiene, Kathleen Winsor's sex scenes seem mainly to contribute to the striptease imagination of the leisure-class consumer. Yet the discourses of science and celebrity are often closely woven in the 1940s, and both novels help us to understand what female desire looks like in these years.

Substitute Sexuality in *Till the Boys Come Home*

Diana Trilling opens her review of Hannah Lees's *Till the Boys Come Home* by noting how few books inhabit this genre. "I have been surprised at the dearth of novels on a theme which I should have thought would be particularly appealing for wartime fiction, the predicament of wives whose husbands have gone off to war."[10] Magazines and newspaper columns favored practical and moral advice for the wife. In "How to Live without Your Husband," Leslie B. Hohman advises wives to "keep busy."[11] As we have already seen, home-front movies often translate into feature-length advice columns. Thus film historian Thomas Doherty writes, "With a ham-handedness typical of an [Office of War Information] OWI-stamped melodrama, *Since You Went Away* taught a dozen-odd lessons in proper homefront behavior."[12] Although outwardly occupying the disparate genres of comedy, melodrama, and romance, *Swing Shift Maisie*, *Tender Comrade*, and *The Very Thought of You* can be understood as wishing, above all, to convey home-front guidance in general, and sexual guidance in specific.

Wartime novels were freer to address the wife's situation more openly than magazines or movies, and yet, as Diana Trilling observed, they rarely brought up the subject. When the theme was broached, it tended to be handled magazine-style anyway, as in Ethel Gorham's book, *So Your Husband's Gone to War!* or Margaret Buell Wilder's *Since You Went Away . . . Letters to a Soldier from His Wife* (1943).[13] As cheery and cute a set of letters as can be imagined, Wilder's novel appeared in condensed form in *Ladies' Home Journal*. That these letters follow "official" guidelines does not diminish the enthusiasm of a reviewer in the *New York Times*. "Following official advice about soldier morale, [Wilder] gives hilarious accounts of her adventures with Brig and Jen, the high-school daughter, and the family pets."[14] David Selznick's film version of Wilder's book makes Joseph Cotten's character more sexualized; at dinner he wonders if he can say the word "body," and afterward he presents Anne with a painting of herself in pinup mode. By contrast, Wilder's novel has basically nothing sexual in it. The author is an adult good sport about girls in "Petty drawings," Tony's naked Godiva picture, and Havelock Ellis.[15] Since the letters are all addressed to her husband, no wayward sexual energy is likely to emerge. But no husband-directed sexual energy emerges either. The numerous cultural references (James Thurber, James Joyce, Arthur Clough, Charles Dickens, Homer's Penelope) do not deepen the story into literary thought, but mix effortlessly into a chatty bubble of dogs and horses and getting ready for school. The book is completely well-behaved, a happy mood, with neither body nor brain. The wife even looks toward her husband's pleasures with only the lightest regard. Anne imagines their future "fun" conversations together: "And sometimes I'll be polite and say did you see so-and-so? And were the girls attractive? So you'll have the fun of telling me. And you'll never tell me quite all, but that'll be fun too because I'll pretend not to know; then you'll feel secret and masculine—the way gentlemen should who've been to the wars!"[16]

It is with novels like Wilder's apparently in mind that Diana Trilling admits to a doubled surprise. Not only is she surprised at the "dearth of novels" about war wives, but "now that one has finally arrived, Hannah Lees's *Till the Boys Come Home*, I admit even greater surprise at its content."[17] For Lees's novel has none of the magazine-style advice for home-front women that found its way into books and films. Even more surprising, her book represents female sexual desire in extended detail. "*Till the Boys Come Home* is remarkably free of the expected sentimental and patriotic clichés, and in sexual matters it is unselfconsciously courageous."[18] Trilling continues, "Without any intention of sensationalism, Miss Lees describes with extraordinary frankness the sexual substitutes for a husband which are available to the women left behind."[19] Trilling once again appreciates the candor around female sexuality, while realizing that the book might not strike others the same way. "If its matter is similarly acceptable to a wide popular audience," she writes, "this country has gone further in recent years than we commonly suppose."[20]

Trilling guessed correctly that not all readers would accept this frank, unclichéd picture of the sexualized war wife. In her review for the *Saturday Review of Literature*, Sarah Henderson Hay judges that the main character, Sophie, is "not a normal woman." And ordinary readers, Hay surmises, will have no choice but to condemn her:

> The problem with which this book deals is certainly a real one, and millions of women have had to make a more drastic adjustment than Sophie Harbor faced. Most of these women have done a much better job; they have brought up their children, worked at much less interesting occupations than Sophie's medical research, coped with meagre finances, kept busy and relatively happy. They have put a part of their lives in abeyance and still maintained their emotional balance, they have been both physically and mentally chaste, and Sophie's reaction to their common problems will both shock and disgust them. It is obvious, however, that Miss Lees's story is not about a normal woman. Sophie's physical need verges on a nymphomania.[21]

This reviewer meets the novel's unconventionality with magazine-style condemnation. Hay idealizes millions of women into a land of heroic purity ("physically and mentally chaste"), those good women who kept themselves busy with work and children. And then, in the assured manner of contemporary psychologists, she pushes Sophie out of "normal" and into pathological. Yet to diagnose the patient's illness will not gain the patient the reader's understanding. Hence Hay concludes her review: "*Till the Boys Come Home* will, as the blurb says, 'shock some people' and it will repel a great many more, not because of its frankness and honesty in dealing with abnormal psychology, but because Sophie herself, in her weakness, her selfishness, her condonement of vulgarity and promiscuity, and her lack of any sort of integrity, is a character for whom the reader will have no liking and very little sympathy."[22] Where Diana Trilling celebrated the novel's "courageousness," Hay sees the novel as an insult to the war's real heroines, to those millions of wives who kept their minds and bodies chaste and strong.

Hannah Lees was the nom de plume of Elizabeth Head Fetter (1904–1973). From the late 1930s to the early 1960s she published many articles and stories in such magazines as the *Saturday Evening Post* and *Collier's*. She published seven books over the course of her career, and taught writing at Bryn Mawr College from 1953 to 1956. She was married to a doctor, and her early books were praised for the precision of their medical discourse. *Women Will Be Doctors* (1939) and *Prescription for Murder* (1941) show her ability to set detailed knowledge of physician and hospital goings-on into recognizable genres of romance and mystery. In addition to her magazine stories, she wrote factual articles such as "Prophylactic Pill" (1943), "So You Had a Virus" (1949), and "What Men Can Learn about Women" (1953), a response to the second Kinsey report.[23] These contributions to mental and physical hygiene lead naturally to a guidebook for marriage, *Help Your Husband Stay Alive* (1957). Over the course of her career, Hannah Lees moved from representing what she knows about doctors through her husband, toward representing what she knows about husbands and wives through a scientific and personal understanding of marriage.

With her usual astonishing perceptiveness, Diana Trilling places *Till the Boys Come Home* in the context of domestic sexual education. Knowing Lees's wider and future bibliography, this is an easier case to make, but Trilling draws this conclusion based only on the novel and the biographical fact of Lees's doctor husband. "[The novel] serves as a liaison between theory and practice and has the potentiality of performing an invaluable educative function. Recently there have been several instances in which the women's magazines have recognized their educative power and broken through the old sexual taboos to tell small but difficult truths. One can guess that these steps in progress are directly to be traced to the influence of young writers and editors of the same cultural cast as Miss Lees, with perhaps no special artistic gift but with the same seriousness and conscience."[24]

Trilling aligns the sexual frankness of *Till the Boys Come Home* with recent breakthroughs in women's magazine discourse. Here she points to an increase in sexual education articles in these magazines. Until now, women's magazines appeared to think nothing of the contradictions between the chaste moralizing of the columnists, the cute kissing of couples in the romantic fiction, and the theatrical displays of flesh in ads for lingerie. Women began to see these contradictions more and more clearly, and one might imagine that a more explicit sexual discourse in the 1940s comes in part from a desire to bridge the gap between Victorian moral purity and burlesque show sexual display. The realities of the war also contributed to more open talk about sexuality. Surgeon General Thomas Parran made venereal disease home-front enemy number one, and adolescent promiscuity became a greater concern as the war went on.

An article published about the same time as *Till the Boys Come Home* confirms Lees's intent to contribute to the dialogue around sex education. In "The Word You Can't Say" (1944), Hannah Lees says a word that is rarely spoken or read at the time—"masturbation." The article is published in *Hygeia*, which is not a women's magazine, but Lees takes an approach that would be found more and more often in those journals.[25] She hopes that parents will associate less guilt and shame with masturbation—that it will be seen as part of a child's normal sexual development. Masturbation, says Lees, should not be called "self abuse" and it does not cause insanity. But she is, like all of her contemporaries, concerned with what is sexually normal. "Excessive" masturbation needs to be dealt with, and while masturbation does not cause insanity, insanity might well cause excessive masturbation. Overall her article seeks to remove the "censorship" from a "whole body of important scientific facts." From now on, not just the biology, but also the psychology and sociology of sexuality would be regarded as areas of teachable, empirical facts.

Till the Boys Come Home can thus be considered as an experiment in sexual candor. Just as masturbation cannot be thought if it cannot be spoken or read, female sexual desire cannot be thought if it is not spoken or read. It is an unenlightened, unscientific version of sexuality that simply treats female desire as invisible. Masturbation is part of a child's life, regardless of whether a parent chooses to admit that it is.[26] Just so, sexual desire is part of an adult woman's life, whether anyone else chooses to admit that it is. Conventional morality simply shames adolescent masturbation out of existence. Likewise, conventional morality shames the sexual desires of soldiers' wives out of existence. Masturbation substitutes for the sexuality of the couple; a main subject of *Till the Boys Come Home* is, as Diana Trilling says, the "sexual substitutes for a husband which are available to the women left behind."[27] If masturbation is the word you can't say, then *Till the Boys Come Home* is the novel you cannot write.

We should note that the topic of unfaithful war wives is one that, at the time, psychologists mostly choose to ignore. The sexual desire of lonely war wives is treated regularly in pulp romance magazines and in newspaper advice columns. What most worries the medical establishment, however, is the sexual delinquency of adolescents. *Women in Wartime* (1943), a brief pamphlet published by the Institute for Psychoanalysis, spends a good deal of time explaining "the present trend of [teenage] promiscuity."[28] Much less attention is given to war's tendency to "loosen inhibitions," where married women may rationalize "illegitimate sexual experiences."[29] Articles in the academic journal *Marriage and Family Living* make the same division of emphasis. The journal regularly runs articles on sex education and dedicates an entire wartime issue to juvenile delinquency. But the journal leaves the topic of a war wife's sexuality almost entirely to the tabloids. An article on "Loneliness and the Serviceman's Wife" only talks about loneliness, not sexual desire.[30] A 1944 article on "War and the Family" argues that sex is a problem only if given too much emphasis ("the erection of the home on the narrow basis of a biological structure makes the superstructure insecure").[31] The 1944 article "Medical Aspects of War Time Marriages" promotes mature "ideals," which will help to prevent a mature woman from falling into "the fixation of the sex pattern of the childhood or early adolescent level of autoeroticism or homosexuality."[32] In other words, keep yourself pure and mature, otherwise you are obsessed, childishly backward, or queer.

Till the Boys Come Home displaces the shame and blame structure of the conventional war wife's narrative. In an enlightened world, parents are asked not to shame their masturbating children, while in Lees's novel, readers are asked not to shame—at least in conventional ways—the cheating war wife. Sophie Harbor is the "bad wife," who in a moralizing Hollywood film would suffer public humiliation and shame. The narrative might kill off her husband (as in *Tender Comrade*) or might force her to repent and beg forgiveness (*The Very Thought of You*). In *Till the Boys Come Home*, the husbands of the faithful wives are killed, while Sophie's husband is wounded. In this courageous novel, Sophie's second affair makes her feel guilty and ashamed, but also vital and loved. Her repentance and guilt are all suffered privately, and the novel ends before the wounded husband returns home. There is no indication that the husband will ever find out, nor that Sophie will suffer any long-term consequence. Thus the novel concludes by indicating its difference from the conventional war wife plot: "She got up from the bed and found *Crime and Punishment* in the bookcase between the windows and stood holding it, looking out the window, grinning a little wrily [*sic*] at the title" (329). She has not read Dostoevsky's book, and she is no testing, amoral Raskolnikov. But the title strikes her as a bit funny, a bit ironic, since if she has committed a crime, she has not really been punished. The novel declines to shame her in any conventionally recognizable way.

The displacement of narrative punishment is seen most clearly in the wake of her first sexual transgression. With an ease that surprises her, she goes to bed with a not too obviously wolfish newspaper man, Wish Curly. "It was all just as she had known it would be: his hands on her breasts and thighs, his warmth, his weight, his body close against hers there on the couch she and Neb had so carefully chosen two years before. Only it was all more wonderful and terrible and sordid and joyous than she had ever thought it would be" (144). In this scene the physical act of sex is given spare detail, and emotion is expressed through a set of forced paradoxes. But most fictional works would name this act "adultery," with all of its scandalous baggage, whereas what this novel wants us to consider is something more concrete and specific—substitute sexuality. In this latter, less sensational form, female sexual desire can be taken more seriously.

At this point Sophie makes a large mistake, but it is a military mistake, not a sexual mistake. Over drinks she tells the newspaper man about her classified scientific project, and soon the details of that project are published in the papers. Students of this time period will remember the many posters that advised women to keep silent about the activities of their loved ones overseas.[33] But Sophie is much nearer the war than most wives since she is a technician on a research project with military significance. She suffers emotionally and professionally for her security leak, but she is also clear about exactly what her mistake was. Since it was her husband Neb's project to begin with, she has betrayed her husband's lab, but not his bed. "She kept feeling Neb's eyes on her. She had betrayed him too. She had betrayed him more by that drunken impulse to share her thought than she had ever for a moment felt she had betrayed him by sharing her body" (157). Thus the novel treats Sophie's home-front war with the same set of values as a war-front novel would. A military blunder is a terrible mistake, which deserves punishment, whereas a sexual encounter is worth some regret, perhaps, but does not indicate any great moral weakness.

That the novel intends to put Sophie on a war front of her own is made clear in her second transgression. After sleeping just once with the newspaper man, she begins a very intense affair with the head scientist at the lab, Sam Wolmuth. Wolmuth is—to everyone in the novel—pronouncedly Jewish, and Sophie must get past not only the regular bouts of narrow-minded anti-Semitism spewed by her sister, Julia, but also the built-up stereotypes of Jews she finds in her own head. "She hated it in

Julia and she hated in herself" (209). The book's Jewish character serves as another way of putting Sophie closer to the European front. "Now [the Jewish element] had come into her personal life and pricking her lightly had brought some reality to the horror she read about in Poland and Germany" (209). Diana Trilling wrote that "even the name of the novel's heroine strikes a new note in popular realism: she is not Sandra or Michele but Sophie."[34] One might say that the name "Sophie" works like the presence of the Jewish scientist and like her military research project. The novel consistently pushes her out of home-front feminine isolation and into the wider European scale of conflict. By doing so, the novel makes judging her by conventionally domestic standards more difficult.

That Sam Wolmuth is a Jew also emphasizes the more-than-physical aspect of Sophie's sexuality. Physically, she is not particularly attracted to him; his face ("his wide thin lips," 216) strikes her racially rather than romantically. He is certainly not the handsome, authoritative doctor of romance novels. Instead, she wants to protect him from his self-loathing, from his neurotic vulnerability. As Sophie says toward the end of the novel: "All my life [I've been] going around asking for comfort, asking people to love me and keep me warm and safe. You've done it, Sam, oh you've done it, and twice as well because you managed to give me the illusion that I was giving comfort to you. I'll always love you because you gave me that, but I wish—I wish like hell now—I hadn't needed it" (322). Since it is linked so closely to long-term feelings of security and love, Sophie's sexual desire goes far beyond outbursts of physical attraction and release. Any romance novel would equally insist that love is what gives sexuality both its beauty and its propriety. But Sophie's love is not the love of romance fiction heroines. Her love is too individualistic, too sensual, and socially too wrong. She ought to be the "bad girl," but the novel refuses to break down its moral categories into easy opposites. The novel wants us to feel that the struggle with loneliness is a complex and fierce battle, a struggle that will not be bought off by folksy sayings or even by a few flings.

Till the Boys Come Home emphasizes the physicality of Sophie's desire, but manages to frame that desire with an almost unique lack of sensationalism. In the absence of their husbands, female bodies hum with desire. Milla and Sophie are so wound up they throw themselves at one another ("there was fright in both their eyes and then they were kissing wildly," 59). Afterward both women buzz with sexual excitement. The omniscient narrator says that Sophie's desire fills her with "horror," while Milla's "body was tingling too but without panic" (61). The added presence of Milla shows that the book's focus is not on Sophie's strange case of "nymphomania," but instead on female desire in general. There is a lot of sex in 1940s literature, or at least enough for essayists to complain about it; "I am one of those many readers who are usually bored and sometimes disgusted by the crudity and coarseness in the treatment of sex which is now so widespread in American fiction" ("Sex in American Fiction" [1948]).[35] But where else can one find descriptions of female sexual desire that are not simply stereotyped as exotica or nymphomania? In hard-boiled authors such as Cain or Spillane, in historical romance writers such as Winsor, the approach to sex comes through a hyperbolic sensibility, as if sex cannot take place outside a sensationalist framework.

For example, take this passage from Libbie Block's *Wild Calendar* (1946), a novel full of adult reflections on sex, and one that falls into no particular genre. Here the heroine looks at herself in a mirror: "Rosy breasts with russet nipples, a lovely concave space above her waist, thighs like two vases. Am I nice enough for him? Am I appetizing enough outside and good enough inside? She threw a robe over her steaming fresh body and left the bathroom, content and expectant. But not before she had rejected, defiantly, the bit of rubber and metal that Sonny had hated, 'the gadget.' "[36] Birth control devices do not make regular appearances in 1940s fiction, and there is some sexual actuality here and elsewhere in the book. But the woman's sexual consciousness is represented by strange literariness ("rosy breasts with russet nipples") and almost pornographic exuberance ("steaming fresh body"). Such passages make imagining a sexual awareness shorn away from melodrama seem difficult.

But this is what Lees is able to do. As Diana Trilling observed, the sex scenes in *Till the Boys Come Home* come "without any intention of sensationalism." The primary intention, as in "The Word You Can't Say," is therapeutic honesty. Let us represent, not repress, sexual desire.

> She put her own hand experimentally on her breast and rubbed it gently, trying to recapture the sensation [of being with her husband]. The pain eased a little. She rubbed the other breast and pinched the nipple till it hurt. And suddenly her hand was Pete caressing her, soothing her, loving her. She moved it slowly down along her thigh and back up across the softness of her stomach and down toward her thigh again. And maybe this is the solution, she thought a little wearily, maybe this is the way to peace and sleep. "Pete," she moaned, "Pete darling."
>
> For moments, for two or three long forgetful moments she thought perhaps it was, perhaps it could be. But then it

> was gone. There was nothing. Pete wasn't there, he just wasn't there, and she couldn't even cry (62).

In the logic of the book, this passage helps the reader to understand why women—in this case, Milla—miss their men. Physical desire is intense, but quieting physical desire is only a momentary solution. The almost scientific necessity for this passage is clear, once the novel's pedagogical intent is grasped. For the 1940s this is a virtually unique description of female masturbation, all the more remarkable for its lack of tabloid motivation.[37] Given the lack of precedent, it should not surprise that scenes like these gave rise to readerly bewilderment. Such a scene typifies the book's challenging and asystematic nature. Even though there is a liberating, even liberal, program around the issue of sexual candor, sex scenes and their consequences continually find themselves outside any simple or even comprehensible evaluation.

Kathleen Winsor's Bosomy Feminism

According to legend, Kathleen Winsor sent off the *Forever Amber* (1944) manuscript on the same day that her husband was shipped overseas. Her novel, dedicated to her husband, Lieutenant Robert John Herwig, U.S.M.C.R., would sell 100,000 copies in the first week of its appearance and almost three million copies by the end of 1945. Supported by an aggressive advertising campaign and helped out, too, by a ban in Boston, *Forever Amber* made a celebrity of the first-time author.[38] Immediately signed to a three-year deal at Twentieth Century-Fox, Winsor became as famous as any movie star, and gossip columns avidly followed her personal comings and goings. Winsor obliged the scandal sheets by soon divorcing her soldier husband and marrying jazz band leader Artie Shaw in 1946. (Shaw had previously been married to, among others, Lana Turner and Ava Gardner.) Winsor tells a version of her spectacular rise to literary stardom in her second novel, *Star Money* (1950), which is the main focus of this section.

In 1949 Lady Astor criticized the period's obsession with sex, calling it "the modern striptease age."[39] Lady Astor had Hollywood in mind, but *Forever Amber* could be the central exhibit in a critique that would find purchase throughout the 1940s. Milton Caniff punningly admitted that *Male Call*, his comic for soldiers, was "a comic strip-tease."[40] The pinup craze was so ubiquitous that leading models could be found regularly not just in girlie magazines such as *See*, but also in *Time* and *Life*.[41] Hence in Niven

Busch's war novel *They Dream of Home* (1944), a bored soldier can pass the time by looking at the living-room magazines. "There was a *Life* on Mrs. Fricke's desk, and he took it and glanced over it, studying the pictures of the girls."[42] Comic drawings in the classy, high-culture *New Yorker* regularly featured farcical sex jokes with naked or half-naked women. Lingerie ads in women's magazines were just as explicit as the pinup drawings by Varga for the men's magazine *Esquire*. It is into this sort of visual culture that *Forever Amber* steps, chest out, fancy dresses falling to the floor. Much more even than Gypsy Rose Lee's *The G-String Murders* (1941), *Forever Amber* is a striptease novel and the most famous of its age.

Gypsy Rose Lee was a philosophical stripper, but a stripped-down Amber approaches a blank slate, a tabula rasa. In a famous monologue, Gypsy Rose Lee says that when she strips she thinks "of a landscape by Van Gogh, or a landscape by Cézanne." And she answers the big question—"Do you believe for one moment that I am thinking of sex? . . . well, I certainly am."[43] In her turn, Amber appears in a scrupulously researched seventeenth-century England, in an England inspired by the diaries of Samuel Pepys and the novels of Daniel Defoe (*Moll Flanders*, *A Journal of the Plague Year*), and peopled by Cavalier poets and the courtiers of Charles II. But the author's self-education does not translate to her novel's heroine; "she had become so desperate for entertainment that she was finally willing to read a book."[44] Amber's whole life is devoted to "entertainment," to pleasure, and to sexual adventure. She rejects moral codes, not through any process of reasoning, but simply because they stand in the way of her fun. "Adultery's no crime," she says, having slept with her stepson, "it's an amusement."[45] The scandalous matter of the book comes through much more in her rebellious attitude than through the physical details of her acts since the sex scenes are almost completely obscured. The novel operates primarily as a striptease encyclopedia of women's breasts in every state of fullness and exposure, with erotic assistance provided by several dozen legs and a few buttocks. As Amber makes her way toward the King's court, her logic is the logic of the pinup and the lingerie advertisement—I want him to desire me. Sex is a pleasurable amusement for Amber, but her main desire is to take part in the world of male desire, to be seen, to be the favorite, to be the most beautiful, to be the most passionately desired. Even though Amber is the main character in a sex novel that truly does go on forever—972 pages—her own sexual desire comes through more like the unknown blank of a pinup than as a detailed subjectivity of one's own.

Readers of *Forever Amber* were apparently too busy thinking about other things to see that the book could easily be read into a contemporary wartime setting. Winsor's second novel, *Star Money*, is set explicitly during World War II. *Star Money* is just as sexed up as *Forever Amber* and a wartime setting helps to explain the disintegration of sexual morality. Likewise, Amber's England is a civil-war–torn mess, with the consequence that widespread sexual depravity should not surprise. The novel begins by producing Amber as the product of a wartime liaison; her father says to her mother, "We'll be married, Judith, when the war's over."[46] And so illegitimate Amber makes her way through an England as uprooted and confused as America during World War II. Many social commentators saw the war as causing rampant juvenile delinquency and sexual immorality.

In her 1944 book, for example, journalist Agnes E. Meyer called her trip across the United States a "journey through chaos." Here she describes the Los Angeles zoot-suiters, who give into "uninhibited and ostentatious sex behavior": "To anyone who has encountered as many unhappy, maladjusted youngsters as I have during my tour of the war areas, the zoot-suiters are only an extreme and articulate expression of the cynicism and rebellion which characterize many of our adolescents in all walks of life."[47] Amber seems happier than the zoot-suitors, but almost as cynical and every bit as rebellious. Thus even as it shows its heroine climbing up the social ladder toward Charles II and his bed, the novel exculpates its heroine from any serious moral judgment by implicitly blaming the social chaos around her. In the best tradition of novels that have it both ways, *Forever Amber* has it both ways. Like the contemporary United States, it blames "bad" female sexuality on a chaotic social structure. But then (unlike the United States here) it also calls that social structure ordered and good so that it can remake morally problematic female sexual behavior into an instrument of Horatio Alger–like self-reliance. Society is both broken and not broken. *Forever Amber* goes to seventeenth-century England in order to enact a sexy version of the American rags to riches story. *Star Money* tells the same story, but now without going abroad.

Reviewers did not offer universal praise for *Forever Amber*, but they did offer some praise—and a good deal of condescending patience. Writing in the *Saturday Review of Literature*, Arthur D. Howden Smith enjoyed the bawdiness and said that the novel "seethes with life. Its action never flags."[48] And regardless of whether it was literature or not, *Forever Amber* was the blockbuster of the decade, whose form and bravado inspired countless imitations. "The financial success of 'Forever Amber' touched off an overnight assembly-line production of contrived historical novels, their most conspicuous features being not literary quality but the presence of lacteal apparatus, to which the full-color jackets paid ample tribute."[49]

When Winsor's second novel, *Star Money* (1950), appeared, patience had worn off and condescension had turned to mockery. *Time* treats her as a celebrity, not an author, and predicts that this book, too, will become a bestseller, due to the "shrewd" use of "prose so obvious that it can (and almost has to) be read under a hair-dryer."[50] Testing the book for literature, not popularity, the *Atlantic Monthly* finds that its heroine "Shireen is without doubt the dullest, silliest, and generally most objectionable beauty in contemporary fiction."[51] Richard H. Rovere, in a *Harper's* survey of new books that also included Lionel Trilling's *The Liberal Imagination*, reported that he could not make it past page 360, "quite a distance from the finish line." Nonetheless, using only this partial evidence, Rovere found himself able to pronounce that *Star Money* "is a dull book, a quite unimaginably dull book."[52]

Star Money is, in fact, a terrifically dull book, but it also represents female desire and sexuality with methodical candor. Interestingly, Rovere in his review can only barely stoop to point out that *Star Money* is, like *Forever Amber*, drenched with teasing, exploitative sex. He refers to the novel's "spice," but otherwise does not say a word about sex. Perhaps that theme is too obvious to mention. But it becomes especially striking when his survey turns to the latest book by Charles Jackson, *The Sunnier Side* (1950). Rovere calls all of the stories in this collection "delightful," and some of them "powerful."[53] He concludes his review by quoting a large chunk of Jackson's prose on the art of fiction; Rovere says that the passage is as rewarding as anything found in "Comfort, DeVoto, or Trilling."[54] But Rovere quotes a completely generic passage about the relationship between literary artifice and real life, whereas the main impulse of the title story is to show that literature usually does not dwell on the sunnier side, but rather on the darker side. *The Sunnier Side* is a straightforwardly ironic title; as the *New York Times* reviewer observed, these stories are "post-Kinseyean tales," which might have been called "The Steamier Side."[55] Indeed, all of Jackson's novels focus on dark topics, from his famous study of an alcoholic, *The Lost Weekend* (1944), to *The Fall of Valor* (1946), in which a married man discovers his homosexuality, to *The Outer Edges* (1948), which centers a fragmented narrative on a rape-murder case. Jackson concentrates on sexual extremes just as methodically as Winsor, but once again, a reader would not get a glimmer of this from Rovere.[56] As thuddingly commercial as *Star Money* is, then, its ability to talk about sex with clarity still seems praiseworthy compared to the strange repressions of Rovere's review.

Star Money tells the story of an author's rise to celebrity. In person, Winsor denied that the story was autobiographical, and the sexual adventures need not be read that way. But Winsor also plants clear references to her own nearly unprecedented success story throughout the book. For example, the writer-heroine of *Star Money* has written a historical novel set in Jamaica—instead of England—during the 1700s. And Shireen, just like her creator, did a lot of research: "I read four hundred books—or not really four hundred. Three hundred and ninety-two, actually."[57] The autobiographical parallel works to provide *Star Money* with the same hard-won authority that Winsor's much-publicized research gave *Forever Amber*. *Star Money* is not just an attempt to create another sexy bestseller. It is also a novel that defends the legitimacy of sex as both a topic for fiction and as a human activity. As Shireen becomes increasingly well-known because of her sex-obsessed novel, she is shown defending herself against criticisms that were previously addressed to *Forever Amber*. In either case, Winsor defends the sex novel by empirical research (I know what seventeenth-century England is like; I know what it is like to be a literary celebrity). The research gestures less toward a realistic aesthetic than toward the seriousness of a work ethic. The work ethic insists that there is more Ben Franklin here than James M. Cain. And if sex is everywhere, it is not because everyone is a dirty animal, but because humans are godlike:

> "To me a roll in the hay is just a roll in the hay. But you always want to make something big and cosmic out of it."
>
> "But it *is* something big and cosmic," said Shireen. "What else do we have? There's birth and death and the union of two people—and sex is the only one that happens to us more than once. Maybe that why we're careless with it, but we shouldn't be."[58]

Shireen defends her sexy novel two ways: by showing how much she knows and by showing how much she does not know. In his review, Richard Rovere gets this exactly right, although I will draw a different conclusion. "Does Miss Winsor take herself seriously as a literary person? As we have it here, she both does and does not."[59] Like so many other sex-themed books from the 1940s, *Star Money* defends itself with citations from high culture. An epigraph from the Roman poet, Horace, begins the novel, while a quotation from Emily Dickinson springs readily to Shireen's mind a few pages later ("I remember so much—too much").[60] But Shireen also reminds press critics that she has little literary experience, hence they should not be too hard on her. She wants, in other words, credit for knowing all kinds of things and credit for not knowing very much. This combination of naïveté, encyclopedia, and stunning beauty is what struck audiences when Winsor went on her *Forever Amber* tour.

> The new author who got the most glamorous treatment of all was Kathleen Winsor of *Forever Amber* fame. Kathleen was young and beautiful, and the experts dressed her in long, mystery-provoking veils and slinky dresses with heavy eye shadow and exotic foundation make-up.
>
> It was a shock to find this spectacular looking woman almost tongue-tied with fright. She said afterward that if I hadn't known her book so well she couldn't have gone on. But I found, midway in the broadcast, that Kathleen had a phenomenal memory for an incredible array of dates and statistics from her research for the turbulent plague and disaster-ridden period of Amber's career.[61]

This combination of innocence and braininess may have been fact or stratagem, and it does come off as illogical prevarication in *Star Money*—wanting to have it both ways. But it also makes for a wider reading of sexuality, one that goes beyond anatomical cynicism.

Winsor uses Shireen to defend her right to talk about sex from a woman's point of view. As a character Shireen is so concerned with her appearance, so in love with money and power, and so desperately needy that she seems an unlikely messenger for feminist politics. But from a contemporary vantage point, Elaine Showalter sees political resistance in both *Forever Amber* and *Star Money*; "*Star Money* suggests Winsor's awareness of Amber's feminist energy and of the social obstacles to creative and active women."[62] This is yet another feminism that would have been invisible to readers at the time and probably unnamed as such by Winsor herself. At number five on the best-seller list for 1950, *Star Money* was yet another "bosom novel," most suitable for the hair dryer. The last thing it appeared to be was a political or philosophical tract.

Yet although Shireen is stereotypically flighty and contradictory, she is also quite consistent in her approach to sex. She demands the right to want what she wants; unattractively, this means her right to want magazine looks, pretty clothes, and fame. More substantially—although just as unattractive to many 1950s readers—she demands the right to equal sexual expression. Whereas the patriotic war wife is supposed to wait for her soldier husband to return, Shireen sleeps with one man after another. She does not do so indifferently, and she falls prey to self-blinding love and tormented guilt. But Shireen rejects all moralistic hypocrisy and all sexual double standards for men and women. "What is this nonsense, anyway? This eighth grade attitude we have toward sex in this country?"[63] She dislikes male and female role-playing—of courtship and pursuit, of women making men wait for an hour—when both people want the same thing. She feels "triumphant" after sex and is proud that she is good at it ("I've been told I'm a good lay").[64] Winsor uses *Star Money* to defend her right to write about sex; in doing so, she also insists on a woman's equal right to sexual self-expression.

In his *New York Times* book review of *Star Money*, Charles Poore wrote that he had seen this kind of novel too many times already: "It is merely one more forlornly elaborated tale of a wartime grass widow who conducted a sort of biological warfare at home while her husband was otherwise at sea."[65] And this subject was relatively familiar; other novels by women include *I Know What I'd Do* (1946) by Alice Beal Parsons and Ann Petry's *Country Place* (1947), which Poore also reviewed for the *New York Times*. Parsons's novel is a sensationalized murder and trial story, where the Ku Klux Klan takes revenge on the wife's seducer.[66] Petry's novel is more low-key, but concludes nonetheless with the wronged soldier's overwrought death. In a loud mingling of eros and thanatos, Ed falls down the stairs to his death, even as he equates each bump with sexual desire. "He began to think that this fast, whirling, downward plunging was like making love to Glory. It was like reaching and reaching for the very heart of the world, the heart he had sought inside a woman's body, a never-ending forward thrusting which could not cease until he found respite, surcease."[67] Here the wronged soldier is given not only a bizarre, spectacular, tragic death, but also a cosmic insight into the depths of his sexuality. Petry tells the story from a male point of view and ends with an emphasis on male desire and anguish. By contrast, the wife's sexual desires are given no parallel representation. It will take Kathleen Winsor, of all people, to paint female desire with a similarly epic brush.

The feminist energy in *Star Money* critiques not only a general, perhaps timeless, sense that men treat women poorly, but also culturally specific ideas about sexual freedom and behavior. Yet even though Shireen fights against moral and sexual conventions, she is helpless to fight against psychoanalytic conventions. She feels obliged to insist that she is average, typical, and above all, "normal," to ward off the notion that she is neurotic or nymphomaniac ("I'm the most normal person there is").[68] Hannah Lees's Sophie also thinks readily outside of conventional moralisms. Yet both Sophie and Shireen have internalized an authoritarian psychoanalytic discourse that attacks them for their deviancy, their maladjustedness. These women are remarkably unburdened by social interpretations of female sexual desire, yet they cannot escape the scientific evaluation of female sexual desire. While Shireen wants to redefine the terms of psychoanalytic discourse, discarding those terms entirely seems unimaginable for her. Hence in one of her last fights with Ed, she demands that he go see a psychologist because *he* is clearly not adjusted to civilian life ("your present trouble is clearly neurotic").[69] One of the most frightening aspects of 1940s culture is the way that psychological discourse embeds itself in women's heads, like some kind of judging parasite. To describe the psychological invader—which lives in people's heads, while knowing nothing about people's heads—is the task of the chapter's next section.

Wartime Psychology and the Attack on Women

The traumas of war gave psychological discourse newfound authority. Doctors were needed to repair the battle wounds of soldiers, and these wounds were as often mental as physical. The entire home-front population was traumatized by the displacements and losses of war, hence every American was a potential neurotic. Psychologists not only addressed the situation in papers to themselves, but they also appeared in newspapers and popular magazines as bearers of good health. And writers of every kind borrowed the authority of psychological discourse in order to make their cases. Key terms in psychological understanding are simply taken as given, even by unconventional thinkers.

Writers such as Hannah Lees and Kathleen Winsor, who approach sexuality from opposite ends of the tabloid spectrum, allow their heroines to think outside conventionally gendered categories. Whatever else is going on, Lees and Winsor want us to rethink moral prejudices about female sexual desire. Neither Sophie nor Shireen have internalized a conventional moral conscience. Yet both heroines have so internalized psychological discourse that it now functions as a kind of conscience. Neither woman is worried in conventional ways about whether she is an adulteress. But each woman is quite worried about whether she is "normal." Thus when Sophie feels momentarily attracted to a woman, her self-condemnation expresses itself in psychological terms: "All the abnormal psychology she had ever read or heard rose up in her mind in huge distorted shapes. Perhaps I have always been abnormal, she thought, and that is why I've never quite been able to feel and appreciate Neb's simple and direct love as much as it deserved."[70] The horrors of war may have undermined family stability and even structures of belief, but psychological discourse holds on because it helps hold people together.

The psychological categories of normalcy, deviance, and adjustment are culturally omnipresent in the 1940s. They filter down from the psychological heights to appear everywhere in popular culture. In an article in *Pageant* magazine, a 35-year-old woman wants to defend her right to remain single; she writes, "I didn't start out life as a misfit. I was a perfectly normal girl with a normal number of boyfriends and also my share of sweethearts."[71] One of the key lesbian novels of the period, *Diana: A Strange Autobiography* (1939), is shaped by the main character's anxieties about whether she is "normal" or "abnormal."[72] Women's magazines ran numerous questionnaires with titles such as "Is Your Man Normal?"[73] "What makes a successful marriage?" asks marriage counselor Paul Popenoe. A main foundation, he says, is "sexual normality."[74] Ethical categories of "good" and "bad" have in some contexts been modernized and relativized away. But psychological categories of "normal" and "abnormal" can perform the same work of sexual judgmentalism.

Until thinkers can see around and through these psychological categories, there is no way to think gender and sexuality outside of "norms." Ruth Benedict intended her article "Anthropology and the Abnormal" (1934) to make a dent in the usefulness of these categories. Yet while her essay had some impact on the anthropologically inclined, psychologists and mainstream culture continued to put everything in those boxes. This is why, at the end of the decade, Ruth Herschberger still needed to begin her feminist polemic *Adam's Rib* (1948) with one more attack on the categories of "normal" and "abnormal."[75] A feminist redescription of sexuality has to begin there because such evaluative, stigmatizing language—from scientific discourse to popular culture—stands at the center of patriarchal surveillance.

In the guise of an optimistic, salvific science, psychological discourse does very effective work on behalf of men and equally effective work against women. On behalf of men, psychology is sexually liberating; it argues that man's nature-given libido must be satisfied. Philip Wylie, who we will meet more extendedly next chapter, based his misogynistic diatribes on this psychological "truth." Although Wylie's *Generation of Vipers* (1942) takes its title from the Bible, it founds its wartime Jeremiad on a reading of Freud and Jung. "True morality" requires that "we remove the fetid incrustations of ages from our sexual instinct"; until then "our sex attitude is insane."[76] While sexual chastity is everywhere promoted, says Wylie the prophet, radio, fiction, and above all, magazine advertisers exploit sex for their commercial ends, as when they "prostrate [women] in the position of copulative thrall."[77] Hence wholesome sex is absent, and sexual impulse is instead relieved with prostitutes ("harlots are ubiquitous everywhere in the U.S.") or through homosexuality, with a resulting plague of pederasty and syphilis. Wylie's fulminations against the sexual hypocrisy of popular culture are not wrong, but they are certainly misogynistic. Like most writers who want more sexual freedom, he means male sexual freedom. When Wylie, prophetically and liberatingly, speaks of "our hidden sexuality," he has no interest in the "hidden sexuality" of women.

Psychological terminology could also be used to attack women. *Modern Woman: The Lost Sex* (1947), by Ferdinand Lundberg and Marynia F. Farnham, supports its misogynistic assault with "clinical work in psychiatry carried on over a long period by Dr. Farnham."[78] As stated in the foreword, "the central thesis of the book is that contemporary women in very large numbers are psychologically disordered and that their disorder is having terrible social and personal effects involving men in all departments of their lives as well as women."[79] *Modern Woman* contains wide-ranging descriptions, evaluations, and condemnations of modern female sexuality. For example, the authors say that female sexual desire must be linked to childbearing; "the greater her desire to emulate the male in seeking a sense of personal value by objective exploit the less will be her enjoyment of the sex act and the greater her general neuroticism."[80] In this typical pronouncement, the authors use psychology as a seemingly objective instrument in order to police the contours of female sexual desire. Although *Modern Woman: The Lost Sex* seems outrageously judgmental, it was a widely known and not particularly controversial book. With *Anything but Love* (1948) and *Adam's Rib* (1948), Elizabeth Hawes and Ruth Herschberger replied directly to the terms of sexual crisis outlined by *Modern Woman*, but it was Hawes and Herschberger who disappeared.

What links *Modern Woman* to the novels by Lees and Winsor is the near inescapability of its psychological terms. In the decade itself it was quite apparent that moralists were using psychological categories to do their moral work for them. For example, Marjorie Farber concludes her *New York Times* review of Allan Seager's *Equinox* (1943) by noting, "Exposing the incorrigible moralism of our culture (in its latest disguise) he has seen how we use psychiatric definitions to hide moral judgments."[81] Likewise, in her 1947 article "Woman's Place: The New Alliance of 'Science' and 'Anti-Feminism,'" Ethel Goldwater writes an extraordinarily clear-eyed rebuttal to *Modern Woman: The Lost Sex*. With a critique of the book's misogyny as cogent as any twenty-first-century reader might hope for, Goldwater shows how Lundberg and Farnham use the "science" of psychoanalysis to blame women for culture-wide problems, and so push modern career women back into traditional domestic roles.

Yet Goldwater herself still has no desire to get outside the psychological "science." She continues to trust the field of psychiatry; what her review rejects is the use to which that otherwise respectable field has been put. Goldwater can still write sentences such as: "More women than men in our society express neurosis in the form of disturbed sexuality." And then: "It does not follow that there are more maladjusted women than men, but only that men will tend to express neurosis in some non-sexual way."[82] Unlike the 1940s feminist critiques of advertising, which undermine the whole façade, feminist critiques of psychoanalysis leave the edifice standing. Hence even though a brave feminist energy rolls through Hannah Lees, Kathleen Winsor, and Ethel Goldwater, the omnicultural discourse of psychoanalysis is so internalized that it easily survives the questions and reexaminations of these writers.

The most illuminating psychological reading of the war wife's sexual desire appears in Therese Benedek's *Insight and Personality Adjustment: A Study of the Psychological Effects of War* (1946). Benedek addresses her book to "professionals," so that, even though it is written in a largely nontechnical way, it was scarcely reviewed in the mainstream press. In the chapter, "Soldiers and Wives: During Separation," Benedek discusses the psychological effects of waiting and sexual deprivation. As noted earlier, many medical authorities declined to talk about the sexual desire of war wives outside a framework of conventional moralism. Benedek, however, gives the topic a much more detailed discussion. She recognizes that adult women, not just adolescents, may feel strong sexual desire, such that "there are women as well as men who are unable to ward off their sexual needs and who submit to their urgency."[83] Women's many responses to wartime separation have one "common denominator: they all represent variations of adjustments to sexual deprivation."[84] Benedek gives adult female sexual desire more actuality and intensity than most other scientific authorities.

In Benedek's analysis, however, female psychology revenges itself on socially transgressive sexual desire. Society's judgment aims itself squarely at unfaithful wives, which Benedek sums up in italics: "*sexual freedom is a dangerous liberty for women*, since its consequences rebound upon them mainly."[85] Benedek appears to be at the edge of questioning society's sexual double standard. "These women do not do anything other than what men, probably their own husbands, are doing and doing without much reprimand. Why then are we so shocked?"[86] But instead of questioning the social sphere, Benedek turns condemnation inward. Whatever societal judgment takes place, it cannot compare with the psychological condemnation of the women themselves. Benedek's model of female consciousness describes the sexually transgressive women as children, who are afraid of punishment, who suffer "total regression" and come to hate not only their husbands, but their children as well. "With this, the woman puts herself outside of society; she becomes criminal."[87] By the end of Benedek's psychological narrative, the woman has been as ruthlessly punished and humiliated as any bad woman in a true confessions magazine. As usual, even in the work of an innovator, psychological discourse grounds its authority in the conventional and unquestioned morals of the wider society.

One more novelist will round out this discussion of the waiting wartime wife. Although she is scarcely mentioned today, Nancy Wilson Ross wrote avowedly feminist books during the 1940s. Her nonfiction histories, *The Waves, the Story of the Girls in Blue* (1943) and *Westward the Women* (1944), are written from a polemical perspective.[88] As she writes in the concluding chapter to *Westward the Women*, "the reason for the alleged discontent, laziness, parasitism, and neuroticism of the American-woman-in-the-home is that—unlike the pioneer woman—she feels that the way she lives her life is no longer necessary; no longer meaningful."[89] Ernest Groves, a founding figure in marriage education, perceptively reviews *Westward the Women* next to another of the decade's major polemics on gender, Amram Scheinfeld's *Women and Men* (1944).[90] Groves chooses—with rare explicitness for the time—Ross's defense of women over Scheinfeld's misogyny. "It is refreshing," writes Groves, "to turn from an attempt to determine the social status of women by biological assumptions to the historical record of what actually some women have done."[91]

In her 1947 novel, *The Left Hand of the Dreamer*, Ross made her own contribution to the genre of the waiting wife. Like the books by Lees and Winsor, it too shows how hard escaping psychological conventions and discourse can be. As a wartime wife during World War II, Fredericka falls in love with a European refugee. At the end of the book, she faces down her returned soldier husband, and saying that she has lived an "unconscious," "immature" life up to now, breaks off their marriage. Franz Allers, the European refugee, teaches history not psychology, but he hails from Vienna and his thought is shot through with psychoanalytic language. The world war is a product of anxiety and tension, and "the whole world, he said to himself, is now like a patient undergoing a psychoanalytic treatment."[92] The plot of the book frees Fredericka from her superficial marriage, and she says bold, culturally subversive things in her final speeches to her husband. She not only rejects an attachment to nature, but she also rejects an attachment to her own children ("we should never have had them").[93] In the concluding stretch, the novel bravely undermines one female stereotype after another.

But the overall shape of the wife's liberation nonetheless buys into the most hoary of the period's maturation myths. Fredericka's life-saving change is figured repeatedly as an "awakening"; she was "unconscious" before, but now she is awake and alive. It has taken an older, more experienced man to awaken the woman. This narrative is taken precisely from the decade's standard sex story, that men awaken women into sexual awareness. These are the terms that Fredericka herself uses when she thinks about her adolescence; she wonders why she could spend so much time with Greg "without any love-making." "Now," thinks Fredericka, looking back, she "understood it. She was unawakened."[94] As a young woman, it took a man to awaken her sexuality; as an older woman, it again takes a man to awaken herself to life. That it takes a man to awaken female sexuality means that women, by themselves, do not know their own desires, do not know what they want. And the logic of Ross's novel is the same; Fredericka has to figure out what she wants from adult life, but only a man can awaken these desires and make them concrete. As in Lees, Winsor, and Goldwater, Ross provides some very brave ideas about female autonomy, dignity, and equality, and this time in the hands of a self-identified feminist. Yet the female heroine frees herself from a man only because of a man, and then escapes directly into the arms of yet another Viennese scholar of the world's neuroses.

4

He-Wolves and She-Wolves

From Tex Avery to Jackson Pollock

As we saw in the previous chapter, 1940s authorities tend to evaluate human sexuality on a spectrum of normal to abnormal. Science (medical hygiene, psychology, sociology) thus bolsters mainstream morality by supporting gender norms for men and women, and heterosexual norms for their interaction. A less authoritative, but equally ubiquitous way of understanding sexuality employed the term "wolf." The term had no particular scientific associations, but it too stemmed from a desire to organize society around sexual categories. The popular term implied opinions about normalcy and ethics since the wolf answers only to his animal desires. Yet the use of the word is interestingly fluid and often much less judgmental than science's "abnormal." Women are advised to avoid "wolves" because social honor and respect can vanish in the face of male wolfish lust. But since masculine sexuality is understood as innately aggressive, all men verge on being wolves. Hence wolves are often tolerated, cajoled, and humored rather than demonized.

This chapter begins with a survey of wolves in order to provide the category with some linguistic and cultural context. I then look at the way that sexually predatory wolves appear in cartoons and comics. Along the way we will meet several she-wolves who will take us back to this book's central question: If male sexual desire is imaged as animalistic—the wolf—what does female sexual desire look like? How do cultural forms evaluate the female animal? After considering several films, a radio show, and some pulp fiction, we will take the man-animal theme into the high-culture realm of philosophy. A main point of this chapter, as elsewhere, is to show continuity between the way figures appear in mass media and the way they appear in scientific discourse like psychology or academic discourse like philosophy. There are differences, of course, but also important links between the she-wolf in *Li'l Abner*, the cat women in *Cat People* (1942), and Jackson Pollock's early abstraction, *The She-Wolf* (1943). These works speak to different audiences, but all emerge from a society that depends heavily on the language and figuration of the wolf.

Wolves and Wolfing

The 2006 *Partridge Dictionary of Slang and Unconventional English* defines a "wolf" as a "sexually aggressive man." The dictionary's given date of first usage, 1945, is years too late, since the term is used throughout the decade.[1] A salacious 1948 guidebook, *New York Confidential*, which the *Partridge Dictionary* cites in one of its examples, says that "the subject of wolves has been written about ad nauseam and to most people it's an old and tedious joke."[2] The chapter, "White Way Wolves," is intended to help out-of-town men pick up city women. In their pose as world-weary sex guides, the authors exaggerate how nauseatingly "old" and "tedious" is the "subject of wolves." But it is certain that by 1948 wolf talk has been going on for some years and across a wide cultural spectrum. The tabloid city guide writes about "wolves" as part of its slangy, knowing sex talk. And yet, contrary to Partridge once again, one might say that "wolf" is neither "slang" nor "unconventional" since the word is culturally ubiquitous. Only prisoners know that "to cop a bean" means to have sexual intercourse with a virgin, while only urban jive talkers know that a "bow wow" is a gun.[3] But everyone in the United States knows what a "wolf" is; the only question is what to do with him.

Who is afraid of a wolf? Young women are told repeatedly to avoid pushy, wolfish young men, while lonely war wives are warned to watch out for potentially wolfish male friends. In a book of advice for the war wife, *So Your Husband's Gone To War!*, Ethel Gorham tells women to watch out for "wolves in Friend's Clothing."[4] Male "wolves" constantly try to take advantage of women, so that women need their wolf radar up. Does he love me or is he only a wolf? Or, as the blurb to a 1945 *Saturday Evening Post* story puts it, "[this is about] the romance of a girl who thought she could tell a wolf when she saw one. But could she?"[5]

In most instances, however, wolves are not too dangerous, or, to frame it somewhat differently, society accommodates itself to the wolf's sexual aggressiveness. On *Command Performance*, Bob Hope is introduced as "chief scout of the wolf patrol" (11–13–43), and his girl-chasing jokes support his title. But the Bob Hope wolf is not scary since on this radio show for soldiers, men leer at women and women's scripts tell them to welcome those leers. In the B-movie *Crime Inc.* (1945), a nightclub singer (Martha Tilton) welcomes the advances of a self-identified wolf. When her new male acquaintance says kiddingly that "there's a little wolf in every reporter," the singer, without any appearance of seeming hard-boiled, replies, "I'll take my chance." "Wolves" like Bob Hope and this journalist are not regarded as dangerous, even if they are on a sexual prowl. *Orchestra Wives* (1942), according to *Billboard*, "glorifies recordings, music machines, one nighters, and wolfing."[6] And indeed, after their concerts, "wolfing" band members chase around young women. Yet as is so often the case, the "wolves" come off as regular folks and even cute. Wolfing ought to come with a clear set of ethics, such as when Julie London, a model in *Esquire*, says that she is interested in gentlemen, and "a gentleman is a man who isn't a wolf."[7] But wolf morality is not always that clear-cut, as witnessed by another *Esquire* model, Betty Jane Hess: "I didn't know what I wanted—but I knew it was right when I found it. It—six foot three of it—came into my life just three weeks after I came to New York. I had never met a wolf, and until then I had no opportunity to meet one. But from what I hear they sound like fun."[8]

Women are thus represented as surprisingly tolerant of wolves, while men tend to be even more self-forgiving. For instance, the 1944 *Time* magazine article "Wolf! Wolf!" gives its own version of a *Washington Post* story:

> The *Washington Post* last week printed a sensational report that started a great cackling among Washington newshens. According to the report, there is a secret list which Capitol Hill's 135 female reporters are supposed to keep of U.S. Senators and Representatives "to stay on the other side of the desk from." Appended to prominent names on the list were such descriptive names as "Garter Snapper"; "Revolving Door Romeo" (he "gets into the same compartment of a revolving door [and] . . . pinches"); "Elevator Lothario"; "Gooser Gander"; and "Desk Athlete" ("He jumps. See him only with your gang").[9]

By our standards all this "wolfish" behavior looks, at the minimum, deeply inappropriate. But the women apparently tolerate it by thinking up clever names for the men, while the article itself has the tone of "no big deal." Female journalists are regarded as "newshens" and the article's title, "Wolf! Wolf!," implies that the women are "crying wolf." As elsewhere, male wolfishness can look threatening, yet people—especially women—are expected to accommodate themselves to it.

Wolfish desire broadcasts itself through the wolf-whistle. Visual culture allows men to stare and leer, while audio culture allows men to whistle. A fancy version occurs in the Rodgers and Hart musical *Pal Joey* (1940). First Vera Simpson sings, "What is a man?"—a question that this chapter answers through both animal cartoons and Jung-inspired philosophy. Vera also invokes the animal: "Is he an animal? Is he a wolf, is he a mouse?"[10] "Wolf" and "mouse" would seem equally unacceptable extremes—too aggressive, too shy. But Joey himself has the next song, "Happy Hunting Horn." It turns out that Joey is a wolf, not a mouse, and he sounds his hunting song for all to hear. The "happy hunting horn" is the musical's elaborate version of the wolf-whistle, the sound that lets women know the man is on a sexual hunt.[11]

In a culture that encourages male sexual desire to make itself known, wolf-whistles are heard regularly on the radio. Most episodes of *Command Performance* cannot be heard stateside, but Jack Benny's shows at U.S. military camps and bases are broadcast to families nationwide. On wartime radio programs like these, soldiers welcome nearly every female guest with whistles. And even without soldiers, audiences often whistle at women, encouraged no doubt by the male hosts' relentless appraisals of female sexuality. Radio comedy makes good use of inappropriate wolf-whistles, too, such as when Dennis Day—the archetypal sexual naïf—whistles at what he thinks are dirty words, or when young Leroy whistles at a woman on *The Great Gildersleeve* (5–26–46). In reply, a somewhat shocked Gildersleeve says that Leroy has been spending too much time at the bus station.

The wolf-whistle not only allows male desire to make its presence known, it also allows women to respond to overt expressions of sexual desire. When Maisie (Ann Sothern) takes her first walk through the airplane factory in *Swing Shift Maisie* (1943), the male workers hoot and whistle at her. The film review in *Time* singles out this moment for its photograph: "She draws wolf calls from welders."[12] Once again, these wolf calls are hardly frightening, and Maisie obviously enjoys them. When Ann Sothern's radio show comes out (*Maisie*, 1947–1953), the opening theme begins with two long wolf-whistles. A man says, "Hi ya Babe, how 'bout—," and with the sound of a slap, Maisie says, "does that answer your question?" A classic "good–bad girl," Maisie is both sexually attractive and morally pure. Indeed, she seems stronger than the wolves, completely self-controlled, and without any tinge of she-wolfishness herself.

In contrast to the many friendly male wolves, she-wolves tend to be social outcasts, misfits, hard women, or nymphomaniacs. Teenage she-wolves steal your boyfriend, while adult she-wolves are promiscuous "dames on the make." Whereas male wolves are sometimes bad and sometimes loveable, female wolves rarely merit sympathy. Female wolves are kin to film noir's femme fatale ("Ned quickly succumbs to the she-wolf calls of an exquisitely dressed war correspondent");[13] she-wolves readily metamorphose into all those spider women, tiger girls, and female werecats of the decade's adventure and horror films. Few she-wolves are attractive since the sexual aggressiveness that seems natural and understandable in men is not judged the same way when it appears in women.[14]

The decade's most straightforward she-wolf polemic is Abner Silver's *All Women Are Wolves* (1945), which makes the provocative claim that female sexual desire is as ever-present as male. Abner Silver, a prolific composer of popular songs during the 1920s and 1930s, begins the book with celebrity witnesses (Milton Berle, Dale Carnegie, W. C. Handy, Arthur Murray), who judge the validity of the title's premise. Most everyone agrees that "all women are wolves," including singer Jo Stafford, who says that when she sings, "that's my wolf cry, set to music."[15] It is a comedy book, and the celebrities come off as good humored in their descriptions of female sexuality. But when the celebrities stop testifying, Silver comes in with the usual collection of misogynistic she-wolf types: the society wolf, the autograph hunter, baby face, the gold digger, Hollywood career girl, the divorcee, the dowager wolf. In this view, she-wolves are aggressive women who seduce and trap men. To acknowledge female sexual desire could join women to men by means of an equitable sexual hunger. But instead the statement that "all women are wolves" turns women into a catalogue of predatory she-beasts—some cute, some ugly—all requiring male vigilance and supervision. This unevenly balanced collection of he-wolves and she-wolves takes many forms over the course of the decade.

Tex Avery, Al Capp, and Cartoon Wolves

The U.S. military made pinup art an official part of its media for soldiers. *Yank* not only contained centerfolds, but also featured comics with scantily clad women. Milton Caniff's *Male Call* offered the revealingly dressed "Miss Lace," "a confection of femininity which put all the 'pinups' in the shade."[16] Pinup women appeared not only in *Yank* and *Stars and Stripes*, but even in training materials. The Private Snafu animated training films sometimes used sexy women as part of the program. For example, that any soldier would ever find two bombs where a woman's breasts should be was unlikely, but that is what happens at the end of *Private Snafu: Booby Traps* (1944).[17] With a similar pedagogical intent, some soldiers learned to read maps by first studying a crosshatched grid over a Betty Grable picture.[18] The female images in the service magazines and training films are not only sexy, but also official productions of the war department. What the pictures communicate is not subterranean eroticism or sensuality, but a visually direct, above-board recognition of male-controlled heterosexuality. The women of *Male Call* and elsewhere did exactly that—their morale-boosting purpose was to call the men "male."[19]

One of the better known GI cartoons was called, quite bluntly, "The Wolf."[20] Authored by Sergeant Leonard Sansone, the Wolf was a soldier with a wolf's head who seemed to spend most of his time pursuing women. The Wolf sometimes looks silly, mooning after pictures or statues, and sometimes he gets his comeuppance when women punch him out or their boyfriend comes home. But mostly the hunt seems quite agreeable to him and mostly agreeable to the women. Many of his flirting techniques are ancient—pretending to be sick so a pretty nurse will take care of him, or supplying his own mouse so a frightened girl will jump into his arms. But some of his methods are extremely coercive; in one panel he drags a woman down the street with handcuffs, while an onlooking soldier says "He has a peculiar hold on women!" In another cartoon a soldier says to his date, "His girl will be along any minute!" while the Wolf leans nonchalantly against a telephone pole, an open bear trap nearby on the sidewalk. The Wolf always smokes a cigarette and is drawn with slightly leering eyebrows, but basically he is fuzzy and cute with a friendly smile. The cute façade helps to offset his consistently nonchivalric behavior, such as when he leaves a trail of money on the ground for pretty women to follow or when we see a young woman washing a child's mouth out with soap, saying, "What else did he tell you?"

In his "Foreword" to an edition of *The Wolf* for a civilian audience, Milton Caniff defends the Wolf from any negative moralisms: "This sort of thing has been going for a good many centuries, but Sansone is the first cartoonist to make capital stock of the fact that in the army a young man's fancy turns to what the girls have been thinking about all along. No matter how snootily she tossed her head, I have yet to see a woman who did not betray that secretly pleased expression around the eyes when whistled at or wolf-called by a man in uniform." Caniff looks into the minds of both Wolf and pretty women and sees the same thing—that Wolves desire pretty women and that women desire men in uniforms. Caniff argues that the military uniform saves the Wolf from critique: "[A woman] wants that cold spot on her neck to be the U.S. lapel insignia, not a lodge button."

In the same way that women's breasts and legs inspire male sexual desire, so too does a soldier's uniform serve as springboard for female sexual desire. A wartime *New Yorker* cartoon makes the same claim: a buxom chorus girl looks down at a row of attentive soldiers in the audience and says: "The second one from the left's not bad."[21]

In his introductory pages, Caniff not only defends the Wolf's aggressive behavior, but also proclaims the intelligence of the cartoon—"Sansone did not write down to his audience." Since the cartoon is mainly sex gags, Caniff's main exhibit for the comic's sophistication is that the Wolf's head is a metaphorical head, not a literal one. "[Sansone] pictured his wolf character in full makeup for the part, assuming the reader to be pixie enough to realize that the animal head was not evident to the other pen-and-ink people in the cartoon." Indeed, sometimes the cartoon depends on the irony that we know the soldier is a Wolf, while the woman about to sit next to him on the bus does not. Oh, is she in for a surprise! So his wolfishness is really not there (he's not really a Wolf or a Wolfman), and yet it is. Everything he does is wolfish, so much so that he looks like a wolf. Women who know about him already react strongly—one cowers behind a trashcan, one punches him, one even gives him a pair of handcuffs (meaning, I know you are a wolf, but I can tame you a bit). The Wolf represents male sexual desire with the same graphic clarity as any female pinup. Caniff claims that the soldier Wolf is the realization of female sexual desire, but what her desire looks like remains unclear. For pinup women and the Wolf both visually display the reign of male desire.

A number of Tex Avery cartoons display a similarly exteriorized, wolfish male libido.[22] During the 1940s Avery directed a whole series of cartoons for Metro-Goldwyn-Mayer Studios (MGM) that played small changes on a sex-crazy wolf and a sexy showgirl. Both *The Shooting of Dan McGoo* (1945) and *Swing Shift Cinderella* (1945) place the wolf-and-girl plot in a wartime setting. But *Red Hot Riding Hood* (1943), *Wild and Woolfy* (1945), and *Little Rural Riding Hood* (1949) need no war references to justify the wolf's head-banging lust. The sex comedy is always based on the pyrotechnics of his arousal—the wolf sees the gorgeous female singer and goes bonkers, floating up in the air, hitting himself with a hammer, eyes popping out of his head, tongue hanging down to the ground. The woman not only looks like a pinup model, but she also sings inviting lyrics. In two of the cartoons she sings to the wolf directly, "Put your arms around me, Wolfie." But her show is an entertaining act, not autobiography, and when the wolf tries to interact with her outside the song she always resists. Female desire thus comes across as an ambiguous fabrication. By contrast, male sexual desire is overt and enthusiastic. All of Avery's wolf cartoons are basically ridiculous celebrations of the male erection.

In *Little 'Tinker* (1948), Avery works up a parallel treatment of female sexual desire.[23] A male skunk scares all the female animals away until he starts crooning like Frank Sinatra. Now *he* is the act on stage, the cynosure of desire, and a dozen female rabbits make like the sex-crazy wolf. The cartoon's parody draws on the thousands of swooning teenage girl Sinatra fans. But these female rabbits do not just swoon, they hit themselves in the head with their feet, bang their heads against fence posts, hit each other with hammers, and wham one another into the ground. The cartoon thus reads the swooning of contemporary teenage girls directly into the sexual lunacy of the wolf. The she-rabbits turned she-crazies storm the Sinatra skunk by the dozens.

In comparison with the all-out libido of the wolf series, the makers of *Little 'Tinker* do not know quite how to represent female sexual desire. On the one hand, it is exactly the same as male desire, which is to say, head-banging craziness. But again and again, the wolf is given a hugely inventive, baroque phallicism, whereas the rabbits are much less wildly insane. Female modesty or moderation, one might say, although Avery likes crossing provocative lines. In a telling contrast, however, *Little 'Tinker* constantly pokes fun at skunk Sinatra, teasing him twelve ways for his beanpole skinniness. Throughout the 1940s, every radio show would harass Sinatra with the same set of gags, but in the cartoon it amounts to an attack on the erotic object. The wolf cartoons do not satirize or render nonsensical the pinup girl singer; she remains statically gorgeous.[24] But with the sexes reversed, Avery uses most of his baroque kookiness to skewer Sinatra. In other words, why the male wolf would go wildly crazy over a living pinup is perfectly clear, but why female rabbits would go crazy over Frank Sinatra is basically incomprehensible. Male sexuality is coherent and representable, whereas if female desire can be shown, it probably does not make sense.

The most interesting version of the cartoon he-wolves and she-wolves appears in Al Capp's *Li'l Abner*. Al Capp appeared on the November 6, 1950, cover of *Time* magazine, the first cartoonist ever to merit this honor. The cover story aligns him with other great innovators in the popular arts: "Capp fills a niche in comics comparable to Gershwin's in jazz, or D. W. Griffith's in the movies. From an instrument which had seemed as crude and monotonous as a dime-store flute, he produces noisy bass blats of comedy, a skirling of irony and satire such as the comic page had never known."[25] A caption to one of the cartoons says in fragmented *Time*-speak, "in gobbets of sex, the absurder aspects of mayhem," but otherwise the article talks about his "endless enchantment with yokels and pretty girls."[26] Since this canonizing essay wants to set Capp alongside Gershwin and Griffith, it emphasizes the strip's range of comic tone and variety of target. "Capp tries to give his readers not only a daily belly laugh, satirical Cappian comment on politics, sex, law enforcement, the housing situation and human rapacity, but surrealistic gobbets of action, mystery, horror, and adventure as well."[27]

The emphasis on the satirical range of *Li'l Abner* makes for a good, civilizing argument, but to a contemporary eye whole stretches of the strip seem, above all, to be focused on sex. Rick Marschall stresses this aspect in his introduction to a 1991 reprint: "We see in 1946 a strip so bursting with vitality that it overflows with blatant sexual symbolism, suggestive elements, and—oh, hell, bathroom-wall scatology."[28] Daisy Mae's desire to marry Li'l Abner shapes the basic plot of the strip. Daisy Mae is a "pretty girl," yes, but one who constantly appears in a revealing shirt and cut-off shorts. And while Daisy Mae clothes her visually provocative looks with a very pure mind, many other women appear who are not so innocent. *Li'l Abner*'s women are often not just pretty women, they are pinup women, clearly readable as glamorous, erotic figures. But since they live in Dogpatch—and not in an *Esquire* photo gallery—they tend to show a surprising degree of ambition.

The comic law in Dogpatch is that women chase men, and not the other way around. Al Capp thought this was a quintessentially funny theme, and explained it as follows: "I try to make a disappointed lover feel better by having 'Li'l Abner' never know what to do about a succession of eager luscious girls who throw their juicy selves at him. 'Li'l Abner' doesn't know what to do, and so he does nothing. And that makes every male who reads 'Li'l Abner' feel fine. Because *he* would know what to do."[29] The "succession of girls" is "eager," "luscious," and "juicy," and Capp implies that a male reader will imagine having sex with his comic-strip women. In saying so, Capp is more straightforward about the sex-centeredness of his comic than most of his contemporary critics.

The motif of girl chasing boy not only works psychologically, it also works satirically by exploding the polite convention that men may show aggressively physical desire, whereas women must remain passive. Sadie Hawkins Day first appeared in *Li'l Abner* in 1937, and throughout the 1940s hundreds of U.S. colleges celebrated their own version. The topsy-turvy holiday reverses the deeply held societal norm whereby men ask out women; now women can initiate and select. This temporary gender swap is still a big thing for the 1940s real world, but it is close to the norm in the universe of *Li'l Abner*. Daisy Mae pursues Li'l Abner regardless of whether it is a holiday. And then the strip multiplies Daisy Mae into many other versions of female desire—a "succession of eager, luscious girls." In 1946, which is where I focus this brief discussion, an extended plotline is devoted to Miss Fortune, who must marry before she is nineteen or lose her legacy. She is very attractive, but also jinxed, which obliges her to pursue one man after another until a final collision with Li'l Abner.

This is also the year that Wolf Gal is introduced to the strip. Wolf Gal is aggressive to the point of cannibalism, but she begins her story by wanting to find out about human love. Since she is outwardly stunning, men are happy to talk to her. One of her impressed interlocutors is named "dateless" Brown, who wears a preposterously phallic long nose. In a crucial stage of her development, Wolf Gal decides she needs to become outwardly civilized in order to learn about love. So she coerces a wealthy woman to teach her how to dress and behave:

> Wolf Gal: Are you quite sure "people" won't realize that—underneath—I still feel like a she-wolf?
>
> Wealthy Woman: Q-Quite sure!
>
> Wolf Gal: Are there any other girls who look like "ladies" on the outside—and feel like she-wolves inside?
>
> Wealthy Woman: Yes! Oh, *sob!* Most of them![30]

1940s society wants women to look good on the outside, in order to engage a man's sexual desire. Meanwhile, her sexual desire is left comparatively vague. But in his science fiction universe, Capp shows women with a range of much more aggressively concrete desires. Insofar as alterative worlds reflect the actual world, the character of Wolf Gal suggests that more animal desire is in women than 1940s society ordinarily allowed itself to imagine.

Li'l Abner is a fascinatingly chaotic comic strip that invites, indeed, seems to insist on, contradictory readings. Some have argued that Wolf Gal works as a feminist character—"strong, beautiful, independent"—who successfully subverts all middle-class norms of work, gender, and sexuality.[31] But her appearance also works to bring out all the social contradictions around female sexuality so that her independence and beauty are to be feared as much as admired. On the one hand, she is the fantasy pinup girl, the pinup with desire, unlike so many "frigid" women who suffocate men in their marriages. But she also tends to eat people. When the casualty list is drawn up at the end of the Sadie Hawkins Day race, twelve men have committed suicide to avoid being caught, while six are "missin', suspected o' bein et by wolf-pack."[32] While naive Li'l Abner does not know what to do with "luscious" girls, ferocious Wolf Gal is quite sure what to do with luscious boys. Li'l Abner sometimes eats a sandwich instead of making love with a woman; this expresses an innocent sexuality. Wolf Gal's men are themselves eaten like sandwiches; this expresses a dangerous sexuality. If Wolf Gal is a feminist character, then she is more like contradictory, violent Medea than, say, Susan B. Anthony.

In the upsy-downsy world of *Li'l Abner*, Abner himself plays the role of the contemporary woman. He is a pinup boy, but without obvious sexual proclivities. He is a hunky handsome young man, often shirtless, who would stand out anywhere, but who becomes especially handsome next to all the gnarled, skinny, and fat inhabitants of Dogpatch. Behind the good looks his character is both generous and dumb. He is heroically self-sacrificing, such as when he volunteers to marry Lena the Hyena, so that his idol, Fearless Fosdick, will not have to. He also offers to bring the hungry workers of Dogpatch 6,000 sandwiches, a Herculean labor unto itself. But Abner is as dumb as he is heroic, and he loses his 6,000 sandwiches twice, once when a very capacious dog eats them all at night, and once when he mistakenly carries home a giant rock instead of the sandwiches. He is not as clued into romance as a woman would be—much to Daisy Mae's chagrin—but in other respects he makes a rather good woman. Both intellectually dim and spiritually generous, he is at once spectacularly attractive to the opposite sex while harboring no particular desires of his own. He is very silly, but very likeable. He is as American, in other words, as Mom.

The Female Animal from *Cat People* to *Tiger Girl*

The animalistic man is not strange or particularly noteworthy. He is perhaps uncivilized or a "wolf," but he might also be "frank" or admirably natural. Animalistic men might be monsters or brutes, or they might simply be rugged or tautologically masculine. The animalistic woman, however, signals both sexuality and otherness. Sexualized women are compared to animals; these similes indicate both physical instinct and physical threat. In adventure and horror genres, animal women are close kin to all forms of exotic women. The leopard girl emerges from the same sexual landscape as the sarong girl and the jungle girl. The animal woman is primitive, closer to nature, and thus judged to be more sexual, like people in the tropics or in the jungle. The animal woman is often given nonwhite racial characteristics, which shows the degree to which sexual desire others white women away from a sexually controlled self.

The animal woman appears as a sexualized and aggressive figure in a variety of cultural forms. Before *Dragnet*, Jack Webb's radio show, *Pat Novak for Hire* (1946–1947, 1949) was a linguistically exuberant parody of the hard-boiled detective genre. Pat Novak would always run into a sexy woman; his voiceover often draped her in some kind of animal simile. She was "a 1949 Panther model" (2–20–49), "she looked like a wasp with a nice sting" (3–6–49), she was a "nice little mouse that made you want to go home and test all the old traps" (3–13–49). Novak's similes accurately indicate the female zoo of 1940s sexual culture. Maria Montez appeared in films such as *Cobra Woman* (1944) and *Gypsy Wildcat* (1944), while Acquanetta starred as the ape-woman in *Captive Wild Woman* (1943) and as Lea, the High Priestess, in *Tarzan and the Leopard Woman* (1946). Young comic book readers thrilled to energetic female protagonists such as Tiger Girl and Princess Pantha.[33] Western enthusiasts found a formidable antagonist in a series from the 1944 *Action Stories*—Señorita Scorpion.[34]

These figures could be read as coming from a landscape of sheer fantasy, from the man-animal planets of Edgar Rice Burroughs; they appear to have little connection to the realities of home-front America. But the sexual culture of women's magazines is continuous with the sexual culture of jungle comics and monster movies. Because radio shows justified their adventures as romantic escapism ("Want to get away from it all? We offer you . . . Escape!")[35] does not mean that their fantasies and their horror do not map back onto the cultural imaginary of everyday life. In his introduction to William B. Seabrook's "The Caged White Werewolf of the Saraban," Boris Karloff—who edited numerous horror anthologies—wonders, "Is it possible that Seabrook in this story intended a subtle criticism of the average man's domestic arrangements, with a veiled suggestion for their improvement?"[36] Based on the introductory notes elsewhere in the anthology, the question here is asked relatively seriously, not with the mad, black laughter of a radio show horror host. In the story itself, the husband keeps his wife in a cage since from "time to time, she becomes demoniac, possessed. She becomes a wild beast."[37] On the one hand, this story is fantastic nonsense, and it explains the wife's symptoms as "jungle madness." But Karloff suggests that this situation speaks also to the "average man" since that man always has to wonder, what happens if I have a wild woman in my house? What if she turns out to be a she-wolf?

Cat People (Tourneur, 1942) is built around similar fears, although here the "average man" says he is not afraid. Instead it is the woman who fears her inner animal. With *Cat People*, producer Val Lewton inaugurates a new style of horror picture, which takes a much subtler approach than the Universal Studios monster movies of the 1930s. Lewton's new style of quiet, offscreen menace has so captivated later critics that they often forget to talk about what is actually on the screen. *Cat People* has received numerous interpretations over the years, along with a general recognition that it ushers in the most original approach to horror in the forties. But almost no one has tried to read the film as a 1940s film, as a film that speaks to culturally specific ideas about sexuality and marriage.

Cat People exposes the period's contradictory and nightmarish discourse around female sexual desire. In *Adam's Rib* (1948), Ruth Herschberger described 1940s sexual culture as an "education for frigidity," in that its emphasis on female chastity and daintiness before marriage left women with nothing to draw on when the sweaty, physical act of sex finally arrived. Marriage manuals explained how young women were to "adjust" to marriage, when they went from the dating girl who restrains the boy's desire to the wife who submitted to it. At this point, if all went well, the experienced man would "awaken" the woman's sexual desire. The marriage psychologists thought the problem could be solved; Herschberger thought the problem was man-made. What both agreed is that due to cultural training—"look sexy, but don't think sexy"—women have a big bridge to cross from premarital prettiness to actual sex in marriage.

And there is nothing offscreen or subtle about the way that *Cat People* takes place in the exact center of this sexual narrative. The motivating crisis is that newly married Irena (Simone Simon) cannot adjust to her marriage. Confused by her feelings of sexual desire, she refuses to sleep with her husband. This is the crisis moment that marriage textbooks repeatedly aim at, but where movies, censored by the Hays Code, rarely arrive.

The cultural particularity of this plot is signaled through the psychoanalytic language of normalcy. The decade's inhabitants, as observed in the previous chapter, have internalized this language, and it appears throughout the film. Irena wants to be a wife like other wives; she says, "they make their husbands happy. They live normal, happy lives." Just as Sophie Harbor wondered if she was "normal" when she sought erotic substitutes for her husband, Irena also wonders if she is normal. "Normal" does not mean "average"; in this context it means sexually adjusted, and a viewer must understand the language in that light. Her husband Oliver tries to convince her that she is not linked to the cat people legends, and, above all, that she is normal: "You're so normal you're even in love with me, Oliver Reed, a good plain Americano. You're so normal you're going to marry me."[38] But the marriage does not work out normally. She cannot manage to sleep with her husband. When she cannot adjust to marriage, she asks for patience and Oliver gives it to her. And he has her see a psychiatrist.

Just as the film takes the psychological terms seriously, but also undermines them, it presents a reasonably authoritative psychiatrist, Dr. Judd (Tom Conway), but also substantially complicates him. "Normal" and "abnormal" matter deeply to both the film and the film's characters; Oliver and his female friend from work, Alice, both appear preposterously average.[39] By contrast, Irena Dubrovna is strange twice over, a Serbian character played by a French actress. Oliver and Alice are almost parodies of sexually well-adjusted people, while Irena's apparent lack of interest in Oliver has sometimes been read as a sign of lesbianism.[40] Likewise, the authority of Dr. Judd is both supported and questioned. The film begins with a quotation that sounds like Freud, but is attributed to Judd, and the doctor seems to represent a reasonable (if overly confident) perspective. At the end, however, he crosses the doctor-patient boundary by trying to kiss his vulnerable client, and this makes some critics view him as an unmitigated creep.[41] William Paul gives the most balanced reading, arguing that Dr. Judd is "both sinister and humane," and that judgment seems right.[42] When Dr. Judd tries to kiss Irena at the end—after he deceives Oliver and Alice in order to get Irena alone—her homicidal panther rage is understandable. Yet just a few scenes earlier, Dr. Judd had given Irena a rousing speech, to which she responded with gratitude and optimism: "for the first time you have been kind to me." His speech ended with an exhortation to "lead a normal life."

Cat People follows, exaggerates, and revises the standard 1940s stories about female desire. The film represents the real difficulties of marital adjustment as belonging primarily to the woman, a wife who can yet be helped by a patient, understanding husband and a knowledgeable psychiatrist. The usual story, however, is that the wife needs her husband's patient help to discover her sexual desire, to build her small inexperienced fire into something that burns as strongly as the husband's own. But Irena's desire is so immense that she can only imagine it as a predatory animal, a ferocious beast. Since the men in the film, Dr. Judd and Oliver, refuse to believe in the cat people legend, it is implied that the wild beast of female desire appears because men cannot understand female desire or have no interest in doing so. In the face of masculine incredulity, female desire appears as a threatening nymphomania, as a monstrosity.[43] Like the sexualized ethnic others of jungle comics and westerns, Irena's double foreignness allows her to represent and feel the power of sexual desire.[44] But the film's violent conclusion—both Dr. Judd and Irena horribly killed—shows how dangerous the stories were that the decade told itself about female sexual desire.

She-wolves and she-beasts appear throughout 1940s culture as commentaries on the period's conventions of gender and domesticity. "The House in Cypress Canyon" (12–5–46), an-oft praised episode of the radio thriller, *Suspense*, offers a particularly interesting interpretive problem. In this story, a couple move into a new home but they are soon disturbed by ambiguous sounds; it might be dogs or a "wildcat," but at other times the cries sound human. Eventually the husband, James A. Woods (Robert Taylor), finds his wife, Ellen (Cathy Lewis), inside a mysterious closet. As he reports in a manuscript that keeps track of these strange events: "She stood there rigid, her arms at her side. Her fingers, extended like claws. Her hair was over her face. Her eyes stared out of it. Her lips were drawn back in a grin like an animal at bay. Very deliberately, she sunk her teeth until they met, into the flesh of my forearm. I'd raised my hand to strike at her . . . but already she'd relaxed her hold and gone utterly limp." Even though the word is never used, all critics assume that Ellen has become a werewolf, that this episode is "a masterful tale of lycanthropy."[45] But since Ellen has gone "rigid," "deliberate," and robotic, I prefer to name her as some species of zombie. She is clearly lost in an involuntary trance.

In the best analysis so far of gender in the 1940s radio thriller, Allison McCracken says that "it is easy" to read the above scene "in terms of the husband's fear of the wife's deviant sexuality."[46] McCracken reads the sequence of biting the husband's arm, going limp, and then waking up refreshed the following day as a version of the male orgasm. The main problem with this otherwise strong reading is that little evidence supports the woman's "sexual deviancy." In other contexts, female sexual desire does turn women into monsters, but here we see no sign that Ellen is anything but completely typical. McCracken notes that even though the couple has been married for seven years, they have no children, which means they are "perverse, far from the 'ordinary family' Jim describes them being at the start of the narrative."[47] And while postwar society might look askance at a single woman or a childless couple, this couple's childlessness is not weighted enough to make an issue of it. They themselves do not talk about their lack of children, nor does any other character, and their seven-year marriage is noted so quickly that an otherwise trustworthy radio critic calls them "newlyweds."[48]

If we read she-wolf Ellen as a she-wolf zombie, however, we can take into account much more of what the radio play actually gives us. The atmosphere of the story is one of luckless, soul-crushing fate, where the couple are dragged down inevitably to their demise. What is important to account for is not only the episode's female monster, but also the circular structure of the episode. A framing narrative has a real estate agent discover Jim's story in a still unfinished house at the beginning; after he reads the story—a story which concludes with Jim shooting his wife and then turning the gun on himself—Jim and Ellen show up alive at the real estate office and ask to see the just finished house. In other words, Jim and Ellen have been caught in a mysterious time loop. Richard J. Hand sees the time loop as extraneous, a "device that seems almost redundant next to the genuine horror and social resonance of the central story."[49] But getting caught in a trance in the form of a wolf zombie is very much like getting caught in an endless time loop. Both the zombie and the time loop emphasize passivity and fatality, a living death. From the beginning, when Jim calls their search for a place to live a "geometrical progression of discouragement," to the end, where Jim gives up all hope, "powerless, helpless now, deadened in thought and will, empty as the house itself," the story is buried in the same bleak fatalism as a postwar film noir. "The House in Cypress Canyon" exposes the wreck of postwar domesticity, not through anything the couple have done themselves (by failing to have children), but simply through the melancholy of postwar gloom. Whereas the murderous "werecat" in *Cat People* signals an out-of-(male-)control female sexual desire, the zombie she-wolf in "The House in Cypress Canyon" signals the lack of control felt by both male and female in postwar American society.

A she-wolf story that allows the woman much more control is Jane Rice's "The Refugee" (1943). In the early 1940s, Rice published regularly in *Unknown Worlds*, a fantasy pulp magazine edited by John W. Campbell from 1939 to 1943. "The Refugee" gives its American heroine, Milli Cushman, two related wartime problems—a lack of food and a lack of men. For some reason, Milli has declined to leave Paris, where wartime exigencies are pressing indeed. Fortunately, just when the wolf of hunger is growling at her door, a beautiful wolf of a man appears outside her window.[50] In a genre where men usually peruse female bodies, Milli's sexual attraction to her visitor is described with both physical detail and enraptured emotion. He is shirtless, and Milli admires his "excellent anatomy" and "extraordinarily well-shaped head." "He was, Milli thought, rather like a young panther, or a half-awakened leopard. He was, Milli admitted, entranced, beautiful. Perfectly *beautiful*."[51] They peer at one another and "his eyes were tawny and filled with a flickering inward fire that made suet pudding of her knees." Eventually Milli "shook herself out of her trance."

Although at first overcome with sexual attraction, Milli soon gains control of the situation. She seductively invites him inside, giving "him her most delectable glance." He says his name is "Lupus," which he explains means "wolf"; cocksure, he does not think she can figure him out. But she is smarter than he is. At the end of the story, she kills him by feeding him a silver bullet, and in the tale's innovative fantasy, the proximity to that same bullet changes her into a werewolf. Having intentionally changed herself into a werewolf, she then eats him. Milli is not the most likeable character; she has a prissy, judgmental attitude about her Parisian surroundings, and she criticizes her "refugee" victim for continuing to fight the Nazis ("What good does it do? It just makes them angrier."). Nonetheless, the conclusion does not feel like one where we realize what a monster Milli was after all, a she-wolf who uses her sexual wiles to seduce and then murder poor refugees. On the contrary, the upbeat last line ("Down to the last delicious morsel.") implies that we should credit her wits and resourcefulness as a refugee herself, as an American woman in wartime Paris. This monstrous woman feels less like a criminal and more like a confident victor. Milli has shown that she can outwolf the wolves of lust, hunger, and war.

She-animals are usually highly sexualized women, but how that sexuality is deployed can differ greatly from example to example. One of the decade's most bizarre female animals appears in *Captive Wild Woman* (Dmytryk, 1943), in which a mad doctor (John Carradine) infuses "sex hormones" into a captive ape. This explicitly sexualized transfusion causes the gorilla to change into Paula Dupree, a lovely woman played by Acquanetta. It is generally understood today that whereas the studios fabricated a South American origin for Acquanetta ("the Venezuelan Volcano"), her parents were actually Arapaho Indians who lived in Wyoming.[52] In her relatively brief career she was always cast in exotic roles, where her "Latin" looks would tie into the sexy primitivism of films like *Jungle Woman* (1944, the sequel to *Captive Wild Woman*) and *Tarzan and the Leopard Woman* (1946), where her high priestess character rules over the Leopard men. In *Captive Wild Woman* Paula Dupree helps a circus lion tamer keep his animals under control.

In a strange refinement of the "male gaze" structure, men stare at Acquanetta while she stares at the animals. In *Captive Wild Woman*, Acquanetta wears a spangly two-piece circus outfit that viewers found quite stunning. In a dismissive review of several monster movies, *Los Angeles Times* critic Philip Scheuer admitted that Acquanetta had "a lulu of a figure."[53] Meanwhile Paula Dupree's simian origins give her a powerful hold over other wild animals. Thus while portions of the audience stare at her, she is shown in close-ups staring wide-eyed at the animals, holding them in check, so that they will not kill the lion tamer, Fred Mason. Eventually her looking passes into desire; Paula likes helping Fred and feels they have a bond. But when she finds out that Fred has a girlfriend, she literally goes ape, and her jealousy turns her back into a gorilla. The transformation scene turns her darker and darker with racist associations (it is as if she turns African and then ape) that even contemporary viewers found offensive.[54]

In *Captive Wild Woman*, femininity is displayed in the form of poise and control, as Paula Dupree has power over other animals and over the animal in herself. But female sexual desire turns her into an angry beast, although the creature still has the presence of mind to charge into the cage and rescue the stunned lion tamer. *Captive Wild Woman* thus works out with revelatory clarity the period's monstrous attitude toward female desire. The quiet beautiful woman can be gazed on indefinitely, but sexual desire renders her grotesquely animal with nightmarish consequences.

One way that Universal Studios kept generating horror movies was by finding female versions of male monsters, so *Bride of Frankenstein* (1935) follows *Frankenstein* (1931), *The Invisible Woman* (1940) follows *The Invisible Man* (1933), and *The She-Wolf of London* (1946) follows *The Wolf Man* (1941). *Captive Wild Woman* is, to be sure, the female version of ape-man movies such as *The Ape* (1940). But the sequels, *Jungle Woman* (1944) and *Jungle Captive* (1945), show that *Captive Wild Woman* is linked not only to horror, but also to exotic adventure. The focus on the human-animal boundary is associated not just with diabolical scientists, but also with powerful humans who live on strange islands or in mysterious jungles. Whether claustrophobic horror or tropical adventure, to which we now turn, the cultural logic of the female animal looks quite similar.

Cobra Woman (Robert Siodmak, 1944) is a blue-skied Technicolor adventure, but the female animal is just as beautiful and just as dangerous as Paula Dupree. The Cobra Woman is played by Maria Montez, Universal's queen of exotica during the first half of the forties.[55] She made five movies in 1941, including a part as Melahi in *South of Tahiti* where she displays strange powers over her pet leopard. On show for her romantic beauty in *Arabian Nights* (1942) and *Ali Baba and the Forty Thieves* (1944), Montez also played a princess who ruled an island in *White Savage* (1943). *Cobra Woman* was a double fantasy for Maria Montez fans since she was cast as two main characters, the bad sister, Naja, who tyrannically rules over the Cobra island people, and the good sister, Tollea, who finds herself in position to drive her sister out of power.

The bad sister reveals her badness through episodes of increasingly aggressive sexuality. At first, Tollea's betrothed, Ramu (Jon Hall), mistakes bad sister for good sister and kisses Naja. Naja, however, shows her sexual experience and unfeminine directness by kissing him back and asking for more. Her sexual aggressiveness then takes on a public dimension when she performs a writhing dance in front of a giant cobra. Hays Code or no, the sexuality of this scene is blatant. Yet Naja's behavior is easy to read because while she writhes around the snake, she also points out future candidates for human sacrifice. In other words, the sexy snake dance is so dangerous it leads directly to religious blasphemy and serial murder. Now Hays is happy.

The snake ritual stages a clear contrast between the good and bad sisters in terms of their sexuality. With a sexual logic that recalls *Cat People*, good sister Tollea disappears from her village just before her marriage. Whereas *Cat People*'s Irena does not wish to sleep with her new husband, Tollea's absence postpones her entrance into adult sexuality. In 1940s terms, both women display sexual adjustment issues. And Tollea's sexuality will remain innocent, even dormant. At the end of *Cobra Woman*, Tollea impersonates her now dead sister in the cobra ceremony. But the giant serpent terrifies her, she cannot manage to do the sexy dance, and she faints dead away, at which point she is rescued by Ramu and Kado (Sabu), who are also rescued—as in a Tarzan movie—by a monkey. Altogether, then, the sexual logic of *Cobra Woman* is stereotypic and familiar. Female sexual desire is associated with cruelty and murder, while the good woman faints unconscious in the face of sex and desire. As in *Cat People* exactly how a woman is supposed to adjust to the sexual exigencies of marriage is not clear. It is just as well, then, that the movie's conclusion provides the shy version of Maria Montez with some premade children, namely Sabu and the chimpanzee. Perhaps they can render moot the primitive need for sexual reproduction.

After playfully mocking the silliness and spectacle of *Cobra Woman*, *New York Times* reviewer Bosley Crowther managed to conclude with a kind of recommendation: "It is better than the funny papers, on which it is obviously based."[56] And it is true that the comic books were filled to the brim with female animal people and male animal people as well. The comic book version of the female animal adds some interesting twists to what we have already observed in fantasy fiction, radio, and the movies. *Tiger Girl* is one of many jungle women who ran barefoot through the pages of Fiction House comics. Dependent on its bevy of half-clad jungle heroines, Fiction House publications would be driven out of business by the 1954 comics code.[57] But through the contorted tangle of racism, sexual display, and violence, one can see that Fiction House has its own kind of self-justifying code, a code that overlaps with other contradictory structures of female sexuality during the 1940s.

Tiger Girl began in the Fiction House work *Fight Comics*, in 1944, alongside other fighting heroes such as "Rip Carson, Chute Trooper"; "Hooks Devlin, Special Agent"; "Shark Brodie"; and "Señorita Rio," a glamorous model turned international spy. In any particular issue, each character gets an eight- to ten-page story. By April 1947, *Tiger Girl* was elevated to the cover of *Fight Comics* and shortly thereafter she became the lead comic, where she would remain for the rest of the decade. *Tiger Girl* followed on the 1938 debut of "Sheena, Queen of the Jungle" in Fiction House's *Jumbo Comics*. Meanwhile, another main Fiction House magazine, *Jungle Comics*, featured male, female, and even animal heroes. With a view to promote maximum mayhem and maximum female nudity, Fiction House kept putting barely clothed women into savage Africa. The rise of *Tiger Girl* to prominence among all these competing titles must be attributed in part to its illustrator, Matt Baker, who has since been recognized as one of the period's most skillful artists. Baker not only showed *Tiger Girl* in her best light, but also drew one of the most sensational figures in 1940s comics, *Phantom Lady*.

The shape of the racism in *Tiger Girl* and other Fiction House jungle comics is relatively clear. Although Tiger Girl sometimes refers to tribes who have lived in peace for hundreds of years, there is more often the sense that the African natives are constantly at war. The blonde white woman is called into save both individuals and communities from harm. The evildoers are often white men who kidnap the natives for slaves or exploit them in dangerous mines. But while the golden-haired princess often refers to the natives as her "friends," she is unsympathetic to their superstitious ways. A repeated plot has white men playing on native credulity by setting up false idols; she then punishes the white men, but also gives the Africans a tongue-lashing. As she tells the natives in a typically severe conclusion, "Now it is time for your lesson, duped ones!" (63).[58] Tiger Girl regularly discovers wayward lawlessness and then imposes a ferocious penalty. At the end, the evil "spawn of jackals" are dead and she triumphantly—though calmly—announces that justice has been accomplished. "They perished amidst the gold they worshipped" is a characteristic last thought (52). This repeated story is a fundamentally racist story since it assumes that only a white woman can adjudicate and execute the law in savage Africa.[59]

While the structure of racism is clear, the structure of sexuality is open to discussion. The commercial reason for Tiger Girl's comic book existence is obvious: the comic heroine is required to look sexy, to pose and bend in various directions while wearing just a tiger-skin bikini. But this inarguable premise has numerous complications. A first observation is that no characters in the comic book itself regard her as in any way sexualized. Her looks are scarcely ever referred to by anyone. She is the least vain pretty girl in the comic kingdom and offers no opinion about her face or figure. The narrator calls her "shadowy, elusive, and lovely" about three times in the whole run, but otherwise says little about her appearance. Most remarkably, Tiger Girl often runs into the toughest, crudest-looking white men, yet they almost never comment on her looks. In *Tiger Girl* 61, a sympathetic white man arrives on a quest "for a beautiful jungle girl" about whom he's heard; in two issues from the late forties, the bad guys refer to her as a "blonde babe" (63, 64). Otherwise, the thugs and slave traders talk about her fearsome strength or her tiresome meddling, but they never dismiss her threat because she is a woman and, even when they have captured her, they do not comment on what is so obvious to the reader, that she is a leggy model who looks well in tiger underwear. The paradoxical, probably hypocritical, result is that *Tiger Girl* offers up its heroine for the transparent purpose of providing a sexual object for the viewer, but then the diegetic space of the narrative itself refuses to admit that there is anything sexual about her.

This is where the comic seems to have invoked its own kind of code before the 1954 comic code. The repeated emphasis on justice at the end of each story captures the "crime doesn't pay" attitude of Hollywood's Hays Code and seeks to offset the often gruesome violence in what has come before. What's more, by limiting the sexiness of Tiger Girl to the viewer's mind—unassisted by any general leering in the comic population itself—the comic potentially (although hypocritically) shifts the moral onus to the reader. Tiger Girl's sexuality is what *you* make of her; as for us here in the comic book, we are completely neutral.

A main emphasis in the animal women of *Cat People* and *Cobra Woman* is that the animal makes the woman more instinctual, more sexually aggressive. But there is no sexual aggressiveness at all in Tiger Girl. On the contrary, she is romantically unattached and exhibits no sexual desire whatsoever. Just as Tarzan has a female companion named Jane, Sheena the Jungle Queen has a male companion named Bob Reynolds. But Tiger Girl's associates consist of Abdola, a Sikh servant, and two pet tigers. There is affection and loyalty to spare, but not a flicker of sexuality. Just as it is striking that no one in the comic seems to notice that she wears a nice-looking bikini, it is equally striking that such a person takes no interest in men. In one of the stranger episodes (65), Tiger Girl attacks the wrong people, not realizing that some white merchants have kidnapped native women. She sits with the men while they admire the women dance. Tiger Girl says, "The dancing girls are those who this day have attained woman status and may now marry . . . do you find it interesting white ones?" Tiger Girl is clever as well as courageous, so she is not dumb. But this is the most sexually naïve question imaginable. She often does battle with those who "lust for gold," but she apparently has no understanding of sexual lust. The strangeness of this episode—where she first attacks the good guys, pals around with the bad guys, and then apologizes to the good guys—is an apt framework for what looks like the comic's brief recognition of its bizarrely restrained treatment of Tiger Girl's sexual awareness.

The sexual psychology of jungle comics is open to dispute. If the main goal of the comic book makers is to offer teenage boys some sexy women to look at, why put the women into a primitive war zone where many of the characters are witch doctors with rhino masks or black men carrying spears? One would think it would be easier—and much closer to home—just to think up stories about showgirls and detectives, and certainly that was done. In that case sexuality is associated with danger as well as glamour. But the jungle comics serve to emphasize both the fearful and the othering aspects of sexuality; that sex is not easy, but surrounded by tumult and alienation. Why does the December 15, 1944, issue of *Vogue* offer perfumes named "Danger" and "Shanghai"; promote a shade of "Chinese Red" on the back cover; style clothes after Greek, Roman, Chinese, and East Indian traditions; model Hindu pants; and advertise a suit made with "genuine python" called "Jungle Allure"? Because it follows the same logic as Serbian (and French) Irena in *Cat People*, namely that female sexuality is elsewhere, is not everyday, and is potentially powerful and terrifying.

And what is a teenage boy supposed to think about such a formidable and authoritative woman? Maybe the hormone-swamped teenager is just happy to possess the images and does not worry about the characters or the plot. In the entire run of 1940s episodes, Tiger Girl smiles unambiguously just once, early on, when she is playing with her tigers (36). Otherwise she is almost always angry and serious; occasionally she looks surprised. While her body is presented to the male viewer for his sexual fantasizing, everything else about Tiger Girl, both the comic book and the woman, does not cooperate with a male desire to possess her as a figure in a sexual narrative. Tiger Girl is regularly captured, so that the viewer can see her lying down, passive, and if it suits his proclivities, tied up. But most of the time Tiger Girl is both physically powerful and morally authoritative, in clear contrast to everything the 1940s linked to conventional femininity. This kind of active confidence could rarely be found outside of comic books.

We should probably understand these comics, then, as being read both by teenage boys *and* teenage girls. To say that the jungle women were "primarily cheesecake," that they "catered to what passed for prurient interest among adolescent male readers," is obvious, but it is not the whole story.[60] Statistical demographics on who is reading what remains scarce, but the magazines themselves give some indication of who they think their audience is. Yes, there are ads for "how to be a radio technician" and how to look like Charles Atlas. But there are also ads for things like seed packets and piano lessons. Most strikingly, in two consecutive issues of *Tiger Girl* (55, 56), placed on the same page as the conclusion of the story, is an advertisement for "Brilliant Blondie," a baby doll, who "drinks and wets." It is hard to imagine that many self-respecting adolescent boys would be happy to conclude their meditation on Tiger Girl with that unmanly picture. But it is quite easy to imagine the baby doll directed at a conventionally domestic young woman who might well have been fascinated by the powerful jungle princess. Whereas male superheroes are likely to exclude female readers, the enterprising comic publisher can get both male and female readers by flooding the market with female superheroes. Because of the period's obsession with the female model, both young men and young women are potentially interested in attractive female bodies. From our perspective, this might also be a way of seeing Tiger Girl as a protofeminist heroine who in her world is treated by men not for her good looks, but for her strength and decisiveness.[61] The same kind of complex power (is it feminism or sexploitation?) that emanates from Buffy the Vampire Slayer when she looks toward the camera over her bloody axe is recalled when Tiger Girl glares at her collapsing victim, knife in hand, blood dripping from its point (53).

Philip Wylie, Vardis Fisher, and the Female Human

Early on in his 1949 autobiographical fiction, *Opus 21* (subtitled, *Descriptive Music for the Lower Kinsey Epoch of the Atomic Age/A Concerto for a One-Man Band/Six Arias for Soap Operas/Fugues, Anthems, and a Barrelhouse*), the main character, Philip Wylie, meets a pretty girl in a restaurant who is apparently reading *Ape and Essence* by Aldous Huxley. In fact, the book jacket is just a front for the book underneath—the Kinsey report. The book and its cover are chosen well by Wylie since each recently published text harmonizes with his own. In the form of a film script, Huxley's *Ape and Essence* (1948) stages a science fiction story in which intelligent apes destroy the world with atomic bombs. Huxley's attacks on religion, science, and sexual repression parallel those Wylie launched. Wylie also cheers the recent publication of the Kinsey report, which "had accomplished what hundreds of psychologists and scores of writers like myself had been unable to do: he had convinced multitudes that the sexual behavior of people is mammalian in every respect."[62] Altogether, then, the novel's Wylie runs into a fantasy woman whose reading falls exactly in line with the novelist's pet subject—the idea that man is an animal.

Wylie the *Opus 21* character then proceeds to entertain the young woman with stories of his animal past. He tells her that some years ago he "was an animal-horror man" in Hollywood. As he explains: "Those were the days of animal pictures and horror pictures. Frank Buck and Osa Johnson and Tarzan. Frankenstein. Paramount was trying to combine the grisliest features of all of them. They were making [H. G.] Wells's *Island of Dr. Moreau*—for instance. And I was doing some of the writing." And indeed Wylie was cowriter on Paramount's *King of the Jungle* (1933, whose hero is Kaspa the Lion Man), *Murders in the Zoo* (1933), and the adaptation of Wells's *Moreau* called *Island of Lost Souls* (1932). As the opening of *Opus 21* makes clear with its strategic collection of Huxley, Kinsey, and Dr. Moreau, there is a straight path from 1930s Wylie to the 1940s. He was once an "animal-horror" screenwriter, but when he transformed himself into one of the nation's most well-known philosophers, he continued to emphasize both the "animal" and the "horror." Never shy about repeating himself, all of his 1940s books focus on man-as-animal, from the best-selling prose prophecy, *Generation of Vipers* (1942), to the novelization of his ideas, *Night unto Night* (1944), to his philosophical clarification, *An Essay on Morals* (1947), to *Opus 21*.[63]

Wylie's *Essay on Morals* attempts to clarify the main ideas of *Generation of Vipers* and *Night unto Night*. Instead of a table of contents, the book once again has a collection of subtitles, one of which is *A Popular Explanation of the Jungian Theory of Human Instinct*. Wylie's central point in all his books, repeated again and again, is that man is an animal, thus we must accept our animal nature and origins. To know that we are animals is a blow to the ego, and strikes down the narcissistic confidence of both religion and science. But his main polemic around the animal is that the chaos of the world—transparently obvious during the global conflagration of World War II—is attributable to sexual frustration and repression. By citing the increase in divorce rate, juvenile delinquency, adultery, inchastity of minors, number of homosexuals, prostitution, and, since V-E Day, "the lack of scruples against cohabitation with the enemy's women," Wylie argues that "the sex life of the United States of America is very close to ruin."[64] This list of ruinous symptoms could come from any conservative commentator, who would then conclude that America needs to shore up moral values by aiming for lifelong heterosexual monogamy. But even as he expresses his alarm about the supposed increase in homosexuality, Wylie proposes that our true sexuality is as yet unknown. In earlier eras men lived "polygamous, polyandrous, promiscuous," and "less bitterly, less despairfully" than we do now.[65] Hence to return knowingly to our animal instincts is to discover our true sexuality, not the sexuality prescribed to us by church or law. "Until he designs his own latitudes and duties," writes Wylie, "he is no man at all, but a bred sheep—a fodder for the cannon he forges with the rage forever rising from his guilty shame that he is an animal and denies it."[66] A man who is not a man is less than human.

Wylie argues that the rise in homosexuality is due to women who do not allow men to express their animal selves sexually. Men desire women, but women do not answer men's desire, leaving men no choice but to have sex with one another. The idea that male homosexuality was a choice of last resort was surprisingly common. Hubert Creekmore's *The Welcome* (1948), for example, works out Wylie's formula rather scrupulously. Standing before an empty church, Don tells his friend Jim: " 'And mostly it's women. Nobody has remembered that women are animals, too, like us. Or they haven't remembered that they ought to be more than fine pieces of interior decoration. Women, or somebody, ought to remember that they're human. They've made themselves'—turning with a drunken, dramatic gesture about the church—'this.' "[67] Jim's wife thinks sex is dirty, too bestial—"I'm not a common woman, James, I won't be pawed over."[68] She rejects the animal and so drives Jim into the arms of his friend. In Jim's overloaded but also telling comparisons, the "empty church" of womanhood needs to become more animal and therefore more human. But these contradictory metaphors also get to the heart of the problem. And the problem is this: a more animal man is a more complete man, but a more animal woman may be monstrous or impossible to imagine.

Wylie's call for self-conscious animalism is aimed squarely at feminized men. It is men who need to bring out their inner animal. *Generation of Vipers* famously lays the blame for the state of the male nation on women. First, Wylie attacks women for buying into mass culture's promotion of the "Cinderella myth"—the myth that men should work for women who do not have anything to do. "Woman as an idle class, a spending class, a candy-craving class, never existed before."[69] Second, and most famously, Wylie attacks American mothers for their fawning, sentimental, tyrannically possessive rule over their sons. Although we cannot see them for what they are, American mothers are nothing less than monsters: "Consequently no Gorgons are ever clearly seen, let alone slain, in our society. Mom dishes out her sweetness to all fugitives, and it turns them not to stone, but to slime."[70] *Generation of Vipers* appeared at the beginning of the war, when thousands of sons were off fighting for the American way—Mom and apple pie. Its astonishingly vituperative style and choice of critical targets were therefore calculated to offend. But *Generation of Vipers* also found traction in a teetering, confused nation whose collective masculinity was at stake.

The comic version of Wylie's call for male animality occurs in *The Male Animal*, a play coauthored by James Thurber and Elliott Nugent, which appeared on Broadway in 1940. In the 1942 film version, which closely follows the play, Professor Tommy Turner (Henry Fonda) tries to summon the nerve to defend his wife from the advances of a former all-star football player while he tries to defend his right to read a controversial piece of writing in class. Surrounded by hulking football players who sit next to his wife and push the college as a whole toward stadiums and championships rather than academic study, Turner drunkenly exhorts himself to an animal ferocity:

> TOMMY: Let us say that the tiger wakes up one morning and finds that the wolf has come down on the fold. What does he? Before I tell you what he does, I will tell you what does not do.
>
> MICHAEL: Yes sir.
>
> TOMMY: He does not expose everyone to a humiliating intellectual analysis. He comes out of his corner like this . . . the bull elephant in him is aroused.[71]

After passing through a stage of clumsy fisticuffs, shy professor Turner eventually works himself into a powerful defense of free speech, which succeeds in winning back his wife's affections.

The Male Animal can be read as a lighthearted play, as mere farce.[72] But even though the film version is very similar to the play, it appeared after America entered the war. Now the Professor's defense of free speech in the face of bullying comes off as substantial and patriotic, like a Norman Corwin radio polemic. "The male animal" is not just a cartoon, but an ideal, a combination of intellect and courage. The film's resolution does not just give back the man his wife, it gives the man his proper human balance—he is a better man than he was before. This conclusion agrees with the diagnosis of Lewis Mumford, who in *The Condition of Man* (1944) argued "the need for human balance" and supported his description by quoting "a profound reader of the modern soul, Dr. C. G. Jung, who has sought to combat this unfortunate lopsidedness and disparity by counseling his patients to cultivate their weaker sides."[73] In Professor Turner's case, he needs to cultivate his animal.

Men become more human by growing closer to their instincts, their desires, but what of women? Are women animals? Are women human? In a radio revamping of the Jack and Jill story, Jack Paar says: "I knew I had to kill her [Jill], but could I? After all, she was a human being and a woman, a rare combination."[74] The audience laughs heartily at such silliness, but really you have to cry. On November 13, 1942, women from Vassar College and Brooklyn College debated "The Value of the College Woman to Society." Since women ideally were supposed to be good wives and mothers, the purpose of educating women in versions of male colleges had been questioned for years, all the more so during the war. Following the debate, however, a Professor Sattler raises his hand to frame the debate somewhat differently:

> The topic of tonight's discussion probably could have been changed to read: "Are Women Human Beings?" (Laughter) As a man, therefore an amateur on the subject, I would be willing to say at once they are, very much so. (Applause) Now that we are in agreement that women are human beings as much as men are, I believe that they are subject to the same frailties. There is a class story told about a couple of Vassar girls who met, ten years after graduation, at a reunion, and, said the first to the second, "Did you get your Ph.D."? And the second one said, "Yes, I got him!" (Laughter)[75]

Even though he generously grants women admission into the human race, Professor Sattler's inequitable conclusion does make one wonder. One wonders, for example, what "frailty" which women share with men does his humorous anecdote illustrate? And one also wonders, with respect to 1940s culture, whether women are, after all, human beings.

This question runs parallel to the experiment in *Island of Lost Souls* (1932), which Wylie and Waldemar Young adapted from H. G. Wells's *The Island of Dr. Moreau*. Although the film is unflinchingly framed as horror—the beast-men are quite scary—the adaptation adds key female characters to answer Hollywood's perpetual need for coupledom. One is the shipwrecked hero's fiancée, Ruth; it is she who comes to the rescue when Edward fails to appear on the mainland. And the second major addition is a female character

Lola, the Panther Woman (Kathleen Burke). With the other beast-men looking mostly tribal and hairy, the Panther Woman becomes the focus of the movie's revised plot. Dr. Moreau (Charles Laughton) sees that he can use uninvited Edward to find out whether Lola, the Panther Woman, will be attracted to a man. Has the doctor created a female who possesses sexual desire? And the answer is yes since the Panther Woman quickly becomes fascinated by Edward. Moreau then tries to strand Edward on the island so he can find out if Lola is "capable of loving, mating, having children." How "nearly a perfect woman she is," says Moreau, who now wants to find out if Lola is biologically a woman.

But the movie is more ambitious than Dr. Moreau and makes sure we know that Lola is not only a woman, but also a human. Before they attack Moreau at the film's end, the horrific man-beasts all chant a nightmarish lament: "we are things, not men, not beasts." Yet the audience understands that the Panther Woman is also the Panther Human. Like jealous Paula Dupree in *Captive Wild Woman*, Lola regresses to beastliness when sexual emotions stir within her. Moreau cries out: "This time I'll burn out all the animal in her!" But just as Paula Dupree sacrifices herself for her beloved at the end of *Captive Wild Woman*, Lola sees a beast-man chasing Edward through the forest and she battles the creature to their mutual death. If showing sexual desire for a man proves that Lola is a woman, then this act of loving self-sacrifice shows her to be, at last, a human.

World War II encouraged philosophers, anthropologists, and psychologists of all types to ask themselves, what was man? What did it mean to be a man, a human man? Much more rarely they asked, what does it mean to be a human woman? An abstract polemic such as *What Man Can Make of Man* (1942), by William E. Hocking, talks at length about how "our flagging liberalisms, democracies, and freedoms can recover their virility," but a woman is let into this book about "man" only once in order to measure her "deficit of head and feeling."[76] In *Nature and Man* (1947), the academic philosopher Paul Weiss aims his argument toward the "task of man," which is to "plumb the foundations of ethics and make evident to himself what he ought to do."[77] But Weiss's deep ethical foundations apparently do not include women since when he drops down to specifics, he says things such as: "Not all can be professional athletes, mathematicians or political leaders," or "the growth and development of most men involves the production of a sexual impulse so powerful that it can be repressed only at the risk of creating a new mode of expression."[78] In 1947 few women were professional athletes, political leaders, or were conceived of as possessing an overwhelming sexual impulse. But the abstract philosopher has no problems about modeling his deepest thoughts about humanity on male humans. The question of whether women are human is therefore, at this point, a real question and not a silly joke.

Vardis Fisher undertook one of the most ambitious fictional representations of man's humanity in this period in his twelve-volume series *The Testament of Man*, which would not conclude until 1960. During the 1940s, Fisher issued the first five volumes of the series: *Darkness and the Deep* (1943), *The Golden Rooms* (1944), *Intimations of Eve* (1946), *Adam and the Serpent* (1947), and *The Divine Passion* (1948).[79] This anthropological epic seeks to show the development of human culture from the very beginning in part to discover what makes humans human. In *The Golden Rooms*, Neanderthal men discover the use of fire, but are still, in the words of a reviewer, "subhuman animal men."[80] *Intimations of Eve* and *Adam and the Serpent* take mankind through a period of matriarchal rule. *The Divine Passion* brings the story to the beginnings of ancient Hebraic culture. Whereas academic philosophy about mankind was often so abstract that women were nowhere to be found, Fisher's *The Testament of Man* focuses almost entirely on the role of gender and sexuality in the development of human culture.

Just as *Island of Lost Souls* and *Captive Wild Woman* use female love to indicate the acquisition of selfless humanity, *Darkness and the Deep* appears to credit women with mankind's development toward civilization. In Fisher's *Testament of Man*, biology is destiny, and culture emerges as a direct result of male and female sexuality. Men are depicted as not only permanently lustful ("Wuh lived day and night with the passion of it consuming him"),[81] but also sexually frustrated since women rarely evidence sexual desire. Women are too busy with their children, with nursing, with being pregnant once again to desire sex or do much of anything else. Hence women want to stay in one place and take care of their children, in contrast to men, who wander and who sublimate their sexual urges into art and invention. If left to nomadic, restless, frustrated men, mankind would never evolve, but female domesticity is credited with making mankind human. "In the centuries preceding this time, it had been chiefly mother love that had impelled one of the beasts to become a man."[82]

But this "mother love" soon becomes as treacherous and emasculating as that professed by Wylie's saccharine devil-Mom. Motherhood gives women the central place in Fisher's version of human prehistory. Men are sexually frustrated and have no obvious value. In *Intimations of Eve*, old women, who have no interest in sex, hold the political and religious power. In *Adam and the Serpent*, the one woman who shows sexual desire for men is mockingly named Passion, and is ugly and barren. Because the role of the father in sexual reproduction is not understood, women possess all magic and meaning, and they use it to sexually oppress the men. These two volumes are designed to make the reader sympathize with beleaguered men and pray for an end to tyrannical matriarchy. By refusing the advances of the sexually aggressive but foul-smelling Passion, Dove, the book's hero, gains confidence in himself as a sexually autonomous man. The book's narrator cheers Dove's heretical skepticism about female power: "[He] was also a confused and unhappy prophet of a new order, who, in spite of all persecution, would keep striving to find for men a position comparable with that of women. He lived under the curse of a woman who spurned him and no longer admitted him to her bed; but he also lived under the prodding of a restless mind that would strive in spite of contempt and curses to find a respectable destiny for men. In this he would contribute to the greatest social revolution in the history of the human race."[83] Although Fisher gave momentary credit to biological motherhood for its stability and affection, men's innate restlessness will ultimately save mankind from these excesses of female power. Humans will become more properly human, it appears, with the much-desired dawn of the patriarchy.

One of the decade's most profound meditations on humanity—but this time told from a woman's point of view—occurs in "No Woman Born" (1944) by the great science fiction writer C. L. Moore (Catherine Lucile Moore).[84] Here, in what the story itself sees as another version of Mary Shelley's *Frankenstein*, a famous dancer has her destroyed body entirely replaced by a machine. Deirdre was renowned worldwide for her extraordinary beauty ("never before Deirdre's day had the entire world been able to take one woman so wholly to its heart" [200]), but while her mind has recuperated from a terrible fire, every atom of her body has been replaced by mechanical parts. In dialogues between Deirdre and the male scientists who made the body, the story tackles directly the philosophical questions raised by this brain without a corporeal body. Is Deirdre still Deirdre? Is she still a woman? Is she still human? Contemporary critics have seen this much-anthologized and much-interpreted tale as an exemplary representative of Donna Haraway's cyborg feminism.[85] "No Woman Born" has also been taken to demonstrate Judith Butler's notion of performative sexuality since Deirdre has no biologically sexed body, but instead must perform her femininity.[86]

While this beautifully conceived story may indeed look forward to our most prestigious contemporary theorists, it can and should be read as an investigation into 1940s sexual culture. The story situates itself at the heart of 1940s celebrity glamour fantasy by focusing on a woman who is held to be the most beautiful in the world. It is a mass medium that is responsible for Deirdre's global popularity, in this case a futuristic form of television ("Deirdre's image had once moved glowingly across the television screens of every home in the civilized world" [200]). A 1940s star image could be built up and transmitted across the country via film or magazine. But we would not expect that such glamour girls would be great actresses or artists; on the contrary, such beauties need no attributes beyond good looks and a good figure. But "No Woman Born" idealizes both the mass media as well as the masses of the future world of television. In this imagining of the future, the "civilized world" has kept its culture apace with its technology. Technology is advanced enough to build both a global television network and a new body for Deirdre. And future culture is just as developed as its science since the masses admire a woman who is not just another pretty girl, but one who is an extraordinarily talented actress and dancer. The "civilized world" thus looks at Deirdre not with a sexualized masculine gaze, but with the disinterested eyes of a civilized aesthete.

The "high culture" framework for the story is crucial to its meaning and omitted by most contemporary readings. Just as Vardis Fisher's *The Testament of Man* equates humanity with civilization—we are more human the more civilized we are—the story's questions about identity and humanity are linked inextricably to a conceptual sense of civilization's development. Instead of going back to the past and watching the cave-dwellers become more civilized and more human, this story interrogates the concept of humanity in the context of an extraordinarily advanced civilization. The story's idealized vision of high culture—that in the future everyone in the world will want to watch a broadcast of Shakespeare—can also be read as a science fiction version of patriotism. It is 1944 and the whole point of the ongoing world war is to save civilization. If the future of mass media were represented by dumb comics and bubble-headed blondes, then what happened to the civilization that so many died to save? In this improbable future, Deirdre is globally popular without succumbing to the vulgarities of pop culture: "It was Deirdre's song. She had sung it first upon the airways a month before the theater fire that had consumed her. It was a commonplace little melody, simple enough to take first place in the fancy of a nation that had always liked its songs simple. But it had a certain sincerity too, and no taint of the vulgarity of tune and rhythm that foredooms so many popular songs to oblivion after their novelty fades" (124).

That she is a high culture star *before* her accident means that the masses could see her for her true beauty. Even though she had a "wonderful dancer's body" and a "soft and husky voice," there is no sense that Deirdre is a sex symbol. In this future society her sexuality is processed as part of her artistry, as part of her beauty. After the accident, it appears that "her beauty is gone," but the "collaboration of artists, sculptors, designers, [and] scientists" have given her a new body, a new beauty, and "Brancusi himself had never made anything more simple or more subtle than the modeling of Deirdre's head" (207). In this world—so unlike our own—Deirdre's true beauty is seen both before and after; the audience loves her dances in her woman's body, and they love her dances in the mechanical body. And as the audience is moved, so is she: "And she was a woman now. Humanity had dropped over her like a tangible garment." One of her male interlocutors tells the other, "she hasn't any sex, she isn't female any more" (218). But when the audience responds to her beauty conceptually and aesthetically, not sexually, then that is when she is most a woman and most human. As we have seen throughout, the sexualized woman is dehumanized, and the question of whether women are also humans is a real question. Even as Deirdre must come to grips with a whole new relationship to her body, so too does the story ask us to wholly rethink the female body on display. In "No Woman Born" the female body is extraordinarily powerful and beautiful, but only when seen by the eyes of a sophisticated human.

As we turn from this chapter's wolves to next chapter's ghosts, it is interesting to see how Vardis Fisher describes the passage of man in *The Golden Rooms*. During this very early segment of mankind's history, Fisher emphasizes two key moments. First, because women ignore him, Cro-Magnon Gode adopts a wolf for a pet. After he kills the she-wolf mother, he stuns the community by declining to kill the offspring, thus making their enemy his friend. The *New York Times* reviewer has some fun at Gode's expense ("He also invented dogs . . . quite a remarkable person, Gode!");[87] but this adoption signals a major culture shift through the domestication of animals. The second key cultural development occurs when Gode begins to believe in ghosts. Once again, women are too busy and practical to consider the "other world," but artistic, sublimating Gode readily conjures up some spirits. The novel concludes with a dreadful storm in an atmosphere of terror: "He was making the dry and terrible sound of a man choked by terrors, of a man driven by unutterable dread to abase himself in the strangled and heartbroken humility of what in its own way was the first human prayer."[88] After a matriarchal phase where women ruled society through mystery and magic, this fearful, humble "first human prayer" must be the origin of true religion in contrast to primitive superstition.

In the origin myth of Rome, orphans Romulus and Remus are suckled by a she-wolf and Romulus founds Rome. In an origin myth for mankind,

Vardis Fisher's protoman kills a she-wolf and raises her pup. The animal gives him strength and companionship in contrast to his fellow women. But even as his consciousness and power expand into the animal kingdom, he is haunted by the spirit world, visited by ghosts. Oppressed and ignored by women, men claim close kinship to animals. Forever afterward, the animal woman will seem less human than the animal man. But the man's physical, animal prowess is far from everything since he also grows into a world of imagination and spirit. Now the animal man is also the man of myth, belief, and art.

One can understand, therefore, that a work such as Jackson Pollock's *She-Wolf* (1943) emerges from the same set of gendered themes and questions that produced *Cat People*, *Tiger Girl*, and Vardis Fisher's anthropological history. The visible basis for Pollock's *She-Wolf* is the bronze Capitoline She-Wolf; the wolf's udders are instantly recognizable, although the painting omits the twin brothers beneath the bronze.[89] As critics have noted, marks around the wolf's form recall cave paintings; the picture feels primitive, messy, and dreamlike. In a book-length argument, Michael Leja argues that Pollock's paintings of the 1940s can be seen as coming from what he calls "Modern Man" literature. In Leja's view, a key figure in this school is Philip Wylie, whose emphasis on the unconscious finds a parallel in Pollock.[90]

One could, therefore, expand the already expansive canon of Modern Man literature to include Vardis Fisher, and then perhaps add Al Capp and C. L. Moore. For Pollock's works of the 1940s—paintings such as *Mad Moon Woman* (1941), *The Moon Woman* (1942), *Male and Female* (1942), *Moon Woman Cuts the Circle* (1943), *Pasiphae* (1943), and *The She-Wolf* (1943)—all present the world in terms of gender, sexuality, fantasy, and violence. Like Capp's aggressive females or Tiger Girl in the comics, Pollock's female figures are both powerful and dangerous. The Capitoline She-Wolf visualizes the foundation myth of Rome, but in Pollock's version, instead of children, several strange monsters perch around. And pointing away from the head and toward the hips, an aggressive, phallic red arrow is painted across the she-wolf. The arrow indicates a sexual narrative since the arrow points into the womb. But the arrow also represents a combative narrative since the male painter has nearly crossed out this dangerous female. Pollock's chaotic lines work both to energize and to erase. Take that crossing arrow for the 1940s plot of plots, as we turn now from the dangerously visible to the invisible, from wolf-women to phantom ladies.

5

Phantom Ladies

On the Radio and Out of the Closet

On March 27, 1944, *Lux Radio Theatre* adapted its play from a recent Universal Studios release, *Phantom Lady* (1944). Since the program sold toilet soap, host Cecil B. DeMille made his usual pitch toward women. In protofeminist mode, he laments the absence of "feminine sleuths" in the mystery genre, but says that his program will remedy this since "the young lady in the play turns out to be a very competent detective." The feminist edge on these remarks soon dulls, however, when DeMille notes that women have been detectives all along. After all, every woman has had to solve her own mystery—"the mystery of a lovely complexion." DeMille's commercial responsibilities oblige him to turn a rare and competent female detective into a "beauty detective" who solves her problems with Lux toilet soap. The woman starts out as somebody—a real heroine in the line of Sherlock Holmes and Philo Vance—but then turns into everybody or nobody, just another pretty face.

The female detective in the story performs the same vanishing act. When her boss, Scott Henderson, is wrongly sent to jail for murder, Carole Richman tries to find the "phantom lady," the only person who can provide him with an alibi. At first Carole comes on so strong that she frightens a bartender, first staring at him in his bar, then stalking after him down the street. She is so intimidating that the bartender flees right into traffic and is killed. Sympathetic Inspector Burgess gives Carole advice about how to confront her next witness, a tough nightclub hood ("He's not what you would call a gentleman"). He tells her, contradictorily, to "play up to him" ("put on some flashy clothes, splash on some perfume, and go to work"), but also not to take any chances: "It may be pretty risky." Her feminine disguise produces results and she gains information, but the hood also figures her out, so she runs away panicked and screaming. This back and forth of strong detective and weak woman continues throughout the program; Carole cleverly tracks down the killer, but has to be rescued from his strangling grasp by the police inspector. The last sequence has freed boss and faithful secretary returned to happy hierarchy, and he instructs her—romantically—that she will be having dinner with him tonight, and the evening after, and the evening after. As happens again and again in the 1940s, a woman may reveal some strength, intellect, or initiative, but not so much that she disturbs the basic social structure on which America depends.

This chapter looks at two kinds of phantom women. First, there are the phantom women of radio, a "blind" medium that supposedly equals invisibility for all. In actuality, radio takes part in the same sexual regime as movies or magazines. Hence radio women are often rounded into sexual visibility, only to be put back into their barely visible social space by episode's end. After a description of Norman Corwin's asexual radio, I turn to sexual themes in radio comedy, with a particular focus on *Our Miss Brooks*. The second section of this chapter looks at what the period barely allowed itself to see—lesbian visibility. If female heterosexual desire is often eclipsed by male wolfishness in 1940s popular culture, then it follows that female same-sex desire will be almost invisible. But we can collect examples nonetheless just like Lisa Ben did in the late 1940s. Films and books offer implied and explicit representations of female same-sex desire, and several examples include women who were not morally condemned by society or themselves. The final section of this chapter returns to the idea that invisible radio is substantially different than visible movies. Several 1940s writers imply that radio's invisibility allows it to become productively queer.

Radio Bodied and Disembodied

An article in the May 20, 1944, issue of the *Pittsburgh Post-Gazette* described the radio shows of several local women.[1] These women had managed to squeeze themselves in on some of the still rarely used FM stations. They said that they were "helping to break down the old-time prejudice against women's voices on the air."

Of course women's voices were obviously on the air all the time—in every soap opera, in every comedy, in every dramatization of a Hollywood film. But women were rarely heard as news announcers or commentators because of a long-term prejudice against women speaking from any position of authority. In her chapter "The Disembodied Woman," Michele Hilmes recounts the arguments against female announcers in the 1920s; she quotes the blunt statement of one executive: "I do not believe that women are fitted for radio announcers. They need body to their voices."[2] If anything, the bias against female announcers had hardened by the 1940s. A 1947 report by the Women's Bureau of the Department of Labor gave this historical summary:

> During the war a few women went into control room work, hitherto considered a masculine stronghold, while others became announcers, directors, sales and publicity representatives, and executives. As the men returned from service, women faded out of these jobs except for a few who made an outstanding success and permanent place for themselves, with the networks, radio stations, and advertising agencies. The public has turned a deaf ear to women announcers, except in certain sections of the South where "announcerettes" are well received. At the present time, except for musical and dramatic programs, women's main chances in broadcasting are on daytime programs for women and children.[3]

In a medium where bodies make no impression, women's "bodiless" voices apparently carry no weight.

In his ambitious, artistic, and sometimes experimental exploration of radio, Norman Corwin repeatedly came back to this "bodiless" conception.[4] In a typical contrast of radio to film, he wrote, "There is no help at all from sets, lighting, composition, gesticulation, costume, make-up or sex appeal."[5] Instead of supplying physical specificity through description, Corwin celebrates radio's lack of physicality by sending his stories everywhere through time and space. Specializing in magic, panorama, patriotism, and music, Corwin's radio plays create an ethereal, global world. The sweeping geography of plays such as "Daybreak" (*Columbia Workshop*, 6–22–41) and "We Hold These Truths" (broadcast 12–15–41 on all major networks) recalls the capaciousness of Whitman's epic lists.[6] Whitman even appears in "Seems Radio Is Here to Stay" (*Columbia Workshop*, 4–24–39), where he finds that radio's godlike ability to send signals "spinning round the globe / Not once, but seven times" is as much a "wonder" and a "miracle" as anything he finds in nature.[7] But Whitman's poetry is always embodied, physically detailed, and made sensual in a way that Corwin's never is. As a way of drawing an essential contrast between radio and visual arts such as film and theater, Corwin both disembodies and desexualizes radio.

Sexuality appears rarely enough in Corwin's radio, and when it does, it often appears negatively. In one of his books, Corwin complains enviously about the sexual freedom granted the comics. "How do newspapers get away with their comic-strip girls, by the way? If radio one day decided to exhibit as much sex for Junior as the ordinary newspaper page of comic strips, there would be a pincers movement against the network by the F.C.C. [Federal Communications Commission] the very next morning."[8] But despite his formal experiments and the vast expanse of his democratic vision, Corwin shows little interest in sex. In "Descent of the Gods" (*Columbia Workshop*, 8–3–41), Venus speaks a little about love, but more about primping: "they all want good looks; each last one likes the smell of new, clean things to wear and pretty baubles for his best girl or her best fellow."[9] Peanut-brained Mary in "Mary and the Fairy" (*Columbia Workshop*, 8–31–41) would like "to buy a pretty dress and look more attractive, so's I'd maybe get a steady boy friend and not be so lonely."[10] In his notes to this play, Corwin says Mary is "not sexy. Yet not sexless. She has small breasts, probably."[11] In "Appointment" (*Columbia Workshop*, 6–1–41), to show that dictator-hating Vincent understands life, we get what is probably the most sensuous description in all of Corwin. Two lovers pass:

> Here's such indifference to earth and its affairs
> As only clouds know, upwards of ten thousand feet:
> The moist, clasped palms, the gently-bumping hips,
> The spring of foot, the pride of bosom,
> Body scent, the texture of the kiss—
> Here, with this easy and domestic gait.[12]

But the play critiques their sensual isolationism. Unlike these passing lovers, Vincent pays attention to the wider affairs of the earth—namely, Hitler's ever-expanding threat. Corwin uses the same logic in *Samson* (*Columbia Workshop*, 8–10–41), where Delilah's sensuality makes Samson into a pacifist ("Yes," she says, "the wars are over").[13] So pure in his conception of patriotic fighting strength (masculine power is diminished by feminine sexuality) and so pure in his ideal of the medium (radio is not the sexually glamorous movies), Corwin performs "bodiless" radio with remarkable moral and theoretical consistency.

To some writers, radio would never work as a vehicle for the representation of sex. In contrast to newspapers or books, which are experienced by individuals, radios are obliged to program for families. For these reasons, says Paul W. White in 1947, compared to the press, "radio is rather namby-pamby in regard to sex."[14] In one of radio's most scandalous incidents, the FCC reprimanded NBC for the "Charlie McCarthy spoof (1937) on Adam and Eve as written by Arch Oboler and 'sexed up' by Mae West."[15] But compared to movies, magazines, or comics, radio did not draw much attention from official censors of sexuality. With no pictures to affront and provoke, the worst potential offenders were ad-libbing comedians such as George Burns and Fred Allen. As far as sex goes, censors mostly had to watch out for dirty jokes.[16]

Yet one might also emphasize a much less disembodied and a much more sexualized radio. The Great Gildersleeve's signature laugh replied to a variety of situations, but it was especially good at sexual insinuation and innuendo around women. Danny Kaye's program regularly featured a sketch where an aggressively sexy woman melted him into nonsensical babble. Bob Hope's radio persona was half grinning satyr; the "road" movies made with "sarong girl" Dorothy Lamour (*Road to Singapore* [1940], *Road to Zanzibar* [1941], *Road to Morocco* [1942]), *Road to Utopia* [1946]) only bolstered that image. In a how-to-write-for-radio essay, one of Bob Hope's writers, Sherwood Schwartz, begins by looking for a topic that might lend itself to humorous treatment. "There are quite a few such topics, of course, but the one which seems to stand out in front of everything else is Lana Turner's sweater. Here, indeed, are a few yards of fuzz that have continued to tickle a great many fancies. So we stop to consider Lana's sweater."[17] Schwartz is right to begin with Lana Turner's sweater since Bob Hope's mile-a-minute jokes never get too far away from that kind of topic.

During the war, radio programs performed for soldiers were basically obliged to furnish sexual content, which ranged from low-key banter to the equivalent of an *Esquire* centerfold.[18] Ordinarily, the *Jack Benny Program* barely depends on sex for its humor; one running gag has two old women talk about how attractive Jack is. But when the show performs live on military bases, Mary Livingstone nonetheless invites wolf-whistles and applause by talking about her dates with soldiers.[19] And this is because during the war almost every woman on the air becomes a potential audio pinup girl whose voice serves the same consoling, patriotic, and sexy purpose as the women in *Yank* magazine. The sound pinup is most explicit in shows such as *Mail Call* and *G.I. Jive*, where the female disc jockeys were in fact sometimes pinup girls. Soldiers not only wanted to hear swing tunes from back home, they also wanted to hear women's voices.

On these shows soldiers not only requested certain songs, but they also requested certain sounds. In particular, soldiers want to hear women sigh, which they obediently do. The wartime film *Four Jills in a Jeep* (1943) begins with a staged taping of *Command Performance*, the most well-known radio program for soldiers. Carole Landis adds to the program's farewell by saying, "I'll be here to ahhhhhh [drawn out descending sigh] sigh for you." Then the film cuts to soldiers listening to the radio and blissfully rolling their eyes. On the *Command Performance* radio show from April 23, 1943, Wee Bonnie Baker reads a soldier's request: "Bonnie, please sing, talk, whistle, and sigh." And Bonnie proceeds to both whistle and sigh. The sigh is a transparently sexual morale booster, just like pinup photographs.

During the war musical numbers could get more explicitly sexual than any double entendre by Bob Hope or Jimmy Durante. For example, after her requested sigh, Wee Bonnie Baker sings two little songs, and they are both sex songs. The first song is a sex joke:

> When I walk, I always walk with Billy, 'cause Billy knows just where to walk,
> And when I talk, I always talk with Billy, 'cause Billy knows just how to talk,
> . . . .
> But when I sleep [long pause]
> But when I sleep [two winking pizzicato plucks from the violins]
> I always dream of Bill.

Bonnie Baker sings in a wide-eyed, innocent Betty Boop voice, so maybe she does not quite know what she says. But the following song makes her character proud and happy about sex:

> He's not so good in a crowd, but when you get him alone,
> You'd be surprised,
> He isn't much at a dance, but when he takes you home,
> You'd be surprised.

The whole song records the woman's happy surprise to find that her man is—despite appearances—a sexually aggressive wolf ("but in a taxi cab, you'd be surprised").

Wartime songs are sometimes straightforwardly sexual, although an added explanation often allows the listener to forgive the woman for her desires and behavior. For example, at the beginning of a *Mail Call* program (4–25–45), Betty Hutton sings a fun, fast-paced song about her physical wants:

I want some hugging, and some squeezing, and some
mugging, and some teasing,
And some stuff like that there.
I want some petting, and some spooning, and some happy
honeymooning,
And some stuff like that there.

The repeated chorus, "some stuff like that there," sounds like ellipses that mean the stuff that happens after "petting" and "spooning." In the end, though, the lyrics save its singer's virtue by aiming toward marriage ("some happy honeymooning"). And the whole song is introduced by a brief story in which the female singer reports that she was "taught" these "words of ecstasy" by a man, which helps the audience understand how a woman could possibly come out with these desires ("when I get a certain feeling I confess it").

After the war there are numerous sexy radio actresses, such as Ann Sothern, whose radio show, *Maisie* (1945–1953), always began with a long wolf-whistle, and *Candy Matson* (1949–1951), whose opening had her answer a phone in a sexy voice. Most notoriously, perhaps, *Lonesome Gal* addressed her listeners with a " 'come hither' style, referring to her listeners as 'muffin' and 'baby.' "[20] Gilbert Seldes called her show a "striptease for the imagination."[21]

Instead of viewing radio as a comparatively asexual medium, then, we may consider that sexual desire is as present on the 1940s radio as it is in movies, comics, or magazines. As in other media, male sexual desire is ubiquitous and normal, expressed openly by men of every age and class, whereas women desire to be the beautiful girl desired by those men. Once again the question is: what does female sexual desire look like? The following section focuses on radio comedy, reserving daytime serials for a later chapter. As the 1940s move on, women often go from sidekick to star in radio comedies. With women in more central roles, sexual comedy—at least potentially—can emerge from a woman's point of view.

Female comedy roles became more substantial during the 1940s. A woman was half of the *Fibber McGee and Molly* comedy team and of the loopy daytime serial *Vic and Sade*. Women such as Mary Livingstone and Portland Hoffa had important roles in the comedy routines of Jack Benny and Fred Allen, while Gracie Allen got most of the laughs at the expense of straight man George Burns. Starting in the early forties, Joan Davis and Judy Canova starred in their own comedy shows. And as radio comedy turned away from its roots in vaudeville and toward a sitcom format, women more often took leading roles. A landmark program in this transition was *My Friend Irma* (1947–1954), whose two main characters were ditzy Irma and her much more rational roommate, Jane. *My Favorite Husband* (1948–1951) gave Lucille Ball the same kind of comic star power that she would have in her television series *I Love Lucy*. More successful and long-lasting than either of these programs, *Our Miss Brooks* (1948–1957) put a woman squarely and solely in the lead role. *Our Miss Brooks* was not only a popular hit, it also presented radio's most detailed treatment of female sexual desire.

As we have seen in other media, wolfishness is neither strange nor immoral in a 1940s male, whereas a she-wolf might well be monstrous. The same holds true for radio, where sexually aggressive women are sometimes more freak than human. The two main sidekicks on Bob Hope's programs were both much stranger than he was—Jerry Colonna, the crazy professor (among other things), and Vera Vague, the "man-crazy" old maid. Bob Hope could leer up and down, flirt with female guests, and talk about picking up women. A "girl crazy" man is normal, not crazy. Yet when a woman chased men, she was routinely called "man crazy," a term which equates female sexual desire with social deviance.

The tradition of the sexually aggressive spinster goes back many years, and Barbara Jo Allen had created the character of Vera Vague before appearing on the Bob Hope show. But that is where her character became famous, with further incarnations in various feature-length films and shorts throughout the 1940s. By 1944 Jack Gould, radio critic for the *New York Times*, could say not only that Edgar Bergen's new character Effie Klinker was a direct borrowing from Vera Vague, but also that she was a "much-copied character already."[22] Barbara Jo Allen would usually appear as Vera Vague in film credits, and Vera Vague guest starred on numerous radio shows. For example, on the short-lived program *Blue Ribbon Town*, host Groucho Marx has already made numerous lewd comments, including a two-way invitation to another female guest: "Just sign on the back of my neck, or neck on the back of my sign." Yet when Vera Vague's arrival is announced, Groucho feigns panic: "Lock all the windows, bar the entrances! I've got to keep that she-wolf from my door!"[23] As usual, male sexual desire can stand center stage and judge women's faces and figures ("What a dish!"), while an equivalent female voice is rendered clownish and bizarre ("she-wolf," "man-crazy").

Although she appears in program after program as a target for sexist hostility, Vera Vague is always given a chance to fight back. Apparently she is so unattractive that no one will date her; hence her absurd desperation to find any man at all (Groucho: "How do you know you'd want me for a husband?" Vera: "You're alive aren't you?"). So the men viciously mock her looks, while the audience laughs at her indiscriminate desire. Unlike the Margaret Dumont sketches where the Marx brothers torture an aristocratic woman until steam comes out of her ears, Vera Vague does not lose her temper; instead, her desperation to stay on good terms with men provides her with a silly, but poignant patience. And the routines let her rebut her persecutors; when Bob Hope insults her looks, she does the same to him.

> Bob Hope: I'm a member of the opposite sex.
>
> Vera Vague: I guess you are, Mr. Hope; the question is, opposite of what?
>
> Bob Hope: Being here with you it's a little hard to tell.[24]

Unlike the numerous airhead comediennes (Gracie in *Burns and Allen*, Irma in *My Friend Irma*) who are stupid about everything, Vera Vague is stupid about sex, but reasonably strong and intelligent in her own defense. Her humor is based not on unintentional malapropisms, but on the same insulting wit that men use. The logic may be that since she is sexually so aggressive—like a man—it follows that she will be verbally aggressive—just like a man. Their amiable but cruel fights also show that Bob Hope does not take his own sexual prowess too seriously. Vera Vague's comebacks hit the mark since the audience has seen all along the difference between Hope's ogling persona and the real strength of a confident man. Above all, when Vera Vague comes on stage, it allows the show to keep talking about sex, but from a different angle. Men can ogle in only so many ways.

> Bob Hope: How do I stack up?
>
> Eddie Cantor: With Dorothy Lamour in the picture, who cares how *you* stack up?[25]

The comedy of *Our Miss Brooks* descends from the racy sexual banter of male comedians such as Groucho Marx, as well as from the man-hungry antics of characters such as Vera Vague. On the radio, Eve Arden had previously played a supporting role in the *Danny Kaye Show* (1945–1946), where she cracked a few sarcastic jokes, but mostly served as a sober, clear-headed ground for Danny Kaye's flights of nonsense and hysteria. "In the movies," according to a *Cosmopolitan* article, "Eve Arden got typed as a sort of female Alexander Woollcott, with a caustic wit and cruel, acid tongue."[26] The masculine quality of Eve Arden's hard-edged sarcasm is underlined in *Mildred Pierce* (1945), where Jack Carson's character continually refers to her as a man.[27] Nonetheless, when *Our Miss Brooks* first came on the air, *New Republic* radio critic Saul Carson compared the show to the best-known program with a female lead, predicting that CBS "could have another 'Irma' " on its hands.[28]

In his affectionate and thoughtful survey of old-time radio, Gerald Nachman gives this description of Eve Arden's heroine: "Given today's smart aleck sitcom characters like Murphy Brown, it's easy to take Arden's Connie Brooks for granted. But she was her own woman fifty years ago, decidedly female and non-threatening, yet a feminist before it was in fashion. Miss (Ms.?) Brooks was feminine, single, and marriage-minded, but never man-crazy, like most sitcom women, or anti-male."[29] I agree that our Miss Brooks often comes off as surprisingly independent, so that the show's title is really "Her Own Miss Brooks." Unconscious feminist energy appears throughout the series. But contrary to Nachman's description, contemporary listeners did in fact regard her as one more "man-crazy" single lady. True, she was so witty and potentially self-controlled that her character did not make coherent sense. Since, argued Jack Gould, Arden was a "rare comedienne" who could "convey a sense of wonderful worldliness" and brings a "spirit of impish urbanity," it was all the more "puzzling that CBS chose to cast Miss Arden, as, of all things, a man crazy and slightly daft schoolmarm."[30] Connie Brooks is rounded into humanity and more discriminating in her affections, but her masculine sarcasm and sometimes desperate desire places her not that far away from the man craziest of them all, Vera Vague.

Our Miss Brooks is not just a romantic comedy; it is a sex comedy. The foundation of the never-ending plot is a sex joke. Connie Brooks does not just pursue a generic teacher, or even the French teacher, she pursues the biology teacher.[31] Connie's heartthrob, Philip Boynton, is the "bashful biologist"—so bashful that hormones, pregnancy, and above all, the birds and the bees, make him blush and run. Every time they meet in his biology lab, sex is the overt if unspoken topic. The boy in Boynton needs not just to admit his love, he needs to grow up and come to terms with sex. Miss Brooks's urbane wit implies that she knows what's what in that department; ironically it is the biologist who never figures it out. *Our Miss Brooks* works as a suburban version of *Li'l Abner*, in which a desiring—and desirable—female pursues a cute but absurdly naïve male.

Some episodes are relatively tame and turn mechanically through the required elements: a breakfast from Mrs. Davis, who specializes in bizarre cuisine, a chat with teenage student Walter, who usually drives her to school, where there is likely a brush-up with the tyrannical principal, Mr. Conklin. But some episodes become racy, in terms of both plot and language. In a description of the 1954 television version of *Our Miss Brooks*, *Time* said that innocent remarks were "turned into leering double entendres by Actress Arden."[32] The basic premise of the radio show is that the biologist is innocent, but Connie Brooks is not, so that leering and double entendre are, more or less, built in.

The high school setting often produces very clean-minded Americana, where Miss Brooks plays a grown-up Mom figure to teens Walter and Harriet.[33] But unlike Kate Smith, whose wartime maternal character was defined by her domestic, asexual lack of glamour, Connie Brooks is both sexually forward and clumsily domestic.[34] Several episodes show how badly she cooks, and in this she resembles a man (and explains why she depends on the food collages prepared by Mrs. Davis). Thus the high school provides its own kind of biology lab where the lovestruck adults fit right in with the percolating adolescents. Teens Harriet and Walter form a nominal couple, and they sometimes manage to kiss through their hysterical giggling. But they also regularly crush on their teachers—Walter on Miss Brooks, Harriet on Mr. Boynton—so that the whole school bubbles over with passion. Except for Mr. Boynton, who acts like a boy, the adults act like frisky teenagers. Sex has more authority than the authorities.

Our Miss Brooks often pushes language and plot right to the edge of acceptability. A repeated motif has characters censor their own foul language, thus silencing themselves like a contemporary bleep.[35] While showing his bachelor apartment to Miss Brooks, Boynton says, "What can you do with a bachelor?" To which Miss Brooks says, under her breath, "There must be a non-censorable answer to that" (12–31–50), and the implication is clear. Later in the same episode Boynton surprises Miss Brooks in a store; "What in the ———," he says, and she interrupts with mock surprise, "Mr. Boynton!" "I was just going to say 'blazes,' " he returns, and Miss Brooks sighs, "Oh," in disappointment. Here she hopes for a better swear word, just as she always hopes that something more sexy will spring into Boynton's head. Every episode is told from the perspective of Miss Brooks; she frames coming events with an opening voiceover. Thus while screwball comedy elsewhere regularly turns physical or sexual (where are my pants? who kicked me in the rear end? how about the figure on that girl?), here the repeated turn to racy puns, imagery, or plot twists might be read as produced by Miss Brooks herself, as if her needful, verbally acrobatic sexuality had supercharged the incidents.

A brief survey of the show's characteristically sexual humor is in order. Women's lingerie and swimsuits make regular appearances, with much leering and excitement in their wake. In one show (5–8–49), Boynton's mother mistakenly opens a gift box containing a black silk negligee. She is surprised, but her husband is most enthusiastic: "Happy Mother's Day!" he exclaims triumphantly. And when Miss Brooks sees the negligee, she whistles approvingly. The gift is really from Mr. Conklin to his wife, which means that everyone has sex on their minds.

Another episode (10–29–50) has Principal Conklin arranging a bachelor's party for the evening; a mix-up puts a swimsuited dancer in his office instead of his new secretary. Apparently the dancer does tricks with balloons; this allows for a suggestive exchange: "What's this woman doing in that get-up?" To which Miss Brooks replies, "She's just blowing up her balloons." Soon the dancer is forced to hide in a closet; surprisingly, the bashful biologist offers to hide in there with her. This makes Miss Brooks terribly jealous, since she not only tries to impress Boynton with new dresses, but also with swimsuits. In another episode, she wants Boynton to see her in a swimsuit, but when she asks him to go swimming, they cannot find a place to go. No matter, she insists, "we'll put on bathing suits and water your window box" (5–15–49).[36] In another episode she puts on a bathing suit and visits Boynton in his office. He blushes and turns around. Miss Brooks encourages him to look at her: "Oh, don't be so modest, Mr. Boynton. Turn around and live a little" (7–31–49). All the swimsuits at the high school prove that *Our Miss Brooks* does not aim for realism. Instead, the show is more like a fantasy dreamt by Miss Brooks where the imagery keeps turning sexual to reflect her sexual desires.

Indeed, several fantasy sequences shed light on the structure of sexual desire in *Our Miss Brooks*. In one such fantasy, Mr. Boynton brings out his college ukulele, and following the magic logic of a musical, he suddenly becomes a whole new man. And he lets loose an amazing riff: "If I had a girl to squeeze / I would burn my BVDs" (4–30–50). Miss Brooks is happily stunned: "Did that come out of you?" Her main project in life is to find some sort of human biology, some sort of sexual desire in Mr. Boynton, and finally, here it is. Miss Brooks adds her riff to the jam session: "We would make a lovely pair / I'm so round and you're so square." At which point Principal Conklin thunders into the room; "What is the meaning of this scandalous conduct?" But this is the scandal that Miss Brooks always hopes for, the scandal of her dreams.

In an age where psychoanalysis holds popular sway, Miss Brooks dreams a dream that goes far toward explaining the political structure of her sexual desire. Like both Gildersleeve and Jack Benny, Miss Brooks sometimes falls into dreams that both process the day's anxieties and create a hoped-for fantasy. In a particularly elaborate vision (7–31–49), Miss Brooks not only dreams that Mr. Boynton desires her, but she also imagines that she is the mayor, with power over both Mr. Boynton and Principal Conklin. In her fantasy, Boynton addresses her as "your honor, Mayor Brooks," and calls her "so wonderful, so desirable." He expresses his love for her; he also barks at her like a dog ("Pardon me for baying at you," he says). Her dream is that Mr. Boynton's desires match her own, that his desire has finally become visible. He says, "I'll kiss you on the roof of the chamber of commerce, the steps of the city hall, at a light on Main Street." With the seductive confidence of a Groucho Marx, she replies, "Try my lips, there's less traffic there." What is especially striking about this fantasy is that it not only sees Boynton's desire flame into light, but it also dreams of power. When it is visible, female sexuality sometimes just looks male; the she-wolf and the he-wolf both answer to their animalistic biology. But here female sexuality is not just about biological desire, it is also about social power. This dream takes into account the economic and social powerlessness that is at the heart of the schoolteacher's life.

Before Kinsey's 1953 book on female sexuality, a key study was Abraham Maslow's "Self-Esteem (Dominance Feeling) and Sexuality in Women" (1942).[37] Working to combine biological drive with social relationships, Maslow argued that women with stronger sex drives were also more "dominant," which meant that they had more confidence, self-esteem, and were even "more masculine."[38] In sexual practice, this might mean that a homosexual woman would be more interested in her partner's climax than her own; "At times I get a feeling of smug power, and of great satisfaction."[39] This kind of analysis not only makes female desire visible, but it also places it within a social network of power relations. Maslow concludes that the best marriages are the result of equal dominance feeling between partners; what is definitely to be avoided is the situation where the woman has more dominance feeling than the man.

Now clearly the structure of desire in *Our Miss Brooks* falls into Maslow's foredoomed category. Mr. Boynton is timid, shy, quiet, self-conscious, more inhibited—to use the categories from Maslow's list—which is to say, he is the exact opposite of the "dominant" Miss Brooks. But Miss Brooks does not necessarily feel dominant. She expresses her desire, and through racy jokes and plotlines, the show expresses her sexual desire with a great deal of clarity. Yet she is constantly running up against Principal Conklin, who invariably puts her in her place, reducing her to squeaky helplessness. Sometimes the comedy overthrows Conklin's authority and his pomposity is deflated; perhaps one of *his* bosses shows up to yell at him. But there may be an authority even wider and more permanent than Conklin, namely the hard rule of penury. Teachers across the country loved Miss Brooks not just because she was funny, but because she reminded listeners about how little teachers were paid.

Reading the radio series in an overly methodical way, then, one might see *Our Miss Brooks* as following the rule that when female sexual desire appears it looks like male desire. Eve Arden's lower-than-usual voice frames a knowing, eye-rolling comic attitude that is much more easily associated with male comics. But the series puts this sexual comedy into a power structure. A main question is: why does Miss Brooks continue to pursue the bashful biologist year after year? In part, the answer is that this is how you make the show continue; the basic premise of female pursuit and male restraint must be kept up. But this "absurd" structure of dominant woman and shy man also makes sense if one sees that the sexual plot compensates for a lack of power everywhere else. In this reading, *Our Miss Brooks* shows female desire as not just another wolfish version of male desire, but as emerging out of fundamentally different social circumstances. Female desire does not just float around the stage—as it does, say, in Bob Hope—instead it is part of a lived world and comes accompanied by disappointments and by dreams.

Ghosts and Goblins in the Heterosexual House

From June 1947 to February 1948, Lisa Ben—an anagrammatic pen name—published *Vice Versa*, a journal intended for lesbian readers. Her magazine was not mailed since she feared arrest for sending obscene materials through the post. Nor did she mimeograph her text, although, as a secretary in a Hollywood movie studio, she had access to this equipment. She thought that others would discover her activities if she used the mimeograph. Instead, her journal was copied using several carbon papers and distributed by hand.[40] *Vice Versa* is usually regarded as the first lesbian magazine in the United States. It was subtitled, "America's Gayest Magazine." *Vice Versa* was also one of America's most forward-looking magazines.

Most of *Vice Versa* is devoted to looking at and evaluating the representation of lesbians in high and popular culture. Book reviews predominate, but reviews of films and plays are also included. Typically, Ben provides a plot summary, then talks about whether the lesbian characters are positively or negatively portrayed. That she can summon numerous examples shows that lesbians in 1940s culture were not completely invisible. A main problem, however, is that when lesbian characters do appear, they fall into a familiar plot, the same guilt-swamped, "abnormal" plot into which male homosexuals would also be thrown. In this kind of story, the lesbian character is deviant unto madness and probably winds up dead at the end. This plot is so pervasive that Ben calls the suicidal end of Dorothy Baker's novel *Trio* (1943) "inevitable." More important even than the fatalistic plot, however, is the idea that these characters are socially unhelpful: "The characterization of the lesbian as a selfish, deceitful woman is not very likely to go far in promoting tolerance towards lesbianism by the general public."[41] In her reviews, Ben methodically judges whether each representation of a lesbian character makes a useful contribution to contemporary culture.

For a positive portrayal of a lesbian character, Lisa Ben makes the case for Sartre's *No Exit*. Ben discusses not only the play, but also the audience members who came to see the play. Since the play's characters had been discussed in newspaper reviews, Ben looks for and sees both male and female homosexuals in the audience. And she imagines their response: "If they expected an exhibition of unreserved lesbian affection, they were disappointed. The gestures, mannerisms, attitudes, and frank, unmistakable significances of the lesbian's dialogue, however, are quite satisfying. It is refreshing indeed to find the presence of such a character presented in a drama without apology or subterfuge."[42] Queer audience members could not see everything they might have wanted ("unreserved lesbian affection"), and twenty-first–century readers may not be happy that Sartre's lesbian character is trapped for eternity in hell. But in this instance Ben is willing to accept an infernal stage for the sake of unapologetic visibility.

Since Terry Castle's influential essay "The Apparitional Lesbian," we understand that same-sex female desire will often come in the form of ghostly apparitions. Insofar as it has been situated on the bounds of social and cultural impossibility, the expression of lesbian desire has taken spectral, ghostly forms. In eighteenth- and nineteenth-century literature, Castle writes, "Homophobia is the order of the day, entertains itself (wryly or gothically) with phantoms, then exorcises them."[43] In the largely homophobic literature of the 1940s, if homosexual characters are invoked, then they are also exorcised by flooding guilt and killing punishments. But the phantom metaphor may stress invisibility at the expense of visibility. In "The Apparitional Lesbian," Castle says that "mainstream" writing—in contrast to the "shadow" of pornographic writing—"derealizes" the lesbian characters, while a footnote to that sentence admits that the distinction between "mainstream" and "pornographic" is "artificial."[44] Thus the distinction between absent lesbians in mainstream literature and present lesbians in pornographic literature can be rendered more complexly. After all, the main point of Castle's "polemical introduction" to a book called *The Apparitional Lesbian* is to remind the reader of lesbian multitudes: "It is time, I maintain, to focus on presence instead of absence, plenitude instead of scarcity."[45]

In that spirit, one could emphasize the multitude of women in 1940s culture who disturbed the conventional portrayals of desire in the heterosexist regime. In *Beyond Rosie the Riveter: Women of World War II in American Popular Graphic Art*, Donna B. Knaff collects numerous images from comics and posters that portray troublingly masculine women whose visible physical strength threatens the contours of 1940s femininity.[46] In *Uninvited: Classical Hollywood Cinema and Lesbian Representability*, Patricia White finds many characters who challenge heterosexual norms. For example, White reads women's films as potentially framed in terms of lesbian address, and she convincingly shows how a supporting actress such as Agnes Morehead typically falls outside expected gender roles for women.[47] In *A Problem Like Maria: Gender and Sexuality in the American Musical*, Stacy Wolf shows how Broadway actresses such as Mary Martin and Ethel Merman refuse magazine models of feminine deportment.[48] In none of these examples do women kiss one another; from that perspective, lesbian desire has been rendered invisible, a phantom, by patriarchal culture. Yet there is also a sense that despite the fact that men insist that female desire is directed toward them, mainstream culture is nonetheless well populated with women who refuse to comply. And even though it is a patriarchal culture that generates these stories about women who do not fit, who are "odd," it is not the case that all odd or masculine women are converted to femininity or punished.

A film that Lisa Ben finds particularly attractive is the Hal Roach sex-switch comedy *Turnabout* (1940). In her "cinema ramblings" for the third issue of *Vice Versa*, Ben says that this film "should be of special interest to readers of *Vice Versa*." The gender exchange is "fraught with amusing innuendoes and ambiguous significance." For the most part, Lisa Ben does not ponder "significance," satisfied in this case with enthusiastic plot summary: "The husband finds that he is firmly ensconced in the curvaceous young body of his wife. As further evidence of this miraculous transformation, his wrinkled pyjamas grace the lithe figure of his spouse. The effect is startling as his man's voice booms out a morning greeting to his wife, Sally. The result is no less strange when Sally, her sheer clinging nightgown stretched around her husband's large brawny body, replies in an unmistakably feminine voice!" The commentary continues in this vein, playing up comic fun and emphasizing the sensual physicality of bodies. As we have noted, Ben often makes extremely clear judgments about a work's treatment of sexuality. But here she encourages her readers to watch the film and sort out its "ambiguous significance" for themselves.

The sexual ambiguity of *Turnabout* is important since 1940s films are supposed to keep to the straight and normal. Although both sexes swap, *Turnabout* turns the man into a visible queer, while the woman is less obviously homosexual. Or to put it another way: the movie knows how to represent and work with male same-sex desire, whereas it does not have an equal vocabulary of visual types to attach to the woman. The man not only speaks with a woman's voice, he also flounces around in an identifiably gay way. As Thomas Doherty has documented, the Hays administration let the nonstop sexual innuendos in *Turnabout* slip through. Hays objected to the "pansy humor" of the script, but most of it remains in the film.[49] In one sequence, the feminized husband sells an account for nylon stockings to a man who is also, as Lisa Ben notes, "effeminate." As they coo and warble over the stockings, this is purely to be read as a scene between two gay men. None of the characters names the womanly husband as some species of homosexual, but probably no other film during the 1940s keeps up a queer premise so clearly and to such an extent.

By contrast, the film does not frame the masculinized wife as homosexual. Hays recognizes the man as a "pansy," but the low-voiced, cross-dressing woman is not given a name. There is an opportunity for the wife to show sexual desire. When she has two girlfriends visiting, one can easily imagine a scene where the man inside the wife's body expresses his desire for the women. But instead this sequence is given over to quarreling; the movie seems at pains to avoid playing with lesbian desire or humor. Yet even though the film does not identify or work with female homosexuality, one can see how Lisa Ben might wish to celebrate the film's "ambiguous significance." The woman with a man's voice and clothes is deeply disturbing to all around her. Although the movie makes comic fun of the sex swap and returns the couple to heterosexual normalcy in the end, the gender bending provides a potentially liberating vision. Most importantly, *Turnabout* reminds us how often similar disruptions take place elsewhere in 1940s culture.

Although *Turnabout* provides a rare image of a cross-dressing woman in 1940s cinema, the period contains numerous images that disturb heterosexist norms.[50] The low-voiced cross-dressing woman—alongside the masculine woman or the tomboy—can be read as visual codes for lesbian desire. But the cross-dressing can also be read as sexual disguise, as a mask that refuses to take part in heterosexual norms. In other words, these examples can be read as *code for*, or *mask against*, where either reading challenges sexual norms and hierarchy. Most of these examples are comic, which allow society to laugh at the disturbing exception and then resolve the disruption.

Theater and film actress Virginia O'Brien provides an extraordinary example of a disruptive female. O' Brien's decade-long shtick—performed in plays, movies, and revues—was to sing her songs without any facial expression. She even appeared on radio programs and released records using her "deadpan singing" or "undersinging," as one record reviewer put it.[51] In the end, the deadpan was a visual effect, not a voice effect, so it helped to sit toward the front in a theater or better yet to see her in a movie. The songs she sings are chosen to bring out the deadpan even more. In *The Big Store* (1941) O'Brien sings a swing version of "Rock-a-Bye Baby"; in *Panama Hattie* (1942) her song is "Did I Get Stinkin' at the Club Savoy"; in *Du Barry was a Lady* (1943) she sings about Salome as the origin of stripping. All of these songs come with feminine associations—motherhood, (non-)moderation, sexual display. Her deadpan delivery, however, rejects the smiling, emotional female we expect for the delivery of a song. And then the song itself plays up the feminine absences even more strongly. In *Meet the People* (1944) her deadpan number sounds like a sentimental love song, but actually compiles a dossier of domestic violence ("I tried to be aloof / When you pushed me off the roof"). As O'Brien moves around a kitchen set, dressed in an apron, she addresses an empty chair. She also looks into the camera throughout the sequence, and at the end the camera actually pushes her, now horrified, up against a wall ("No love can match it / Please put down that hatchet"). The song is a terrific critique of vapid love songs and male violence, and it goes together perfectly with a deadpan look that refuses to participate in amiable codes of femininity. Although her parts in films were usually small, O'Brien's look was popular and recognizable. She often appeared in the repertoire of female mimics; for example, impressionist Virginia Layne imitated Bonnie Baker, O'Brien, Baby Snooks, Betty Hutton, and Carmen Miranda. I do not see that anyone read O'Brien's act as anything but silliness, as silly as Red Skelton or the music of Spike Jones. But women like O'Brien, Betty Hutton, and Cass Daley must strike us now as questioning conventional femininity by refusing to comply with gendered rules.

Betty Hutton was a widely recognized actress who stood out because she differentiated herself so radically from conventional models of femininity. Whereas O'Brien refused to emote, Hutton was unrestrained tumult, wide-eyed and shadow boxing. Hutton's yelling, howling songs were hugely popular, and by the mid-1940s she was one of Hollywood's leading stars. Yet if her behavior was so eccentric, so challenging to feminine norms, why would a national audience approve? One might say that her "masculine" fits go well with the strength and freedom of wartime women, who flex their muscles like Rosie the Riveter. Perhaps her youthful vigor corresponds to a new conception of young women who consider themselves to be energetic and autonomous. More pessimistically, one might say that Hutton's violent explosions confirm the expectation that women are overemotional and out of control. One can easily argue that, in the end, her wild woman act only served to placate gender anxiety insofar as audiences could see the wildness tamed, the femininity restored.

Hutton ended the decade playing the triumphant lead role in the film version of *Annie Get Your Gun* (1950). That Hollywood first cast Judy Garland in the lead shows that the studios were not trying to scare anyone about gender. But Hutton took over when Garland could not continue. Garland is the bigger star, but Hutton makes more sense for the part. After all, Hutton had been doing versions of that part for almost ten years. In her typical film, she would disrupt gender roles and then be corralled back into obedience. As both play and film, *Annie Get Your Gun* serves as a parable of how 1940s society treats disruptive women. The 1946 play starred Ethel Merman as Annie; as Stacy Wolf has shown, Ethel Merman is a major example of a woman who does not fit conventional gender norms.[52] In each case, both with Merman and with Hutton, the play takes Annie—masculine, independent, and candid about sexual desire ("doin' what comes natur'lly")—and domesticates her.[53]

In a plot repeated endlessly through the decade, independent, sharp-shooting Annie is obliged to change herself into someone suitable for a man. Frank Butler, narcissistic and annoying, sings a song about his desire for "a pink and white lady." And his desire wins out in the end. As the movie goes on, Annie gets pinker and whiter, cleaning herself up in the manner of a thousand women's magazines. The story ends up amidst stuffy, disagreeable society women, so one can see that a person should not take hygiene *too* far. Although Annie and Frank sing their famously competitive song to a draw ("Anything you can do I can do better"), smug, idealizing Frank cannot countenance their equality. So Annie can only win Frank by losing to him on purpose in a shooting match; she is required to give up her identity as a sharpshooter ("You can't win a man with a gun" is an early song) in order to satisfy his dream of the pink and white lady. The energetic pleasure in sex with which Annie began ends up as an exuberant performance for an approving audience ("There's no business like show business").

With the providential logic of cultural determinism, Hutton's 1940s films look like a version of *Annie Get Your Gun*. Her wild woman character passes through the same stages found in the play and movie. For example, her wildness had already been read as tomboyishness and masculinity. As a guest on the *Danny Kaye Show* (1–4–46), Hutton says that she did not want to be this "crazy" character, that she would prefer to take "quiet and refined" roles. But when she tried to obtain such a part, alas, Paul Lukas got it. This comic bit is based on the audience's understanding that Hutton's wildness is masculine and not likely to go away. As in *Annie Get Your Gun*, Annie's wildness is not just gendered as masculine, it is racialized as nonwhite. One of Annie's big musical numbers is "I'm an Indian, too." But in 1945 Hutton had already made a huge hit out of "Doctor, Lawyer, Indian Chief" ("Send the injun chief and his tommyhawk back to little Rain-in-the-Face"); the war drums in the chorus map onto Hutton's unfeminine exuberance, which she tops off with Indian whoops at the end. That Hutton's wild woman act was not just unfeminine, but even nonwhite, is implied by the title of a 1944 *Saturday Evening Post*'s article outlining her meteoric success: "The Huttontot."[54]

Hutton's 1940s films repeatedly give her Annie's masculinity and wildness, but then take them away. Her decade's overall title should be, "Annie Hand Over Your Gun." *The Perils of Pauline* (1947) unfolds the plot most clearly. At the outset, Pauline (Hutton) works in a sewing factory and sings a rowdy song that rejects the link between sewing and femininity. When the boss tries to make a pass at her, she decks him. When she performs another rowdy song at a theater, the patrons throw tomatoes at her, and she throws them right back. But the movie refocuses this unfeminine, rebellious energy into passionate admiration for the theater director. Potentially antimale fractiousness is thus transformed into the purest heterosexual love. At the end, Pauline is diagnosed with a crippling illness, which she willingly makes worse for one more dance with her beloved. The final image has him picking up her weakened body. No other film corrects Betty Hutton's physical and emotional exuberance with such complete decisiveness.

Other films perform versions of this pattern. Like *The Perils of Pauline*, *Red, Hot, and Blue* (1949) allows Hutton a knockabout opening, but then refocuses her energy as the movie continues. In the opening sequence, aspiring actress Eleanor (Hutton) wakens her two female roommates by throwing them out of bed and jumping all over the room. Like the man in *Turnabout* who always does calisthenics first thing, Hutton's exuberance is registered as masculine. When she suggests that their troupe perform "Charlie's Aunt" (a male cross-dressing play), a roommate asks, "So you could play Charlie?" *Red, Hot, and Blue* lets Hutton get rambunctious several more times in a crazy anti-Hamlet, where she punches out all the other characters, and at the end, where she helps her boyfriend take down gangsters. But once again her energy is repeatedly refocused on hypercool Victor Mature, who singlehandedly vacuums emotion out of the film. Although she is used less idiomatically in Preston Sturges's *The Miracle of Morgan's Creek* (1944), she still begins by lip-syncing a man's voice in a record shop (with the same gender bending comedy found in *Turnabout*) and ends prostrate in a hospital bed after giving birth to six(!) children. And while her boyfriend in *Morgan's Creek* is stumbling 4–F Norval Jones (Eddie Bracken), Hutton's Trudy Kockenlocker, despite the name, is not emasculating or scary. Perhaps Hutton's submerged wild woman character allows Hays to miss what is right there before his eyes, namely that the fantastic "miracle" is that Trudy is pregnant out-of-wedlock.[55] So while Trudy is constrained to maternity at the end, she is not exactly the picture of American motherhood.

Here Come the Waves (1944) also sets Hutton's craziness into a controlling narrative, but with a twist. First the movie cancels out her transgressive energy right from the start by casting Hutton as each of two twin sisters, one unstable, one perfectly staid. Like the good girl/bad girl twins played by Maria Montez in *Cobra Woman*, *Here Come the Waves* allows the immodest woman to cancel herself out at every moment. *Here Come the Waves* now reads Hutton's energy not as a masculine threat, but as ultrafeminine emotional weakness. The crazy sister, Rosemary, is one of ten thousand swooners, whose luscious love object is not Sinatra, but Bing Crosby. This Hutton character seems pathetically insecure rather than strong. The plot maintains that since Crosby's Johnny Cabot has girls swooning in the aisles, he should be able to recruit women by the droves. So both twins join the WAVES (Women Accepted for Volunteer Emergency Service), and many sequences show WAVES training and talking in their dormitories. These all-woman spaces could become sanctuaries of same-sex desire, but the movie makes sure that women constantly talk about men whenever they are together by themselves.

As if to compensate for the absence of a masculine Hutton, the recruiting troupe stages a gender turnabout of its own. A title card says "If Waves Acted Like Soldiers," and the curtains fall away to reveal a group of WAVES pressed up against a bar. (Over the bar is a large cartoon of a hunky man in a caveman suit.) Hutton leads the women in an imitation of male soldier bravado; using hand gestures to indicate the shapely form of men, she sings about all the boys she has waiting for her in Poughkeepsie, Pomona, Daytona, and Decatur. The scene then cuts to two of her waiting men. Unlike the female man in *Turnabout*, Bing Crosby plays the woman's part with no hint of effeminacy. Yet Hutton's presence—and the strength of her fellow female soldiers—have at least generated a dream of masculine women.

But soon the show is over, and macho Hutton reverts to immature, swooning Hutton. At the end of the film, the WAVES cross the stage in perfect military order and the composed twin sister gets Bing Crosby.

Although Lisa Ben reviews movies and plays, she finds much more material to reflect on in the form of books. Julie Abraham writes that "before Stonewall, novels were the primary (textual) source of popular understandings of lesbianism."[56] In her sarcastic critique of society's erasure of female desire, Elizabeth Hawes claims that lesbians are *only* found in novels: "Females only become homosexuals—before the age of eighteen, or after thirty-five—in books. So relax about that."[57] In one issue of *Vice Versa*, Lisa Ben publishes a list of novels, each one evaluated according to whether its representation of lesbian characters meets at least some of her ideals. *Diana* (1939) is "excellent"; Dorothy Baker's *Trio* is "boring"; Gale Wilhelm's *We Too Are Drifting* (1938) is "drifting . . . but not far enough!"; and *We Are Fires Unquenchable* (1942) is "not so hot."[58] And Lisa Ben would probably not have found several other novels published in the 1940s too inspirational. In her indispensable survey, *Sex Variant Women in Literature*, Jeannette H. Foster notes a "disparaging" section in Nora Lofts's *Jassy* (1945), in addition to the "ruthless egomaniac" heroine of M. F. K. Fisher's *Not Now But Now* (1947), who starts up a "lesbian scandal" in one part of the novel.[59]

It is worth saying a few words about *We Are Fires Unquenchable* because even though Ben thought it "not so hot," the book was at least familiar enough to annotate. Since then, however, the book has almost entirely vanished from surveys of queer literature. In a rare notice, Marion Zimmer Bradley calls the book "a badly written, almost illiterate novel, the first few scenes of which are laid in a girl's [*sic*] college swarming with luridly treated lesbians and in an assortment of Bohemian settings."[60] The book is "illiterate" in the sense that it is not literature, but instead some species of sex novel. Yet it is also a book that sets its erotica into an interesting scientific framework. As we will see in Jo Sinclair's *Wasteland*, a scientist is often required to bring an invisible lesbian into the light.

We Are Fires Unquenchable begins with a preface supposedly written by "H. K. Bonaparta, Ph.C."[61] This doctor of pharmaceutical chemistry introduces the book thusly: "I am glad to state that I believe this is a novel for which the medical profession has long waited, because it deals with a subject completely understood by the medical world today, yet, one which heretofore has not been translated into novel form in the language of the layman." This authoritative, scientific preface may serve to ward off the pornography police since the publishers, Murray and Gee, are not otherwise dirty book peddlers. The supposed doctor then tells a lie when he says, "I would like to make it clear to parents, teachers and the reading public, that in no sense does the medical man consider 'sex reverse'—'moral reverse.'" The good doctor (not very objectively) assumes that parents and teachers are reading the book for its educational value and falsely says that medical authorities do not equate sexual abnormality with moral derangement. In actuality, most psychologists see only varying degrees of failure in the homosexual. What the novel itself proceeds to do, however, is take a widely held psychological "fact" and present it with a great deal more sympathy than any psychologist.

In the standard psychological model, bisexuality and homosexuality are adolescent stages that normal people pass through on their way to adult heterosexuality. In one of the many nightmarish psychological studies of the period, *Personality and Sexuality of the Physically Handicapped Woman* (1942) applies these widely understood categories to various kinds of handicapped women (chronic heart disease, spastic paralysis, epilepsy, and orthopedic disabilities) in order to assess their "psychosexual development."[62] Homoerotic and autoerotic practices have a place in sexual development, but a normal adult sets them aside. "Masculine protest," the desire to rebel against the normal feminine role, is also a stage that women must overcome. By grading the handicapped women on each of these behaviors, the scientists assemble overall scores that reveal each subject's psychosexual maturity or immaturity.

We Are Fires Unquenchable rather brilliantly—if not very literately—performs psychology's understanding of adolescence. If adolescence really is a stage of polymorphous sexuality, what does that look like? Most of the characters in the book are either high school or college students; most of them are also unsure about their sexuality. "Masculine" and "feminine" qualities float around and inhabit different characters at different times. The first section of the novel is given over to female same-sex desire, but male homosexuality takes center stage for most of what follows. The characters in the book are completely aware of their role in the psychological experiment. Corisande knows that "the pattern of a girl's sex life could be diverted during the stages of sex development," while Kenith is appalled by his potential bisexuality.[63] The novel may use psychological science as an opportunistic ground for sexual sensationalizing, but there is real poignancy in the way that the tremulous but desiring gay characters are treated. Since Lisa Ben does not believe the psychological model on which this novel is based, one can see why she would not recommend it. But as an example of how inescapable psychological discourse has become, *We Are Fires Unquenchable* has much in common with the far more literate novel by Jo Sinclair, to which we come now.

In a later issue of *Vice Versa*, Ben writes one of her most enthusiastic reviews, for Jo Sinclair's recently published *Wasteland* (1946). Just as Lisa Ben put her finger on one of the more interesting films to interrogate gender conventions in *Turnabout*, she also draws attention to one of the most remarkable depictions of female same-sex desire in the 1940s. "Jo Sinclair" was the less feminine-sounding pen-name of Ruth Seid. Like the novel's Deborah, who writes as "D. B. Brown," Sinclair's earliest stories take African American experience as their subject.

What is striking about Sinclair's *Wasteland* is that the lesbian character Deborah is treated as a rounded human being and not as a stereotype for kicking around. She is neither a psychotic exhibit of "abnormal" psychology nor does she fall into the usual punishing plot. As Lisa Ben writes approvingly, "There is none of the mental sickness, the morbidity too frequently associated with such characters in most current fiction."[64] Monica Bachmann has excerpted numerous letters sent to Sinclair from readers "like Debby," which all attest to the fact that they had never seen such a real and positive description of a lesbian.[65] These readers would agree with Lisa Ben's conclusion that "thinking people" must now accept that "the homosexual may be an intelligent, healthy, decent member of society rather than a degenerate."

Sinclair's *Wasteland* was an extraordinarily popular book. It won the 1946 Harper Prize novel and was widely reviewed and widely praised. It was on best-seller lists for months. On a bestseller list from mid-January 1946 to mid-February 1946, *Wasteland* is ranked number thirteen, with *Forever Amber* (still on the list since 1944!) at number nine, and similarly sexy historical novels at number five (Anya Seton's *The Turquoise*, "on her glamorous, foreveramberish road to success")[66] and number eleven (Frank Yerby's *The Foxes of Harrow*; "for the devotee of the plush, over-heated romance, this book should provide nothing less than an orgy").[67] Closer in genre to Sinclair's novel is Ann Petry's *The Street* at number ten. Petry's novel would be the most famous and critically well-received novel about African American experience for 1946. In a period that also saw a great deal of postwar, post-Holocaust literary reflection on Jewish identity, Sinclair's *Wasteland* would be the year's most prominent contribution, preparing the way for Laura Hobson's *Gentleman's Agreement* in 1947.[68]

For the serious-minded reader at the beginning of 1946, no topic was more timely than a consideration of what it meant to be Jewish in America, and Sinclair's book filled this need perfectly. The book is structured around a series of consultations between the main character, Jake, and his psychoanalyst. Over the course of the novel, the psychoanalyst leads Jake from an angry fragmented "wasteland" toward a more integrated understanding of his Jewish identity, family, and tradition. After the horrors of World War II, Sinclair's novel gave readers a cathartic vision of Jewish identity reassembled. And it was no sociologist or politician that managed to knit together the pieces, but instead an all-powerful psychoanalyst, who was never more authoritative than at this cultural moment.

Why readers bought and read the book seems relatively clear; what they read in the book, however, is harder to say. The male protagonist is the main focus of the book's attention, no doubt, but his sister is an important secondary character. As Gertrude Springer wrote in her *Survey Graphic* review, "Gradually it becomes Deborah's story, too, and through her the story of all the others."[69] Of all the members of their family, Jake's relationship with Debby is the strongest and most explanatory. His psychological crisis and the book's themes have everything to do with her. She is a writer who has black friends and who writes stories about black characters. Hence the novel shows Jake's progress toward integration, but in relationship to sexual and racial issues that go beyond Jake. A reviewer in *Christian Century* sees the thematic connections more clearly than most: "The author is intensely interested in the social and spiritual problems of suppressed minorities."[70]

But many reviewers manage to suppress entirely the minority status of everyone but Jake. Most reviews go into detail about Jake's crisis of Jewish identity, but most also leave out Deborah's lesbianism and her interest in African American issues. When Deborah's sexuality is brought into a review, it comes as an aside: "Strong-willed daughter Deborah had to back up her mother and made herself the 'father' of the family—and a Lesbian to boot" (*Time*).[71] For the most part, reviewers follow the path of the psychoanalyst and see Deborah as strong, not flawed. Only the reviewer in the *Boston Globe* (whose ecstatic praise, "tremendously moving," was borrowed for ads) uses judgmental scientific language that the book's psychoanalyst notably refuses: "Deborah is an intellectual and the one abnormal person in the family."[72] While the reviewers, then, read the novel correctly, by agreeing that Deborah is a significant and impressive character, they read the book incorrectly insofar as they fail to talk about the central role of sexuality and race in the book.

While these issues were invisible to many readers, they were quite visible to a few. In a contemporary reflection on the way that critics had received his recent novel, *If He Hollers Let Him Go* (1945), Chester Himes noted the "sly manner in which many critics evaded the racial-sexual conflict."[73] For us today, such evasion would amount to a complete misreading of Himes's novel. Ironically, Himes's reflection appears five pages away from the *Saturday Review of Literature*'s review of Sinclair's *Wasteland*. Their review allows Deborah one sentence, and makes no mention of her sexuality or the book's concern with black experience.[74] This is, of course, exactly what Himes was talking about. It is no wonder, then, that Himes wrote Sinclair a fan letter congratulating her on her honesty.[75] Nor should it surprise us that in the newspaper *P. M.*, Richard Wright enthusiastically praised Sinclair's *Wasteland*, at one point equating it with masterworks by Stein, Proust, and Joyce. Lisa Ben, Chester Himes, Richard Wright, and those women readers who identified with Debby could see the book in something like its totality, while many eyes saw only pieces.

A comparison to Himes's *If He Hollers Let Him Go* allows us to see what Sinclair was and was not willing to do with sexual and racial issues in her novel. In Himes white racism works violently against black masculinity; racism produces not just economic inequality but sexual humiliation. Racism's sexual boundaries mean that the novel's protagonist cannot "make a polite pass at Lana Turner at Ciro's without having the gendarmes beat the black off you."[76] As he explains in the *Saturday Review of Literature*, Himes emphasized black male "frustration" and "compulsive behavior." Although his critics may have preferred a more collected protagonist, Himes intentionally refused to give Bob Jones "powers of calm ratiocination."[77] By contrast, "calm ratiocination" is exactly the quality that Jo Sinclair gives her queer protagonist. Sinclair does not share the risks that authors such as Wright and Himes take by showing Bigger Thomas and Bob Jones sexually out of control. On the contrary, Sinclair's Deborah is always poised, always balanced. Thus whereas the relationship between sexuality and race in Himes is dynamic and intense, the relationship between sexuality and race in Sinclair is structural and theoretical. Himes's novel represents the way that white racism violently penetrates the African American male's psychology, whereas a fantastically skillful psychologist has helped Sinclair's Deborah overcome her feelings of abnormality in order to achieve balance and happiness.

Deborah's sexual identity is supported—not critiqued—by the narrative, but it is also given a psychological origin. In the book's logic, Deborah *becomes* a lesbian due to the shape and character of her family. It begins when she is a young girl: "Jake remembered that when Debby was a kid, everybody on the street called her Tomboy."[78] The tomboy is a potentially dangerous category for young women; like the effeminate young man, these boyish girls must be watched.[79] But in the period's psychological understanding, sexuality remains to be determined. Deborah's sexual identity solidifies only because of her weak father. The father is weak and repeatedly characterized as dirty. Deborah thus takes over the father's place in the family, at the same time that she is driven away from "dirty" men. And the psychologist sees it all: "[Deborah] had to throw off all weakness and softness, all femininity" (130). The abandonment of her womanhood explains why Deborah becomes a lesbian.

While Lisa Ben lauds the well-rounded and positive portrayal of the lesbian character in Sinclair's *Wasteland*, she quietly questions the psychological explanation. After citing the passage that contains the quote above, Ben writes, "Whether or not the reader accepts this diagnosis, this novel, an excellent psychological novel on all counts, has won an important literary prize." Since it shows great insight into the psychology of the sister, the prize-winning novel will help enlarge a general understanding of female homosexuality. But even as she celebrates the psychology, Ben questions the psychologist himself ("whether or not the reader accepts this diagnosis"). The implication is that although the novel's lesbian character is credible and dignified, the psychoanalytic understanding of where lesbian desire comes from is still open to question. This is a crucial objection, and one that flies in the face of both the novel's psychologist as well as a wider cultural discourse that saw homosexuality as created in just such family vacuums as Sinclair portrayed in the *Wasteland*. From our vantage point, we can see that Lisa Ben points toward a conceptualization of sexual identity that looks more genetic ("born this way") than developmental.

It is striking that such a politically progressive book feels the need to ground its human generosity in the authoritative figure of the psychologist. In addition to the very detailed portrayal of Jewish psychology, Sinclair's *Wasteland* shows an almost uniquely three-dimensional representation of a lesbian character. Through Deborah, the book argues movingly that homosexuals are an oppressed, marginalized group with political affinities to African Americans. "I went to them first because they seemed—yes, wounded. I felt that way too," says Deborah (145). Yet framing all this leftist social realism is the psychologist, who is not just a scientific character but also a figure of absolute authority. The novel never questions his judgment. The psychoanalyst sees that Jake is going to integrate his personality and he sees exactly when and how. He identifies and interprets Deborah's homosexuality in a revelatory and indisputable way. Thus even as Sinclair's *Wasteland* challenges major social assumptions and structures of postwar American society, it frames these social challenges with a remarkably unrealistic—because preternaturally authoritative—psychoanalyst.

In several postwar essays, Siegfried Kracauer attempts to explain the ubiquity of authoritative psychologists and psychoanalysts in films. Kracauer gives 1944 as a beginning date for Hollywood's "psychological films," and with the advent of postwar "bewilderment," exemplified by Fred Derry in *The Best Years of Our Lives* (1946), the phenomenon can only continue. As seen in films such as *The Lost Weekend* (1945), "inner disintegration has become a widespread phenomenon."[80] This disintegration is often repaired by a psychoanalyst, "half-magician, half mechanic," who can put the "scattered fragments of the soul together again."[81] But why is a psychoanalyst the savior? In his essay "Psychiatry for Everything and Everybody" (1948), Kracauer argues that the authoritative psychoanalyst is a particularly American figure.[82] In a European culture with more extended traditional structures, other social and religious figures could play this reintegrating role. But the psychoanalyst occupies and underlines an abyss in American culture. He is the only one who Americans can imagine occupying this salvific role. By pointing out the psychological investment that Americans have made in psychologists, Kracauer means to undermine this figure's credibility and authority.

And the psychoanalyst serves a similarly vexed function in Sinclair's *Wasteland*. Up through the 1940s, psychoanalytic discourse has carried nothing but pain and punishment for those outside the heterosexual standard. The stigmatizing and moralizing language of "abnormality" remained a powerful source of social shame and individual guilt. If a homosexual character is going to be granted a dignified humanity, then surely the novel's psychoanalyst needs to be provided with far less authority. Yet this is not what happens. In an earlier chapter we saw how intentional and intuitive feminists such as Nancy Wilson Ross and Kathleen Winsor could rebel against so many cultural conventions, yet still be unable to see past and through the authority of psychoanalysis. *Wasteland* takes place at a similar crossroads of revelation and obsequiousness. Even though Deborah's basically unique character could come into a fictional universe in many other ways, amidst many other plots and contexts, Sinclair's *Wasteland*, almost fatalistically, can only announce Deborah's arrival inside the completely authoritative framework of the psychoanalyst's surveillance. As Kracauer argues, the psychoanalyst is not necessary, and surely he is even less necessary to a novel about lesbian personhood. But apparently the 1940s cultural imaginary insists that Deborah appear alongside a psychoanalyst, whereupon he appears more magical and perfect than he ever has before. The novel makes him a benevolent authority since he does not judge Deborah as "abnormal." In so doing, the novel quietly but firmly revises psychoanalytic tradition. Yet his unnecessary presence also implies that readers would not come to their own benevolent conclusions about Deborah's sexuality without the doctor's medical adjudication. The psychoanalyst not only integrates his patients, he integrates the novel's readers, by making sure they think the generous, sympathetic thoughts that they are supposed to think.

Sinclair's *Wasteland* gives us a psychologist who can see into the darkest recesses of human minds; the novel then makes sure that we can *see* what he sees. The psychologist can see what is hidden, but what the mind hides and what society hides are two different things. American culture in the 1940s has conjured into its abyss the magical character of the psychoanalyst, whose power of sight and insight is unmatchable. But this is still a culture that itself wants to see and only believes what it sees; it is above all a visual culture. Mainstream culture can barely see the African American ("the invisible man") or the female homosexual ("the apparitional lesbian"). Jake's developmental integration, then, depends not only on the psychoanalyst's insight but also on Jake's actual sight. To highlight the point as clearly as possible, the novel makes Jake a photographer. As an interpretation of the 1940s culture of sexual visibility and invisibility, this may be the novel's most substantial gesture.

Jake's integration concludes not just when he joins the family's Passover Seder, but even more significantly, when he photographs it. Now it feels "easy to take these pictures he had always been afraid to take" (317). Cultural space in the 1940s is almost incomprehensible without the framing male gaze on it. Earlier Jake had broken through by taking a picture of Deborah and accepting her for what she is: "I used to wonder what a picture of Debby would look like. Maybe I was afraid it wouldn't look right. Because I didn't know what right was, for her" (221). After taking this photograph of Deborah, which he captions a "young writer" not a "young lesbian," he can see her as a whole person. And even though the resolution of the novel depends on what Jakes sees, what Jake photographs, Deborah's gaze is included too: "Her eyes were wonderful. He could not keep feeling afraid, looking at her eyes. They were full of different expressions, like the colors of a rainbow but not bright, just soft and changing. Her eyes were a lot like the voice of their father, sad and yet, a second later, hopeful, strong as the walls of sound and yet lamenting what had gone before, grave and devout and yet full of a passionate, searching look" (320). The novel laments missing coherence, absent fathers, and credible authorities, and it fills the gap in part with the psychoanalyst. With her masculine strength, Deborah replaces the weak father, a distress to both Jake and herself. As the book rounds to a conclusion and the father is given his place at the ritual table, Deborah eyes are beautifully compared to the "voice of their father" in all of its wide-ranging complexity. Deborah is the most vital character in the book, and Jake's description grants her at the end, "a passionate, searching look." Amidst a culture that equates the male gaze with authoritative desire, Deborah looks out with patriarchal strength and passionate desire of her own.

Queer Radio

Scholars such as Steven Capsuto and Matthew Murray have collected numerous examples of swishy, effeminate men in 1940s radio.[83] These male "homosexual" characters appear with some frequency and Capsuto's and Murray's examples could be multiplied. A good deal of radio comedy humor is based on what Capsuto calls "radio drag," where male characters assume female roles at the cost of their masculinity. In a typical gag Dennis Day claims to be jealous that Robert Taylor kissed Mary Livingstone but not him ("he wouldn't even put his arm around me"): "I may not look like much, but he ought to taste my potato pancakes."[84] The concluding section of this chapter argues that 1940s radio not only includes these laughably effeminate voices, but it also can, in a more positive light, be conceived of as sexually queer. Like all other mass media, radio either excludes homosexuality or mocks it. But several key cultural artifacts also figure radio as uniquely and productively queer.

As we have seen, "invisible" radio takes over the male evaluating gaze from visual culture. The bodies of female characters are still subjected to male scrutiny—as they are in movies and advertisements—even though radio's audience cannot actually see these women. This unblinking, ever-present masculine gaze blurs the boundaries between visual culture and radio culture, between the visible and the invisible.

But radio's invisibility also produces real differences with other media. As the previous examples from radio comedy demonstrate, "masculinity" can be more loosely embodied on radio than in films. Male movie stars come in a variety of masculine forms, from the American toughness of Humphrey Bogart, Gary Cooper, and John Wayne to the European glamour of Cary Grant and the emotional sensitivity of James Stewart. But the top male radio comedy stars all play against the masculine movie star image: Jack Benny, Fred Allen, Groucho Marx, the Great Gildersleeve. Radio's invisibility helps these stars to parody Hollywood films and explode their own masculine ambitions.

It is important, of course, to keep track of sexually disruptive and recognizably homosexual characters as they make their appearances, one by one. But we can also consider the various figurations that attach to the medium itself. What kind of object is a radio?[85] A common analogy has the radio equated to a family member. Unlike a movie, which performs in an outsized and grandiose manner, a radio sits in the living room with you and talks to you like an uncle or a brother. If one conceives of the radio as a person who is just like you or like a member of your family, then the radio is likely to transmit stability and conformity. This radio is as comfortable and as comforting as your home. To emphasize the familiar domesticity of radio was a typical way to contrast it with the potentially overblown thrills of movies and theater. I would suggest that *Lux Radio Theatre* "domesticates" its films when it adapts them; daytime serials such as *The Goldbergs* and *One Man's Family* fill the listener's house with more family sounds; a "fireside chat" by President Roosevelt emerges from this domestic space in order to connect the listener with a broader public sphere.[86]

But the period offers important alternatives to this familiar and friendly radio. After all, World War II radio was linked closely to global power and national propaganda; Roosevelt's fireside chats were intended *not* to occupy the radio space of Axis authoritarianism or newscast crisis. In these alternative models, radio is not so familiar or friendly; instead the global network of radio transmits powerful, possibly frightening voices. Orson Welles's 1938 "War of the Worlds" broadcast made terrifying use of a global and apocalyptic radio. Listeners knew well what horrors wartime radio had broadcast and even wrought; the frightening "voice" in *Sherlock Holmes and the Voice of Terror* (1942) is the voice of Nazi radio propaganda. In *The Next Voice You Hear* (1950), a film based on a short story in *Cosmopolitan*, God takes over the radio airwaves to admonish mankind.[87] The film audience never hears what God sounds like, but he fills the average family with fear, which He well realizes ("I also see many expressions of fear").

John Cheever's short story "The Enormous Radio" (1947) combines several radio metaphors to create a household monster.[88] Like Frankenstein's creature, the newly delivered radio is big and ugly, its dials "flooded with a malevolent green light," as it stands among Irene Wescott's "intimate possessions like an aggressive intruder." This radio is as frighteningly powerful as the globally capacious radio that can broadcast war news and war sounds from across Europe and the Pacific. Yet this radio instead uses its magical power to broadcast sounds from nearby apartments. The "enormous radio" overhears and broadcasts family quarrels, and so upends the idea that the family radio is an amiable, comforting member of a family. Even when the Wescotts send back the radio, the breach has been made, and they fight about things that had formerly remained hidden. "Where was all your piety and your virtue when you went to that abortionist?" asks the husband. This radio is frightening not because it transmits Nazi propaganda from distant lands, but because it knows and reveals private secrets.

In Jo Sinclair's *Wasteland*, *We Are Fires Unquenchable*, and Carson McCullers's *The Heart Is a Lonely Hunter*, a "queer radio" is associated with each of the main characters. Like Cheever's "enormous radio," the queer radio undermines the idea that a radio is just one more happy family member. The queer radio emphasizes difference and distance rather than self-replicating sameness. Yet in these examples distance brings hope rather than horror. Instead of eviscerating the family, as in Cheever, opening up its private wounds to death and destruction, the queer radio is a hopeful image, which dreams of a satisfyingly queer elsewhere.

Carson McCullers's novels *The Heart Is a Lonely Hunter* (1940) and *The Member of the Wedding* (1946) both experiment with the same psychological territory as *We Are Fires Unquenchable*. Each novel uses adolescent tomboy characters, Mick and Frankie respectively, in order to explore bisexual impulses. Like *We Are Fires Unquenchable*, these novels test the potentially polymorphous sexuality that characterizes the preadult stage of development. Although whether these novels overthrow the sexual framework of 1940s psychology is not clear, for contemporary critics both books seem, on our terms, queer.[89] Heterosexual and even homosexual categories cannot contain the fluidity of sexual desire in these novels.

In *The Heart Is a Lonely Hunter*, Mick is regularly drawn to the magical distance of radios. She loves Mozart and piano music plays in her head. But the music is more than music; it brings a liberating elsewhere to mind: "After a while she knew which houses tuned in for the programs she wanted to hear. There was one special house that got all the good orchestras. And at night she would go to this house and sneak around into the dark yard to listen. There was beautiful shrubbery around this house, and she would sit under a bush near the window. And after it was over she would stand in the dark yard with her hands in her pockets and think for a long time. That was the realest part of the all the summer—her listening to this music on the radio and studying about it."[90] Since she listens to someone else's radio outside and in the dark, Mick's radio does not reinforce a sense of boundaries and containment. Several times in the novel she pauses on stairways and on streets to listen to other people's radios.[91] Radio's passionate, but boundaryless music goes with her inchoate desires—"The Thing I Want, I Know Not What."[92]

In *We Are Fires Unquenchable*, Corisande and her friends work to produce a radio show. She wants to play folk songs, which are both old and foreign. She sees herself as an agent of cultural transmission: "How could she take these little stories and make American-born people like them?"[93] The parallel interest in folk music and sexual experimentation implies that homosexuality is not an accidental deviation from the true path, but rather a deep truth in itself, like a traditional melody. Again radio's distances represent a utopian elsewhere; "Norman's voice was coming to her through miles of darkness, coming clear and sweet to her."[94] Unfortunately, this novel cannot escape the punishing plot that chases down social deviants, and Corisande drowns in a flood at the end. But even as she dies, the soundtrack reaches down to ancient and distant truths, just like a radio: "treading over the primitive valley—treading to the distant sound of African drum-beats—drum-beats—drum-beats."[95]

In *Wasteland*, Jake links Deborah's sexuality to her absorption in radio music. "Secret, coming from the radio into this room, like the restless, powerful rush of waters" (34). From Jake's perspective, the mysterious radio music is suspicious and discomforting, but ultimately strong and empowering. Deborah is "strange," like her music: "that music low and solemn and strange as she was" (134). But he respects her strangeness since she is strong; he associates her "unwavering," "clean blue" strength with "that special kind of radio music she listened to" (87). Instead of being swept away by the radio's "powerful rush of waters," like Corisande at the end of *We Are Fires Unquenchable*, Deborah gives over her paternal place to her father and to Jake. But even as she recedes, she retains her power and strength; "her eyes were a lot like the voice of their father, sad and yet, a second later, hopeful, strong as the walls of sound" (320). Deborah joins Mick and Corisande in their connection to a queer radio, where invisibility does not mean erasure and death, but instead connotes a hopeful elsewhere more open to multiply directed desires.

6

White Female Desire
Wearing the Masks of Color

This chapter takes on the pervasive relationship between sexuality and race by looking at two related motifs in 1940s popular culture. First is the cultural impulse to mark female sexuality by turning white women into women of color. This book began with a description of Pearl Chavez in *Duel in the Sun* (1946); since Chavez is a "half-breed" her sexual passion is both understandable and visually verifiable. As a white woman, Jennifer Jones is a European saint in *The Song of Bernadette* (1943), but as a brown-faced woman in *Duel in the Sun*, the same actress becomes a lustful, self-destructive pagan. Although surrounded by the Hays Code, which intends to whitewash sex, Hollywood films can still sex up their fantasies by painting their angels with dirty faces. In Hollywood white women are pushed across ethnic boundary lines, not for the sake of blackface comedy but in the service of brownface sexuality.

But the whiteness of white women is not about to blur across the color line for very long. On the contrary, the white woman rules over airwaves and jukeboxes with remarkable authority. Whereas the white woman's sexuality is potentially seen as ethnically brown (Latin American, Polynesian, Native American), she must nonetheless be shielded from blackness at all costs. Hence popular music is overseen in a very real and coercive way by the image of a sacrosanct white woman, now more Bernadette than Pearl Chavez. African American male singers and musicians are widely heard and hugely influential in the 1940s; popular music gives black expression a scope far greater than what Hollywood allows in movies. Audiences understand that swing music is black music, swing orchestras become increasingly integrated, and white youth listen eagerly to both white and black musicians.

Yet despite a sense that music is the most racially progressive of all the popular arts, what African American men are allowed to do is still largely governed by an ideal white woman whose sexual honor must be defended from the approaches of black men.

In order to organize this description of the blackface and brownface masks that white women wear or are made to wear, I discuss two key figures in 1940s culture. First, I use the example of Gene Tierney in order to examine ways that the sexuality of white women can be ethnically and racially marked. Tierney's early films at Twentieth Century–Fox show the studio repeatedly trying to build the young actress into a star by casting her in brownface and yellowface roles. Then I turn to Ella Mae Morse, a popular singer who helped newly formed Capitol Records get started. Her "black" voice and songs stand at the center of a discussion of how the 1940s music industry strategically negotiates race and sexuality.

Gene Tierney, "Half-Breed": Sexual Star Making at Twentieth Century-Fox

Wearing an outfit from her recent film, *Sundown* (1941), Gene Tierney "seductively bedecked" the cover of the November 10, 1941, issue of *Life*.[1] The article inside notes that star Tierney "makes four films a year." What are those four films? "In *Tobacco Road* she was a tattered poor white. This fall in *Belle Starr* she is a bandit queen. This month she appears in *Sundown* (cover) as an exotic African half-breed. Now at work in *Shanghai Gesture* she appears again as a half-breed, this time the daughter of an Oriental vice queen."[2] The one-paragraph article—more like a long caption than an article—comments neither on the roles she has been given, nor on the unlikely chance that two of her four roles have come as "half-breeds." And Tierney would soon play full-blooded Asian characters in *Son of Fury* (1942) and *China Girl* (1942). In outward appearance, Tierney is just a shy, pretty white woman, so there is no apparent physical reason why she keeps appearing in these roles. But of course there is a logical cultural reason. In the 1940s culture of sexual visibility, Twentieth Century-Fox wants to make their new star into a sexy leading lady by aiming her toward the sure-fire sexiness of the nonwhite woman.

At about the same time (1939–1940), Twentieth Century-Fox signed three women who would become major and emblematic stars of the 1940s: Betty Grable, Carmen Miranda, and Gene Tierney.[3] At Fox, Grable and Miranda made musical after Technicolor musical, sometimes with one another (*Down Argentine Way* [1940], *Springtime in the Rockies* [1942]), and which were often set in sunny or tropical locales (Grable: *Moon over Miami* [1941], *Song of the Islands* [1942]; Miranda: *That Night in Rio* [1941], *Weekend in Havana* [1941]). Miranda is preposterously and almost incomprehensibly exotic, while Betty Grable is radiantly wholesome, the girl next door. Yet Fox promotes them both as glamorously sexy stars who love to display and express themselves in the over-the-top world of the musical. Carmen Miranda would become the most famous Latin actress to take part in Hollywood's "good neighbor" policy of the early 1940s. Meanwhile Grable became the war's most famous pinup, which Fox was happy to cash in on with *Pin-Up Girl* (1944). The studio executives at Twentieth Century-Fox quickly figure out how to sell and promote each actress as a sexual commodity.[4]

In the early 1940s Fox executives also attempt to create a sexualized niche for recently signed Gene Tierney. By giving Tierney an early role as a poor white seductress in the adaptation of Erskine Caldwell's scandalous novel *Tobacco Road* (the long-running play was even more notorious) or by loaning her out for "half-breed" roles in *Sundown* and *The Shanghai Gesture*, Fox blatantly intends to manufacture an aura of provocative sexuality around the actress. Dirty white and "half-breed" roles each remove the burden of sexual restraint that ordinary whiteness entails. Musical numbers let girl-next-door Betty Grable compete with Carmen Miranda's exoticism by allowing a transcendence of everyday self. In the dreamworld of the musical, feminine constraint can be left behind, given over to sexual display and passionate expression. Yet in contrast to both Miranda and Grable, Tierney is not going to sing and is thus unable to sing her whiteness away. Hence Tierney's ethnic masks serve as a means to display her sexuality for her.

By the mid-1940s, Tierney would eventually find stable, glamorous stardom in vehicles such as *Laura* (1944), *Leave Her to Heaven* (1945), and *Dragonwyck* (1946). But her career starts with this deluge of "exotic" roles, where the studios repeatedly force white prettiness into provocative ethnic otherness. *Life* cooperates with Tierney's publicity agents by putting her on the cover, but Fox's racial manipulations also draw fire from the press. Bosley Crowther, for example, sees this whole series of roles as "ruinous," and reads Tierney's ethnic otherness as inhuman: "Having escorted Gene Tierney through a series of ruinous roles attired in anything from a hula skirt to a muttonchop sleeve, Twentieth Century-Fox is currently letting her have a fling in tailored dress and bathing suits, 1942 models. It is an improvement, however slight. At least, in 'Rings on Her Fingers,' Miss Tierney is allowed to resemble a human being if not an actress."[5] In *Son of Fury* (1942) Tierney played a tropical native in "a hula skirt," but now, in *Rings on Her Fingers* (1942), she is an up-to-date white American woman in a bathing suit. In Crowther's view, the update grants Tierney not just modernity, but humanity. Hollywood's treatment of race holds numerous contradictions, but in Crowther's overview we see two major strains at work. Here the racism that sees the racial other as sexually attractive crashes into the racism that sees the racial other as intrinsically monstrous. It is a nightmare either way, but once again the details are well worth investigating.

The roles given to Tierney in her early career provide key insights into the corporate construction of female sexuality during the 1940s. Darryl Zanuck and Twentieth Century-Fox do not just put Tierney's body on display, they repeatedly rename and relocate her body by placing her in ambiguous, exotic contexts. In these films we see Fox struggling with her cinematic identity. How should they publicize this actress? How should they make the most of their contract with her? Will she be promoted as another "sarong girl" like Universal's Maria Montez? Figuring out what to do with Carmen Miranda and Maria Montez is easier since their visible ethnicity makes a sexual case on their behalf. Fox's strategy is, in essence, to repeatedly label Tierney as an ethnic or racial other, even in the absence of such visible signs. Since in the early forties a racist America allied itself with ethnic and racial others in Latin America and China, Fox's ethnic othering of Gene Tierney makes for some complex and intriguing political outcomes.

In some cases, Fox offers Tierney's body not just as a racialized spectacle, but as a patriotic merging of nations. In May 1941, for example, a South American sculptor—but surely also Twentieth Century-Fox—chose Tierney as "Miss Pan-America," whose "dark brown hair and fiery temperament are typical of the South," while her "green eyes, clear white skin, and athletic ability typify the best of North American womanhood."[6] This *Los Angeles Times* article gives the impression that it closely follows a press release. The article is accompanied by a photograph—which is larger than the article itself—of the twenty-year-old Tierney posing by a swimming pool. Soon, as the article says, her life-sized image will be "carved out of Central American mahogany." In the photograph, Tierney smiles what has been labeled a Pan-American smile, unaware that this geographical parceling out of her body will characterize her cinematic future for this year and the next.

Some of Tierney's "ruinous roles" in the early 1940s have no obvious connection to the contemporary state of world affairs. Tierney plays a Polynesian native in *Son of Fury* (1942), a nineteenth-century costume film that invites no link to the furious ocean wars taking place beyond the theater. Subtitled *The Story of Benjamin Blake, Son of Fury* sends Blake (Tyrone Power) from England to the South Seas to make his fortune pearl diving. Here he meets Tierney in native sarong; he names her "Eve." From beginning to end, Eve is the smiling, brainless, barely verbal, and barely clothed embodiment of a Polynesian paradise. In this instance Fox hopes that Tierney can match the race-changed success of Dorothy Lamour in films such as *The Hurricane* (1937), *Her Jungle Love* (1938), and *Tropic Holiday* (1938). That a 1941 newspaper article on the Hays Code and sarongs mentions Tierney in the same breath as Lamour and Montez suggests that Fox publicity is having the desired effect.[7]

Son of Fury provides a solid helping of ethical incoherence when Blake returns to England after his tropical romance with Eve. Now that he has money, Blake seeks to marry the English woman he left behind. Because of his business acumen and because his English girlfriend is white, the audience is asked to sympathize with Power's two-timing hero. *Son of Fury* appears to aim for the moral Patty O'Brien found in her study of tropical exoticism: "Love does not last across racial divides; it is fleeting and cannot be sustained."[8] But in fact Blake discovers that his white girlfriend is bad, and so returns, after all, to a happy ending with the native girl. In this case, love easily overcomes the color line. Overall, the film is ethically incoherent since the hero flits back and forth between two women. But the real moral is that Hollywood will play quite flexibly with all color lines except the white-black divide.

Likewise, Josef von Sternberg's *The Shanghai Gesture* (1941) is a bravura display of style and sensuousness, but has little to do with contemporary geopolitical realities (and a prefacing title card claims exactly that). Here Tierney plays a lost young woman, Poppy, who finds out in the end that she is the daughter of a white father and a Chinese mother. Whereas a number of Hollywood films in the thirties and early forties were set in China in solidarity with that country, *The Shanghai Gesture* is not *The Good Earth* (1937), *Dragon Seed* (1944), or *The Keys of the Kingdom* (1944). On the contrary, von Sternberg's Shanghai is an international pit of corruption where all nations look equally terrible. The film concludes when Poppy's newly revealed Chinese mother inexplicably shoots her dead. Whereas Eve survives to live happily ever after with Benjamin Blake in *Son of Fury*, Hollywood can also decide that white race-mixing with Asians is as taboo as whites mixing with blacks.

Although the mixed-race character in 1940s films may appear as a relatively simple sexual convention drawn from dime novels, it often takes on all the manifold contradictions that come with miscegenation in 1940s society in general. In westerns and adventure fiction, the mixed-race character is usually scandalous, and racial mingling signals sexual abnormality. Two of the most sexually explosive films of the decade, *The Outlaw* (1943) and *Duel in the Sun* (1946), exploit the notion that the desire of "half-breed" women is socially transgressive. Shanghai stands as an image of decadence and corruption not because of historical fact, but because clear boundaries of nation and race have disappeared. In the original play, *The Shanghai Gesture* put Poppy into a sexual couple with a Japanese man. But in von Sternberg's 1941 film, according to the *New York Times*: "Victor Mature is appearing as Dr. Omar, a Levantine scoundrel, replacing Prince Oshima, the Japanese debaucher of a young English girl in the play. The change was made out of deference to the Hays office's distaste for miscegenation."[9] On the one hand, then, racial mixing appears as a simple way to denote scandal and corruption, but on the other, it is not so simple if Hays thinks that Poppy with a Japanese man counts as miscegenation, but that Poppy with an Arab man does not. And although the Hays office vetoes (some) mixed-race romances, it does not veto their mixed-race offspring. Thus the play's scandalous conclusion remains in the film, where Poppy is revealed as the daughter of a white father and a Chinese mother.

As Susan Courtney shows in her study of miscegenation in Hollywood film, the Hays Code was applied inconsistently.[10] In the Code's written form, the miscegenation clause refers explicitly to white and black characters. In a list of subjects prohibited in order "to protect the sanctity of the institution of marriage and the home," the sixth rule is this: "Miscegenation (sex relations between the white and black races) is forbidden." Courtney points out the inconsistency of approving a movie focused on a mixed-race character (as in *Pinky* [1949]), when Hays at the same time refuses to allow the mixed-race couple who produced such a child to be shown. Courtney also shows that while Hays systematically refused to allow black and white desire on screen, it was not always clear whether white characters could desire characters identified with other races. She notes that white desire for Mexican, Native American, and Asian characters is usually acceptable, but not always.[11] In the *New York Times* article quoted earlier, the Hays office reads "Japanese" as racially out-of-bounds for white desire. That a white actress such as Gene Tierney so often plays these ethnic or racial others only adds to the ethical confusion surrounding an audience's interpretation of sexual desire in these films.

With these ideas in mind, the most instructive film in Tierney's early career is undoubtedly *Sundown* (1941). For this film, Twentieth Century-Fox has loaned Tierney to Walter Wanger's independent production company. As head of Walter Wanger Productions, Wanger has, up to this point, managed to add some political edge to otherwise ordinary Hollywood fare. *Blockade* (1938), unlike most every other film of the time, questions American neutrality during the European crisis. And the coda to Hitchcock's *Foreign Correspondent* (1940), in which Joel McCrea's character also reminds Americans of their role in the European war, allows a viewer to read that whole film in a more pressing, less escapist way.[12] After the financial failure of *Sundown*, Wanger would score a huge hit with the Maria Montez fantasy, *Arabian Nights* (1942). In *Sundown*, then, we see Wanger following both the Twentieth Century-Fox program and his own, as he combines the contemporary relevance of African warfare with Near Eastern fantasy. True to Fox's pattern of star exploitation, while looking ahead to his own desert dreamland, Wanger now casts Gene Tierney as Zia, the beautiful half-breed Arab.

Sundown was adapted from a six-part serial in the *Saturday Evening Post*. If one recalls only the Norman Rockwell covers, one might imagine the *Post* as all sugar and sentimentality with the whole family as the target audience. But Tom Pendergast calls *Saturday Evening Post* "the first magazine for men," and it retains signs of its nineteenth-century origins well into the 1940s.[13] In a thoroughgoing patriarchy, as a later chapter argues, many mainstream magazines also function as men's magazines. And such is the case here. When the first installment of *Sundown* appears in the January 18, 1941, issue, the other ongoing serial novel is a cattle-rustling western. Authored by Barré Lyndon (a pen-name derived from Thackeray), and subtitled *White Empires Fight for Africa*, *Sundown* is indeed a pulpy adventure tale, set into the contemporary struggle of British and German forces in Africa. Pulp genre comes through most strongly in the mysterious woman Zia, who runs an enormous trading operation throughout the region. With the appearance of Zia, the story loses any pretense of contemporary wartime realism and turns into a comic. The pulp element is often felt in the illustrations; the large picture for the February 15 installment makes Zia into a pinup.

Following the logic of pulp fiction, Zia is a sexually provocative figure, but the *Post* story deals with her in a scrupulous and also contradictory way. At the outset, some of the characters assume that she is "half native." When she brings news to the outpost, "she is never wrong"; "that was why Turner was convinced she had native blood."[14] The men argue over whether she is sexually desirable: "She won't get anywhere with Bill, she's half native."[15] Hence the story contains its own miscegenation code, where, despite inarguable beauty, her native blood puts her beyond male desire. Yet

Zia manifests her own desire; she has clear designs on one of the men. Her aggressiveness apparently goes with her exotic appearance and mixed race: "She knows a lot she didn't learn in any convent!" But even as the men observe Zia's provocative desire and appearance, the narrator makes it obvious that she is, in fact, not "half native." In the magazine's plot synopses and in phrases like "that was why Turner was convinced she had native blood," the story wants its audience to know that white male desire for her is in fact entirely authorized. Thus the story gets to work both ways: it presents a racially othered, sexually alluring woman, who is at the same time really a white woman and can therefore receive the sexual attentions of a white man. And somehow, even though her racial otherness is not real, it still serves as an explanation for her notably aggressive behavior. She not only operates her giant shopping network, she also, at the end, gets the man she wants. Like every American housewife, Zia alternates between white and nonwhite in order to provide an explanatory framework for her social ambitions and sexual desire.

As if the *Saturday Evening Post* story were not already contradictory enough, the film adaptation turns *Sundown* into a message movie. With some especially patriotic speeches at the end, Wanger's 1941 production makes the pulp story feel more like other inspirational films of the time. In *Making Movies Black: The Hollywood Message Movie from World War II to the Civil Rights Era*, Thomas Cripps shows how Wanger adds a strong emphasis on racial discrimination.[16] The black African characters are not treated as racist cartoons, and the film stages an ongoing debate about racial discrimination where the racists clearly lose. In these additions and emphases, the film version gains contemporary relevance and point. Yet at the center of this contemporary debate remains, nonetheless, the pulp figure of the supposed half-breed, Zia. Her presence does not help to clarify what the film wants to say about race.

To make the movie's point about racial discrimination more palatable, it is the beautiful Zia who suffers from discrimination. When she arrives in spectacular garb for a birthday party, the new outpost commander, Coombes (George Sanders), puts her at a special table apart from the main group. Only one brave white officer, Crawford (Bruce Cabot), soon to be her suitor, is willing to cross the racial line. When she sits down at her separate table, Zia knows what they have done: "I was born in Africa. I know what this little table really means." The strongest form of the movie's antidiscrimination message thus comes when white British officers segregate a beautiful (white) woman. The antiracist message is clear, but the movie has pitched its political tent in an Arabian fantasy, many miles away from the real and vicious segregation practiced throughout 1940s America.

Like the *Saturday Evening Post* story, Wanger's *Sundown* deploys the mixed-race (and white-raced) Zia in contradictory ways. The film's Zia is a powerful figure who strides confidently through the desert alongside the native people. We see in Zia's demeanor the intelligence and strength that running her commercial network must require. Whereas the *Post* story aligns her apparent mixed-race status with sexual aggressiveness, the film's Zia is constantly on display, but not aggressive. Instead her apparent mixed-race nature allows us to understand why she can so confidently and serenely interact with potentially dangerous tribes. Zia shows her intellectual strength on the white man's terms when she solves a gun-running mystery. She not only fingers the European culprit, but she continues to investigate the degree of his influence. Toward the film's end, she is imprisoned with Crawford, and she finally loses her Arabian cool when he does not believe her version of events. After showing so much strength and determination, she now cries and collapses in a heap.

But of course Zia is not an Arab and the movie needs to return her to her western self. The movie thus preaches antidiscrimination and multiracial understanding while also ensuring that Zia is white enough to be part of an English couple. When her purely white ancestry is revealed, Zia turns more conventionally feminine. In the final sequence, an English church minister delivers an elegy for Coombs, his deceased son. Now Coombs is a hero, with no taint of racism, and Zia sits in the pew next to Crawford. No longer a fantasy half-breed in a harem outfit, Zia is dressed like every other modest British woman in a wartime church. Now she can behave properly, and she looks up at the minister glassy-eyed and passive. At the very end she repeats half of the minister's closing phrase and her husband repeats the other half. Following a well-travelled path of political economy, *Sundown* first allows Zia power and strength at the cost of racial ambiguity and physical display. Then the film shuts down her character by returning her to whiteness, domesticity, religion, and teary-eyed mush. *Sundown* may be a message movie, but in terms of the way it treats female sexuality, it is also an exploitation movie.

Tierney's main contributions to Hollywood's wave of patriotic films are *Thunder Birds* (1942) and, in her final Asian role, *China Girl* (1942). In *Thunder Birds* we can see Twentieth Century-Fox still struggling to make Tierney a star through sex appeal. Tierney is given top billing and the film is shot in Technicolor. The aerial sequences are skillfully handled, not surprisingly, since the director is William Wellman, himself a World War I aviator. Indeed, Fox may be trying to bring back the glory and glamour of Wellman's famous silent film, *Wings* (1927), which won the first Academy Award for best picture. *Wings* stars an earlier decade's "it" girl, Clara Bow, as the love object of two pilots. As we have seen, Fox spends several years promoting Tierney as the 1940's "it" girl and that dream is still present in the film's combination of romance with chest-thumping patriotism.

In *Thunder Birds* Tierney plays an ordinary whiteface American; hence she is sexualized not through mystery and exoticism, but by openly submitting her body to the masculine gaze. The first time we see her, she is unclothed in an outdoor bath, while the grinning, heroic pilot dives at her in his plane. "Why you peeping Tom!" she says, without seeming too scandalized. Later, in a clothing store, two soldiers drop a coin on the floor in order to look at Tierney's ankles. When she catches them, they admit "we were just trying to have a look at your legs." "Did you like them?" she asks. When they say yes, she says "thank you," and walks off, happy to cooperate with the needs of the military. "I hope you're not angry," says a prospective pilot and future suitor. "That you are interested in my legs? Why not at all. That's what they're there for." Tierney's name may top the credits, but in *Thunder Birds* her character is decorative rather than substantial.

Given that Twentieth Century-Fox is about to return Tierney to an exotic role in China, we should note briefly how *Thunder Birds* deals with sexuality and race. *Thunder Birds* begins in documentary newsreel mode as if instead of the romantic triangle about to unfold, we are watching an objective description of a military training camp. The credits say, "commentary by John Gunther"; Gunther was a well-known journalist and author of books such as *Inside Asia* (1939) and *Inside Latin America* (1941). Fox apparently wants to ground both romance and patriotism in documentary substantiality. Widely admired for his international analyses, Gunther provides the voiceover for the opening section of the film. He says that this camp trains not only American pilots, but also the pilots of U.S. allies, the British and the Chinese. "Chinese, British, and American boys work together, study together, play together." By using Gunther's commentary, the producers intend to give this patriotic "one world" idealism a real world authenticity.

And we can see that this international contingent of boys can work and play with one another; but can these diverse boys play with the hometown girls? An interesting sequence proposes to answer this question. Some female nurses want to practice their medical technique on a group of male soldiers. Both women and men are happy to work and play with one another in this way. Thus far in the sequence the soldiers are American and British, but then we see Chinese soldiers hanging back, looking through the window. A cheery old man says to the Chinese soldiers: "Hey you! Come in here. You've been bleeding to death by yourselves long enough." The men come into the room, but all the nurses have been paired off already. Or all the nurses but one, and she looms into view, a six-and-a-half-foot giantess. One of the Chinese soldiers tries to run, but she grabs him and drags him off. In this sequence, then, the movie treats the Chinese men as "one of the boys"; the soldiers are enthusiastically invited to join the boy-girl fun with no qualms about race or color lines. But the plot makes sure, nonetheless, that the Chinese men are not allowed close contact with white women. The movie pairs just one Chinese man with a woman, and she is barely a woman—a woman so tall and monstrous that all the men are afraid of her. In this way *Thunder Birds* can spout its patriotic internationalism while also respecting the social realities of sexual color lines.

China Girl (1942), which features Tierney's last "exotic" role, negotiates some of this same racial terrain since the film proclaims America's military alliance with China, while treading carefully around potential sexual alliances. Tierney now plays Haoli Young, the full-blooded Chinese daughter of Doctor Young (Philip Ahn). In playing such a role, Tierney takes her place among the pantheon of white actresses who have played Asian characters in "yellowface," actresses such as Myrna Loy (*The Mask of Fu Manchu*, 1932), Loretta Young (*The Hatchet Man*, 1932), Lana Turner (*Dramatic School*, 1938), and Dorothy Lamour. But *China Girl* is produced beneath a new political banner. The "yellow peril," the monstrous Asian still exists, but is now limited to the invading Japanese. By contrast, the Chinese characters that Americans have represented in films, radio programs, and pulp magazines as monstrous others, are now American allies and therefore people. Indeed, Tierney's Chinese girl is so human—so nonmonstrous—that she barely looks Chinese. In her book on actor Philip Ahn, Hye Seung Chung notes that the Fox pressbook boasted that Tierney could play the Chinese role "without racial makeup or eye-tape."[17] Clearly the film's producers want Tierney *not* to look like a threatening Asian other. And the characters in the film agree with the audience's perception; the protagonist, Johnny Williams (George Montgomery) thinks that she is an American. It is not until she stands next to her obviously Asian father, played by Philip Ahn, that Johnny and the audience understand her racial identity.[18]

In the early 1940s, American films, radio shows, and magazines often wish to show solidarity with China. Even before Pearl Harbor the November 1941 cover of *Woman's Home Companion* shows a pretty white Red Cross nurse holding a Chinese girl. Propaganda attacks on the Japanese invaders often focused on their ruthless killing of Chinese children. But what will the uniformed nurse say to the little girl after her supportive hug? The *Woman's Home Companion* does not speculate since it gives the photograph no caption and no accompanying article within the magazine. Films, radio shows, and comics that want to represent this same sense of good will and solidarity need to provide narrative context for the image.[19] Because Hollywood's structures demand a heterosexual couple, the iconic pair will no longer be a white nurse and a Chinese child, but instead a white male hero alongside a Chinese woman.

Two analogous films shed light on the dynamics of sexuality and race found in *China Girl*. *China* (1943) begins with a long sequence shot that captures the terror of a Japanese bombing raid. The camera follows an American, Johnny Sparrow (William Bendix), as he works his way through the explosions. The sequence concludes when he finds an orphaned Chinese baby and carries it off. Thus far *China* replicates the iconic emotions of the nurse and child cover of the *Woman's Home Companion*, and William Bendix will carry the Chinese baby around with him for half the film. But the movie is more obviously an adventure vehicle for Alan Ladd. Ladd's character begins as an amoral truck driver who has no qualms about selling gasoline to the Japanese. By the end, however, he helps the Chinese to fight the Japanese, inspired by the violence he has seen and by the companionship of a right-thinking American teacher, Carolyn Grant (Loretta Young).[20]

Ladd and Young make up Hollywood's requisite couple, but the film does not want to omit Chinese women from its conventions. So the plot has truck driver Ladd obliged to transport a dozen of Young's female students. There is political work going on here since the young women represent a modern, democratic approach to the Chinese future. Their presence assures U.S. audiences that Ladd fights for modern American values. But if the viewers are to support the women's political ideas, they must also acknowledge the women as women. Hence when the women are discovered in the back of the truck, Bendix says admiringly to Ladd, "Not bad. I don't know how you do it." In Hollywood's version of racial solidarity, the white heroes grade the native women approvingly on their looks. In a later sequence, a very Western-looking Kwan Su (Iris Wong) tells Ladd, "I like you," and it seems she has a teenage crush on him. She soon dispels that notion by asking, "When are you going to kiss Miss Caroline?" But the movie has at least troubled itself to make the Chinese girls possible partners for the men. Later, Japanese soldiers kill the orphan baby and rape Kwan Su, who dies shortly thereafter. Her death awakens Ladd's dormant sense of injustice and eliminates any possibility of cross-racial romance. As happens so often, the movie's "one world" politics invites the sexual crossing of racial borders, but a fatalistic plot defers that crossing to a later time.

Bombs over Burma (1942) also navigates some of these sexual and racial relationships. Here the Chinese heroine, Lin Yang, is not played by a white actress in yellowface, but by silent movie star Anna May Wong. Now with the potential of a *visibly* mixed-race romance, the romantic elements are handled even more delicately. Lin Yang is a schoolteacher who works with the Chinese guerillas; she is freed to go on a long mission when her school is bombed. The opening sequence concludes with the death of an innocent Chinese child, which provides Lin Yang and the audience once again with iconic motivation to fight the Japanese.

In several key sequences Lin Yang is paired with the standard tough-guy American, Slim Jenkins (Nedrick Young). Early on Slim tells Lin that he identifies with China because they have both been beaten up by bullies, and now both of them are learning to fight back. "Them coolies out there working in the mud and rain," says Slim, "they're all blood brothers of mine." Lin Yang is clearly moved by Slim's speech and by his full-blooded identification with the Chinese. But even though the emotion is there, the camera refuses to frame the pair as a romantic couple; talking with his back turned and then from several feet higher up, Slim is not shown in the same cinematic space as Lin Yang. Later, when Lin Yang is suspected of betraying her own people, Slim reacts like a wounded lover: "Boy what a chump I am. I ought to get a blue ribbon and pin it on myself. I like you. I like the way you talked about things. China was going to be proud of me. That's what you told me." And eventually Slim and Lin Yang find the real traitor—a German spy pretending to be British—and save the day. In the penultimate sequence, Lin Yang explains her successful plan to an astonished Slim and they walk out of frame together. In the final sequence, Lin Yang says goodbye to an old Chinese man, and then gets on a bus in the background; Slim, barely recognizable, holds the bus door for her. *Bombs over Burma* thus uses its main characters to highlight Chinese and American solidarity, all while treating the potentially romantic couple in such a restrained manner that they are much more likely to be friends than lovers at the end.

Thanks to Tierney's lack of Asian features, *China Girl* can heighten the romantic element between its American protagonist, Johnny Williams, and its Chinese heroine, Haoli. Whereas *China* put the Japanese bombing of children at the film's beginning, *China Girl* saves the bombing for the end, when a whole classroom of children are buried under rubble. Johnny and Haoli help the children escape, but Haoli is killed. Now romantic sympathies can take precedence over maternal sympathies. The film's opening epigraph says: "An American will fight for three things—for a woman, for himself, and for a better world. He was fighting for only two of these things when the story begins, November, 1941." By the end of the story, having fallen in love with the Chinese woman, the American hero can now fight for her and China as well. After Haoli dies in his arms, Johnny jumps onto a roof and mans an antiaircraft gun. With a small Chinese boy feeding him ammunition, the American shoots down a Japanese plane. "We got that one, China Girl," says Johnny, and he keeps fighting. Now America can fight for the beautiful woman that is China.

Racial masking often serves to sexualize white women or explain their sexual aggressiveness. But that is not the case in *China Girl*. Wearing no mask at all, Tierney's Chinese girl remains chaste and passive. The film contrasts chaste Haoli with worldly, sexually available Fifi (Lynn Bari), the dangerous white woman. At first Johnny's impatient lovemaking offends Haoli, but then she forgives him and soon falls in love. But it is a contemplative, abstract love. Since he wants to go back to America and she needs to stay in China, she does not think their love can find a place on earth. So she imagines their inevitable parting: "My spirit will belong to you forever." Johnny wants physicality, not abstraction: "I don't want your spirit. . . . I don't want a spirit bride." But the movie's plot converts Johnny to her way of thinking; at the end, he dedicates himself to her spirit and to the spirit of China. *China Girl* thus takes the tradition of racial othering and desexualizes it, making Haoli beautiful but without sexual desire, while causing the American tough-guy to reroute his sexual priorities. Wartime ideals asked waiting wives and fighting soldiers to put sexual desire on hold, and *China Girl* revises the traditions of racial masking in order to enact these ideals.

All major studios in the 1940s had huge publicity departments that sent biographies, anecdotes, and photographs to newspapers and magazines across the country. Publicity, or "ballyhoo," was a major wheel in the studio's star-making machine.[21] Twentieth Century-Fox filled fan magazines and newspaper gossip columns with planted stories about Gene Tierney, but their uncertainty about how to promote her inevitably comes through. She was immaculately photogenic, no doubt, and would appear in countless photo galleries and on dozens of magazine covers. But what kind of personality was she? A 1942 *Mademoiselle* film article assumes that everyone knows about Tierney's early publicity: "You may remember the nature of her early build-up—many pages of pictures being rural at her Connecticut country seat."[22] That is one kind of identity—beautiful, wealthy, "natural." The 1940 *Collier's* article "Preview of a Star" makes an early attempt to claim her as an actress; after filming her screen test, a "hardened technician" supposedly tells Tierney, "I've been shooting these tests for twenty years, but that's the first one I ever wept over."[23] But her acting was so often disreputable that Fox had to fall back on her looks. So in an article that displays great indignation against mere glamour girls, Hedda Hopper begins with Tierney's example: "With great pomp and rolling of drums, Twentieth Century-Fox reports that Gene Tierney has taken two inches off her ankles and at least four from her hips—and in consequence will be in fine shape shortly to make glamour art for the newspapers."[24]

Fox's desire to sexualize Tierney's good looks was never-ending. In a 1946 fan magazine article, a "studio official" is quoted as saying: "Gene must have had something to sustain her through so many bad pictures. Perhaps no other actress would have been able to survive such turkeys as *Sundown*, *Shanghai Gesture* and *China Girl.* She had something and that something was sex."[25] Publicity, no doubt, trails clouds of irony. But it seems especially ironic here, when even as he sexualizes Tierney once more, the studio official claims that her sexuality has survived her earlier sexualizations. We sexualized her by means of these terrible ethnic roles, yet her innate sexuality somehow shines through.

And there is a neat plot here, too, in which Tierney passes through these awkward ethnic incarnations in order to arrive finally at the dignified whiteness of *Heaven Can Wait* (1943), *Laura* (1944), and *Leave Her to Heaven* (1945). Supposedly Tierney "was so fed up with playing natives that she went to Ernst Lubitsch and put on a crying scene," which won her a role in Lubitsch's *Heaven Can Wait.*[26] But as Hedda Hopper points out, Tierney has still not graduated from "native" roles since even after *Heaven Can Wait,* "poor Gene will be molded right back into that sarong again for a remake of *Bird of Paradise.*"[27] Although Fox announced this film numerous times ("Gene Tierney Cast as 'Ultimate' Sarong Girl"), a remade *Bird of Paradise* did not appear until 1951—and without Tierney.[28] But it shows how persistent Fox was in its determination to clinch Tierney's stardom through ethnic sexualization.

This determination still holds even during the production of *Laura* (1944). Tierney's Laura is unambiguously white, although apparently dead at the beginning of the film. Since her fate is mysterious, a trailer proclaims of Tierney's character: "Few women have been so beautiful, so exotic, so dangerous to know." In the picture itself Tierney is not obliged to go native. Instead, the film reserves its exoticism for witty narcissist Waldo Lydecker (Clifton Webb). After the opening credits, the camera pans around Lydecker's apartment, starting with an elaborate Buddha and then turning to a wall covered with strange ceremonial masks. The non-Western artifacts provide an exotic ground for a character who is as openly gay as anyone can be in a 1940s movie.

Still, Zanuck would have liked to do more with Tierney's character. He wanted to make sure that Tierney's Laura would not be too ordinary, too everyday. Laura, he wrote in a memo, "should come into the story like a breath of spring, like something out of this world."[29] And how to ensure that Laura appears "like something out of this world"? Zanuck has an idea (from a memo dated March 20, 1944): "I want to dissolve to Mark in front of a little New York Newsreel Theatre. He goes into the theatre and sits down in the darkness. A newsreel is on, of course, and the woman in the newsreel dissolves into Laura. Madame Chiang Kai-shek dissolves into Laura."[30] This idea was not used in the final film, but it says much about the way Zanuck deployed race on behalf of cinematic meaning. Madame Chiang Kai-shek visited the United States in early 1943 in order to appeal for more U.S. military aid to China; a *Fortune* article from the time began by saying that "Mme. Chiang Kai-Shek has made a deeper impression upon the American consciousness than any public figure since the appearance of Franklin Roosevelt."[31] Zanuck wants to appropriate this woman, who gracefully and poignantly told the American people about China's wartime horrors in order to bolster his heroine's otherworldliness and exoticism. Although critics had panned Tierney's earlier racial masks, Zanuck still wants to make her into a China girl.

Of course this discussion is not just about what Zanuck or Fox wants to do with Tierney or some other of their female stars. When Richard Harland (Cornel West) first meets Ellen (Gene Tierney) on a train in *Leave Her to Heaven* (1945), he says her appearance made "exotic words drift across the mirror of my mind" and that he "thought of tales of the *Arabian Nights*." This exotic language has been foisted on Tierney since before *Sundown*. But in this case the words are not for Tierney, but for all beautiful women since they are drawn directly from the novel on which the film is based.[32] Tierney's Fox career looks like it does because everyone knows that a white woman's sexual desirability renders her exotic and even nonwhite. In *Leave Her to Heaven*, Ellen marries Richard Harland, and then she jealously kills anyone who gets in the way of her possessive desire. As an advertisement for the book says, "her lovely face became a mask for a diabolical heart."[33]

Thus beautiful, photogenic Tierney is provided with a series of ethnic masks to confirm her sexual desirability. Although racial and ethnic masks sometimes signal tropical or primitive sexual desire, Tierney's ethnic masks signal desirability but not desire. Her ethnic characters are usually sexually restrained "good girls." These masks are signs but not concealments. By contrast, Tierney's purely white mask in *Leave Her to Heaven* conceals sexual desire that will kill for what it wants and possesses.[34] Tierney's career reenacts the period's basic duality around female desire: there is either a pretty picture without desire, or there is female desire that is maniacal and destructive. Hence studios provide their actresses with a wide range of masks, but without enlarging the range of possible desires.

Ella Mae Morse's Sultry Voice: Cultural Blackness and Blackface at Capitol Records

Ella Mae Morse is a key figure in 1940s popular music. The huge success of "Cow Cow Boogie" (1942) helped launch newly formed Capitol Records. During 1943 her version of "Shoo Shoo Baby" appeared on the charts for weeks at a time alongside a version by the Andrews Sisters. She scored another hit with "No Love No Nothin'" (1943), which crystallized the patriotic home-front sentiment of "I'll wait for you—chastely—until you come home." And music scholars frequently place her 1946 song "House of Blue Lights" amidst the first wave of rock-and-roll.

But beyond this rock-and-roll acknowledgement, scholars have not studied her cultural presence in any detail. Music historians have scrutinized very carefully the racial dynamics that structure many aspects of 1940s music, but Ella Mae Morse has not received her due. This section tries to remedy this omission. Morse challenges our critical ability to describe the racial elements of music, and she certainly challenged listeners during the 1940s. As a white singer who not only sang black music but also sounded black, she allows us to see how the color line is administered in 1940s cultural discourse. The following examines how critics talked about her music and looks into some fascinating ways that her contemporaries processed her identity in radio, film, and music culture. Generalizing from her example, I provide a compressed reading of how race and sexuality figures into Capitol recordings during the 1940s.

Morse's forays into boogie-woogie and blues allow her to express sexual desire with a forthrightness rarely approached by any other white female performer. But whereas white yellowface and even blackface minstrelsy are conventional in Hollywood films, Morse's "black" voice and music are more difficult to categorize. What we see in the examples that follow are various ways that her contemporary culture tried to come to terms with what she said and how she sounded. I argue that Morse's race-crossing music is not a species of blackface minstrelsy, where white performers mimic black language and music at the expense of African Americans. I compare her practice to fellow white musicians such as Johnny Mercer, who do frame the blackness of their music in a minstrelsy tradition. Instead Morse's music may be said to emblematize a crisis in racial integration, where musical audiences are now required to recognize that black and white music and musicians exist in equal social spheres. This recognition is performed with varying degrees of anxiety and awkwardness across music's industrial spectrum.

Cultural discourse and the music industry must come to terms with the fact that 1940s popular music is racially much more integrated than Hollywood.[35] Whereas black film roles are inevitably undignified, black musicians are promoted just as vigorously as their white counterparts. In some respects, it is as if music and film take place on different cultural planets. Nonetheless, even though white and black musicians can share the stage in a way that will never happen in a film, authorities still maintain a full-scale monitoring of the color line. That is, even though racial integration is increasingly common in many aspects of music—from the composition of bands, to the juxtaposition of hit songs—criticism and the wider industry continue to foreground racial contours. Such racial vigilance is due in large part to the fact that the racial color line is always a sexual line. Hence the cultural administrators of 1940s music feel obliged to keep track of both race and sexuality.

Billboard magazine provides important insights into how the music business organizes racial and sexual categories. The magazine contains much objective, statistical information about the entertainment industry, but it also contains numerous subjective reviews of nightclub acts, burlesque shows, radio programs, and record releases. The reviews imply straightforwardly that race and sexuality play significant roles in a performer's success. Reviewers must therefore keep track of these categories. The advertisements in *Billboard* magazine are also crucial to this analysis since they allow us to see how record labels want to promote their artists. Here too race and sexuality are often overtly marked.

In many respects, *Billboard* magazine appears to uphold an ideal model of racial integration. In part, business actuality has made this an obligation since young listeners hunger for swing played by both white and black bands. To take a characteristic example, the cover of the 1944 *Billboard* Music Yearbook is admirably integrated: Jimmie Lunceford, Count Basie, Duke Ellington, Cab Calloway, Louis Armstrong, the Ink Spots, and Louis Jordan are not much outnumbered by popular white music acts. The visual and quantitative certainty of this racial mingling is echoed throughout the

Billboard Yearbook, where black music stars are promoted with exactly the same kind of glamorous bravura as white. But it is one thing for musicians to appear on the same cover or to have their promotional photographs on adjoining pages, and another thing entirely when it comes to the subjective reviews. Black music is still not treated as a cultural equal with white music. And ideals of racial integration are put to the greatest test when sexuality enters into the equation. How will these white male reviewers—who are obsessed with glamour and appearance—evaluate black women? And with white women so close—both as artists and as listeners—how do critics represent and evaluate black men?

Since the 1920s record companies had labeled music by African Americans that was intended for African Americans as "race music."[36] As music culture became more integrated some modifications to this designation took place, but much remained the same. The newly formed Capitol Records had no official line of "race records," but Glen Wallichs, one of Capitol's founders, still thought of his offerings in those terms: "We plan a complete catalogue that will offer sweet music, swing music, Hawaiian, hillbilly and race music."[37] "Race music" in the 1930s often meant "blues," but in the 1940s black artists were deemed more likely to gain broader appeal. In the first half of the 1940s, therefore, Decca released a "sepia" series of recordings. The new "sepia" label still refers to black performers, but indicates that the music is closer to "popular," meaning "white." Or, as a 1942 *Billboard* review has it, the "sepia" label is a "cross between the race and pop listings," which makes a contrast with "unadulterated race songs."[38] Even as the musical landscape becomes more integrated, then, this industrial categorizing shows the ongoing intent to measure blackness in music.

As a publication that serves the entertainment industry, *Billboard* reproduces this desire to measure blackness. The most obvious adjustment to the commercial realities of the 1940s is their introduction of "The Harlem Hit Parade" in October 1942.[39] This list acknowledges the importance of African Americans as consumers of music. From February 1945 to June 1949 the title of this list changes to "Race Records," which follows the labeling practice of record companies. These lists often appear on the same page as lists for "popular" categories, thus giving black listeners a newfound visibility alongside white consumers. But the music is still segregated, still marked as "black," and the reviews elaborate what "black" means. As it turns out, these reviews target records with a discrimination (pun intended) that record companies cannot hope to match. Making sure to leave no racial indicator unmarked, *Billboard* reviews sometimes conclude with the directive that certain songs are best for "race locations."

While *Billboard* reviews both white and black performers, they often treat black acts with a distance that amounts to disdain. Their reviewers seem permanently exhausted by the blues; blues tunes are inevitably "usual" or "typical," as if white popular songs do not follow conventional forms. A small handful of words are repeatedly used to signal African American blues; blues singers are "shouters," while black voices and material are "sultry." White music is refined, while black music is "low-down." Thus *Billboard* can measure the blackness of music in terms of class and cultivation. They approve when white singer, Peggy Lee, changes from blackness to whiteness; after first performing a "typical race blues," she then "goes in for the finer lyrical projection [of] "That Old Feeling."[40] Similarly, *Billboard* appreciates the racial accommodation of Lucky Millinder, who apparently has left his blackness at home; "Millinder's band is off the usual sepia track, in a much more commercial groove . . . the melody is carefully preserved thru [*sic*] all, and the jive seldom exceeds radio bounds."[41] Black means jive, noise, and shouting, while white means popular, melodic, and listenable. In these ways, the details of the reviews overturn *Billboard*'s outwardly integrated appearance.

Billboard's need to negotiate a sexualized color line obliges the magazine to perform numerous hypocrisies and contradictions. For instance, while the magazine's high-culture/low-culture dichotomy associates sexuality with black music, the magazine simultaneously declines in almost all cases to grant sexual attractiveness to black women. On the one hand, delicate white sensibilities need protection from the sensual content of black music; hence music with sexual innuendo is often limited to "race locations." On the other hand, the magazine looks out with the same leering male eyeballs as every other 1940s magazine and is therefore obsessed with female sexiness. Sexuality is partitioned into two halves—the dangerous, dirty sexuality of race music and the glamorous sexuality of white women.

Billboard, subtitled *The World's Foremost Amusement Weekly*, not only reviews music, but also nightclubs, burlesque shows, vaudeville acts, Broadway theater, casinos, carnivals, and circuses. Since sex sells, sexy female acts are given their enthusiastic due, so long as they are not black. White women are often described as "sexy": "a sexy, blond warbler"; Yvonne De Carlo (in a 1942 Soundie) is a "sexy brunette working in a nightgown"; a dancer is described as a "sexy black-haired tapper."[42] Latin women are also allowed sexiness by white reviewers: a "Latin-American canary . . . shows a sexy shape"; "Estralita, a sexy Latin, is vastly entertaining"; "This show has its torrid moments with Amelia Vargas, a sexy-looking individual whose vocalizing is incidental to her torrid torso work."[43] Since sexually attractive women apparently make or break a show, these examples could be multiplied indefinitely.

Although *Billboard* reviewers find numerous "sexy" blondes and Latin Americans in vaudeville, nightclubs, and Soundies, they are much more hesitant to ascribe sexiness to black women. Even though black women are singing, dancing, and dressing with the same intent and function as white women, white reviewers respect the color line of sexual desire. Enthusiasm is usually kept away from black female bodies, although black women's *voices* can be sexy: "Billie Holiday, the sepia songbird with a sexy quality to her sultry chanting."[44] Sexuality is emphasized in the music, with no connection to the singer, as in the next example, where the writer cringes at the singer's body, but hears sexuality nonetheless in her song: "Miss [Ethel] Waters, back on the variety stage after a successful fling in the legit field, is not the trim figure she used to be. However, she still has much of her sultry vocal qualities in selling the blues songs, especially those on the sexy side."[45] In the 1946 review of Soundie program 1224, the Janette Hackett Dancers are "attractive," Jean Ivory is a "lush blonde," the "cinema cuties" are "torso twisting," and "pretty gals add interest" to a Lawrence Welk number. By contrast, Mabel Lee is merely "a sepia entertainer who both sings and dances."[46] *Billboard* is obsessed with finding sexy female looks, but when they see black women a kind of Hays Code comes in to cordon off sexual attractiveness.

Billboard's racial anxieties coincide with the ways that the music industry treats race. Hollywood films and radio programs rarely show African Americans on an equal social plane with whites; movie studios and radio networks always point to the bellicose South in order to explain why black actors cannot get better parts. Music in the 1940s looks much more integrated, yet the racism that constrains film and radio also constrains music. For example, the archetypal legend that black men present a sexual threat to white women keeps black men from singing romantic ballads. Billy Eckstine, who would become a kind of "sepia Sinatra" in the late 1940s, said: "They weren't ready for black singers singing love songs. It sounds ridiculous, but it's true. We weren't supposed to sing about love, we were supposed to sing about work or blues."[47]

With a romantic persona rendered taboo, black men are often obliged to behave like comic buffoons. Hence there is a clownish aspect to popular black performers such as Cab Calloway and Louis Armstrong. Contemporary music historians often find themselves debating about how deeply a black male singer has given himself over to minstrelsy stereotypes.[48] Louis Jordan, one of the most popular black singers of the period, turns out hit after hit, but nearly all of them are comic. He plays regularly in white clubs and white consumers sweep up his records. With so much race-crossing at stake, record companies promote him in the most nonthreatening way possible. This means, apparently, making him into a kind of clown; his iconic image is a spectacle-wearing, grinning face.[49] It is a modern-looking ad campaign, but the grinning face is as racist as it is hip. This comically smiling face is there, above all, to make sure everyone knows that this extraordinarily popular black man poses no erotic threat to white women.

Billboard's manner of marking songs and performers for race and sexuality is, then, an extension of an industrywide practice. Music has no official Hays Code to tell it to avoid sexual race-mixing, but music's practice looks just as code-abiding as any Hollywood film. White radio announcers and record reviewers do not flirt with or ogle black women, and it is almost illegal for black men to sing romantic songs. Both *Billboard* and the music industry mark race and sexuality in an obsessive and even paranoid fashion. And it is amidst this industrial landscape that Ella Mae Morse's racially challenging and sexually provocative songs appear.

That Ella Mae Morse's voice is a black voice is agreed on after the fact. Liner notes to her issue of the Capitol Collectors Series call Morse a "rhythm singer who phrased like no other white chanteuse in the mainstream pop of the era."[50] In later years, Morse proudly recollected that Sammy Davis Jr. told her he thought she was "one of his people" when he first heard her voice.[51] In 1952 Ethel Waters said there were only two white singers who could challenge the "negro monopoly" on the blues: Ella Mae Morse and Mel Torme.[52] "I don't know what it is that they've got," said Waters, "but my ear tells me they've got it." At about the same time, African American journalist Frank Marshall Davis wrote: "White performers who can do justice to R & B are few and far between. There are Ella Mae Morse, Vicki Young, Tennessee Ernie Ford and one or two more, but the rest are pale imitations of the real thing."[53] Obituaries and later critics could agree that Morse not only sang black music, she sounded black. Descriptions from the 1940s are not quite this straightforward. Yet in a culture devoted to measuring whiteness and blackness, Morse's contemporaries agreed that she "phrased like no other white chanteuse."

Morse sprang into national prominence with the release of "Cow Cow Boogie" in 1942. "Cow Cow Boogie" (Capitol 102) was among the first recordings Capitol Records released. Capitol's initial offerings were a smash success; they sold 17,000 records in the first two weeks. The biggest hit was Johnny Mercer's novelty song "Strip Polka," but not far behind was "Cow Cow Boogie."[54] At this point newcomer Morse sings as the vocalist for the well-established Freddie Slack orchestra. But "Cow Cow Boogie" makes Morse a star, and even when she goes solo, she will continue to be linked with her hit song for years afterward. Promotions invariably refer to her as the "Cow Cow Boogie girl." The song comes to serve as iconic branding for a singer who might otherwise be hard to describe.

The song itself provides a startlingly specific reading of Morse's vocal style. "Cow Cow Boogie" was intended to be sung by Ella Fitzgerald in the Abbott and Costello film *Ride 'em Cowboy* (1942). In the finished film, Fitzgerald jives up a "square" dance and sings some other songs, but "Cow Cow Boogie" does not appear. "Cow Cow Boogie" was written for a black singer, then, and black singers would return to the song after Morse. Ella Fitzgerald released a version with the Ink Spots (1943), Dorothy Dandridge made a Soundie (1942), and Maurice Rocco played "Cow Cow Boogie" on *Jubilee* in 1944. But even though "Cow Cow Boogie" is adopted as a kind of black song, a song sung most appropriately by a black singer, it is even more appropriately performed by Ella Mae Morse.

"Cow Cow Boogie" provides a self-aware comment on music's cross-cultural inclinations. The lyricist, Don Raye, had already written a song with similar ideas for the Andrews Sisters—"Rhumboogie"—for the musical *Argentine Nights* (1940). That song, along with the same film's "Brooklynonga," each reflect on the cultural melding that takes place when Latin American musical genres cross paths with big city swing. Both songs are froth, but serve also as authentic sensors of musical migration. In its turn, "Cow Cow Boogie" takes two widely divergent genres—the cowboy song and the boogie-woogie tune—and puts them together. From a strictly musical perspective this is not a likely combination in 1942; Capitol's main cowboy, Tex Ritter, does not sing boogie-woogie. But from a wider cultural perspective, the song musically performs an idea of racial integration since it combines white cowboy music with black boogie-woogie. And as it does so, "Cow Cow Boogie" almost too perfectly sums up what is at stake for Ella Mae Morse when this young Texas woman puts her "husky" voice on a record.

"Cow Cow Boogie" tells the story of a black man, whom the speaker finds herding cattle "down near Santa Fe." The man jive talks to his cattle ("git hip little dogies"), which the speaker finds odd ("in the strangest way"). The combination of western and urban is admired ("He's got a knocked out western accent with a Harlem touch"), although a stereotyped vice is also noted ("he was raised on loco weed"). Just as Decca issued a "sepia" middle-ground between popular and "race records," the cowboy's mixed-race music is also marked: "He's what you call a swing half-breed." Altogether, the song makes a comic narrative out of racial and musical integration with a minimum of racist stereotyping and violence.[55]

There is, however, potential for racist violence in "Cow Cow Boogie." A cute song about a hip black cowboy can easily go wrong. The song's potential for comic disaster is realized in a 1943 Walter Lantz cartoon. Although the soundtrack's piano is performed by the great black pianist Meade "Lux" Lewis, the cartoon is one of many hideously racist cartoons from the period.[56] In this version of "Cow Cow Boogie," the big-lipped black cowboy sings the song about himself; his legs are so long that he actually walks over his donkey instead of riding on him. A white cowboy hears "Cow Cow Boogie" and wants the black cowboy to sing some more, so he throws a lasso over the black man and drags him closer. In the process, the black man loses all his clothes except his long johns and ends up playing the piano for the rest of the short in his underwear.

One would like to think that Morse's hit song is more enlightened about race than this nightmarish cartoon, but the racism of white culture goes very deep. In the *Ella Mae Morse Songbook* ("The Cow Cow Boogie Girl Sings," 1944), the songs acquire greater prestige when linked to a Hollywood movie.[57] Hence the songbook proudly points out that "Cow Cow Boogie" is "from the Columbia Picture—'Reveille with Beverly,' " where it is sung by Morse. With equal pride it says that the song is "from the Waltz Cartune—'Cow Cow Boogie,' " thus happily aligning Morse's signature tune with Lantz's animated horror. The cartoon's racism is not the racism of Morse's song, but it does show that Morse's "black voice" is a precarious medium at the precipice of racial injury.

Billboard, not surprisingly, makes certain to mark the racial elements in Morse's music. They approve of "Milkman, Keep Those Bottles Quiet" (1944), which they say is in the "better EMM shouting manner."[58] Even though "Milkman" is hardly a "race records" blues, *Billboard* has already decided that Morse is a blues shouter and will be judged on those terms. *Billboard* calls "Buzz Me" (1945) a "slow and low-down race blues" and Morse is "just as sultry" on the reverse side, a "jive" version of "Rip Van Winkle."[59] This review begins by noting that her "tunes are tailored to her vocal talents," and then describes her songs as "race blues" and sultry jive. In other words, she sounds black. As is often the case in *Billboard*, low-down black sultriness can be dangerously sexual; therefore they draw a line around "Buzz Me." They recommend "race locations" as a "match" for her " 'Buzz Me' buzzings."

During the 1940s black female blues singers were much more likely to express sexual desire than white female pop singers. The female blues tradition begun in the 1920s and 1930s by singers such as Bessie Smith, "Ma" Rainey, and Ethel Waters was carried on in the 1940s by black artists such as Dinah Washington, Helen Humes, Julia Lee, and Nellie Lutcher. In a culture that otherwise doomed women to sexual silence and that limited black women to the maid's "Yes, ma'ams," African American women could sing straightforwardly and humorously about sexual desire.[60] Most songs were not as sexually blatant as Dinah Washington's 1949 hit, "Long John Blues." Here the singer finds herself at a dentist where her "cavity just needed fillin,' " and what a skillful dentist he is—"you thrill me when you drill me." More typical and less graphic are songs such as Julia Lee's "Snatch It and Grab It" (1947) where the "it" is left open, or Lee's 1946 release "Gotta Gimme Whatcha Got," which renders desire more concretely ("Let me tell how I feel / I'm crazy about your sex appeal"). Helen Humes's 1947 hit "Jet Propelled Papa" falls entirely within the conventions of African American blues; Papa's powers are admirably sexual powers ("fast like a rocket / He's built for any need"). The *Billboard* reviewer makes certain to underline the song's sexual humor: "words pull the kind of chuckles that race fans like on wax."[61] When reviewers and audiences read Ella Mae Morse's songs as black, then, they locate her sexual humor as closer to this tradition of black female blues than to anything found in songs by white women.

Billboard processes the sexuality in Morse's songs with varying degrees of enthusiasm and vigilance. After Morse's patriotic vow of female chastity in "No Love, No Nothin' " (1943), "Hello Suzanne" (1944) imagines the soldier's rambunctious return home—"now we'll do all the things that we both waited for," sings Morse. As the closing line to the song's chorus, that sentiment is as sexually explicit as a popular tune will get. *Billboard* likes the song, but needs to signal the degree of sexiness through code words: "It's a hot hymnal as Ella Mae Morse sings out with sizzles."[62] They might as well have called the record "spicy." Presumably the song is allowed its sexual explicitness for two reasons; first, sexual desire is expressed from a man's point of view, and second, a marriage is announced ("I foresee a wedding—soon").

Interestingly, *Billboard* does not even wink at Morse's most sexually explicit song, "Get Off It and Go" (1947). Their main comment is: "a contagious rhythm ditty cut from typical blues cloth."[63] But the sentiments expressed are hardly typical for a white singer. Morse encourages other women to get off their rear ends and "have yourself a ball." White women in 1947 do not generally offer advice this straightforward: "Some men are wrong / Some men are right / They all act the same when you turn out the lights." Using their powerful assets, women should do what they want:

"You're born with something no man can forget / Get off it and go." Such sexual candor would be at home on a "race record," but *Billboard*'s sex and race alarm does not buzz. Could it be that white female sexual desire is once again too incomprehensible for the authorities to notice?

Like *Billboard*, the wider 1940s culture is also interested in marking and measuring blackness, and it processes Morse's music from various directions. This section looks at the ways that Morse is characterized through sheet music, radio appearances, and a film role that aims to interpret her cultural presence.

The Leeds Music Ella Mae Morse songbook (1944) is an obvious attempt to capitalize on Morse's stardom, but it also presents her in an interestingly racialized way. As always, Morse is "the Cow Cow Boogie Girl" on the cover, where a happy cartoon cow plays the piano. The "foreword" says that Morse is "known to millions as the Cow Cow Boogie Girl," and that song comes first in the folio of eighteen songs. On the back cover, Leeds calls itself "the home of boogie woogie," and here it advertises numerous instruction books for boogie-woogie piano. Leeds also offers music scores transcribed from solos played by "the most famous 'boogie woogie' and 'blues' pianists," including Pine Top Smith and Meade "Lux" Lewis. Leeds has a commercial interest, then, in promoting the "Cow Cow Boogie Girl" since they want to keep the musical fad going strong, while, as the Leeds copy says, "Boogie Woogie carves more and more niches of fame for itself."

The songbook's minibiography of Morse begins with racial euphemism: "In her early career, though appreciated by specialized fans, the 'big time' eluded her, until she chanced upon the tune, 'Cow Cow Boogie.' Her treatment of this tune established her as a sensation overnight. From this point on, she was definitely on her way towards a Boogie Woogie vocal technique, unique to her." The first sentence is nonsensical publicity; Morse is too young to have an "early career" where the "big time" eluded her. Apparently the rise to the top needs a story of struggle. "Cow Cow Boogie" did, however, make her a "sensation overnight," whereupon she developed a vocal technique "unique to her." As elsewhere, it is not difficult to read this "unique" vocal technique as a way to say that her voice sounds black.

Although the folio's introduction reeks of publicity and euphemism, there is an interesting willingness to promote the blackness in Morse's music. The paragraph ends with: "The songs in this folio are Ella Mae's favorites and she personally selected them. You'll note how they fall easily within her style." The last sentence continues the racial euphemism; it means "you will notice how often this music is race music." Of course, amid all the publicity and commercialism, no one can believe that Morse "personally selected" these songs. Yet, remarkably, the blackness of the folio's sheet music makes it appear that Morse *did* select the songs. Critics identified Morse's "black" vocal style right away, which is why the 1944 *Billboard* review could say that Morse's "shouting manner" was "typical" for her. But Capitol kept her blues on the swinging, popular side of things, so that *Down Beat* could write, exhausted with her commercialism, "it would appear that Capitol is out for blood, determined to tap the till with a succession of commercial bellringers."[64] The commercial side of the Leeds songbook is more than apparent since it is filled with tunes by Don Raye and Gene DePaul, the composers of "Cow Cow Boogie." After "Cow Cow Boogie" comes "Boogie Woogie Conga," which makes the same kind of point about music genre mixing: "First the Latin had it— / Harlem's gone and added / Boogie syncopation."[65] But while the songbook wants to continue the "Cow Cow Boogie" commercial success story, it also unapologetically presents a Morse much closer to a "race records" persona.

The Ella Mae Morse songbook provides a condensed historical overview of African American music. The collection contains two blues classics, "See See Rider," composed by "Ma" Rainey, and "Lonesome Mama Blues," introduced in 1922.[66] The folio also contains blues songs that had recently been recorded by black female vocalists: "Please Mr. Johnson" (1941, Buddy Johnson with Ella Johnson) and "Fare Thee Honey, Fare Thee Well" (1943, Andy Kirk with June Richmond). The book concludes with the Raye/DePaul song, "You Don't Know What Love Is," which had been recorded by Ella Fitzgerald in 1941 and would go on to become one of the great jazz standards.[67] "Just Another Blues," which traces blues from 1922 up to boogie and jive in 1943, provides historical self-awareness. "Just Another Blues" got its debut airing in the 1944 film *Beautiful but Broke*, where the (white) Bryan sisters sing it in an upbeat style. But Nat King Cole released a 1944 version that gives the song a melancholy feel; now jive and boogie-woogie have dissipated the blues ("I'm just another blues") in a sad way.[68] Morse would never record any of these songs, but their selection pays thoughtful and passionate homage to the African American music that was so important to her.

A few examples in the Morse songbook also show a willingness to push sexual themes. The song "On Time" comes from the variety show *Lunchtime Follies*, produced by Broadway's patriotic division during the war, the American Theatre Wing. Several of Morse's wartime recordings are patriotic and inspirational ("Shoo Shoo Baby," "No Love, No Nothin' "), while others are comic or even risqué ("Milkman, Keep Those Bottles Quiet," "Hello Suzanne," "The Patty Cake Man").[69] "On Time" does both patriotic and sexual work as a female singer encourages men to work harder. The songbook lyrics have been bowdlerized compared to the blatant sexual innuendo of the original: "The man who stays home and lets his pals down / Won't get in my plant to turn my wheels around."[70] But the Morse songbook version still stages a clear sexual invitation, which trades male work for female favors ("I can see by your smiles boys, see by your style, / That all of you have something I'd find worthwhile"). Another song filled with sexual innuendo is "That's Her Mason Dixon Line," with lyrics by Don Raye. Literally, the "line" is a southern woman's sweet drawl ("Honey, you're sweeter than the honeysuckle vine"), but it is also a sexual line that divides north from south. Both songs are true to Morse's willingness to cross sexual lines in some of her recordings.

The Ella Mae Morse songbook represents one way that 1940s cultural institutions processed her "unique" voice and musical choices. Like many popular singers, Morse was also a frequent guest on radio programs. These shows framed her work by providing a context for what the listeners were about to hear. For an investigation of race and sexuality, her most interesting radio performances took place on *Jubilee*, an Armed Forces Radio Service (AFRS) broadcast. *Jubilee* began as an all-black musical program, but it then changed into a racially integrated show. As it did so, *Jubilee* highlights all the vexed problems of putting black and white acts together on the same stage. Morse's appearance on *Jubilee* is historically important since she is one of the first white women to bring a solo act to the show. I propose that the timing of *Jubilee*'s invitation to Morse amounts to a positive recognition of her musical blackness.

The musically brilliant and politically progressive *Jubilee* had to tackle significant programming issues.[71] Although it is at first an all-black entertainment show, in January 1944 with the appearance of Bing Crosby, *Jubilee* enters an integrated phase. Most integrated radio shows keep peace with the South by making sure that African Americans never occupy the same social space as the white characters. The intent is to administer not only racial segregation, but also sexual segregation; the bogeyman scenario occurs when black men and white women occupy the same social space. Radio programs make certain that this never happens. Thus Jack Benny's butler Rochester can share the stage with Mary Livingstone; on *Duffy's Tavern*, Eddie the waiter (Eddie Green) shares the stage with Miss Duffy and female guest stars; on the Andrews Sisters radio show, *Eight to the Bar* (1944–1945), Pigmeat Markham plays Alamo the Cook. The clearly marked separation in the social status of white and black characters serves to appease segregationists. Yet integrated music shows—which come without socially contextualized characters or a narrative—are necessarily more difficult to divide into culturally acceptable zones.

The awkwardness of well-intentioned radio integration comes through in an early installment of *Command Performance* (9–29–42). This program clearly intends to demonstrate that white and black acts can occupy the same socially equal space. The show features four famous bands under the direction of Count Basie, Lionel Hampton, Tommy Dorsey, and Spike Jones. With two black acts on the same program—a rare event outside of *Jubilee*—the program is a patriotic attempt to perform racial integration. But the master of ceremonies for the evening is Bob Burns, who specializes in southern hick humor. At the beginning of the show he asks the question on everyone's mind: why would anyone choose him as the emcee? He provides no answer, but we can surmise the reason. When black acts appear on equal footing with white acts, southern audiences inevitably object, so we may assume that the show's producers are trying to ward off southern objections by having Bob Burns host.

As it turns out, however, Burns's introductions are extraordinarily awkward. He calls Count Basie, "Count Bassy," and then makes a joke of the mispronunciation when the song is over. Of Lionel Hampton he says, "That boy's as hot as a two-dollar bill," and when the song is done he compares it to a milk truck crash. Burns makes no such nervous remarks about Tommy Dorsey. At the show's end, in a readably emblematic gesture, all the bandleaders provide the musical backup for Burns (on his "bazooka") and Dinah Shore. This has been the goal all along, to show an integrated band playing alongside a southern man and a white woman. But in practice this utopian image is hard to construct.

The integrated phase of *Jubilee* needs to keep track of the same difficult question: How will black men and white women appear on the same program? This hard question is made even more intractable since, as on *Command Performance*, sexual banter or flirtation often occurs between the male emcee and the female guests. Will the black emcee treat his white female guests more distantly? In part, *Jubilee* solves this problem by producing an integrated program, but without white women. As far as I can determine, the first white woman on *Jubilee* is Gracie Allen (2–14–44), who joins husband George Burns for a comedy routine.[72] On the well-intentioned *Command Performance* program just mentioned, Bob Burns introduced both Count Basie and Lionel Hampton in an awkward, distancing manner, which made integration feel like segregation all over again. Gracie Allen gives something of the same effect by aiming her scatterbrain routine at black jive; "that announcer," she says, "speaks better French than Charles Boyer."

When George explains that jive is a "fad," the language of the "hepcats," Gracie makes up a bunch of crazy jive sentences. Gracie is too silly to come off as mean-spirited, but once again this does not seem like a smooth example of racial integration. For Burns and Allen to joke about how the black musicians talk feels less like joining in and more like another way to reestablish social barriers.

Specifics allow us to see how hard it was to imagine integration across the sexes in an otherwise politically imaginative program. In 1944 the following white women appear on *Jubilee*: Gracie Allen, the International Sweethearts of Rhythm (an integrated all-female band), gossip columnist Hedda Hopper, the Andrews Sisters, and Johnny Mercer backed up by the Pied Pipers (Jo Stafford and three men).[73] There are many fewer white women than white men, and the acts have been methodically chosen to avoid individual female stars. The year 1945 opens up a bit more: the King Sisters, Anita O'Day with Stan Kenton, Kitty Kallen with Harry James, Ella Mae Morse, Peggy Lee, June Christy with Stan Kenton, and Kay Starr.[74] In other words, almost two years of racial integration pass before female soloists such as Ella Mae Morse, Peggy Lee, and Kay Starr find a place on the program.

I read Ella Mae Morse's appearance on *Jubilee* as a cultural validation of her attachment to black music. As shown above, *Jubilee* is transparently concerned about which singers and groups appear together. It seems significant that on the September 6, 1945, program, Morse becomes not only the first white woman to appear as a soloist, but she is also the first white woman to be accompanied by an orchestra led by an African American man. Morse sings "On the Sunny Side of the Street" accompanied by Louis Armstrong and his orchestra. Interracial music-making between white men and black men is relatively common, but the combination of white women and black men is much less frequent. Brief duets break out in a pair of Soundies where Gene Krupa's white vocalist Anita O'Day sings and jive talks with black trumpeter Roy Eldridge; among Soundies this interracial duet has no parallel.[75] Recordings by white singer Libby Holman and black guitarist Josh White made an equally unique contribution to 1940s blues recordings.[76] So Ella Mae Morse singing with Louis Armstrong is hardly an everyday musical event. *Jubilee*, an integrated show that foregrounded black music, would now broadcast more songs performed by black men and white women. In doing so it challenged deeply held racial and sexual standards. And *Jubilee* inaugurated the practice with the appearance of Ella Mae Morse.

Two months after her first visit to *Jubilee*, Morse was back on the show (11–5–45), this time singing "Buzz Me" and "Rip Van Winkle." Recall that

Billboard called "Buzz Me" a "race blues," and recommended the song for "race locations." And indeed, what records I have indicate that, although she was a guest on numerous radio shows, Morse only performed "Buzz Me" on *Jubilee*. In 1946 Louis Jordan would score a number one hit on the "race records" charts with his own version of "Buzz Me." In his introduction, *Jubilee*'s regular emcee, Ernie Whitman, does not prepare the audience for Morse's "black" music; he just rolls out his usual blast of enthusiasm: "I see a package of dynamite sliding under the microphone—it's the ladybird herself, Ella Mae Morse." On her third and final visit to *Jubilee* (10–24–47), however, announcer Gene Norman provides a more specifically "black" context: "Singing in that husky, bouncing voice is one of the greatest rhythm singers, Ella Mae Morse." Her "black" music had been identified in a similar manner in one of her many appearances on *Command Performance* (3–29–45); "Here's that rhythm queen you've been asking for, Ella Mae Morse," and she begins her third visit to *Jubilee* by singing, once again, "Buzz Me."

Ella Mae Morse was far from the "blackest" white person invited on *Jubilee*. On the November 11, 1945, program, *Jubilee*'s interest in celebrating black culture and music puts the show at the edge of a racial and sexual crisis. This show accidentally serves as an explanation for why *Jubilee* is so careful to invite the right combination of black and white, male and female. The program begins with Stan Kenton's orchestra playing "Southern Scandal," and then June Christy adds her voice to Kenton's band for the hit song "Tampico." Emcee Ernie Whitman introduces Christy with his trademark enthusiasm ("Well snap my lids and call me curfew"), but his jive buildup stays away from flirtation ("the little lady with the ration of passion"). However, when her song is over, Whitman wants Christy to stay for the next act, saying, "Don't go away, June; I want you to get a load of this next number, [by] an old friend of mine." And then a gravelly voice comes in: "Step down, brother, let's mess up the joint so a guy can feel at home." The voice sounds like a black voice, and his exchange of familiarities ("old friend," "brother") with Whitman encourages the listener to assume that the speaker is African American. He identifies himself as Harry "The Hipster" Gibson.

Whereas Whitman kept a respectful distance from June Christy, Harry gets personal. "Who's the skinny chick?" asks Harry, jive-talking away. Although he is the master of jive himself, Whitman tries to tone up Harry's line: "Not skinny, Harry, in the best places we say she is slender." But Harry insists on a dirty reading: "In the best places I say she is skinny." Like so many other 1940s women, Christy follows the patriarchal script and responds to the male gaze obediently: "I like your sense of humor,

Mr. Gibson." Whereupon Harry continues his hepcat wolfishness: "Well don't go on the make for me, chick, I'm very particular about my women." Sexual innuendo and flirtation occur regularly between black men and black women on *Jubilee*. But this sexualized exchange between June Christy and Harry Gibson, between a white female voice and a black male voice, is one that the program's careful, strategic sense of integration has always managed to avoid.

And, after all, *Jubilee* has avoided the racial taboo even here. Harry the Hipster talks like a black man and plays black music, but he is a white man. He grew up near Harlem and he identifies deeply with black language and music. His racial identification is so strong that his 1944 album, "Boogie Woogie in Blue," contains a song called, "I Stay Brown All Year Roun'." Blackface minstrelsy is hardly the right word for Harry's music; racial "passing" might be closer to the mark.[77] The song Harry plays on this episode of *Jubilee* is "Slender, Tender, and Tall," a song strongly associated with black acts. Nat King Cole and Velma Middleton have already performed the song on previous episodes of *Jubilee*, and Louis Jordan had recorded the song.

But what was probably not widely known was that Harry Gibson is white. Three Harry the Hipster Soundies appear in 1944, and by the end of 1945 jazz cognoscenti would have known his act from East Coast and West Coast clubs and jazz magazines. But for those many listeners who missed his Soundies—out of hundreds and hundreds of Soundies—and who did not read *Down Beat*, this sexual and racial moment in *Jubilee* must have seemed very strange. From our point of view, we can see that Gibson's multiracial (as it were) identity allows him to occupy tabooed space. He can present himself as a black singer, who plays black music, yet he can also, as a white man, make a legal play for the white woman. And it seems that Gibson enjoys occupying this almost unique racial and sexual space. In his trademark song, "Handsome Harry the Hipster," Gibson brags in the first line that "he's the boy with all the chicks." But he also calms parental fears in a chorus: "He would never marry your sister." This is exactly the language that white segregationists would return to again and again: "But would you let a black man marry your sister?" Gibson knows what sexual and color lines he crosses in his act. For those listeners to *Jubilee* who did not know Gibson's race, they must have thought that social boundaries were dangerously blurred. This was the kind of moment that *Jubilee* had avoided until then and would continue to avoid for the rest of the decade.

A remarkable reading of Morse's cultural presence occurs in a comedy-detective film called *How Doooo You Do?* (1945). Although made by the ultra–low-budget company, Producers Releasing Company (PRC), the film shows moments of real invention and critical acumen. One ideal for low-budget films is that they will risk things that big-budget films will not, and, amid much dreary filler, *How Doooo You Do?* does invent. The film follows a story by Harry Sauber, who is also coscreenwriter and producer. Three of Sauber's earlier scripts were for Columbia B-movies—*Sing for Your Supper* (1941), *Laugh Your Blues Away* (1942), and *Let's Have Fun* (1943)—all vehicles for Bert Gordon as the "Mad Russian." Sauber's PRC production also features Bert Gordon, now with the twist that everyone in the movie appears as themselves. In other words, the Mad Russian is a radio actor, Harry von Zell is a radio announcer, and Ella Mae Morse is a boogie-woogie singer.

The film begins with a sequence that promises some intelligence and risk-taking. Radio announcers Harry von Zell and Harlow Wilcox talk about their radio shows with a surprising lack of respect for the stars. There is a long tradition in which announcers introduce their stars in a mock insulting manner, but von Zell and Wilcox take this to an extreme. Von Zell and Wilcox assume that their radio programs are really focused on them, and they have trouble remembering who the stars actually are. This is an amusing skit, and it even has a point. The announcers want to overthrow the hierarchy of stars over secondary characters; likewise, here comes a B-movie made out of secondary characters, which perhaps can challenge the A-movies and their stars. Making this claim explicitly, von Zell faces the camera and introduces the cast: Harry von Zell, Cheryl Walker, Claire Windsor, Ella Mae Morse, Keye Luke. As von Zell says, "There are many people in radio whose voices are familiar to you, and yet you have never met them in person." What von Zell says is not strictly true, since Walker and Windsor are not radio actresses, and Keye Luke's Asian face was familiar from his many films. But what von Zell says rings true for Ella Mae Morse, since now audiences can finally put a face to the familiar voice of the "Cow Cow Boogie girl."

We can now see that the woman who sounds black is actually white, but the movie takes into account Morse's musical blackness. The film begins with a radio show, and Ella Mae Morse is introduced as the "Cow Cow Boogie girl." She sings "Boogie Woogie Cindy," another song about musical race-mixing, where "dusky maidens" in Harlem combine boogie-woogie with samba. Having established her black musical credentials, the film treats that element as part of her character. The two main male characters (von Zell and the Mad Russian) and the two main female characters (Cheryl Walker and Claire Windsor) form pairs, with Morse as odd woman out. In an early sequence, a black butler helps von Zell and the Mad Russian dress; they do not speak to him and he does not utter a word through the whole scene. But shortly afterward we see the black butler singing to himself, and he opens the door to Morse. She acts superior to him, but the film has gone out of its way to show that she is closer to the African American servant than to the other white people. The plot has the Mad Russian running away after the final radio show of the season; he is afraid of Ella Mae. And that is her role throughout the movie, to pursue the Mad Russian. The clear implication is that women who sing boogie-woogie are sexually aggressive.

In most respects, Ella Mae Morse does not look like a 1940s man-chaser. Stereotypically, the man-hungry woman is ugly and therefore desperate for attention. Vera Vague, Brenda and Cobina, and Cass Daley all based their sexually aggressive routines on the premise that their looks scare men away. The Andrews Sisters were often thought to be unattractive; one sister was thus obliged to play a man-hungry character on their radio show. But Ella Mae Morse is as pretty as any other pretty girl around; it must be her cultural blackness that makes her character so aggressive. When she finds the Mad Russian at the resort, she orders him to be ready at ten a.m. and she gives him his whole day's schedule. When she shows up the next morning, she is dressed in a silly hiking outfit and a hunter's horn is heard on the soundtrack. The same horn attended Joey's wolfish "Happy Hunting Horn" in *Pal Joey* (1940); now Morse is the huntress. As if her sexual aggressiveness were not clear enough, the film has her grab the Mad Russian and say, "Come along my little Russian wolfhound." And then she barks and growls at him. Apparently cultural blackness causes this white woman to behave like an obnoxious she-wolf.

Ella Mae Morse's musical path was closely linked to that of Johnny Mercer, who also fell strongly under the influence of African American music. As a guest star on the final episode of Bob Hope's 1942–1943 Pepsodent show (6–15–43), Mercer explained to Hope that he had not only cofounded a new record company, but that he was also working on a musical, *St. Louis Woman* ("You have your thumb in a lot of pies," says Hope). The reason that Mercer was guesting on Bob Hope's season finale was that his own radio show, *Johnny Mercer's Music Shop*, would take over as the summer replacement program for Bob Hope. *St. Louis Woman*, an all-black musical with words by Mercer and music by Harold Arlen, would eventually play on Broadway in 1946. But the play's production was beleaguered by controversy; most substantially, Lena Horne gave over the main role when the NAACP protested the play's racial stereotypes.[78] *St. Louis Woman* closed after 113 shows. *Johnny Mercer's Music Shop* came back for a second run in the summer and fall of 1944, but eventually it too was cancelled. According to singer Jo Stafford, Mercer's radio show was cancelled because it was "too black."[79] Mercer's music also pushed racial boundaries.

If *Johnny Mercer's Music Shop* is "too black," however, it is not black because of either cast or guests. Mercer's show is "black" because of Mercer's musical blackness. According to the nearly complete records for the second season (June to December 1944), not a single African American guest appeared on the *Music Shop*.[80] On July 25, 1944, the show's guest was Marlin Hurt, a white man who played a black woman named Beulah on *Fibber McGee and Molly*.[81] On this show Mercer sings "Is you is or is you ain't my baby" in a duet with "Beulah." This song—with its absence of good grammar—is thereby marked as "black." And many of Mercer's songs are likewise made out of jive talk, identifiably black musical genres, or feature black characters.

On the very first episode of the *Music Shop*, Mercer sang "Louisville Lou," a song about a black stripper ("when she struts her feminine plumes, / the porters drop their mops and their brooms").[82] This song included a brief minstrelsy show skit in the middle. Mercer's popular song, "Accentuate the Positive" (Capitol 180, *Music Shop* 7–19–44, 11–17–44), was based on the rhetoric of African American sermons; its origins in African American tradition were recognizable even without the blackface performance by Bing Crosby and Sonny Tufts in *Here Come the Waves* (1944). Except for the title, Mercer keeps black dialect to a minimum in his version of "De Camptown Races" (Capitol 217, *Music Shop* 10–6–44, 10–27–44, 12–4–44). Although "Mrs. Wiggs of the Cabbage Patch" (*Music Shop* 11–22–44) is probably a southern white woman, Mercer's dialect performance ("Who dat?") helps make the cabbage patch black.[83] All in all, a listener who read Mercer's jive ("G.I. Jive," Capitol 141, *Music Shop* 6–23–44,7–17–44, 8–25–44, 10–20–44) and blues songs ("Memphis Blues," *Music Shop* 6–30–44, 8–11–44, 10–30–44, 12–8–44; "St. Louis Blues," *Music Shop* 7–21–44, 11–24–44; "Blues in the Night," *Music Shop* 8–7–44, 10–13–44) as black would probably read the whole show as black, if not "too black."

Mercer's culturally black credentials were established early on. Mercer's "Blues in the Night," composed for the 1941 film of the same name, was nominated for an Academy Award for best song. Mercer's successful use of black lyrics ("my momma done tol' me") no doubt helped convince the producers of *St. Louis Woman* to sign him on as the musical's lyricist. Mercer's bluesy "blackness" earned him roles such as that of Memphis in the radio *Screen Guild Theater*'s version of *The Birth of the Blues* (9–13–43). Unfortunately this folksy history of the blues is one that almost eliminates black people. Early on, Jeff Lambert (Bing Crosby) says in exasperation, "I was getting ready to give Dixieland back to the colored folks." As an idea about the development of jazz or as a racial comment suitable for democracy in 1943, that remark is wholly unacceptable. But apparently neither Bing Crosby nor Mercer worried much about racial offense when they sang their beloved black music.[84]

Ella Mae Morse's cultural fate was closely intertwined with Johnny Mercer's. Her "Cow Cow Boogie" (Capitol 102) and his "Strip Polka" (Capitol 103) helped launch Capitol Records. She was a regular cast member in the 1943 summer season of *Johnny Mercer's Music Shop*. While he performed "Louisville Lou" on the first program, Morse (of course) performed "Cow Cow Boogie." Morse from Texas, Mercer from Georgia: they both loved African American music and that love came through in their own performances. But Mercer's cultural blackness is always shadowed by minstrelsy traditions and by a willingness to ridicule black characters and characteristics. I claim here—although a counterargument can easily be imagined—that the comic exuberance of many of Morse's jive-filled, bluesy numbers tends not to come at the expense of African Americans. To take an unfair because unequal comparison: in 1946 Mercer releases his comic song, "Ugly Chile" (Capitol 268), which uses black language and imagery ("your hair is nappy, / who's your pappy?") to substantiate its insults. By contrast, a few months earlier Ella Mae Morse released "The House of Blue Lights" (Capitol 251), which uses black music to make a major contribution to rhythm and blues idiom. "The House of Blue Lights" begins with a jive dialogue between lyricist Don Raye and Morse; it is not just hepcat jive, it is recognizably black jive ("what's that, homey?" asks Morse).[85] In my judgment, Morse's black cultural appropriations stay on an acceptable side of the line, in contrast to Mercer's more stereotyped usages ("who dat?").

However one evaluates Mercer and his deployments of black idiom, it may well be that his deep involvement with African American music helps to expand the musical offerings at Capitol Records. Mercer is only one of several cofounders of Capitol, and his musical tastes do not overdetermine a rather heterogeneous catalogue that issues hundreds of records over the course of the decade. Still, the Mercer stamp is on a large swath of material. Capitol releases numerous records by Mercer, Ella Mae Morse, and Freddie Slack. Many songs in the Capitol catalogue come from Mercer's backup group, the Pied Pipers, and from Jo Stafford, a member of the Pied Pipers who becomes a major solo star on her own. Capitol releases recordings by many top black jazz players—Benny Carter, Coleman Hawkins, Cootie Williams—although the label is hardly a leading producer of black jazz.

Given the success of Ella Mae Morse in black blues mode, one might have expected Capitol to release more blues by black singers, but except for a few acts (Julia Lee and her Boy Friends, Jesse Price), Capitol's blues are sung by whites. Indeed, Capitol's blackness is conveyed more often by Mercer and Morse than by black musicians. The core of the catalogue is white: Martha Tilton, Bobby Sherwood, Gordon Jenkins, and Andy Russell, along with many records from Stan Kenton's swing band and country star Tex Ritter.[86]

Capitol does challenge the racial stereotypes of 1940s music in many of its releases by Nat King Cole.[87] Whereas most black male singers were prohibited from adopting romantic personas, Capitol often allows Cole to sing luxurious love songs. Some of the Capitol songs are jive tunes or nonsense songs, as listeners might expect, songs like "Vom Vim Veedle" (Capitol 139) and "Frim Fram Sauce" (Capitol 224).[88] "Bring Another Drink" (Capitol 192) strategically, not romantically, advises boys to "bring another drink" before they whisper "love words" in their chick's ear. But songs like "All for You" (Capitol 139), "I Realize Now" (Capitol 154), and "You Call It Madness but I Call It Love" (Capitol 274) are unqualifiedly romantic ballads.[89]

If Capitol extends the sexual range of the African American male singer, it also extends the sexual range of the white female singer. Capitol released five records by Betty Hutton (including "Stuff Like That There," Capitol 188), whose persona, as we saw earlier, is one that refuses to occupy standard feminine confines. By adopting black song forms, Ella Mae Morse could sometimes express unusually aggressive sexual desire ("Buzz Me," "Get Off It and Go"). Kay Starr followed in Ella Mae Morse's path by using black blues to advance some straightforward sexual sentiments ("You've Got to See Mama Every Night," Capitol 497).[90] Betty Hutton and Ella Mae Morse adopt gendered and racial masks that allow white women to express sexual desire.

Capitol also released all the songs in the early career of Peggy Lee. In the late 1940s, Lee created a musical style and space that allows for the expression of sexual desire, and now this expression takes place without masks. The clearest example of such a song is "It's Lovin' Time" (Capitol 343), which straightforwardly announces that it is time to go to bed. The singer says that her brother is asleep and that her parents have accommodatingly gone to a movie ("they were once young too"); everything is perfect, but where are you? *Billboard* speaks of Lee's "sensuous, intimate styling" on this record, while *Down Beat* says that there is more of the "shut off the lights" Lee tone.[91] The *Down Beat* comment implies that Lee's songs regularly express sexual desire.

Sometimes Lee, like Morse, adopts a blues form for the purpose; she says a "long, long train with a red caboose" will cure her woes (Capitol 445). But mostly desire is expressed quietly and intently without any Hutton hysterics or Morse masks. Although Margaret Whiting, Jo Stafford, and Martha Tilton all sing romantic ballads, none of their songs take place in the "sensuous, intimate" space Peggy Lee created. How is it that Lee is "allowed" to express sexual desire without a mask? Is it because her songs are always accompanied by her husband, Dave Barbour? Does this help to constrain potentially wayward female desire? In another intimate song, "Don't Smoke in Bed," from the Capitol album *Rendezvous with Peggy Lee* (1948), we learn straight away that the singer is married ("I left a note on the dresser / And my old wedding ring"). This calm, adult overview of activities in bed is rare in 1940s popular music, but at least constrained by some recognizable social regulations. But walking out on your sleeping husband is no one's idea of good behavior, just as the song "Aren't You Kind of Glad We Did?" (Capitol 292) does not promote conservative values. Yet somehow Lee manages to express sexual desire without either punishing herself or framing herself as a sultry femme fatale.[92]

By the end of 1942 Ella Mae Morse was one of the most famous singers in America. In an overview of the year, *Down Beat* said that "the year's sensation of course was Ella Mae Morse."[93] And she was no one-hit wonder since she kept turning out one popular song after another. The July 5, 1945, *Command Performance* is dedicated to celebrating the one thousandth program of *G.I. Jive*. Ella Mae Morse is not only invited to the celebrations, she is also introduced as "the most requested gal singer of them all." Even taking into account show business hyperbole, a good case can made that few female popular singers were more widely known than Morse. Her popularity went hand in hand with an almost unique way of singing. *Billboard*, with its usual clumsy precision, referred to Morse's "tabasco styling."[94] In code—in Morse code—they mean that she sings black, and therefore she sings spicy. Ella Mae Morse was one of the most popular singers of the day, a key player in the development of Capitol Records, and at a nexus of race and sexuality in 1940s culture. Yet she has largely vanished from our contemporary critical consciousness, another 1940s phantom lady. It is hoped that this preliminary overview of her place in 1940s music culture will help us see her and the important issues all around her with more clarity.

I'm equipped for television,
Walkie talkie,
And Morse code too.
("Buzz Me")

7

What Young Women Want

From High School to College

Jon Savage begins *Teenage: the Creation of Youth Culture* (2007) with the following information: "During 1944, Americans began to use the word 'teenager' to describe the category of young people from fourteen to eighteen. From the very start, it was a marketing term used by advertisers and manufacturers that reflected the newly visible spending power of adolescents."[1] Merchants wanted to know what teenagers wanted, but in the fashion of all successful selling, this meant educating the consumer in their wants. What do young women want? What shall we say that young women want?

This chapter pursues a description of female desire in 1940s culture from two related directions. First I look at the way that teenage female desire is represented—openly or obliquely—in books and magazines for teenagers, in magazines for mothers, and through a survey of artifacts from movies to plays to newspapers. Then I examine the astonishing increase in college courses in marital study. With psychologists, scientists, and specialists of all kinds in the ascendant, magazines and newspapers were filled with advice columns that, when combined with advertisements, give the impression that readers needed lessons in every aspect of their lives. Naturally, women needed more instruction than men, and young women needed more instruction than old. College programs in marital studies were the logical outgrowth of an assumption that young women needed formal, scientific training before they were married, especially around issues of sexuality. From *Seventeen* to Missouri's Stephens College, young women knew what they wanted, and were told, even more forcefully, what they really wanted.

Teenage Girls: The Crush and the Billboard

It is absolutely the case that the teenager is invented, to begin with, as a consumer. But this is not a symmetrical moment in which both male and female teenagers are invented at the same time. Instead, the 1940s teenager is much more readily identified as a girl. It is mothers who control the purse in the domestic household, and it is teenage girls who need to shop for teenage things. When Jon Savage's book gets to "The Arrival of the Teenager," the chapter is subtitled, "The Launch of *Seventeen*."[2] There are plenty of boy teenagers, no doubt, but it is female teens who show the country that something different is happening. There is no male equivalent to the hordes of swooning bobby-soxers, which is where Savage announces the "arrival of the teenager." Nor is there a male parallel to *Seventeen* magazine, which starts up in 1944, and serves ever since as the hip, seductive, glossy guide for young female consumers.

A 1945 *March of Time* newsreel, "Teen-Age Girls," gives the period's own sense of the teenager's recent arrival. The famously deep-voiced and judgmental narrator, Westbrook Van Voorhis, introduces the piece: "Of all the phenomena of wartime life in the United States, one of the most fascinating, and mysterious, and one of the most completely irrelevant, has been the emergence of the teenage girl as an institution in her own right." Despite the teenage girl's "complete irrelevance," the narrator soon adds that "teenagers are consumers with minds of their own, as businessmen have discovered to their profit." And the newsreel now shows and praises the manufacturers of products for this newly identified market. As usual, the framing patriarch is all contradictions. He cannot decide whether to see these young women clearly ("one of the most acutely noticeable groups in the nation") or turn them into "completely irrelevant" phantoms.

Indeed, the patriarchal framing of this newsreel is more than usually evident. After the opening section, the film cuts to a seminar room in which five men (none younger than 50 years old) and a prim female stenographer sit around a table with a teenage girl as their focus. Van Voorhis says that "sociologists, psychologists, and students of behaviorism find in the teenage girl of today a stimulating and almost limitless field of study." The men scrutinize the young woman, taking notes, as if she comes from some mysterious, alien tribe. "What are your group's social habits?" they wonder. They want to know what she likes, what she doesn't like, and who she is. It is in this "scientific" context, then, that the teenage girl is allowed to speak. Under this psychological, sociological, and entirely male scrutiny, she now narrates the main section of the newsreel.

In order to introduce these investigators to teenage culture, the young woman shows them her bedroom. There is a brief establishing shot of the family home's exterior, but then the film is inside her room, where it finds her making her bed. Here, as she cleans up, like the future mother she is, she asserts her independence: "We like to live our own lives; we want our own rooms; family keep out." It is hard to imagine that a newsreel on teenage boys would start in his bedroom, but nothing seems more natural than the film's abrupt occupation of the girl's private quarters. We are allowed immediate intimacy, and her wall decorations make evident her culturally shaped desires. "We like to have a lot of our favorite pinups on the walls," she says, "the boys we date and the movie stars we go for." On the left side of her wall, the representative teenage girl has a cork board covered with photographs of high school age boys. On the right side, in a much more artistic display, we see a perfectly arranged double arc of movie star photos: Fred MacMurray, Alan Ladd, Gregory Peck, and the ubiquitous Frank Sinatra. The celebrity photographs arch over her mirror like an altar; she sits down to apply her makeup beneath their exalted presences. With astonishing efficiency, then, the newsreel has entered the girl's bedroom and revealed her innermost (heterosexual) desires.

The newsreel allows our teenager to unveil her innermost desires to a circle of male elders; as they look on, wise yet mystified, it appears that they have never seen anything like her before. But in reality some other circle of men has already created and narrated her desires, so that the main purpose of this investigation is, in the end, to give the impression that she is a free agent, that she "has a mind of her own." Just as she is the representative teenage girl, her room is the perfect blend of teenage psychology and consumerism. When she sits down at her dressing table before her large mirror beneath the celebrity photos, she takes part in the appearance-obsessed culture that magazines such as *Seventeen* have created. First and foremost is to look good (and smell good) for your men. Not only the magazine's advertisements, but also the advice columns are relentless about that. And when the teenage girl covers the wall with her men—half with high school boys and half with movie stars—she demonstrates the decade's recurrent understanding of teenage girl psychology. She does not reveal a mysterious inner world to these men, so much as she narrates a structure of desire that society has already provided her.

The psychology of the 1940s adolescent girl is often put in exactly these terms: the young woman must move past a stage of celebrity idolization toward a relationship with a real boy. This narrative is adopted throughout popular culture and popular psychology. The conflation of psychology and consumerism works perfectly since popular culture becomes so prevalent and so internalized that it forms a recognizable stage in normal psychological development. Instead of an oedipal phase associated with mother or father, this psychological narrative features a phase associated with Frank Sinatra or Van Johnson. Eventually the teenage girl must throw off the Hollywood fantasy in order to accommodate herself to a future husband. But in the meantime her heterosexual desires can be aimed at an impossibly distant object, which helps, among other things, to keep her out of trouble. It also aligns consumer culture (record collecting, movie watching, fan magazine reading) with a completely normal pattern of psychological development. How convenient for shopkeepers everywhere to find that the intensity of adolescent emotion has been aligned with shopping. And this is just where we find the girl in the *March of Time* newsreel, with a perfectly built altar to movie stars on one side and a jumbled bulletin board with pictures of real boys on the other. When time marches on, as it always does, the movie star pictures will be taken down, and the real boys will be filtered down to one.

This psychological narrative, in which teenage girls obsess over celebrity but then throw it over, appears in many forms. A typical magazine story in this regard is "The Star that Fell in Ohio," where the starstruck girl eventually comes to see her real-life boyfriend for the attractive man he is. "And [there was] Johnny, grinning in that devilish way of his, and looking more handsome than Ray Milland, Gregory Peck, and Jimmy Stewart all rolled into one."[3] In the story "Not Like in the Movies," published in *Calling All Girls*, teenage Tommy stops behaving like George Sanders in order to have a real relationship with Nancy: "Bel Ami was suddenly just a make-believe character in a make-believe story. It was part of a childish game that was behind him. But this night was not make-believe. It was very real."[4] In yet another *Calling All Girls* story the same conclusion is reached: "She'd go home and face the real facts of her life and try to be brave and honest, and maybe someday things would work out better for her. Not the way they did in her dreams, because now she saw that they never would. She wasn't ever going to be a movie star, or a glamorous deb."[5]

One of the decade's most inventive versions of this story occurs in *A Date with Judy*, a radio series that ran from 1941 to 1950. In the March 20, 1945 episode, Judy wants to see a Frank Sinatra movie. Since her boyfriend, Oogie, can tell that Judy is out of her mind about Frank, he would rather do anything else ("How about we go down to the fire station and wait for a three-alarm fire?"). But Judy, as intoxicated as every other girl in the bobby-sox brigade, insists: "I'm going to explain how a girl feels," she says, "[there's just] something that when he sings comes over you." And she continues her swoon: "He represents everything that a girl wants out of romance, her ideals of what perfect love is like." Although he claims not to be jealous of "that little peewee," Oogie's high-pitched, permanently cracking voice is no match for "The Voice." As Oogie says, resignedly, "It's mighty tough to live in the same world with Frank Sinatra."

This episode rather brilliantly—in a show not known for brilliance—uses Sinatra himself to undermine his intoxicating hold on young women. After the Sinatra movie, Judy dismisses her date very disdainfully ("just shake my hand and say good night, Oogie"), and goes to bed. But whereas some dreams are wished-for fantasies, Judy's nightdream now shatters her Sinatra daydream. She dreams that Oogie is the star of the Sinatra movie, and that Sinatra is Oogie. Frank Sinatra himself is there to play a needy, pleading teenage boy, but Judy won't listen to him; her heart belongs to screen star Oogie. What her dream tells her is what Oogie told her already, that having a crush on an impossibly distant ideal is no good, and in the end Judy agrees. "The movies and the phonograph are just wonderful of course," she tells Oogie, "but why should a girl keep on dreaming when there's somebody so marvelous and attainable as you around?" By having Sinatra croon two seductive songs, but then also present himself in a silly nonglamorous way, this episode challengingly works out the familiar plot in which a teenage girl throws off her fantasies and grows up into reality.

The Sinatra episode of *A Date with Judy* can also be used to gauge the limits of sexual discourse in the 1940s. As a situation comedy focused on a teenage girl, one might imagine that *A Date with Judy* would work its comedy in a more restrained, circumspect manner than, say, Bob Hope or Jimmy Durante. But in its first two years *A Date with Judy* was in fact a summer replacement for Bob Hope's Pepsodent show. And the Sinatra episode does not shy away from the sexual element in teenage swooning. In his role as dream movie star, Oogie sings a song to counter Sinatra's magnetic, masculine crooning:

> I'm not a wolf,
> I'm just a little drip,
> A little squirt,
> But there's a beast in me.
> CHORUS: I've got a date with Judy, and Judy's got a date with me.

Oogie's song is both cute and preposterous, yet it also manages to speak with some intensity about a skinny teenage boy's desires.

And the whole family plays the game of sexual expression. To many adults, one of the great mysteries about the 1940s teenage girl was what she found compelling in Frank Sinatra. Judy's parents offer a historical explanation. Her mother recalls that father used to "squeal every time Theda Bara came on the screen." Father denies this, "I did not," while admitting, "I might have given a soft little moan every now and then." Later the family adds to their history of swooning; Mom says, "In my day, we didn't squeal, Judy, we moaned." After Judy's father sings a bit of an old tune, Mom and Dad have a funny adult exchange.

> MOTHER: Do you mind if I moan?
>
> FATHER: No, go ahead.
>
> MOTHER: Ooooom.
>
> FATHER: Finished?
>
> MOTHER: Yep. All done.

Like certain episodes of *Our Miss Brooks*, where all the characters—teenagers and adults—are swept up by sex, the Sinatra episode of *A Date with Judy* shows us sensual intoxication across generations, but also mature self-control. Sex has certainly not been edited out of the program—quite the contrary—but it has been restrained.

An important treatment of the adolescent girl's crush occurs also in *The Bachelor and the Bobby-Soxer* (1947). Here teenage Susan (Shirley Temple) falls for bachelor artist Richard Nugent (Cary Grant). In this model of the crush, Nugent is not a movie star, but then again he is, since he is so obviously Cary Grant. As the review in *Movie Teen* puts it, "since the heartbeats are for Playboy Artist, Cary Grant, the problem [the "Great Big Crush"] is not hard to understand."[6] In an early sequence of the film, Grant-Nugent gives a speech about art at the local high school. Beyond this, however, there is no attempt to make Nugent into a character or an artist; indeed, he is just the handsome Hollywood charmer, Cary Grant. He is so good-looking that girls in the high school audience whistle at him even before he gives his speech. When he walks out afterward, girls continue to wolf whistle at him in the halls. The art talk barely matters; what is important is that "he's handsome" (as Susan tells her soon to be ex-boyfriend). And then she—and the film—imagines that this ideal of ideals, Cary Grant, has turned into a shining white knight.

Remarkably, however, the film does not make fun of Susan's crush. Humor in the 1940s is often grotesquely misogynistic, and dumb females of all ages make much of the decade's comedy possible. As noted in a *Time* review of the sitcom *My Friend Irma*, "U.S. radio comedy leans heavily on dumb-belles."[7] Yet although *The Bachelor and the Bobby-Soxer* is a lighthearted comedy, the teenage crush is never treated as silly or absurd. On the contrary, the adults treat Susan respectfully and patiently. The film allows us to see flickering irritation in Grant's eyes, but he holds it in, thus gaining the respect of both the audience and Susan's older sister, Margaret (Myrna Loy). There is even a psychiatrist (Ray Collins) present to authoritatively pronounce that Susan's crush is normal. The psychiatrist responds to the crisis by encouraging Nugent to take Susan out on dates; he predicts that this will allow Susan to see the relationship for what it is. The psychiatrist's prescription is not proper medicine, but instead a plot device to enable screwball mismatches (Nugent is bored at teen functions or he overcompensates by acting like a teenager). Yet the movie does not mock the psychiatrist either, and eventually, after he gives Susan a stern talking to, she comes back down to earth. Altogether, then, even though this comedy could easily make fun of either the girl or the psychiatrist, it does neither, choosing instead to find its comedy elsewhere. The canonical story about a teenage girl's celebrity crush is so normal, so widespread, that to make fun of it in a film would be, in essence, un-American.[8]

The celebrity crush took on epic proportions during the middle of the decade. Teenage girls by the hundreds of thousands swooned over Frank Sinatra in a nationwide craze. Listeners to *Your Hit Parade* during 1943 and 1944 could hear teenage girls screaming at Sinatra throughout the program. Magazines and newspapers kept track of a fad that showed no signs of diminishing. An early story in *Life* was subtitled " 'Bedroom singer' from Hoboken rose from 70 cents to $2,500 a week through voice that makes women swoon."[9] Newspapers regularly reported on near riots when Sinatra appeared. When 17-year-old Rita Stearns won the "Why I Swoon at Sinatra" contest, newspapers copied out her well-crafted reasoning: "If lonesome he reminds you of the guy away from your arms. If waiting for a dream prince, his thrilling voice sings for you alone."[10]

1940s culture encourages young women to display themselves sexually, but it does not encourage them to express their sexual desires. Advertisements and social instruction addressed to teenage girls encourage them to make themselves attractive to boys, but girls are responsible for stopping sex if it goes beyond a kiss. Yet whatever is going on in the Sinatra pandemic, these thousands of swooning girls are expressing sexual desire. In 1943 psychologist Donald Laird judged that these swoons were *not* sexual, but maternal; in his view the rail-thin Sinatra played on the nurturing instincts of the girls.[11] But this view clashed with almost everyone else's, including Artur Rodzinski, conductor of the New York Philharmonic, who called Sinatra's followers "pitiful cases" and linked them to degeneracy and delinquency.[12] To Sinatra's female fans, the sincere, intimate approach of the "bedroom singer" called for a response in kind. Noting that so many young men were away in the war, an editor of the *New Republic* wrote, "Undoubtedly, just plain sex has a great deal to do with the whole matter."[13] Since some of the girls were really too young (age 11 or 12) and because the phenomenon was public and crowd-driven, "just plain sex" would never work as a complete explanation. Psychologists thus added "mass hysteria" and even "mass hypnotism" to "mass frustrated love" as reasons for the wartime craze.[14]

One way of reading the nationwide swoon fad is, indeed, as a symptom of a culture that does not allow women to express themselves sexually. How can a young woman express her desire? The groovy new teen jive makes some room for sexy speech; a teenage dictionary in *Calling All Girls* says, "*Wipe off your chin* means the same as 'Pass the Drool Cup.' Any tall, dark and handsome can bring it on."[15] Like hipster jive generally, teen heptalk provides some language for sexual attraction. But drooling is like swooning—passive, ridiculously overt, self-satirizing. As always, a perfect face and figure may be read by men as invitations, but are *signs* the limit of female expression? Perhaps women are forbidden access to language and must therefore express themselves in nonverbal sighs or swooning moans.

Numerous artifacts turn young women into carriers of signs, signs that mean desire but also imply that verbal speech is off limits. In college, sorority women might wear a boy's pin to signify that they are going steady or are engaged. High school girls, at least in the magazines, could mark themselves in similar ways. Manrey Jewelry advertises the "hi-sign," an ornament that "proclaims your heart to be open for 'Free Parking' or marks it a 'restricted area!' "[16] Similarly, the "date-light" pin is a traffic light that switches between red and green to signal the girl's intentions; "when you want him to give with the dating just push the button and presto—green light!"[17] *Calling All Girls* advises their readers to make "a friendship or jive skirt," where friends' names or jive talk are embroidered on the inside fold of a pleated skirt. "When you stand still, it looks like an untrimmed skirt, but when you walk—hey, watch those boys turn around!"[18] The cover girl on the January 1946 *Calling All Girls* wears a sweater "knit all over with names of boys' colleges."[19] Florida Fashions promotes their "flirt shirt," which features photos of "six divine men" plus a question mark where the buyer can "write in HIS name" on the mystery square.[20] In a 1948 episode of the teen comic *Andy*, one of the two girls wears a shirt covered with the names of boys.[21] Jamboree Jeans are covered with writing—like "you love me"—that "makes 'em Stop, Look and READ as you pass the corner Casbah!"[22] Most of this signage means some version of "I want you" or "please recognize that I desire." But the sheer volume of these body-covering signs and texts points to a planet where the wearers have no clear way of expressing sexual desire. Hence young women swoon by the thousands or dress like billboards.

Teenage advice columns focus on fun, although there is often a moral component. Let's have fun, but not too much. Adult columnists talk from a parental perspective, with perhaps some jive talk thrown in, about how to conduct a job interview, become a musician, or drive a car. Teenage columnists are more oriented toward pleasure and entertainment—how to dress for a date, what games to play at your party. In her syndicated newspaper column, "On the Solid Side," Sheila "Chi Chi" Daly writes about learning to dance, how to study, how to entertain guests, and she warns against catty gossip. Her newspaper columns are both fluffy and sensible, and there is no sign of sex anywhere.[23]

The "Sub-Deb" column in *Ladies' Home Journal* could get more detailed about teenage sexual activity. The *Ladies' Home Journal* supported a fairly robust form of sex education elsewhere in the magazine, and a national audience was concerned with "promiscuous girls" during the war. In a December 1944 column Elizabeth Woodward talks about the "vice" of sex, where "by sex we mean necking, and so on. And by necking, and so on, we mean mostly necking, and very little so on."[24] Woodward does not pretend that sex does not exist, but she certainly wants sexual activity to stop after a certain point. In a July 1945 column, she even encourages girls to kiss—"if you don't get kissed, beat him to it!"—while also insisting that girls slow down, "learn how to say 'no, thank you.' "[25] When Maureen Daly takes over the column in October 1945, she also talks about putting on the brakes. In "No Parking Please," she warns her readers about losing control: "But before you know it, you're necking! You can suddenly find yourself with a lot of emotion just too hot to handle! And don't even try to fool yourself with the smug assumption, 'I'm not that kind of girl!' "[26] Such advice follows the usual formula that female sexual desire is less overwhelming than a man's, so that women become responsible for remaining in control. But such descriptions also acknowledge that female desire can quickly become as overwhelming as a man's. When emotions grow "too hot to handle," everyone becomes a wolf.

Sexual realism reached its peak in 1949 and 1950, when *Ladies' Home Journal* ran a series called "Profile of Youth." When the collected articles were published as a book, it included epigraphs by Margaret Mead and Alfred Kinsey (and Eisenhower!). Moral judgment comes through no doubt in what evidence is used, but a more fact-based, anthropological and sociological study of teenagers is the intent. The article, "Sex Freedom and Morality in the United States" begins with the statement: "What, according to high-school students, is the most important personal problem facing them today? The answer, according to a national survey, is 'What should we do about sex?' "[27] With a nod to Kinsey, the article says that there is often a "vast and disturbing difference between what they are 'told to do' by parents and 'what the crowd really does.' " Another article in the series goes into convincing detail about "Where do teenagers get their sex education?"

Although Mead's rituals and Kinsey's facts are everywhere present, the moral conventions of parents and subdeb editors still oversee these articles. Female sexual desire remains hard to see, while all due diligence must be paid to male sexual desire. A disreputable girl, for example, is the "teaser, a girl who 'courts up a big storm' (kisses a boy until he is passionately aroused)."[28] As in the advice columns, "the boys feel it is up to the girl to keep things under control. She should know how and when to say stop, for 'after all, it's just *natural* for a fellow.' "[29] Although these articles do real Kinseyesque work by showing the discrepancy between prescriptive morality and actual practice, they also reinforce society's sense that female sexual desire is hard to document.

Some advice columns pitch their morality in more sexualized terms. The heavy hand of the parents is clear in *Calling All Girls* or *Ladies' Home Journal*, but other teen columns are not equally constrained. In a long unsigned article for the first issue of *Movie Teen*, "What's the Do with Woo?," the familiar case is made that girls should give in only so far, while remaining always in control. But this article, which cycles between attraction and prohibition for pages and pages, makes female desire seem much stronger than usual. Female desire is not hard to restrain if it is barely there in the first place. But this article begins with the assumption that "necking is nice as any honest gal must admit."[30] And the fireworks of sex keep exploding throughout the article: "before you know it you've got a big POW!, big like anything"; a "four alarm fire"; "heavy artillery"; "delirious with thrills." The "temptations" here seem much more tempting than in *Ladies' Home Journal*, even though the advice is the same: "Know what kinds of magic get you too starry-eyed to recognize a stop signal." Here female desire is registered as positively spicy: "Before long, if you let it, your relationship becomes entirely a matter of experimenting with the wonderful sizzly feeling only He can build up."[31] This is as open and volatile a description of female sexuality as one will find in a magazine for teenage girls.

But female desire in *Movie Teen* looks like this not because of realism, but because of commercialism. Female sexual desire in *Ladies' Home Journal* looks weak or even absent because of neo-Victorian assumptions about female chastity and virginity. Mother is buying the magazine. Even in the more realistic "Profile of Youth" columns, teenage girls do not have much trouble putting boundaries on sexual exploration. The column in *Movie Teen*, by contrast, is a species of erotica. Much longer than the usual advice column, it makes the same point again and again by bringing desire to a boil and then warning against it. As the cover article for the premiere issue of *Movie Teen*—"Are You a Droop? Is Woo Taboo?" are the cover's questions—it intends to spice up the magazine, to make a sexy splash. By admitting that female desire has burning, "sizzly" substance this article may seem more realistic than parallel columns in *Calling All Girls*. But the repetitious structure of the piece is erotic rather than realistic; its goal is to incite patronage rather than represent things as they are.

Seventeen, the archetypal magazine for young American women, is emblematic of all the contradictions surrounding female sexuality during the 1940s. Born in 1944, at the height of wartime frankness about male sexual desire, *Seventeen* presents a more adult teenager than *Calling All Girls*, but a less obsessively sexual teenager than the column from *Movie Teen*. In *Seventeen*, the *verbal* teenager exists in stunning contradiction to the *visual* teenager. The October 1946 issue, for example, offers serious articles and seriously difficult quizzes in both the "Your Mind" and "Having Fun" sections.[32] There are articles on boys, but without too much jive talk, and a whole series of articles that stress the importance of good citizenship ("Two Border Cities Meet Each Other," "Old Enough to Help," "Feed the World Plan," "Send Christmas Overseas"). The young woman constructed in these articles wants to shop, look nice, and go on dates, no doubt, but she is also socially responsible and remarkably brainy. This almost unbelievably mindful teenager has been created, one presumes, in order to balance out the huge proportion of the magazine devoted to fashion advertisements.

Whereas most women's magazines are marked by the contradictions between expectations in female roles (chaste housewife and mother versus sexually voluptuous wife), *Seventeen* is, if possible, even more ambiguous about the place of female sexuality. The magazine is addressed to women in both high school and college, which makes for advertising that is both cute and fuzzy ("Dizzy Wuzzy" sandals by "Oomphies, Inc." are covered in "luxurious bunny fur" [51]), but also as sexually adult as anything found in women's magazines aimed at housewives. As a counseling article says, "you are about to sprout into womanhood" (45). Which means that every growing body part is now controlled by men and the masculine gaze. A "Teentimer show-me-off dress" is a "stag line sensation" (218). Due to Lastex (rubber) yarn, your girdle and bra will attract a man, "bewitched by your pretty silhouette" (63). "Munsingwear Foundettes" have the "power to give even a fuller young figure the curves you covet" (49). High-heeled shoes are "high and haughty and just a bit naughty" (88). A teenage girl exclaims, "Jeepers what a luscious looking bra!" (266). Good citizen or sharp intellect she may well be, but meanwhile the teenage girl is thrown body-first into a highly sexualized world, where her intimate choices are determined by appraising men. The young woman must learn not only that she will be appraised, but also that she desires the appraisal. In one series of advice comics, a man looks away from his date at the legs of a passing girl. Which means a feminine blunder has taken place: "A sagging stocking makes your date / Prefer a gal who keeps hers straight" ("The Low-Down on the Clothes Line" [161]). The man's look at the passing leg is drawn as a devilish leer, but the teenage girl needs to learn—right now—that this wolfish hunger must not just be accepted but aroused.[33]

The strangest ad in the October 1946 issue of *Seventeen* promotes "Chen Yu 'Wolf Gal' " lipstick and nail polish (222). Elsewhere Chen Yu marketed its makeup with classy, exotic advertisements. "Wolf Gal," by contrast, is a kind of novelty item, with a large close-up of Al Capp's Wolf Gal on the box. As we have seen, *Li'l Abner*'s Wolf Gal reverses the usual plot by chasing after men. The sides of this makeup box, however, show men chasing women, while Capp's hillbilly prose reads, "Red-blooded American boys will go outa their minds" for you when you use this "smooch paint" and "paw paint." This *Seventeen* ad thus takes the central and potentially subversive premise of *Li'l Abner* and turns it back around to where it was. Now, despite the scary face of Wolf Gal herself, it is men who are turned into wolves. While promoting heavenly romance, youthful fun, and intellectual self-esteem, then, *Seventeen* also manages to train young women to submit their bodies, and their desires, to a masculine regime. Women seem to know what they want; how else can we interpret these hundreds of pages of advertising? But the most emblematic ad might be for yet another preverbal costume—the "do you love me" dress. "That's what the big question mark asks in bright embroidery on our date dress" (62). And there is the teenage girl in all her self-confident glory; she wears a dress with a giant question mark on her front.

Professor Bowman, Stephens College, and the Education of Female Desire

During the 1940s, *Ladies' Home Journal* staged an ongoing debate around the necessity and purpose of college education. For young women, the question was an especially pointed one. Should a young woman go to college? One repeated concern was that college women would find themselves too smart for their man, thus increasing the odds of marital incompatibility. An investigation by Paul Popenoe, head of the American Institute of Family Relations, found that "girls who go to college often try to assert their individuality in marriage." The result is that "their divorce rate is four times higher than that of college men."[34] Another common complaint was that college courses in literature and science had little relevance to women who were going to be wives and mothers. Thus Leslie B. Hohman insisted that "colleges should give academic courses every possible application to actual life."[35] With its conspicuous lack of interest in intellectual culture, *Ladies' Home Journal* provided a clear sense that a woman's education had primarily to do with her actual life of raising children, pleasing her husband, and running a household. Only in such a context could they recommend, in "New Careers for College Girls," that female college graduates apply for situations as maids. Here their writer spins this work—the housework described so elaborately in women's magazines—into a cultivated and elite profession. "Housework," writes Dorothy Swenson, "is becoming one of the highest-paid, most privileged occupations for girls with intelligence and taste."[36]

Now we might hope that these gestures—of pseudoscience and euphemism—are simply self-serving and local and that they have no particular resonance beyond the consumer-centered empire of one magazine. But these gestures go much wider and appear not just in *Ladies' Home Journal*, but also in numerous college textbooks, college courses, and even in entire colleges. In this section I take a detailed look at the literature of family studies in 1940s higher education. To focus my description, I turn to a school known nationwide and even internationally for its experiment in women's education, Stephens College in Columbia, Missouri. I then discuss a marital textbook by Henry Bowman, who taught at Stephens College from 1931 to 1955. The last section of this chapter surveys a series of education films based on Bowman's textbook. These textbooks, courses, films, and colleges collect numberless scientific authorities—one lecture hall after another—in order to cultivate and organize female desire.

Despite the sheer number of these marital courses, which were offered decade after decade across the nation, few cultural critics have sought to examine this literature in any detail. In her book chapter, "Scientific Truth . . . and Love," Beth L. Bailey presents what remains the best introduction.[37] And even after many years, it is still Betty Friedan, in *The Feminine Mystique*, who makes the most vigorous attack on what she called "the sex-directed educators."[38] In Friedan's parlance, the "sex-directed educators" not only educate female students into an obedient understanding of their "femininity," these educators also literally direct their female students towards sex: "some college presidents and professors charged with the education of women had become more concerned with their students' future capacity for sexual orgasm than with their future use of trained intelligence."[39] I will put the matter somewhat differently, while likewise emphasizing the centrality of female sexual desire in the organization of these programs. Marriage courses still exist when Friedan writes *The Feminine Mystique*; I argue that such courses attain a peak of cultural eminence during the 1940s. In Friedan's history, "education for femininity spread from Mills, Stephens, and the finishing schools to the proudest bastions of the women's Ivy League."[40] And regardless of whether one agrees with Friedan's diasporic narrative, Stephens College certainly serves as a cultural hub for female education during the 1940s.

In 1946 *Social Forces*, a sociology journal based at the University of North Carolina, published two articles back-to-back on the proliferation of marriage courses across American higher education. In "College Courses in Preparation for Marriage," Frances C. Thurman surveyed 270 small and large college universities and found that 39 percent of the colleges (105) offered "practical marriage courses."[41] Thurman did not provide data on the gender of students in these courses, but she did report that "men's colleges, as a whole, seem to have less interest in marriage courses."[42] She found that larger colleges were much more likely to offer such courses than smaller colleges; this meant that "large colleges are the leaders in offering practical marriage courses, while the very small colleges are much slower in offering such courses."[43] Thurman's article accurately reflects the proliferation of marriage courses, although it is biased toward reading these courses as progressive and forward looking.

In an accompanying article, "The Teaching of Marriage Courses by Sociologists and Home Economists," Judson T. Landis provides more logistical detail. Landis surveyed teachers colleges and found that half of all sociology departments provided a marriage course, while one-third of all home economics departments offered one.[44] Of the forty-two sociology departments studied, eleven offered their marriage course for the first time in the 1940s, while twenty-one began the course offering in the 1930s, and ten in the 1920s. The textbook used most widely by the sociologists was *Marriage and the Family* by Raymond E. Baber. Landis reports that one-third of the sociologists say that their marriage course had been added because of student demand, and Landis quotes Ernest Groves's book, *Marriage* (rev. ed. 1941) to support this contention. More so than geology or calculus, marriage courses exist to give the students what they want.

Stephens College claimed much more of the public's attention during the 1940s than its small size might warrant. In contemporary histories of higher education, Stephens College shows up only fitfully. At that time, after all, it was just one two-year junior college among many nationally recognized women's colleges. Yet in the 1940s, Stephens College appeared in the national media with some regularity. In a cultural environment readily drawn to communities of well-groomed young women, Stephens College was made for the age. Displaying all the contradictions of a *Harper's Bazaar*—which published the finest fiction next to the most glamorous models—Stephens College could be made into whatever the viewer wanted. It could be brought forward to represent a conservative viewpoint ("Youth Finds a New Road to Religion," *Reader's Digest*, March 1942; "Triumph in Moral Education," *Newsweek*, November 17, 1941), or a glamorous viewpoint ("Styled by Students," *Collier's*, September 13, 1947; "Every Girl Has a Talent for Beauty," *Ladies' Home Journal*, August 1943). According to Beth L. Bailey, *Mademoiselle* "frequently praised Stephens College for its 'practical' orientation in the 1940s and 1950s."[45] James Wood, president of Stephens College, published polemical articles throughout the decade in *Woman's Home Companion*.[46] And that was the perfect place since Wood had created a kind of woman's magazine finishing school. Like *Ladies' Home Journal*, Stephens College was an exuberant juxtaposition of morality and style; the women were required to take rigorous courses in Bible study at the same time that they learned about fashion and self-beautification. The college also included trips around the country and abroad, and—as if all this were not eccentric enough—it conducted a flying school with eighteen college-owned planes.

The flying school for women helps the college seem both cutting-edge and patriotic. The 1944 *Collier*'s article "Campus in the Sky" shows how well Stephens fits into mainstream American culture at the time.[47] During World War II, stories about flyers and airplanes were enormously popular; this same issue of *Collier's* has a column called "Wing Talk," illustrated by a woman holding a plane deicer (8), a mystery by Mignon G. Eberhart titled "Wings of Fear" (the wings are airplane wings), a cartoon where a plane tunnels underground to escape a crash ("Boy! I was worried there for a moment" [54]), and a full-page ad for airplane manufacturer Curtiss Wright (motto: "Look to the Sky, America!" [65]). A similar swath of aircraft would be sighted in most other popular magazines. Meanwhile, many newspapers ran an adventure comic strip called *Flyin' Jenny*, starring a brave female pilot. Hence the Stephens College flying students ring all the right bells in 1944, and the *Collier's* picture story (twelve photographs in all) can show the women learning to fly planes and fix engines, as well as lounging around on dorm beds. Stephens College appears to have been invented for the sake of a 1940s magazine article.[48]

Stephens College faculty were no ivory tower shut-ins, and they helped to keep the college current in the public's mind. I have already noted the series of articles by President Wood published in the *Woman's Home Companion*. Henry Bowman also contributed a handful of articles to popular journals. In his 1945 article for the *American*, "Are Girls becoming the Pursuers?," Bowman inveighs against modern "huntress tactics"; he hopes that women will wait for a man to make the first move, while in the meantime she can "make herself a still more vibrant and appealing person."[49] In a later article for the *American*, "Looks that Men Like," coauthored with the chairman of the Personal Appearance Department, Priscilla Scott, Bowman and Scott opine that "men want women who look like women, clearly and unmistakably."[50] This article is illustrated with numerous photos of Stephens College women primping. One photo is captioned: "Test: Every Sunday morning Stephens girls, leaving church, pass in review before a line-up of critical University of Missouri men. It's an old college custom."[51] And not just a college custom, but an encapsulation of 1940s society. As the women exit church in order to pass this "test" administered by the masculine gaze, they prepare for a world that ranks physical measurements over everything else. All in all, by using their female students as visual examples, the Stephens College professors have made an unusually coercive contribution to patriarchal culture.

But Stephens College provided more than a photo opportunity for magazines; the school acquired real academic prestige in some circles. Articles in the *New York Times*, for example, helped to legitimate the college in the public eye. The *New York Times* did not treat Stephens College as an oddball finishing school, but instead included it often in general surveys of college life. The school promoted itself vigorously through various institutes, conferences, faculty speeches, and pronouncements, and the *New York Times* often covered these proceedings.[52] The *Times* not only kept track of President Wood's numerous speeches, but it also reported on the college's response to war, new courses offered at the school, trips the students took abroad, and talks given by its professors. The *New York Times* covered a 1941 radio program in which a Vassar College student debated a Stephens College student on the topic of marriage versus career. The paper covered reports from the College's Institute for Consumer Education. A long Sunday article was devoted to a recent Stephens College hiring coup—Maude Adams ("Then and Now—Maude Adams: The Most Glamorous and Enigmatic Figure of the American Stage Thirty Years Ago Is Still a Creature of Mystery").[53] For the most part, the newspaper refrains from evaluating the college's curriculum, although one article does say that the college has "developed a program of general education for women which today is emulated by many schools and colleges throughout the nation."[54]

The respectful tone the *New York Times* adopted toward Stephens College has something to do, one supposes, with the fact that the college's graduates made frequent appearances in the paper's society pages. During the 1940s, several hundred engagement notices announce the imminent marriage of one Stephens College graduate after another. Although only a junior college in Missouri, Stephens had built itself into an Ivy-League–class finishing school, the Yale of marital studies. Where other colleges might keep track of how many graduates went to medical or law school, Stephens College kept track of how many of its graduates were quickly married.

With these kinds of courses and with the college's stated goals in mind, we might have difficulty understanding how so many could take the school seriously as an academic institution. But the school was treated respectfully not only by much of the media, but also by much of academia. The school positioned itself as a "progressive" school, which made it part of a broad movement in the early twentieth century that emphasized experiential learning. With intellectual support from the writings of John Dewey, progressive schools claimed to take a more student-centered approach to education. Theoretically the female student wanted training that would be more relevant to her experiential future as a housewife and mother. While this sounds good, we can see that Stephens College is, after all, a male-centered institute dedicated to foisting predisposed ideas about gender roles and sexuality onto young women.

One of the key figures at Stephens College was Henry Bowman, chairman of the Division of Home and Family in the Department of Marriage Education. With marriage as a stated main goal of both students and institution, it was Bowman—not the airplanes—that made Stephens College what it was. It was his discipline that influenced what Friedan called the "sex-directed educators." His well-respected textbook thus merits our close consideration.

Bowman did not consider that "marital studies" was a quaintly dogmatic appendage to what was otherwise a charm school. On the contrary, he saw himself as an experienced researcher at the cutting-edge of a developing academic discipline. At a 1942 conference he criticized courses in marital relations taught at other colleges by professors who consider the subject "a sideline rather than a profession." According to the *New York Times*, "he deplored the attempts of some institutions to whip up marriage courses in four or five lectures."[55] Bowman conceived of his discipline as one that required the same need for research and experience as any division of science or humanities. Indeed, the expert in marriage will need to bravely cross many disciplinary boundaries; "he will eventually need to be familiar with certain aspects of sociology, psychology, biology, hygiene, obstetrics, consumer problems, economics, and dietetics."[56]

The marriage course at Stephens College, like most courses on marriage, would include some form of sex education. The "one major objective" of such a course is "to give instruction and guidance in meeting the premarital and marital problems of normal young people."[57] In practice, this would break down into topics such as "acceptable standards of conduct" during "courtship and engagement" and "an extended consideration of personality adjustment," which includes a discussion of "the role of sex in marriage."[58] There is a "unit of discussion designed to develop healthy attitudes toward sex" in which "an effort is made to bring the problems of sex into proper perspective, but without unnecessary and superfluous detail."[59] Due to the sensitivity of the topics, free discussion is encouraged, after which "evidences of embarrassment, fear, and emotional stress soon begin to disappear."[60] An important element of pedagogy at Stephens College involves individual counseling, and the article sets forth a list of common discussion topics (broken engagement, parents' divorce, "how can I be sure?"), in addition to helpful hints for potential counselors ("the counselor must learn to listen").[61] Bowman calculates that 4,000 girls have taken the class in the past twelve years, while in his academic obituary he was credited with having "privately counseled over 3,500 students during his teaching career."[62] The marriage course at Stephens College used Bowman's *Marriage for Moderns* as its core textbook, along with 2,000 pages of supplementary reading, usually drawn from current periodicals. When they are married, these women will mostly be reading magazines, so now they are taught "to read discriminatingly."[63]

Bowman's textbook contains substantial representations of female sexuality.[64] Toward the beginning of the chapter on "sex in marriage," Bowman characterizes the typical difference between male and female sexual desire:

> Women have natural sexual desire, just as men do, although it may take a somewhat different form and be aroused by different stimuli. When a woman does not experience such desire, there are two probable explanations. (1) It has been trained out of her. It has been so overlaid with inhibitions that it cannot find expression. She has built up, or has had built up for her, a wall about herself so effectively corralling natural impulses that they have ceased to demand exercise or have atrophied. (2) There has been nothing in her experience up to date to arouse her desire. She is, as we say, "unawakened." Some women remain so until their experiences with loving husbands bring to the fore an urge that they were not aware could exist. There are women who have a sexual urge but do not recognize it as such. (341)

One does not need Foucault to notice the disturbing relationship of power and knowledge in this characterization of female sexuality. The male teacher is progressive, experimental, student-centered; by providing a course in marriage, he is giving these young women what they want. As he says, "educators are responding to this awakening interest."[65] Even though the discipline of study scarcely exists, the teacher claims authority through academic investiture and citation, makes quantitative gestures toward research, coursework, and rigor (2,000 pages of reading beyond the textbook), and uses scientific language and categorization. He tells the unmarried students what they want to know and what they desire. Only a loving husband can "awaken" this desire, "as we say." "As we say"—but who is we? Presumably they are the men who awaken women into sexuality or knowledge, who give women what they want by allowing them to know what they feel.

Bowman's *Marriage for Moderns* uses all the academic, scientific authority it can command in order to reinforce a sense of ethics that is old-fashioned, not modern. Although Bowman continually gestures toward the mutual reciprocity of intimate relationships, the situations often feature a relatively strong husband and a relatively vulnerable wife. Here is one of his suggestions for the wife:

> First of all, she should realize that hers is not the only problem. Her husband has one, too, it is that of helping her to the best start and making her experience as rich as possible. In a sense he has her and her problem. She should help him as much as she can. She must also realize that she has married a man, not

> a neuter organism. He is a masculine being with strong masculine impulses. Probably, however, he has had no direct sexual experience or has had the wrong type. Most wives do not wish their husbands to have had any. (348)

As we saw in the magazine article "Looks that Men Like," Bowman has some clear (and tautological) dispositions about masculinity and femininity. Men are masculine beings who want their women to look like women. Somehow the academic at the leading edge of his field is working with the most stereotyped man (with "strong masculine impulses") and the most stereotyped woman. In this social hierarchy, the helpful, strong, virginal man has bravely to contend with not one, but two sets of problems—"in a sense he has her and her problem."

Every aspect of this discourse is built around patriarchal fantasy gilded by egalitarian rhetoric. A nice instance of fantasy is present right here: "probably, however, he has had no direct sexual experience or has had the wrong type." Like many of the marriage authorities, Bowman does not condone premarital sex.[66] But in the text, he simply wishes it away. And he knows, somehow, that wives want to wish it away, too. In his textbook, Bowman cites authorities when they are agreeable, but not when they contradict his views. Thus he says in an earlier part of the book: "The evidence is inconclusive that youth is as promiscuous as sometimes pictured by his elders, by his contemporaries, or even by himself. Undoubtedly there is more freedom between the sexes today than there was a generation or so ago. There are, however, no extensive and at the same time reliable data available. No one really knows what the present situation is. There are many guesses, many questionable deductions, many broad generalizations based upon incomplete evidence."[67] No one, therefore, can claim that premarital sex has increased over the past generation, although Bowman is nonetheless able to say that "probably [the man] has had no direct sexual experience, or he has had the wrong type." Bowman can say that because his well-researched textbook takes place in a moralizing dream world.

And what is "direct sexual experience"? Are masturbation and petting indirectly sexual? Masturbation is only mentioned once in 544 pages; it takes place during a transitional, "immature" phase that a mature individual soon outgrows (123). And Bowman does not need Kinsey to awaken him to the possibility of premarital intercourse. Other textbooks of the time wrestle with the uncertainty of the data, but are still able to say something more definite than Bowman. For example, in his textbook *Marriage and the Family* (1939), sociology professor Ray E. Baber writes: "At present, there is no way of knowing how extensive is the sex experience of young people before marriage. Some students of the subject state that there is less of it than during the 'mad twenties' following the war. Others say that it is definitely on the increase but that it is more restricted to engaged couples than formerly. At any rate, there is little doubt that premarital sex experience is more widespread than it was a generation ago, as shown by the studies by Dickinson, Terman, and others."[68] As increasingly becomes clear, Bowman aggrandizes his stature as a scientist by deploying a barrage of statistical research, but then he cherry-picks the data in order to support whatever moral point he wants to make.

Despite the scientific apparatus, Bowman's description of human sexuality is founded on an essentialist and traditionalist conception of men and women that accepts contradiction whenever necessary. Bowman deploys a wide array of physiological, psychological, and sociological data to support a traditional patriarchal system. The textbook begins with "A Point of Departure," which argues at length about the differences between men and women: "Undoubtedly there are deep-set biological reasons for this more rapid maturing of girls, but may there not also be social reasons? May it not be partly due to the fact that girls are equipped to accept the traditional feminine role in life sooner than boys are equipped to accept the traditional masculine role, which requires more vocational preparation, and that therefore girls seem to mature earlier?" (3). "Traditional" gender roles include the idea that "in courtship men assume the role of pursuer while women assume the role of pursued" (4). While men are more "pugnacious" and "competitive," women tend to be more "subtle, more indirect in their methods and in achieving their aims" (4). A woman's "subtle" approaches will extend even to her sexual behavior since "in the matter of responding to her husband's love-making a wife should and usually does resort to all the wiles and subtleties that she employed in courtship" (362).

Bowman's descriptions of sexual interaction give men the lead in sexual success and tend to make women the source of most sexual problems. Bowman raises sexuality above mere instinct by claiming that "it is an art" that "transcends the 'natural' and the physical" (346). Men seem to control the artistic process, however, since "the arousing of [a woman's] natural desire is less spontaneous than is the case with a man and depends to a great extent upon her husband, his expression of affection, his own desire, his insight, understanding, and skill as a lover" (344). Before marriage, because of women's weaker sexual desire, women have an easier time controlling a sexual situation: "the girl [has] the greater possibility of rational control" (220). But after marriage, this weak, perhaps "unawakened" desire needs a true artist—masculine, but gentle—to make the act of love a mutually gratifying success. Even when a young woman can get past her relatively weak sexual desire, her moral scruples, her fear of pain and pregnancy, her inhibitions about nakedness, the husband must still "prepare" the wife for sexual union. Here, of course, "technique is important, but not all-important" (360). Using biblical language and words from the marriage vow, Bowman asks each wife to "abandon herself to her husband, [and] to lose herself in this new experience with him" (361). Somehow Bowman knows that "a woman derives pleasure from yielding to the man she loves, a pleasure as remote from masculine experience and understanding as the physical aspect of a man's experience is remote from a woman's comprehension" (361). Masculine men—even the most artistic ones—could not possibly understand what it means to derive pleasure from yielding, although sometimes manly textbook professors can authoritatively convey to their female students the degree to which their masculine understanding is remote from their own.

In Bowman's world there is no male impotence; on the contrary, the man is somehow always prepared, ready to lead the way. Although probably a virgin, he somehow knows what to do from the very start, how to awaken a woman to her own desires. Bowman complains eloquently about the "veil of obscurantism cast about marriage and sex" in education (311). But for all the detail in some areas—like most of the day's sexologists, he recommends simultaneous orgasm as a goal—men do not seem to have erections or even penises. For a textbook that hopes to illuminate sexual obscurantism, this is an interesting, although not atypical emphasis. Men simply accumulate fluid and desire release: "There is nothing in a woman's experience quite analogous to this. She may be subject to nervous or muscular tension, but no more than a man. Because this urge for release is foreign to a woman's experience, it is impossible for her fully to understand how a man feels when his sexual impulses have been aroused" (358). While Bowman does not represent male sexual desire graphically, he does deploy metaphors. "One might say that the man is like a lake; he exhibits waves or calm" (363). Since Bowman works at the leading edge of his discipline, this binary lake-man (waves on, waves off) must be the best way to convey to young women what looms ahead in their sexual future.

By contrast, "the woman is more like an ocean; in addition to waves and calm she exhibits tides" (363). Bowman refers here not just to the cycles of a woman's menstruation, but also to the fact that "many women manifest a so-called *periodicity of sexual desire*" (363). Bowman obviously likes this idea, therefore the scientific studies are now not problematic, but "rather careful." Sexual desire for these "many" women sometimes collapses beyond a mere lack of interest to a place where "sexual union may be repugnant" (365). A husband should not draw premature conclusions about his wife during these dark times. Nor should his wife take her bitter thoughts too seriously: "No wife should conclude that her attitude toward her husband during such a period of depression or irritability is permanent or represents her 'true self.' A woman's 'true self' is what she is over a period of about twenty-eight days, not what she is at a given moment" (366).

What is of interest here is not whether the sexual cycle for women is true, but why Bowman wants it to be true. In their reactionary psychoanalytical treatise, *Modern Woman: The Lost Sex*, Ferdinand Lundberg and Marynia Farnham argue that a woman's sexual desire will always be disordered if not geared toward pregnancy. As Ethel Rosenberg noted in her *Commentary* review, this conclusion, although buttressed with scientific footnotes, becomes an old-fashioned insistence that women identify themselves primarily as mothers. Just so, Bowman cites Amram Scheinfeld's *Women and Men* (1944) when it helps his arguments, but not when Scheinfeld speculates on the possibility of a "sex cycle" in men "with prescribed periods of high and low sex feeling."[69] Scheinfeld reports on evidence for widespread masturbation among girls, as well as "many studies" that report that "young boys are in many instances sexually initiated by girls of their own age or younger."[70] But for Bowman to include these kinds of ideas would be to intrude on the clarity of his idealized plot, in which a man awakens the sexual desire of an innocent young woman on her wedding night. Bowman's attraction to the "cycle of sexual desire" in women may be ascribed to the way it recuperates—in modern language—the oldest kinds of misogynistic representations of female instability—"varium et mutabile semper femina."[71] Women are not ordered, consistent creatures like men, so we (men) need to storehouse our patience. Since Bowman's textbook arose from the practicalities of teaching courses in marriage to an entirely female audience, the "cycle of sexual desire" could also be seen as a way of allowing women to feel their antisexual feelings and still not give up on sex. A lack of desire is only temporary. The rain will fall again, desire will reawaken with the assistance of cyclical hormones and your husband's magic crop duster.

Bowman's textbook not only went through numerous editions over many years, but it also served as the basis for five McGraw-Hill Text-Films on marriage. In the decade of the picture story, the text-film was the logical and modern outcome for Bowman's copious text. The audio-visual age of pedagogy was here, and colleges began to collect A/V materials for the most up-to-date teaching methods.[72] In May 1950 the Protestant Council of New York in New York City debuted the five films, which were then made available for rental to churches, civic organizations, youth groups, and community forums throughout the country.[73] According to the *New York Times*, Bowman gave a talk in which he "deplored the fact that '$2 and fifteen minutes are all that is needed to set up a home under the law,' whereas long training, education, understanding, and patience are required to make a successful marriage."[74] The five films—*This Charming Couple* (1950), *Choosing for Happiness* (1950), *Marriage Today* (1950), *It Takes All Kinds* (1950), and *Who's Boss* (1950)—were deemed effective enough to be offered as "correlated films" for sale fifteen years later with the fifth edition (1965) of Bowman's *Marriage for Moderns*. I close this section by looking at the way that female desire is represented in these instructional films.

Although they approach the problem of marriage from a seeming variety of angles, the films are basically repetitious in their advice. The films assume that marriage is difficult and toilsome—not easy. A successful marriage is the product of labor, not romance. To counteract the rising divorce rate, four of the films provide premarital wisdom. The moral of these films is "look before you leap," think clearly about what you are doing, do not let love and dreams get in the way of a cold, hard look at whom are you marrying. Make realism, practicality, and future responsibility your guiding principles, rather than infatuation and present pleasure. As the couples interact with one another, they learn one more basic theme—you cannot change the other person, you can only change yourself. Since the films all argue that prospective brides and grooms need to think long and hard about marriage, they have the effect of justifying elaborate coursework in marriage. As McGraw-Hill Text-Films, they not only supplement the text, they work like advertisements, by arguing the need for a textbook.

Affiliated Film Producers, a New York City company founded in 1946, produced these five films.[75] Well-respected filmmakers such as Irving Jacoby and Willard Van Dyke appear in the writing and production credits for these films. Van Dyke and Jacoby had recently produced *The Photographer* (1948), a well-received documentary on Edward Weston. Alexander Hammid, best known to contemporary cinephiles as codirector of Maya Deren's *Meshes of the Afternoon* (1943), directed three of these films. Hammid would win widespread critical praise for his film *Angry Boy* (1950), which was scripted by Jacoby and produced under the auspices of the Mental Health Film Board. These films for McGraw-Hill, then, are produced by men at the forefront of their profession.[76]

With men such as Hammid and Jacoby at the helm, these films do look better than comparable educational films. The Affiliated Film Producers make films that are technically and aesthetically more appealing than movies produced by the education film factory at Coronet Films.[77] All five films were not only described in academic journals as teaching resources, but they were also given film reviews in both the *Saturday Review of Literature* and the *Nation*. Yet despite their heightened production values, the films stay on the surface level of sensible problem-solving. In the most interesting film, *The Charming Couple*, one feels the tension between talented, expressive filmmakers and the textbook manufacturer that has hired them. Not surprisingly, whenever this tension appears in these films—and it is relatively rare—it is always resolved on the side of the textbook and its messages.

Cecile Starr reviewed educational films critically—engaging them at a level much beyond the usual plot summary—and she made an interesting point about gender roles in these films. Backing up her claim with case-by-case examples, she writes, "One tendency throughout the films which bothered this reviewer is the fact that the leading women in the films seem excessively dominant."[78] The films make many overt claims about equal responsibility in marriage, so at first it seems Starr is reacting to female characters who express themselves forcefully, who stand up for themselves. But Starr has got it right; the women are often characterized as pushy and ambitious rather than strong. The omniscient voice-overs claim that each partner in a relationship is equally responsible and tries to move the viewer into a more modern understanding of gender roles. In *Marriage Today*, for example, the wife keeps her fulfilling job while the husband helps her with burdensome housework. But the films still tend to scapegoat the women, as if the male voice-over cannot quite come to terms with a woman who speaks for herself.

This scapegoating is evident in *The Charming Couple*, which Starr calls "a most provocative introduction to marriage problems."[79] Directed by Willard Van Dyke and scripted by Irving Jacoby, the film is thoughtfully constructed and shot. The film begins with the couple, Winnie and Ken, in a divorce court, and ends with their marriage. At the beginning, the voice-over asks, "Whose fault was it?" In a long speech at the end, the voice-over doles out blame equally. They each idealized the other, unable to see their partner for who they really were. "Each is a dream in the other's mind," says the voice. Hence this was a marriage "doomed to fail."

Yet once they were in love, and the body of the film shows us the signs of trouble, which we see but they do not. And despite the voice-over's balanced judgment in the end, the film seems intent on making Winnie much less sympathetic than Ken. She is indeed "excessively dominant," as Starr says; she "is the girl who always gets what she wants, including Ken."[80] Winnie has ambitious dreams for her professor boyfriend. She wants him to be “famous” so she can live an exciting life. What is more, she tells him that she will not “play ghost to your Hamlet.”

To give a more objective look at the main characters, the film contains two sequences where secondary characters reflect on Winnie and Ken. The girl who talks about Winnie says that she was always “reaching for something beyond her reach,” and that she “made things go the way she wanted them to.” The boy who reflects on Ken is concerned about his dreamy informality, that he is so “impersonal” and absorbed in his projects that he could never really belong to anyone else. But Winnie comes off as much more abrasive. When Ken invites two of his “East Coast” friends to dinner, Winnie becomes rude and defensive and ends up breaking up with Ken. After they reconcile, she runs the show and makes Ken agree to a whole set of conditions. *The Coordinator*, a conservative academic journal on family life, later published a series of study guides for these and other marriage films. And even to their writer it was obvious that, despite the balance of blame divided up at the end, “many times Winnie receives more severe criticism than Ken.”[81] The film does not want us to like this pushy woman.

The films represent women as “excessively dominant” because the filmmakers do not know how otherwise to represent female desire. The filmmakers want to show a woman who wants things and who is the equal partner to a man, but circulating through the narrative there can still be felt the traditionally gendered ideology in which men desire and women respond to that desire. *Choosing for Happiness* allows the ideology to come through more clearly than the other more circumspect films. In this film Eve tells Mary about all her possible boyfriends, where nothing ever seems to work out; why is that? In perhaps the most telling moment in all of the films, Eve recalls her encounter with Arthur, the math geek. They sit on the ground, birds chirping in the background; Arthur has made a circle out of little stones, while Eve has made a heart.

> ARTHUR: You’re different from other girls.
>
> EVE: That’s what you think.
>
> ARTHUR: You’re smarter, you’re almost like a man.
>
> EVE: Oh no, I’m very much the woman.
>
> ARTHUR: I don’t think of you that way at all.

> EVE: I don't get you at all. You think math is exciting, but you really ought to get yourself straightened out. You'd be surprised at how many things are just as exciting as math.

> ARTHUR: You don't think that there's anything wrong with me do you?

Eve's character throughout is unpleasantly pushy and judgmental, but here the film allows her a self-righteous putdown. Because there really is something wrong with Arthur. For Arthur is not attracted to girls and that's about the worst mistake a man can make in this "modern" world. It is not just Eve who identifies Arthur's problem, but so does her more objective interlocutor, Mary. Mary takes time in her concluding survey to note that Arthur will "need some help" in order to change. That the film needs to put Arthur in this film at all—and then skewer him—shows how important it is for these productions to insist on traditional gender categories.

Thus while Arthur is openly criticized for being insufficiently male, Eve is criticized for her willfulness, that is, for being insufficiently female. The dramatic crisis comes when Mary reveals to Eve her true character, that she wants what she always wants, for people to do what she tells them to do. "That's terrible," says Eve, offended when Mary diagnoses her, but we agree with Mary since we know it is the truth. Provocatively, Mary has told Eve that the best match of all would be John, because at last here is someone Eve can't boss around. John has said to Eve that "someone ought to take you across his knee and give you a good spanking," and the movie wants us to agree. That way there would be a little more manliness in the world, and a little more womanliness, too, now that Eve's bossiness was under tighter control.

The women are scapegoated in these films partly because of Bowman's conservative textbook, but partly because the male artists who made the films cannot transcend deeply held attitudes about women's sexuality. *The Charming Couple* shows Winnie making the first ominous mistake when she flinches from Ken's touch on her hand. "Ow, Ken, the ring, you squeeze so hard," she says, pulling away, then admiring the ring. "Isn't it rich looking and unusual?" she says. The film has barely begun and Winnie has already been accused of trading natural affection for seductive glitter. By contrast, the film gives Ken both a natural air and a real control over that nature. In the most artful sequence of the film, Ken goes far into the rural countryside to record a folk ballad for his scholarship. For a moment, the movie is showing, not selling, and we listen to a woman sing deep in the woods.

As Ken records the woman with his microphone and taping equipment, this sequence may be read as unconscious allegory on the part of the filmmakers. Ken is Thoreau with technology, allowed to connect with both simplicity and complexity, nature and art. The film registers his desire as natural and honest. By contrast, Winnie's desire comes across as distracted and ambitious. Even though the film wants us to see them as equally subjective, equally dreamers, the film, just like Ken the scholar, uses female desire for its own more important male projects.

Willard Van Dyke, the director of *The Charming Couple*, explained his use of nonprofessional actors in these marriage films. Nonprofessionals, "with their untrained spontaneity, can often approach truth more closely than any except the most proficient professionals."[82] Van Dyke interviewed potential actors for ten days, then visited intensely with those finally cast since "when he knows them well he can help them to find the things within themselves which can be used to create the feeling of truth so essential to the film."[83] To talk about the cinematic "truth" this way seems rather pompous from a hired hand—however celebrated—on an instruction film about marriage. But Van Dyke elevates himself as director into a position where he can help his actors and actresses do their best.

> By now the director knew a great many such stories about the actor. He might know that the girl who was playing her first love scene had never kissed a boy until she had gone home for her Christmas vacation that year. He could caution the crew against kidding her and he could sympathize with, and use (if it fitted the script), her flushed embarrassment after she had kissed the handsome young man who played the scene with her.[84]

Van Dyke motivates a male actor by asking him to recall a "particularly difficult problem in his daily life." A standard approach, no doubt. But with the female actor, Van Dyke uses the actual biography of her sexual desire in order to push the film closer to the truth. Van Dyke also exhibits his leadership by cautioning the all-male crew against "kidding her" about it. Admirable foresight and restraint on his part. But the crew does not need to kid the first-time actress about her desire, since the film's narrative will not just mock but sabotage female desire.

When taking a final overview of our brief pass through Stephens College, we can see that the different elements—the flying school, the marital studies program, and the educational films—are all joined under a banner of modernity. The airplanes should not be understood as the popular magazine front for intellectually empty classes in child-rearing and personal appearance. On the contrary, each element represents exactly the same impulse toward contemporary and noticeable relevance. The school basks in newness, reinvention, the latest, the up-to-date. The school's progressive identity rests in experiment and innovation; the airplane school comes into existence at exactly the right time; Bowman's scrupulously researched, interdisciplinary book is aimed at "moderns"; the college extends its substantial interest in the latest audio-visual pedagogy and, with the help of talented directors and producers, makes Bowman's book into text-films.

The obvious irony of all this is that Bowman's "modernism" is so relentlessly old-fashioned. As noted, the psychological and sociological references are used in a completely disingenuous manner, in order to bolster whatever ominously conservative point Bowman needs to make. The section on "Petting," for example, threatens young women with all the same disasters as any magazine advice column: "Some girls pet as a price for popularity" (217); "A girl may acquire a reputation for petting" (218). No scientists uphold these points, however, because they come from *Ladies' Home Journal*. Bowman's committed interest in the modern world can be gleaned from the example he uses to show that "petting is much like a squirrel cage":

> Petting tends to become like riding on a merry-go-round, something that the old Negro refused to do. "No, suh," he said, "I been a-watchin' that Jones boy ride around all afternoon and he allus gits off right where he gits on and I say to him, 'Johnny you done spent your money, but where've you been?' " (218)

In 1948 a more "modern" approach to this argument might not have used a foolish old black man talking in dialect as a way to make young white women reflect on their sex lives.

The less ironic conclusion to be drawn from these examples would be to consider the fictions that the patriarchy generates in order to preserve its own power. In the end, it does not so much matter whether what Stephens College does is really new or really old. The story that Stephens College tells is one where it answers a need; they claim that they are relevant and up-to-date not in order to follow or even create a trend, but rather because they imagine to their audience that they provide the answers to society's questions. In this understanding, Bowman has little to tell us about the actuality of female sexual desire, whether it is masculine, periodic, or requires awakening. But Bowman's giant textbook tells us much about the contours of male desire, whose need for power and control is visible in every airplane, yearbook, press release, and counseling session. We answer America's need, says the college. Yet the patriarchal institution's answer is to mold student desire into a shape of its own liking. The female student is made to want what the patriarchy wants of her.

8

The Power and the Horror

Male and Female Cultural Spaces

This penultimate chapter looks at the way that female desire is represented in cultural spaces conventionally assigned to either male or female. Such designated spaces are for women radio daytime serials, confession magazines such as *Modern Romances* and *True Confessions*, and women's magazines such as *Mademoiselle* and *Ladies' Home Journal*.[1] For male cultural spaces, I survey men's magazines such as *Esquire* and *True*, spicy detective stories, and paperbacks that promise sex. Male cultural spaces are relatively more permeable. For example, few editors or advertisers imagine that men are listening to soap operas or reading the recipes in a woman's magazine. Female cultural spaces are fairly well contained. But male cultural space is more porous. For instance, both men and women read those provocative paperbacks with the increasingly sexy covers. As I suggest more than once over the course of this chapter, male cultural space is not conceptually parallel to female cultural space, since in a thoroughgoing patriarchy *all* general magazines are potentially men's magazines.

When taking a wide view of 1940s culture, there are numerous places where we perceive strong boundaries, where it is clear that editors and audiences have agreed to separate cultural spheres. Such a boundary is apparent, for example, when examining movie magazines. The best-selling movie magazines are fan magazines built around gossip, photographs, and romance. Indeed, popular movie magazines are aimed directly at women and contain all the same ads for lipstick, hair curlers, deodorant, and tampons found in magazines more straightforwardly labeled as such (*Woman's Day*,

Woman's Home Companion). The cover of the July 1949 *Movieland* hypes its contents using the same rhetoric as romance magazines such as *Screen Romances* or *True Confessions*; "Hollywood's Sensational New Romances" and "Confessions of a Cowboy" woo a female consumer. *Photoplay*, which in 1942 claims the "largest circulation of any screen magazine," is unambiguously organized as a woman's magazine, with the table of contents divided into "Glamour" and "Fashion, Beauty Notes and Departments."[2] Articles in the June 1942 *Photoplay* look at Hedy Lamarr's recent engagement, Myrna Loy's marital breakup, the divorce of Anne Shirley and John Payne, Joan Fontaine's "confession of a girl who didn't want to live," and an "exposé of the personal life of the Bill Holdens." These movie magazines cordon off a female space defined by glamour and romance, a space where many male readers would feel uncomfortable and foreign.[3]

Numerous other movie magazines are clearly aimed at men, although these do not rank among top sellers. In their blatantly sexed-up approach, these magazines are allied with spicy detective pulps and with the scores of ribald humor magazines.[4] These film magazines multiply cheesecake photographs until the result is what contemporaries called a girlie magazine.[5] The spicy pulp magazines, which are discussed in the next section, were largely put out of business in 1943; the cheesecake movie magazine, *Film Fun*, met its demise at exactly the same time.[6] But unlike the bloodlust savagery of the spicy detective magazines, which make their worlds wholly from murder and animal lust, *Film Fun* crosses lines of acceptability by accumulation rather than mayhem.

Film Fun is an obsessive scrapbook of cheesecake photos where any single photograph could have been found in most any newspaper. It is the sheer pathological barrage that makes the difference. Add in their "regular Showgirl Revue," which is not obviously a department of film, and the salacious intent becomes clear. In the March 1941 issue, the most instructive (for our purposes) article is "3 Dears for Love"; it shows Kay Winters, Jane Holm, and Susan Hayward jumping around and lying about on the beach.[7] Another publisher might have used just one photograph, but *Film Fun* uses four, including one where the women hop around ecstatically with stick horses between their legs. These women are not movie stars; Winters and Holm would never make a movie, and Susan Hayward had only small parts to this point. Yet they are designated as "Movie Queens" since the "Warner Brothers' personality department" provided them. It is illuminating, then, to consider that Warner Brothers thinks that providing a well-known skin magazine with more female bodies counts as a good marketing device. And why not? In this compressed sexual universe, where deodorant ads and cheesecake all amount to the same thing, it does not matter where the studio's girls go or what they do when they get there.

Thus the gendered and sexualized boundaries blur on and off. *Screen Romances* and *Film Fun* are clearly intended for female and male audiences respectively. "Glamour" photography and gossip columns are held to be distinct from "cheesecake" photography and ribald jokes. Women want more romance and narrative; men want things direct and even dirty. But these boundaries are fragile. One woman's "glamour" shot is another man's "cheesecake" photo. The fact that a film studio willingly supplies female bodies to *Film Fun* shows that there is often not much distance between everyday glamour and borderline pornography. Male sexual desire runs through everything, which means that the same "sexy" photograph can appear with equal probability in a daily newspaper (sometimes with surprisingly lewd captions), in *Look: America's Family Magazine*, in *Movieland*, or in *Esquire*. Even though male and female cultural spaces throw up barriers, 1940s sexual space is compressed and repetitive. In what follows I will once again collect examples of female sexual desire that emerge in a culture organized tyrannically around the centrality of male sexual desire.

Measuring the Patriarchs: Men's Magazines, Spicy Pulp, and Paperbacks

By 1950 the concept of and the empirical history of the "magazine for men" were relatively clear. By 1956, with the publication of Theodore Bernard Peterson's *Magazines in the Twentieth Century*, the genre and genealogy had been made explicit. In brief, the history of the American "magazine for men" goes like this. Since *Esquire* was for so long nearly unique as a cultural artifact, it was not necessarily the case that there were "men's magazines" in the 1930s. But when *True* and *Argosy* reinvent themselves around 1945, the genre of "men's magazines" is made evident. A "magazine for men" is not just a girlie magazine or a spicy detective magazine, although those magazines are intended for men. *Esquire* and *True*, parallel to women's magazines, create a full-scale masculine lifestyle that requires a range of consumable products. Since more players have entered the game, *Time* magazine can outline the post-*Esquire* battle of *True* and *Argosy* in "A Man's World" (2–6–50).[8] Now Peterson's history can provide a detailed evolution of the way that *True* and *Argosy* challenged *Esquire* in the late forties, attended by numerous postwar adventure magazines. In my necessarily brief overview, I stay with the standard view that *Esquire*, *True*, and *Argosy* constitute the main men's magazines during the 1940s. But first I will say a few more things about how *most* magazines can be considered men's magazines.

Peterson observes that many magazines in the 1930s and 1940s were aimed at a largely male audience: *Field and Stream*, *Outdoor Life*, *Popular Mechanics*.[9] In a 1950 trade article on men's magazines, "For Men Only," the author adds "outdoors," "mechanical," detective, and fraternal (that is, publications aimed at the American Legion or the Elks) magazines to the basic triumvirate of *Esquire*, *True*, and *Argosy*.[10]

But from our contemporary perspective, many of the large-scale magazines can also be seen as men's magazines. The three most successful magazines published by Henry Luce—*Time*, *Life*, and *Fortune*—could all be regarded as magazines overwhelmed by a male point of view. Since it focuses on industry, business, and finance, *Fortune* necessarily portrays an almost entirely masculine universe.[11] *Time*'s trademark clipped, cynical style radiates masculine hard-headedness. And even though *Life* seemed out on every middle-class family's coffee table, it could picture sex and violence as sensationally as any men's adventure magazine.

In his 1949 history, *Magazines in the United States*, James Playsted Wood summed up *Life*'s successful "formula": "lavish use of sex pictures and of gruesome pictures displaying slaughter, executions, [and] strewn corpses."[12] Spicy detective pulps were described in exactly the same terms. But since this was journalistic realism, not pulp sensationalism, *Life*'s photographers were allowed to present the graphic horrors of war, as well as peacetime and stateside bloodshed of every variety, all under the banner of education and information. In the August 12, 1946, issue, which contains a picture story showing how Weegee photographs a corpse (using a dummy), an article called "Blood Runs in Palestine Violence" includes a photograph of the hand of a dead victim protruding from rubble, while several pages later, "Bolivian Revolt" shows the "Dictator Villarroel" covered in blood, hanging from a lamppost.[13] Meanwhile *Life* used its market-changing emphasis on pictures to convey countless seminude chorus girls and models into American living rooms. As Richard Rovere wrote in 1944, "By dignifying semi-pornography as sociological inquiry, *Life* brought the undraped female out of the *Police Gazette* and into the family journal."[14] Compared to *True* and *Argosy*, there is less emphasis on bear hunting and shark fishing, but *Life*, *Time*, and *Fortune* equally conspire to produce a hard-edged masculine persona suitable for life in a violent and voluptuous world.

But of course it was *Esquire*, not *Time* or *Life*, which most famously and methodically aimed its content at men during the 1940s. Although its profits began to tumble at the end of the 1930s, the war brought *Esquire* back to the top. Soldiers clamored for Varga girl pinups, which appeared for the first time in October 1940, and the magazine gained nationwide notoriety during a long obscenity suit filed by the U.S. Postal Service.[15] The Varga pinups were the center of public attention, and radio comics added them to their repertoire of sexual innuendo. Meanwhile the magazine created an entire habitat for male sexuality that went far beyond pinups. From the fiction to the articles, from the art galleries to the advertisements, *Esquire* built a detailed portrait of a virile, masculine lifestyle.

Esquire is by far the most culturally schizophrenic of the men's magazines. Like *True* and *Argosy*, it feeds male readers a constant diet of sports, adventuresome travel, position papers on male and female roles, plus pictures of attractive women in varying states of undress. In addition to sometimes multiple pinup paintings are numerous photographs of glamorous women and a barrage of sex-centered cartoons. But juxtaposed with *Esquire*'s onslaught of buxom nurses, secretaries, gold diggers, surprised bathers, and knowing fan dancers—whose multitude far outnumbered any such in competing magazines—was its lineup of high-culture gurus. F. Scott Fitzgerald ran Pat Hobby stories throughout 1940, and literary heavyweights made regular appearances (although their stories were usually not too heavy). Gilbert Seldes had his regular column, "The Lively Arts," while the most famous Broadway critic of them all, George Jean Nathan, held down the theater department. Starting in 1941, Yale Professor William Lyon Phelps penned a book review column that was more likely to talk about Thomas Gray than Thomas Wolfe.[16] The music columns, too, both by Carleton Smith, rarely got around to pop. The cultural distance between the critics talking about poetry and opera on the one hand and the cartoons showing old men chasing naked women around a desk on the other is enormous and often looks more like the *New Yorker* than any other magazine for men.[17] The sexy cartoons by the *New Yorker*'s Peter Arno are close kin to those by Barbara Shermund in *Esquire*. That the sophisticated *New Yorker* and the masculinist *Esquire* have this much in common shows the degree to which most magazines are, after all, men's magazines.

Hence we can read *Esquire*'s cultural heterogeneity in an emblematic way. Instead of viewing *Esquire*'s masculine space as one curtained off from the mainstream, like men drinking beers in the dark, we can recognize the extent to which *Esquire* makes the open-air claim that men's culture is, in essence, all culture. With its big-shot professors and its burlesque humor, *Esquire* does look something like the *New Yorker*. But we might also say that *Esquire* looks like a good deal of mainstream media. *Esquire*'s breadth of culture resembles those radio variety shows whose "variety" intends to represent an expansive sense of American cultural identity, from the heights of highbrow to the dirty lows of lowbrow. *Command Performance* was only heard by soldiers overseas and was thus a kind of radio men's magazine for soldiers; a typical program would follow racy banter by Ann Sheridan with a Chopin recital by José Iturbi. High culture not only provides moral cover for the ribald jokes, but taken together they also proudly stand for the breadth of American taste. The popular *Radio Hall of Fame* (1943–1946) was broadcast domestically; hosted by music critic Deems Taylor—who also provided learned guidance through Disney's *Fantasia* (1940)—it methodically juxtaposed dimwitted comedy routines with long selections from Broadway plays or poetry readings. *Esquire*'s masculinist culture is not subterranean, but capacious, and displays an American culture that is proudly and violently patriarchal.

Esquire becomes especially useful as a critical tool insofar as it makes patriarchal violence so transparent. Other magazines, films, and radio programs are also culturally capacious; they want to ring the bell of high art even as they parade out more dancing girls. But *Esquire* combines its cultural ambitions with an entirely blatant and methodically worked-out misogyny. *Esquire* thus allows us to see the patriarchy in all of its unapologetically imperial splendor.

The most notorious element of *Esquire* world-making is the Varga centerfold. In the editorial pages, male readers would evaluate the salient qualities of each Varga girl. The pictures come with captions and a little poem, but with captions like "Red Means Go" (December 1941) and solicitous poems, whatever the woman says is not likely to obtrude on a male viewer's fantasy. Over the course of this book, I have often highlighted the appraising, measuring quality in the 1940s male gaze. With a clarity obtained from unapologetic masculinism, *Esquire* views its pictorial enterprise in exactly these terms. In the November 1940 issue, *Esquire* promotes December's Varga calendar as follows: "These girls, whose aspects paralyze men's reason, and whose subtle gestures inflict never-closing wounds on the tissue of dreams, have been carefully collected, examined, unveiled, and tattooed for your express pleasure. They have even been classified, in a rough way, according to the season."[18] Revealingly, *Esquire*'s ad reads the measuring, categorizing male gaze as a direct response to male sexual anxiety. It is as if the calendrical ordering of women serves as a balm to the sexual violence that women unleash in men. Hence women must not only be seen, they must also be surveilled and measured. The title for the advertisement—cast in font half a page tall—says everything: "Varga Girl, or A Yardstick for Living."

Esquire keeps female agency and desire under strict supervision. Although the magazine ambitiously surveys vast amounts of cultural terrain, from literature's latest to a cutting-edge interest in jazz, women's voices are rarely allowed to appear in any department. Women are allowed to speak very occasionally in letters to the editor. Even more rarely women are allowed into the articles, as when, in April 1942, an anonymous "herself" responds to some masculinist positions set forth by "himself." From 1940 to 1945, I count no articles or stories of any kind authored by named women, and only one story, written by a man, takes a woman's point of view, Mark Schorer's "The Long Embrace."[19] Schorer's story begins with a car accident and concludes with the woman's death, as she swims toward the abyss "with infinite pleasure."[20] In concluding italics that signal a perspective outside the main story's point of view, a male medical voice sums up: "some want to live, some don't." Thus a male perspective is restored, after all, to help us understand that this woman was so weak, so confused, that she willed herself to death in language ordinarily reserved for sexual desire. If this is what female desire looks like—confused and self-destructive—then it is good that *Esquire* does not work to provide more of it.

Women are allowed to talk in their own voices only under carefully manufactured conditions. Women speak, for example, in paragraph-long boxes that accompany "pictorial features." Here, next to large glamorous photographs, *Esquire* may allow the model to say a few things, invariably about men. So Pat Boyd, in the "American Beauties, Eastern Style" series, says: "I like men who smile a lot (makes you think they're enjoying your company) and who have nice eyes and large hands, preferably manicured."[21] Such comments support the idea that women evaluate men with the same kind of obsessive but superficial analysis that men perform on women. The women may complain about men, as does Chili Williams, one of the decade's most famous pinup models: "My pet peeve is the man who has a preconceived notion of what kind of person I am and stubbornly refuses to change his mind after he gets to know me."[22] But if in their allotted paragraphs these women become unruly, the *Esquire* editor can bring them back under control. The little columns always end with an overview of the woman's "vital statistics," carried out to an accuracy of half an inch. Pat Boyd's vitals are: "Age: 20. Height: 5'6" with heels. Weight: 105. Bust: 32. Waist: 22. Hips: 33 1/2. Hair: Chestnut. Eyes: Green." The concluding statistics once again serve to put the attractively photographed woman in her objectified, barely human place. If the woman still seems too threatening, *Esquire* can drive one more pin through the butterfly. The description of Chili Williams ends: "Favorite indoor sport: talking."

In these ways, *Esquire* methodically reveals the violent misogyny at the heart of the male gaze. "Methodically" is the right word because *Esquire* puts down women as often as it pins them up. From our interpretive vantage point, the implied misogyny—such as when *Esquire* prints picture after picture of women without regard for what they think—is overt enough. But *Esquire* makes sure to include regular and straightforward attacks on women using every stereotype known to men. Women talk too much, women drive badly, women want to trap men into sexless marriages. With a hearty endorsement of the sexual double standard, *Esquire*'s masculinist ethics allow men their freedom, even in marriage. "He does not go out of his way to seek extra-marital experience, but will not promise always to dodge them."[23] Wives are responsible for much of the world's misery, as attractive young women age in horrible ways ("From Babe to Battle-Axe").[24] Since *Esquire*'s masculine privilege is unbounded, and since women older than 24 seem unbearable, it is surprising that there are not more models like "Little Sister Pin-Up," who is only 15 years old (vital statistics also provided).[25] The ideal wife, according to Parke Cummings in "Specifications for Superwife," is one who completely understands how a man does business and who he hangs around with. Since everyone knows that no married woman would behave this generously, the piece is supposed to be funny. In the end, *Esquire*'s two fantasies are the same: the dream of the voluptuous woman is also the dream of the invisible woman. "Superwife then turned up the radio so her husband could hear the prizefight better, and vanished into thin air."[26]

Two recently transformed magazines, *Argosy* and *True: The Man's Magazine*, challenged *Esquire*'s hold on the men's magazine market during the mid-1940s. Both evolved from sleazy pulps into tamer presenters of a masculine lifestyle.[27] The new, more restrained look was commercially successful, although these magazines still created masculinity by sexist and racist means. In *True* there are the usual sorts of manly subjects: hunting and fishing, sports, treasure hunting and adventure, gambling and drinking. A western cowboy emphasis is often linked to tough-guy racism, such as when a border story is hyped with the blurb: "Kill a Texan, did he? They'd get the little Mex . . ." or when an illustration shows an expressionless white man on a horse lassoing a pop-eyed black man.[28] As a change of pace, the magazine encourages its readers to identify with a nonwhite hero in its article about King Ibn Saud, who is a "giant," has 250 wives, and is therefore "the most virile man of modern times."[29]

This is the usual material for 1940s men's magazines, most of which have no interest in the high-class swank of *Esquire*.[30] But *True* also has a centerfold that sets it apart from most other men's magazines—from January 1945 to December 1948 it has a Petty Girl. George Petty was the centerfold artist for *Esquire* until the legendary Varga came along. Even without *Esquire*, Petty's paintings of women were highly sought after throughout the 1940s. At the end of the decade, in order to cash in on his continued notoriety, Hollywood came out with *The Petty Girl* (1950), starring Robert Cummings as George Petty. Like earlier films such as *The Powers Girl* (1943), *Cover Girl* (1944) starring Rita Hayworth, and *Pin-up Girl* (1944) starring Betty Grable, *The Petty Girl* not only trades on the culture-wide obsession with feminine glamour and modeling, it offers a chance to see what mind might lie behind the posed photo.

Although the female centerfold may offer itself as a purely nonverbal object for the masculine gaze, there is often a desire to put the woman into context, into a narrative, to give her a voice. Strippers sometimes talk and often centerfolds do too. At times the context allows the reader to know the woman more intimately; at times the context allows the reader to view the woman more imperiously. For example, the first Varga girl to appear in *Esquire* is accompanied by a poetic monologue, which reveals a changeable, mercenary mind. At first she tells her girlfriend, Irene, that she is giving up on "that guy from Butte." But when she learns that he has money, she says: "As RICH as THAT? He surely doesn't show it . . . MY GOD! I've been in love and didn't know it."[31] In contrast to Gypsy Rose Lee's stripping monologues, which reveal a witty and cultivated mind, a poem like this allows the viewer to dismiss the woman's mind and refocus back on the body. Such a woman is comical at best and stupid at worst, and this knowledge reinforces the viewer's power over her.

The Petty Girls in *True* magazine come with a "psychological analysis" by William Moulton Marston.[32] These analyses take the tradition of poems and extended captions that accompany *Esquire* pinups to another level of detail.[33] Marston was the academic author of hefty tomes on psychology (*Integrative Psychology: A Study of Unit Response* [1931]). He also made major excursions into popular culture by not only inventing the comic heroine, *Wonder Woman*, but also by writing numerous articles for women's magazines.[34] *True* magazine gives his credentials as "noted author and lecturer on female psychology." In his analyses, Marston takes the woman—named Miss Heartsnatcher, Miss Paddywhack, Miss Wrong Number, or Miss Bewitching—and provides an elaborate description of what motivates her. Then he advises men about what to do if they run into such a figure.

Although we cannot know for sure, Marston must see some connection between his work with *Wonder Woman* and his psychological analyses for *True* magazine's Petty Girls. Marston's 1944 *American Scholar* article,

"Why 100,000,000 Americans Read Comics," begins with a drawing of Wonder Woman herself; she is shown breaking chains labeled "prejudice," "prudery," and "man's superiority." The meaning of the last chain is clear because *Wonder Woman* breaks the stereotype that only men can be strong, powerful, or fast. How she breaks the chains of "prudery" or "prejudice" is less obvious. For Marston, as for many psychologists, a main goal of psychology is to combat sexual repression with sexual candor. As A. P. Sperling writes in *Psychology for the Millions* (1946): "Under the influence of psychology, twentieth century America has been having a 'coming out' party. Coquetry, prudery, and suppression have been giving way as men and women are laying bare more of their body and soul than has ever been exposed before."[35] Just as Sperling sees a montage of bathing suit photos in the *Saturday Evening Post* as a "crusade for health-giving sunshine waged against inhibiting traditions of false modesty," Marston may view his half-naked *Wonder Woman* and the all-naked Petty Girls as images aligned with sexual progressiveness. Whatever his thinking, it is his job as psychologist and educator to welcome a discussion of power and sex.

Although Marston writes from an authoritative vantage point, his comments betray considerable anxiety about the pinup girl. To demonstrate his cultural credentials, he brings in historical references; "Miss Bewitching," for example, is compared to witches confronted by "Salem Puritans in the late 1600's."[36] His ultra-accurate version of psychology is part telepathy and part astrology, and he reduces each female type to essential characteristics. Meanwhile, he uses his authoritative position to ward off her seductive powers. He sees each naked pinup as possessing the same "magical net which the Greeks ascribed to Aphrodite," although each enchantress has different motivations. "Unlike Miss She Wolf," he tells Miss Bewitching, "you don't lose interest in a captive when you've got him hog-tied." Marston's "analysis" thus amounts to an attack on the naked woman for her nakedness. "Altogether, you're too smart for your brassiere, and that's where your trouble begins." Then, once he has cut her down to size, Marston can advise male readers on how to break down each woman's dangerous power of seduction. In this case, Marston suggests that men carry her off "cave-man fashion"; "I seldom advise masculine rough stuff, but with Miss Bewitching it's your best bet for breaking her allegiance to the devil of female witching." In "Why 100,000,000 Americans Read Comics" Marston wrote, "Give men an alluring woman stronger than themselves to submit to and they'll be *proud* to become her willing slaves!"[37] But his analyses for *True* make the opposite claim because they show men fighting off powerful, alluring women. The psychologist uses his science to unveil the woman's thoughts and sexual desires, and then he uses those desires as moral evidence against her. The pinups look sexy, but these women really want power, and men must assert their continued dominance over the frozen centerfold.

Argosy continues the sports, adventure, and detective themes of *True*, but in fictional, rather than "true" stories. In his fine description of masculinity and consumerism in *Esquire*, *True*, and *Argosy*, Tom Pendergast calls *Argosy* "*True* minus the misogyny."[38] And it does seem that *Argosy* spends less time openly insulting women and that its descriptions of strong men do not always come at the expense of women. But I would not go so far as to say that *Argosy* "appealed to a man with a more refined sensibility and a greater moral sense" or that the magazine's fiction "offered a fairly enlightened view of manhood."[39] In my understanding, no men's magazine or any 1940s general magazine has particularly enlightened views on manhood: most are deeply misogynistic. The November 1947 issue of *Argosy* provides a calendar pinup girl for November, another photograph of Myra Keck, "model pin-up queen" from July ("O-o-o-o!! Can't we have more of Myra?"), and promises that December's issue will contain the story "The Cabbie, the Bum, and the Beautiful Babe" plus a "picture feature" on "Grappling Gerties" ("Glamazons of the mat, these buxom beauties toss and tussle and pull each other's hair for pay").[40] It appears that this is not yet the age of enlightenment. The only sign of female desire amidst all the sexual display comes in "Sahara She-Wolves," where archeologist-adventurer Byron de Prorok describes a tribe of sexually aggressive African women.[41] As usual, overt female desire appears pathological or laughably primitive ("As a mark of courtesy to my expedition I was assigned three delightfully unsophisticated beauties").

The U.S. Postal Service crackdown that almost shuttered *Esquire* and that caused *Argosy* and *True* to tame themselves also meant the end for "spicy" magazines.[42] "Spicy" pulp magazines flourished in the 1930s and offered themselves as a readily available form of pornography. According to pulp historian Peter Haining, "sexual desire was indulged in full for the first time."[43] During what Haining calls the "spicy decade" (1933–1943), there were "spicy" versions of adventure, western, and mystery stories. For the purposes of this compressed survey, I look at a specific issue of *Spicy Detective Stories* from January 1942.[44]

Like most pornography, *Spicy Detective Stories* is characterized by repetition. Every opportunity is taken to weave a nearly naked woman into the plot. This is hardly realistic, but the point is to provide the reader with unbroken sexual fantasy. With mechanical regularity, then—every few paragraphs—sultry, undressed women appear before the powerfully male protagonist. In addition to rampant verbal nudity, each story comes with illustrations of women in nightgowns, tight dresses, or apparently naked. In this issue there is even a short section of comics starring "Sally the Sleuth." During an era where female detectives were rare, this character could represent a moment of equal opportunity for women. But the only opportunity this magazine gives women is one more chance to appear naked; Sally has to change her clothes in the first half of the story, while in the second half she strip-searches the female criminal. In general, *Spicy Detective Stories* has far more female characters than one might expect—in the form of wives, girlfriends, victims, and often criminals—since every female character represents another chance to show a woman naked.

The visual nudity and the sexy, flirtatious talk come with the "spicy" territory, no doubt, but what is truly remarkable is the level and extent of violence. Mainstream detective plots have men fighting men, with women as victims and women as rewards. But since women are now cast in almost all the nonprotagonist roles, women not only get murdered, they also get into fights with the hero. So there are not only many drawings of the female victims (woman on bed with knife in chest [6], fleeing naked woman in silhouette [23], attractive "skewered" corpse in swimsuit lifted out of water [31], half-naked woman with "knife buried in her throat" [59], partially clothed woman dead on floor [71]), but also many drawings of women fighting with men ("I toss my companion's heels high" [15], woman holding a gun on a man [19], another woman with a gun [38], woman flipping upside down with caption, "It was the first time I'd ever hit a woman, but I got a kick out of it!" [63], another woman with gun, "she brought up her automatic and fired" [75], man tackling gun-toting woman, flipping her over [79]). Some of the fighting pictures show the men and women in clinching poses (with the woman's dress flying up), so they provide more sexual eye-fodder. But the magazine's overall premise holds that the combination of nonstop half-nakedness with nonstop horrific violence makes things even "spicier."

Occasionally the undraped women do reveal their desires to the rough-and-ready heroes. The much-experienced male protagonist, Eel, expresses his desire for Magda Leyder, but in a moral context. "I am the man who fell in the poison ivy," he says, "I itch all over" (9). She is "poison ivy" because she is married. But she says simply, "If you itch that awfully, why not scratch it?" And she moistens her lips to kiss him. He notes that "for a woman to be man-crazy is not exactly according to Hoyle" (10). Attractive women come with come-hither looks (68, 95); their desire matches their appearance. But their sexual desires are punished as ruthlessly as any homicide, since they are usually killed. Masculine sexuality is regarded as part of nature and inside the law, while female desire is pathological ("man crazy") and outside the law. In a few pages Magda will be found with a knife in her throat, and Eel will memorialize her desiring flesh. "It saddens me to think that she will never run a fever again" (13). In *Love and Death* (1949), Gershon Legman noted the central hypocrisy of late 1940s comic books: they were willing and able to show graphic violence, even though murder is illegal, while they were unwilling and unable to show the act of sex, even though everyone agrees that sex is normal.[45] These "spicy" magazines work the same way—with flirty but always unconsummated or interrupted sex ("I had taken a good lead off third base"), combined with one bloodthirsty homicide after another. Anxieties about the violent aggressiveness in sexual desire explode in truly horrific ways in these magazines.

While spicy magazines disappeared, paperback books made a market-shattering appearance. Priced at 25 cents each, they were popular with soldiers and caught on with readers who might otherwise have settled for magazines. Indeed, they were sold like magazines, and a new publisher like Bantam Books modeled both content and covers after the *Saturday Evening Post*.[46] But there were other magazines for models, such as pulp detective and fantasy magazines that had more provocative covers. Competition for market share drove paperback books into an escalating sex war, hence covers and content became increasingly coarse. It was not just a Catholic magazine that in 1950 would label many drugstore pocketbooks "concentrated doses of filth."[47] In 1952 the Gathings Committee of the House of Representatives began an investigation into the obscene nature of comic books, pulp magazines, and paperbacks. One need not side with censor or libertine to agree that paperback books now played a major role in 1940s sexual culture.

And what does female desire look like here? Can we judge a paperback by its flamboyant cover? Let us look at a select few of the hundreds and hundreds of paperbacks that came from publishers such as Avon, Dell, Fawcett, and Pocket Books. As the decade goes on the covers get pulpier and sexier. Many paperbacks turn out tamer than the cover, some paperbacks reproduce or inaugurate hard-boiled sex talk, while some elaborate the sexy decadence of successful historical fiction by Kathleen Winsor and Frank Yerby. The contents of a few paperbacks actually answer the promise of their sensational covers.

Susan Morley's *Mistress Glory* appeared as a Signet paperback in 1949. In 1948 Dial Press published *Mistress Glory* in hardcover; it was promoted as "America's newest sensation, the exciting tale of the adored darling of London's wickedest era. If you enjoyed *Duchess Hotspur*, this is your meat."[48]

After the blockbuster success of *Forever Amber* (1944), the popular genre of historical romance often gave itself over to sensationalism. The Dial Press dust cover portrays Mistress Glory with the usual bosomy display.[49] The hardback version of *Mistress Glory* is promoted as a sexy novel; a *New York Times* ad puts it next to new books such as *The Furies* by Niven Busch ("Even better than his *Duel in the Sun*") and Charles Gorham's *The Future Mr. Dolan* ("a nightmare of casual violence, of sex that preys, and no mercy for the weak"). In its original hardback incarnation, then, *Mistress Glory* is straightforwardly hyped as a sex novel; Dial Press places it in the recognizably salacious genre of historical fiction and then gives it notorious company.

What happens when *Mistress Glory* goes from hardback to paperback? During the late 1940s, paperback reprinting begins with widely varied content and then markets these books—irrespective of content—right out to the edge of pornography. The Avon paperback cover for David Dortort's violent *Burial of the Fruit*—which "injects a belated boy-meets-girl element" according to the *New York Times* review—is not that different in its sexual intensity from the Avon cover for Erskine Caldwell's *Georgia Boy* or Jack Woodford's *The Abortive Hussy.*[50] Erskine Caldwell's scandalous southern tales are Faulknerian literature compared to Woodford's methodical sleaze, but the paperback format pushes every book in the same direction. Likewise, while the Dial Press ad for *Mistress Glory* emphasized sexual content, Signet frames the paperback version as less an amiable bosom novel and more a challenge to public decency. At Signet number 748 *Mistress Glory* appears alongside some particularly sexed-up reissues: Signet 751 is *Love without Fear*, a 1940 sex manual by Eustace Chesser, while Signet 752 is Charles Gorham's *The Future Mister Dolan* once again, but this time marketed as unmistakable smut. The back cover blurb says: "Dolan was a Good Boy—Good enough at nineteen, to seduce a frightened, but affectionate high-school girl in the back seat of a stolen car; fast enough to pick up a sex-hungry housewife in a movie theater; smart enough to loot the pockets of a lonely, middle-aged invert who's taken him to a swank apartment for a night."[51] Both the notorious front covers and the back covers of late 1940s paperbacks promise much spicy business in between.

In a 1949 article for *Commentary*, "The Dream Life of the New Woman: As Mirrored in Current Historical Heroines," David Bazelon argued that heroines like Amber and Glory represent contemporary female fantasies of independence. According to Bazelon, these novels do not just let us see their heroines in varying states of undress, they "let us see the way women have come to regard men, including their husbands."[52] This reading sees female desire as not just erotic but political, and looks ahead to Elaine Showalter's take on Kathleen Winsor; it credits these sensationalist novels with ideological substance. In the end, however, Bazelon disagrees with this brand of female independence because this careerist, sexually aggressive, bed-hopping freedom too closely resembles the priorities of men. Such independence is too "masculine" for Bazelon; in the future women will need a more female version of independence to strive after. Bazelon's article reminds us, once again, that aggressive sexual desire served as a synonym for masculinity. But his article also reminds us that female readers were assumed to be a main contingent of the readership of historical novels.

What the paperbacking of *Mistress Glory* does, then, is turn a potentially sexy romance for female readers into borderline pornography for male readers. Between the covers it is exactly the same book, but the paperback beckons much more overtly to male readers. The picture on the hardback dust cover was bosomy, as befits the historical heroine, but the paperback's cover sharpens the sexual terrain. Unlike her demur hardback predecessor, who cast her eyes down, the paperback's Glory looks directly at the reader, unembarrassed and unashamed. A virtuous lady would at least blush, since Glory is evidently putting on her clothes; her low-cut dress falls off one shoulder and she adjusts her bracelet. Yet there is no blush, no shame; she has just had sex and she looks out at the viewer in her lover's place. Altogether, the paperback portrait takes part in the transformative work of paperback cover art, which aims to sell the book's sex more specifically to a male viewer.

Even as they promise reams of scandalous sex, Signet and Avon paperbacks simultaneously claim that these books provide quality, high-class literature. Just as *Esquire* combined its high-culture gurus with a barrage of undressed women, Signet and Avon emblazon their paperbacks with overt contradictions. On the one hand, the covers promise tawdry hard-boiled lust. Accompanying promotional copy underscores not just sex but violence. The end of Signet's *Mistress Glory* contains several pages of ads for books such as James M. Cain's *The Butterfly*, "an unforgettable story of passion, suspense and violence"; Thomas Savage's *Lona Hanson*, "a bold woman with a lust for power"; Faulkner's *Sanctuary*, "a blood-chilling gangster story centering on a terrifying and macabre killer"; Raymond Radiguet's *Devil in the Flesh*, "the famous French novel of young love"; Ludwig Lewisohn's *The Vehement Flame*, "a bitterly beautiful novel of marriage and adultery"; and William Gardner Smith's *Last of the Conquerors*, which provides a quote from its African American protagonist: "I had lain on the beach many times, but never with a white girl." Everything is pitched at the level of tabloid and taboo. According to the back cover of *Mistress Glory*, the heroine possesses astonishing sexual appetite ("insatiable paramour of men of low estate and high"), although the copy quickly refocuses attention on the power of masculine will ("But finally and forever she was a slave to the lust of Innocent Paradine, king of highwaymen, the man who had fiercely claimed her virgin body").

Yet even though every picture and nearly every word shouts obscenely, the paperback also claims that it is culturally central, not marginal or subterranean. Susan Morley is described as "an actress on the BBC, and the wife of a well-known author . . . and also the mother of three children." One might imagine that this last fact would break the hypererotic spell. The whole Signet series is given the pretentious name "The New American Library of World Literature," and it all looks positively wholesome: "Good Reading in Signet Books—25 cents." Avon books contradict themselves even more preposterously; the Jack Woodford front cover for *The Abortive Hussy* reminds readers that Woodford also authored *The Hard-Boiled Virgin*, while the back cover contains Avon's icon, Shakespeare himself. As Avon back covers regularly say: "In the many years since the 'Shakespeare-Head' first appeared as the imprint on Avon Books, millions of readers have found this trademark represents a high standard of reading entertainment." Since a 1947 Jack Woodford novel is aimed at the same audience that bought the now illegal spicy pulps of the early 1940s, Shakespeare's prestigious face on the back cover tries, absurdly, to cover up the undressed woman on the front.

The contradictory indicators of culture—This is a smutty novel! This is a classy novel!—can be explained in several ways. Legal threats and moral crusades abound, and not just in Boston; hence publishers frame their books for two audiences. The intended reader is promised sensationalism, but the moral crusader is appeased by these gestures of civilization. In his cantankerous autobiography, prolific sleaze author Jack Woodford says exactly that; he surrounded his sex writing with high-culture references to throw moral bloodhounds off the scent: "I wrote some mildly literary stuff such as I am writing now; did a little name dropping like Hogarth, to fool reviewers; grabbed at a word like tergivisation, completely to throw censors; and then went back to the bedside to carry on."[53]

But the contradictory cultural signals can also be viewed along the same lines as my earlier reading of *Esquire*. Instead of relegating *Esquire* to the niche of "men's magazines," its cultural ambitions and capaciousness show, on the contrary, that men's magazines represent all of culture. And although Shakespeare's iconic head is a contrived marketing tool, Avon's paperbacks also perform cultural meaning. Shakespeare's head on a Jack Woodford novel is silly and defensive, but it also makes the same argument that I have made all along: 1940s sexual space is compressed cultural space, and there is not much difference between mainstream sexual discourse and borderline pornographic discourse. Paperbacks not only take varied content and sell it as male-oriented, sensationalist smut, but they also show that there is not much difference between their colorful wares and the magazines that well-mannered ladies leave out on the living room table.

I will turn to those women's magazines after looking at one more paperback mask. For paperback collectors, one of the most famously sought after books is Felice Swados's *Reform School Girl* (Diversey Romance Novel, 1948). The book is rare and the cover is legendary. There a blonde woman in a short dress attaches a garter to her stocking; to round her out moral depravity, a cigarette dangles from her mouth. This is a fallen woman, 1940s style: "A shameful path led her there—scarlet secrets kept her there." The cover's words and picture promise an anthology of scandalous sex. The 1950 Avon paperback reverts to the original title of the 1941 hardcover, *House of Fury*. Now a blonde woman in close-up seemingly prays to be released from her prison. The 1950 front cover is not quite so intent on turning tabloid: "A Powerful Novel about Reform Schools and the Girls behind Its Walls." Even with Shakespeare looking on, however, the back cover is still prepared to sensationalize: "Bursting with desire for which there could be no outlet, these girls formed a volcano of suppressed emotion which was bound to erupt."

Paperback copy is all lies and marketing, but in fact the 1950 version has it right: this is "a powerful novel." Swados is a serious writer. In her 1936 master's thesis for Smith College Felice Swados compared "mechanical materialism" to "dialectical materialism," and in 1941 she published an article on "Negro Health on the Ante Bellum Plantations," which has since been cited regularly by scholars.[54] If Swados had not died of cancer in 1945, we would surely have been left with more novels, and these would have helped to classify her first. *House of Fury* has passed into its afterlife as a scandalous paperback, when in fact it is a seriously complex book that juxtaposes white female sexuality and sexual desire with white and black race relations. For contemporary readers, the well-known paperback cover has turned a remarkable book into a nearly invisible phantom.

What kind of book is *House of Fury*? The paperback's hyperbolic rhetoric is not entirely misplaced, since, as in Richard Wright's *Native Son* (1940), there is plenty of melodrama and pulp violence. The constant juxtaposition of the black women (who escape and are recaptured) and the white women (who are openly racist) leads the reader to reflect on the relationships between power, gender, and race. The novel clearly takes the side of the black women and works against the white women's racism. But it also may be said to use the presence of the black women in order to make the restrictions on white female sexuality appear more substantial. Questions about liberty and sexuality will seem more profound with the black women there.

The anguish of the imprisoned young women has partly to do with the fated power of adolescent sexuality: "Again she felt on the verge of a precipice, on the brink of something empty and enormous, but she knew it was only herself, only her body ripening. Every month she swelled to a climax of trembling fury, then fell abruptly to a plain of despair in which nothing seemed to matter and even the raising of a finger required tremendous effort."[55] Thus the "house of fury" is, on the one hand, the body of adolescent sexual desire. But the "house of fury" is also a nightmarish prison, a space that oppresses women and deprives them of any safe home. In this element the novel has much in common with the gothic horrors of 1940s women's magazine fiction to which we now turn. The paperbacking of *House of Fury* turns the story into a man's story, where a man can contemplate adolescent female desire for his own sexual delectation. But beneath the sensationalist cover, *House of Fury* is a woman's story, and one that already knows about the power men have over women. Instead of reading *House of Fury* next to paperback sleaze by Jack Woodford, read it next to Margaret Shedd's "The Great Fire of 1945" or Hitchcock's *Rebecca* (1940).

The Ladies' Home Nightmare: Soap Operas, Confession Magazines, and Women's Magazine Fiction

In the patriarchal tyranny of the 1940s, male power still oversees female space. Male announcers organize and evaluate what happens in soap operas to ensure that female listeners line up on the right side of characters and products. Whereas a men's magazine such as *Esquire* rarely allows in a woman's perspective, women's magazines often allow in male authors and stories with male protagonists. Society is centered on a male point of view, and women's magazines continually train their female readers to empathize with what men feel and want. Advertisements in women's magazines continue this strain of domination and surveillance, and every female curve and crevice is treated as a masculine possession. In one frame of an ad a stern husband glares off into space, while alone in her own frame the miserable young wife clutches a handkerchief. Alas, she has run into "one of woman's most serious deodorant problems," and her failure to douche regularly has driven her powerful husband away.[56] Female space remains male-dominated space. Yet in some cultural forms aimed at women one might nonetheless perceive a level of resistance or self-consciousness that is entirely absent in publications for male readers.

In this section I take an admittedly biased approach to soap operas, confession magazines, and women's magazine fiction. Whereas one could easily emphasize the substantial differences among the various radio serials and women's magazines—*One Man's Family* is pitched less anxiously than *Backstage Wife*, while *Mademoiselle* is aimed at a more sophisticated readership than *Ladies' Home Journal*—I foreground a common inclination toward horror. In this reading the patriarchal containment of female space is not seen as natural and supportive, but instead as a structure that generates anxiety and fear. When the female body is well-formed and the male viewer approves, then romantic ecstasy follows, but when the male viewer disapproves, then shame and darkness fall on the woman; hence the oscillation between ecstasy and despair that so often characterizes these narratives. In 1942 Max Wylie defended the oft-attacked soap operas by arguing that soaps know things that other cultural forms do not so readily admit. For example, "they presuppose that the great mass of all mankind—with the women worse off than the men—is cramped and poor and troubled and tired."[57] My reading agrees with Wylie; the much-maligned misery of soap operas contains real truths. These stories intended for women regularly represent woman's ghastly plight under patriarchy as the horror show that it is.

Although magazines and daytime serials constitute the main focus of this section, I must first say a few things about that most well-studied female cultural space of the 1940s—the woman's film. The 1940s woman's film has been discussed in some of the most illuminating analyses in all of film studies. Jeanine Basinger's *A Woman's View: How Hollywood Spoke to Women 1930–1960* (1993) takes a properly wide-ranging approach to the woman's film; the British Film Institute collection, *Home Is Where the Heart Is: Studies in Melodrama and the Woman's Film* (1987), assembles some of the best film scholars around; Mary Ann Doane's *The Desire to Desire: The Woman's Film of the 1940s* (1987) remains a classic of psychoanalytic criticism; more recently (2007), Helen Hanson has clarified the long-recognized subgenre of "female gothic" within the woman's film.[58] These texts contain nothing but first-rate readings, and they allow me to turn the bulk of my attention to much less studied cultural terrain. But what the genre of the woman's film needs above all is a link to other cultural forms. The film *for women* has a good deal in common with magazines for women and with radio programs for women. Yet none of these books—as illuminating as they are—take a step outside their respective constellation of films. And so another step needs to be taken. The loosely defined "woman's film" needs to be set next to other cultural artifacts that are also designed for women. In the given space of this chapter, I can only make a start on this contextualizing approach.

My thematic focus now is on horror in the daytime serials and magazines; these nightmares are clearly linked to a main subgenre of the woman's film, the female gothic. In her appendix, Helen Hanson lists the main films in "the female gothic cycle of the 1940s," films such as *Rebecca* (1940), *Suspicion* (1941), *Shadow of a Doubt* (1943), *Dark Waters* (1944), *Experiment Perilous* (1944), *Gaslight* (1944), *Jane Eyre* (1944), *Spellbound* (1945), *Dragonwyck* (1946), and *Undercurrent* (1946).[59] These films often combine "mystery" with "romance," two genres that audience surveys found appealed to women. But this "cycle" is not a self-enclosed set of films that begins with *Rebecca* and then tries to replicate its success. Instead this "female gothic" energy should be seen as circulating throughout 1940s culture. For it is found in abundance in confession magazines, women's magazine fiction, and in daytime serials. Beyond the movies, women's culture often appears in nightmare form.

To draw on a wider range of cultural artifacts also serves to complicate the already complicated genre of the woman's film. Jeanine Basinger's *A Woman's View* has, to my mind, the best sense of where to find women's films, because she finds them practically everywhere. I disagree with individual examples—she sees *China* (1943) as a woman's film—but such a proposal deserves consideration; her larger point is that even war movies and westerns can be women's films.[60] Although Basinger does not validate her choices with contemporary criticism, she could; a review of RKO's *Roughshod* in a 1949 *Movieland*—another fan magazine geared toward women—begins by calling it "a western with plenty of romance," and concludes that "the ladies will go for this western."[61] To look at the way that movie fan magazines represent film culture and the way that women's magazines review films is to substantially expand the possible candidates for a woman's film.

Before turning to radio soap operas, then, I offer a single but important addition to the porous canon of 1940s women's films. Hitchcock's *Rebecca* (1940) plays a key role in most surveys of the 1940s woman's film; Doane and Hanson give it ample treatment. Even though no film critic has used women's magazines to help them contextualize the genre, many candidate women's films were adapted from novels that were serialized or condensed in women's magazines. *Rebecca* appeared as a condensed novel in *Ladies' Home Journal*, a fact that seemingly helps support the idea that Hitchcock's first American film is also a woman's film. Following the success of Daphne du Maurier's *Rebecca* (a bestseller in 1939) and of Hitchcock's

1940 adaptation, *Ladies' Home Journal* then proceeded to serialize du Maurier's next novel, *Frenchman's Creek* (1941), over several months.[62] And this novel was later adapted into a 1944 film, with Joan Fontaine, as in *Rebecca*, once again in the female lead. Should we not then consider that *Frenchman's Creek* is a woman's film? The plot has an unhappily married woman with children fall in love with a charming pirate. In some respects this narrative might provide *the* archetypal fable of female desire. Yet *Frenchman's Creek* goes unmentioned in Doane, Hanson, and the capacious Basinger. Whereas social transgression must at times be interpreted after the fact, *Frenchman's Creek* is blatantly transgressive, and the wife's socially incomprehensible love for the thieving pirate fills her with joy. *Frenchman's Creek* may have more to say about female desire than *Rebecca*, but has it been forgotten because Hitchcock did not film it?

Ladies' Home Journal was not known for its groundbreaking fiction, especially compared to *Mademoiselle* or *Harper's Bazaar*. But with its finger on the pulse of its women readers—or with its masculine hand on their shoulders—the magazine produced its own cycle of female gothic before Hollywood. Not only does it condense du Maurier's *Rebecca*, but on two successive months in 1943 *Ladies' Home Journal* publishes condensations of Margaret Carpenter's *Experiment Perilous* and Anya Seton's *Dragonwyck*.[63] In 1944 and 1946 respectively, these novels would be adapted into two indisputable members of the gothic woman's film.

The tendency to push fiction at least occasionally toward horror seems intentional. During the 1930s and 1940s, *Ladies' Home Journal* published ten novels by Mignon Eberhart, a writer who specialized in romantic mysteries punctuated by bone-chilling scares. These stories are usually murder mysteries, but editorial captions and illustrations always play up the frightful elements. For example, a teaser quotation for a new episode of Eberhart's *Speak No Evil* goes: "Fog was everywhere, pressing in upon her. Then, quite near, there was a sound—horrible and terrifying."[64] And the September 1943 issue looks ahead to next month's Eberhart novel, *The Sisters*: "A thrilling story of two beautiful sisters and the man they both loved, and how that love became the center of a horrible, terrifying web of mystery and emotion!"[65] It is not the case that the 1940s *Ladies' Home Journal* is *Weird Tales* in disguise. Most of its stories are sweet and cute and illustrated with a pretty heterosexual couple in a clinch. But even this brief description should make it apparent that the 1940s "female gothic" films are not a self-enclosed cycle. Nightmare energy cycles throughout female culture. And even though most fiction in women's magazines cannot be classed as horror, what horror there is still feels completely at home. This is because the 1940s woman's magazine—as conservative domestic ideology weirdly combines with the glamorization of female display—has all the trappings of a gothic nightmare.

As critics often noticed, many soap operas took their characters out of an everyday realm of housecleaning and dress mending, and placed them in a heightened world of murder and mayhem. John Crosby, in his January 1951 radio column, heard more and more homicide as the serial form developed. "Murder, which intruded only occasionally in soap opera years ago, has become overwhelmingly fashionable."[66] Crosby sees genre continuity between *Perry Mason*, a 15-minute daytime serial just like the soaps; *Front Page Farrell*, another daytime serial in detective mode; lawyer Portia (of *Portia Faces Life*), who defends accused murderers; and *Backstage Wife*, where Larry Noble "just beat a murder rap." A sociological attempt to distinguish soap opera listeners from nonlisteners confirms the same generic overlap; Herta Herzog found that listeners prefer "mystery novels" more often than nonlisteners.[67] Two main characters on the 1947 *Joyce Jordan, M.D.*, are Mike Malone, reformed gangster, and Doria van Dorn, reformed playgirl, while Vincent in the *Backstage Wife* of 1950 is clearly some kind of hood.[68] Many soap operas, therefore, with their guns, murder trials, and underworld characters, willingly take on the genre trappings of the mystery.

And while this genre overlap between soap opera and mystery was intentional and recognizable, soap operas could also take on elements of horror. Detective mysteries and police procedurals take place in relatively rational worlds where crime and motive can be sorted out. Reason and enlightenment frame a temporary dark passage. By contrast, horror's violence descends from inexplicable madness. And it is certainly the case that the world of the soap opera is often inexplicable and irrational. Daytime serial characters live in a constant state of humming anxiety, which can quickly blossom into fear, despair, and terror. Soap opera heroines are tortured, driven crazy—sometimes right into asylums—by crazy people.

We can contemplate the strange weather of daytime serials by looking through the main radio fan magazine of the day, *Radio Mirror*. Published under several titles during the 1940s, this is the radio version of Macfadden Publications' very successful film magazine, *Photoplay*. Like *Photoplay* it is a fan magazine aimed at women with the same collection of ads selling feminine beautification. *Photoplay* "feminizes" its film coverage by emphasizing the racy biographies of movie stars. Movie plots are mostly ignored; instead the stars' lives are turned into romantic stories. To create the same sensation of romance, *Radio Mirror* mostly ignores radio programs that are not soap operas. Whereas *Photoplay* turns the stars' lives into soap operas, however, *Radio Mirror* just recounts the soap operas. A much less stable magazine than *Photoplay*, *Radio Mirror* changes its approach almost yearly during the decade. In the mid-1940s it devotes itself completely to daytime serials, calling itself *Radio Romances*; by the end of the decade it is called *Radio and Television Mirror* and now offers a wider range of coverage. But because it is a magazine intended for women, all versions of *Radio Mirror* are skewed toward soap operas. This observation allows us to develop some language and imagery for describing this female audio space.

Radio Mirror's selections and illustrations make clear that soap operas overlap with mysteries. A prose fiction version of *The Romance of Helen Trent* is illustrated with a dead body, "staring blankly," on the opening page, and a terrified Helen, "a stifled scream burning her throat," pictured on the facing page.[69] The same issue (May 1940) contains the Ellery Queen mystery "The Adventure of the Haunted Cave"; *Ellery Queen* is not a daytime serial, but occasionally appears in *Radio Mirror* nonetheless. From January to March 1941, *Radio Mirror* serializes *Mystery House*, a 1935 novel by Kathleen Norris and recently adapted for the *Kathleen Norris* radio program. *Radio Mirror* regularly gives a pictorial overview of a serial; often these images find a comfortable home in a mystery genre. In "Through the Years with *Young Widder Brown*" (November 1948), the caption under one picture reads: "Knowing she could not win him, Barbara revenged herself by disappearing after arranging circumstances to make it seem that Ellen had murdered her."[70] Such a plot point is completely run-of-the-mill in the 1940s soap opera.

Yet the genre elements that spell out "mystery" can often be reidentified as coalescing into something closer to "horror." Because serial plots never end, the psychic torment is relentless, irresolvable, and practically unbounded. There are no monstrous demons that attack people, but there are monstrously demonic people who attack people. In the *Young Widder Brown* plot, Barbara is found out and declared insane, yet even in the sanitarium, "she still plots revenge."[71] In its overview of *Big Sister*, *Radio Mirror* says that Neddie's wife, Hope, who is "selfish, grasping, and pitiless, has made life a series of torturing incidents for Ned."[72] In soap operas, crazy people roam the streets like zombies. In a *Radio Mirror* story for *Joyce Jordan, Girl Interne* (before she becomes Joyce Jordan, M.D.), a "pathetically crazy," "strange, neurotic" girl throws a fit in the hospital ("she screamed [and] struck her forehead savagely with both clenched hands"), runs outside, and is struck dead by a car.[73] A *Radio Mirror* adaptation called "Bitter Marriage" starts with a blurb that warns of her "husband's madness, a madness she had never comprehended until too late," and captions its picture with

"My knees gave way to panic, and I knelt beside little Justin."[74] The 1940 *Radio Mirror* version of *Second Husband* begins with the heroine telling her diary how anxious she is: "I'm frightened all the time."[75] Since her second husband will save her from poverty and loneliness, this story ends happily. But many soaps draw the fearful implication that everyone is deeply unstable and that every home verges on a madhouse.

Typical madhouse anxiety characterizes a stretch of *Backstage Wife* from 1950. The "home invasion" theme is so potent that it takes hold of both main plots. Wealthy Rupert Barlow feels obliged to let his long-time assistant, Julia, return from Bermuda with her new boyfriend, Oliver. To have a romantic rival staying on his estate is humiliating for powerful Rupert. But his anguish is nothing compared to that of Mary Noble, who has to play hostess to Claudia Vincent. Claudia transparently manipulates Larry Noble, and everyone except Larry can see this. Mary's husband, as always, is completely untrustworthy, while fawning, terrible Claudia sleeps just down the hall from Mary. The relentless instability of her home soon drives Mary up the wall. Her friend Maude repeatedly reminds Mary to control herself, but to little avail. Mary explodes with righteous anger several times, while on other occasions she gives into prolonged crying. The sense of ongoing anxiety is registered when one episode concludes with "her rising fear," while quite remarkably, another episode begins with Larry startling Mary in her own garden.[76] "Oh! Larry Noble!" exclaims Mary. "You nearly scared me to death." "Why?" asks Larry, in his characteristically unsympathetic way. Mary says that she might put a bell on him "if you [keep] sneaking up like that and scare the wits out of me." But Mary's anxiety is larger than a momentary surprise; she is jumpy because her whole house is—as always—falling down around her.

Amidst the patriarchal horror show of 1940s culture, the gendered structure of many soaps stands out. In a 1951 newspaper article, John Crosby put it like this: "While good women are nobler than anything in your or my experience in soap operas, the bad women are more venomous than anything you'd care to encounter. In either case, the woman are strong, just as men, whether good or bad, are weak or at best rather simple-minded and easily bamboozled by women."[77] Crosby's description goes back at least to Rudolf Arnheim's 1944 article, "The World of the Daytime Serial," which also divides characters into good, bad, and weak.[78] This gendered structure applies to multitudinous soap operas, whose producers clearly regard it as a recipe for success. Crosby has *Backstage Wife* in mind—with strong, good Mary; strong, bad Claudia; and weak, bamboozled Larry. Working along similar lines, *Big Sister* is overseen by strong, good Ruth, while hapless, weak

Neddie is tormented by strong, bad Hope; meanwhile Ruth's weak husband, John, spends 1944 brooding vaguely about who-knows-what. While most critics perceived this gendered structure, neither Crosby nor Arnheim nor anyone else made the point that such strong women and such weak men appeared consistently in no other cultural form. The almost exclusively female audience meant that daytime serials could give women and men attributes that they would not possess in films, music, or even nighttime radio.

But soap operas, with their strong women and weak men, only appear to turn the patriarchy upside down. Strong bad women like Claudia and Hope are misogynistic fantasies; narcissistic, money-grubbing manipulators, they supply more grist to grind down in patriarchy's woman-hating mill. Even strong good women like Mary in *Backstage Wife* and Ruth in *Big Sister* are surprisingly unstable. As Arnheim observes in a footnote: "Remarkably enough, the objects of identification [i.e., the strong heroines] sometimes, in a difficult personal situation, forget their part and show a 'weak' behavior which is quite in contrast with the masculine energy they display while helping others. They take fright at decisions, they burst into tears, they wail around in a hysterical and pitiful way, they take refuge in the unwavering strength of male friends or follow obediently."[79] Arnheim's comment is perceptive and prescient, and it applies to soap opera heroines who threw fits well after his essay. As we have seen during Claudia Vincent's 1950 home invasion, Mary Noble regularly bursts out in anger, tears, or hysterical fear. Whereas she can see clearly that Larry Noble is blind to Claudia's manipulations, she alone cannot see that Rupert Barlow is in love with her. So in her hour of need she repeatedly runs to Rupert for security (he represents Arnheim's "unwavering strength of male friends"), even though everyone else knows that he is far from the "gentleman" Mary takes him to be. Meanwhile strong, ideal Mary asks Rupert to return money that her husband had invested with him—without telling Larry. This dubious behavior—friend Maude tells Mary that she is wrong—is also linked by Arnheim with the idealized characters. They not only forget their strength in emotional outbursts, they themselves can cause nearly as much trouble as the "bad" troublemakers. Once these structural exceptions are fully taken into account, the good, strong, idealized women start to look significantly less powerful.

The soaps were called soaps, of course, because they were often sponsored by companies that sold soap, but these are not clean, refreshing programs. Many of these programs are relentlessly nerve-wracking; as Arnheim writes, "human existence is pictured as continuously threatened by catastrophe."[80] Postum Decaffeinated Coffee ("Are you nervous?") and Bisodol antacid (which cures nervousness so widespread it is called "American stomach") would have made more appropriate sponsors than soap.[81] Big cities make characters feel "restless and jittery," as Diane says on *Big Sister*; cities are filled with "people who have no place to go."[82] But those apparently safe small towns can also turn disorienting and fearful. When strong, good Ruth hears Diane's voice on the other end of the telephone, the announcer tells us that "what [Diane] said sounded completely unreal, like a dialogue in a nightmare."[83] Big Sister's strength and moral goodness can only go so far in a world where her husband is hundreds of miles away, lost, bewildered, and aggressively pursued by another woman.

Sexual desire is parceled out according to the tripartite system of good, bad, and weak. The strong, bad women display themselves sexually in order to get what they want. Sometimes they desire money or power; sometimes they desire men. Sexuality is indicated straightforwardly and sex is certainly not repressed. When eye-dazzling Claudia says that she should "put on something more appropriate," it is clear what she means.[84] When Diane, who is passionately in love with John, wants to sit next to him on his bed, her desire is transparent.[85] Vincent tells Rupert that Julia's new boyfriend is "giving her one hot run," which is appropriately vulgar (Vincent is a gangster), but also candid.[86] Female sexual desire is intensely present, then, but only evidenced in bad women. Sexual desire makes bad women appear unbalanced, and they deploy sexuality in inappropriate ways.[87]

In contrast to the often vampiric seductresses, soap's good female heroines do not express sexual desire. In his 1948 essay "Soapland," James Thurber found only "coy and impregnable chastity in the good women" and opined that "chill Miss Trent has her men frustrated to a point at which a moral male would smack her little mouth."[88] Less violently, but along the same lines, Raymond William Stedman writes: "From a biological standpoint, the virginal heroine was rarely to be found in the daytime serial. From a behavioral standpoint, she was ever present." [89] The conservative, moralistic, and structural aspects of soaps are clearest here because the titular heroines are constructed as total opposites to their man-hungry female rivals. For all their insecurities and instabilities, it is impossible to imagine Mary Noble acting like gun-toting Claudia or Ruth Wayne behaving like either Hope or Diane. In line with the general cast of 1940s sexual ideology, proper women do not exhibit sexual desire, whereas women who do express sexual desire are labeled as some species of neurotic or nymphomaniac.

Where the sexual topology of soaps differs from other 1940s cultural artifacts is in their representation of men. Gilbert Seldes went so far as to name the well-recognized element of male weakness "impotence": "The weak man required by the structure of daytime serial is peculiarly useful because he is, obviously, impotent, and although a woman may weep at suspected infidelities, she is never deceived; her long self-examinations to decide whether she loves him conceal what she knows, that he cannot make love to her."[90] That male weakness literally means impotence is hard to believe; his supposed impotence will not deter Ruth's husband from an adulterous affair.[91] But Seldes is surely right to push masculine weakness into a sexual arena. While soaps maintain the good woman–bad woman (no sexual desire, neurotic sexual desire) distinction drawn from conservative ideology, soaps largely defang the male wolfishness that lurks at the center of 1940s sexual culture. The male sexual gaze is power itself everywhere else, but in daytime serials male sexuality is damaged, crippled, ineffective. In soaps women are in charge of both sexual display and its prohibitions, whereas the looking men are now mostly hapless bystanders.

Soap opera anxiety and horror is if anything elaborated and magnified in women's confessional magazines.[92] Magazines such as *Modern Romances*, *Real Story*, and *Secrets* supply a never-ending maelstrom of intense and varied emotion. A key catalyst in the sensationalistic chemistry of women's confessional magazines is the Macfadden publication, *True Story*. Founded in 1919, *True Story* invented the woman's confession magazine, thereby "changing the woman's magazine niche forever."[93] By 1940 *True Story* is still going strong, but like its masculine cousin *True*, it restrains itself over the course of the decade. Hence a 1943 or 1946 *True Story* looks comparatively tame. But a 1940 *True Story* is a stunningly tabloid romance magazine, where ads for lip gloss and Kleenex are juxtaposed with stories about abortion ("His 10,000 Women Victims") and murder ("She Killed Her Fifth Column Nazi Lover!").[94] A successful and controversial magazine in the 1930s, *True Story* spends the 1940s toning down its tabloid hyperbole and toning up its patriotism.[95] But its notorious example invites other "true story" and confession magazines to adopt wild and terrifying scenarios.

Soap operas and confession magazines overlap and differ in several crucial respects. The anxiety, dislocation, and homelessness that typify soap operas are also prominent in confession magazines. A 1942 *True Experiences* story is pitched from one end to the other in terror—"My life was a nightmare, those days"—in this case, the abject fear of falling into poverty.[96] A story in the same issue takes part in soap opera's disorienting "home invasion" theme; a tensely dramatic picture is captioned—"Pop shouted, 'Paula can stay here if she wants to. It's my house just as much as yours!' "[97] In an important contrast, however, the weak, impotent men of the daytime serial are not a convention followed in confession magazines. This must be due in part to the fact that the sexual censorship that attends daytime radio serials is considerably loosened in confession magazines. Hence the confessions provide formidable records of sexual desire as experienced by both men and women.

What makes women anxious and afraid in these stories varies widely. In the story above the wife is terrified that her family will return to the poverty she had known during the Depression; her wider fear is that her secure house will collapse into ruin. Gothic strains also filter into modern romance, such as when a new bride moves into a large, old house and feels everywhere the presence of her husband's dead wife ("her expressionless voice was like a force which forbade me to touch the chest that had belonged to Maida").[98] Homicidal revenge and tabloid fear-mongering combine in a 1947 *Modern Romances*, as first the "twisted" heroine of "Murder in My Mind" plots to poison the twelve-year-old killer of her four-year-old son, and then an advice column warns teenage girls that "many of the 40,000 sex crimes" in the United States each year start with "Masher Menace."[99] Dangerous men (an illustration shows the masher's hand reaching out of shadows toward the young woman), the "other woman," unstable homes, and hysterical emotions can all sweep through these narratives with fearful effect.

What is perhaps most frightening is female sexual desire itself. Male sexual desire is potentially frightening ("wolfishness"), yet since it is normal, it is likely accommodated. But 1940s culture makes a monster of female desire, and women in these magazine stories are often frightened by their own sexual feelings. It is not that women fear their potential for sexual transgression; it is not that they are tantalizingly afraid that they will give in to gangsters or married men. Instead women fear sexual desire in and of itself, no matter where it is directed. In a culture entirely given over to expressions of male sexual desire, female sexual desire will necessarily appear as a strange intruder into the patriarchal mansion.

Physical sexual contact is concentrated in kisses, which are often tumultuous and intense. A characteristic confession magazine kiss reads: " 'Sweet Nora,' and he kissed me. Not as he had kissed me before to say goodnight. Tonight his lips were demanding and hard on mine, and I was both thrilled and frightened. I was whirling in a black exciting void when I pushed him away slowly. I looked up at him, then away, unable to hide my quick surge of emotion at what I saw smoldering in his eyes. I wasn't so sure of my own feelings. . . ."[100] The female narrator is not unsure of her romantic feelings; she aroused the man's passions by calling him "darling"—"I had never called him darling before, but in that moment I meant it." What she is unsure about are her sexual feelings. The man's lips are sexually "hard" and desire "smolders" visibly in his eyes. The narrator is afraid that sexual desire will be visible in her face as well ("unable to hide my quick surge of emotion"). When she returns, her roommate assumes that her dazed appearance is the result of sex: "You've just been kissed, but good." These intense kisses stand in for acts of sexual intercourse that rarely appear. Women take part in these kisses with a combination of ecstatic willingness and confused terror.

Although passionate kisses are usually the limit, confession magazines sometimes go beyond kisses to represent sex with as much detail and emphasis as in what passes for male erotica. In the 1942 *True Confessions* story "He Took My Love—And Told," narrator Gale is thrilled by Clark's kisses: "I was ashamed of the desire he had kindled in me, afraid of the clamoring demand of my flesh for more. In the abandon of our kiss Clark had awakened me, prodded my slumbering senses to the piercing ecstasy of love."[101] This is the usual sex plot, where an experienced man "awakens" female sexual desire. Gale's newfound desire now wants more than kisses: "with each kiss it was becoming increasingly difficult to pull away." Later Clark asks if they could do more than kiss just once, and she sleeps with him. "That night, the ardor of Clark's passionate wooing gave me a temporary spurious sense of power and desirability, but I had been too strictly reared to find complete happiness in the sin I was committing."[102] Soon Clark's mother tells her mockingly that Clark would never marry "a girl he's already slept with. You must be crazy to think of such a thing." And then the final hammer comes down when her nice new boyfriend, Jud, finds out that Gale has slept with Clark, and he breaks their engagement. Gale concludes the story by admitting that she is the "guilty party" and thus fairly condemned. In this way the confession rounds out a Victorian moral—the fallen woman is excluded from proper society—even as the story renders female sexual desire with an intensity and visibility that rarely appears in other popular media.

Confession magazines render sexual desire transgressive, sinful, criminal. Psychology in the 1940s argues that male sexual desire is normal, not a sin. But there is no normal in a confession magazine since everything has crossed a line: "Blackmailed into a Living Death," "I Am a Fugitive—Shall I Give Myself Up?" "Temptations of an Air Raid Warden," "Wife without Pride," "Second-Hand Love," "Dishonored by Passion," and "There Is Sin on My Soul" are all titles of "dramatic confessions" in one issue of *True Confessions* (June 1942). In men's magazines, masculinity is enhanced through physical daring and prowess—boxing for the championship, steering a ship through foul weather, escaping the jaws of a giant clam. Adventure makes men more manly. In women's confession magazines, sexual desire is aligned with the exotic, the unknown, and the mysterious. But sexual adventure for women is not only exciting, but also destructive. Hence the web of contradictions that structure women's magazines, where glamorous ads appear alongside stories that regret glamour and where homicidally angry stories appear next to cute ads for baby powder. The often terrifying excitement of the confession magazine story makes sense in a culture that cannot imagine female sexual desire as part of a normal, everyday world. Desire is there to burn—frighteningly, confusingly—and then to be regretted, diminished, and abandoned.

Women's service and fashion magazines are financed with many of the same ads as confession magazines, but there is much more heterogeneity in their wider approach and presentation. It is not easy to distinguish *Modern Romances* from *True Experiences*; with their cast of anonymous authors and their similarly melodramatic stories, most confession magazines look the same. But slick magazines such as *Cosmopolitan*, *Ladies' Home Journal*, and *Woman's Home Companion* use fiction, advice columns, journalism, and graphic design to cultivate strategically separate identities. In *The Feminine Mystique*, Betty Friedan famously showed how "the heroines of women's magazine stories" tended to be "career women" in 1939, whereas by 1949 "only one out of three heroines in the women's magazines was a career woman—and she was shown in the act of renouncing her career and discovering that what she really wanted to be was a housewife."[103] As Nancy A. Walker and others have noted, however, Friedan's choice of magazines gave her survey an unnecessarily narrow result.[104] Although many contemporaries viewed "woman's magazine fiction" as a genre unto itself, different magazines published different kinds of fiction. Although my concluding vision of 1940s patriarchy is not any more positive than Friedan's, it seems useful at least to begin by imagining that women's magazines were capable of encompassing a good deal of heterogeneity, especially in the way of fiction.

The strongest way to imagine the heterogeneity of women's magazine fiction is to remember the work contained in *Mademoiselle* and *Harper's Bazaar*. The short stories in *Ladies' Home Journal* and *Woman's Home Companion* are clearly linked to other departments in the magazine; their usually pretty, young fictional heroines concern themselves with what is important beyond the fiction—prettiness, social success, and marriage. But the stories in *Mademoiselle* and *Harper's Bazaar* seem to have little connection to the construction of fashionable femininity that takes place elsewhere in the magazine. What is more, the stories in *Mademoiselle* and *Harper's Bazaar* seemed inarguably good; only the *New Yorker* could match them for quality fiction. Whereas *Esquire* published mediocre fiction by famous writers simply for the sake of a name on the cover, *Mademoiselle* and *Harper's Bazaar* published top-rank fiction by well-known authors, while they also discovered numerous soon-to-be famous writers. *Harper's Bazaar* put fashion aside for an issue in order to publish Carson McCullers's *Ballad of the Sad Cafe*; Ray Bradbury and Truman Capote made names for themselves in these two women's magazines. Martha Foley, who edited *The Best American Short Stories* throughout most of the 1940s, criticized the typical woman's magazine story, where "vaporous characters wander vaguely around in a rose-colored vacuum."[105] But Foley claimed that *Mademoiselle* and *Harper's Bazaar* stories do not come in this typical form, backing up her point by including numerous stories from these magazines both in her *Best American Short Story* anthologies and in the appended lists of "distinctive short stories in American Magazines." All in all, then, the women's magazine story cannot be conceived as a homogenous entity, since there is a wide spectrum from "vaporous" stories to prize-winning stories, with a probable hodgepodge in between.

Now that the heterogeneity of women's magazine fiction has been established, however, it is time to emphasize a homogeneous strain—the strain of horror. Despite the widely held impression that *Mademoiselle* and *Harper's Bazaar* simply provided different sorts of quality fiction, Mary McCarthy and others proposed that their stories were actually quite similar. Their stories were similar insofar as these fashion magazines bought fashionable stories. In her 1950 article "Up the Ladder from *Charm* to *Vogue*," McCarthy provides a devastatingly astute summary of *Harper's Bazaar* fiction:

> The fiction published by *Harper's Bazaar*, to be conned by suburban ladies under the drier, belongs almost exclusively to the mannerist or decadent school of American writing. Truman Capote, Edita Morris, Jane Bowles, Paul Bowles, Eudora Welty, Jean Stafford, Carson McCullers—what these writers have in common, beyond a lack of matter and a consequent leukemia of treatment (taken by the *Bazaar* editors to be the very essence of art), is a potpourri of *fleurs de mal*, a preoccupation with the décor of sorrow, sexual aberration, insanity, and cruelty, a tasteful arrangement of the bric-a-brac of pathology around the whatnot of a central symbol.[106]

In *Love and Death in the American Novel*, Leslie Fiedler calls Welty, McCullers, and especially Capote, "feminizing Fauknerians" whose "tone and style have been accommodated to notions of chic nurtured by such fashion magazines as *Harper's Bazaar*."[107] Fiedler's book emphasizes the dark, gothic origins of American literature, but he sees what some would call Capote's "southern gothic" as an effeminate falling off. Although McCarthy and Fiedler each justify their critiques by an unfortunate appeal to normative standards of masculinity, they provide, nonetheless, a convincing sense that *Harper's Bazaar* fiction is more homogeneous then it might appear.

I characterize the homogeneity of this fiction as one inclined toward the gothic. McCarthy feels a lack of real subject matter in these works, and an overemphasis on madness and cruelty. The stories, indeed, tend toward the subjective, the atmospheric, the inverted fairy tale, the pathologically internalized. The protagonist of Patricia Highsmith's "The Heroine" (*Harper's Bazaar*, August 1945) needs to be part of a heroic story so badly that she sets her house on fire. The protagonist of Margaret Shedd's "The Great Fire of 1945" (*Harper's Bazaar*, July 1946) narrates while her house is burning down all around her. Marianne Hauser, author of the gothic novel *Dark Dominion* (1947), makes "The Other Side of the River" (*Mademoiselle*, April 1948) a weird, interior voyage ("she had lost her speech—at the foot of what burned-out volcano, what stricken tree?").[108] Gladys Schmitt's "The Mourners" (*Harper's Bazaar*, May 1944) makes a marriage as strange and death-bound as possible ("[her eyes] would shine like that in her withered face when he had stepped into nothingness before her and she lay listening to May thunder in an empty bed").[109] Bessie Breuer's "The Skeleton and the Easter Lily" (*Harper's Bazaar*, April 1947) works out a weird, almost experimental romance, where self-involved lovers are observed through a lens of archaic language ("Only his Bride, the dark seraph, floating in light and joy, and forever").[110] Ray Bradbury's fantasies in *Mademoiselle*—"Homecoming" (October 1946) and "The Cistern" (May 1947)—are not pathological or tragic, but they fit right into this highly subjective framework. Bradbury was happy to move from the horror pulps to the well-paying slicks, but *Mademoiselle* did not leave fantasy and horror behind.[111]

The *Harper's Bazaar* critics aim their harshest comments at Truman Capote; even Diana Trilling calls the "trappings of horror" in Capote's *Other Voices, Other Rooms* (1948) "the latest chic example of Southern Gothic."[112] Apparently horror is now so common that it is hip. But once we look past the layers of "chic," what is at stake in Capote's horror? Capote's "Miriam" (*Mademoiselle*, June 1945) is a straightforward nightmare; a little girl named Miriam keeps popping in and out of Mrs. Miller's perception. No explanation is offered in terms of the widow's psychology or genealogy (Miriam is not her deceased or unborn daughter); the little girl's appearances and disappearances render the widow's apartment completely unstable ("the sofa loomed before her with a new strangeness").[113] Compared to Lovecraft and *Weird Tales*, this horror is pared-down and contemporary. "Miriam" looks ahead to both Bradbury's lyrical fantasies and to Shirley Jackson's domestic horror in a story like "Charles" (*Mademoiselle*, July 1948).[114] Capote, Bradbury, and Jackson all rise to prominence at about the same time, but only Capote is attacked for gothic modishness.

Capote's "A Tree of Night" (*Harper's Bazaar*, October 1945) speaks explicitly to the situation of the woman's magazine reader.[115] The main character is an "attractive" girl (191) who carries an "assortment of magazines" (192) on her train ride to college. She is stuck next to a strange-looking woman who orders her not to read; on the woman's other side is an even weirder man, perhaps her husband. At one point the man reaches out to stroke the young woman's cheek; at another he pulls out a "shellacked peach seed" and "caresses the seed in an undefinably obscene manner" (204). The college student tries to escape the pair, but is forced back into her seat. She comes to fear them like a childhood fear, "a childish memory of terrors that once, long ago, had hovered above her like haunted limbs on a tree of night" (207–208). The man stares and stares at her, "not removing his gaze for an instant" (208). When Kay finally stares back at the man, "the man's face seemed to change form and recede before her like a moon-shaped rock sliding downward under a surface of water" (209). As the strange woman takes her purse, Kay "pulled the raincoat like a shroud over her head" (209).

The attractive young woman in "A Tree of Night" is a surrogate for all the pretty and prettifying readers of *Harper's Bazaar*. She is put into the alien, oppressive space of the female gothic, where monstrous men drive women crazy. Capote's scenario is exactly parallel to the illustration for *Experiment Perilous* in *Ladies' Home Journal*, where a pretty blonde stands bewildered in the foreground, while a scary vampire-like man stares ominously at her from behind.[116] This is just what happens to women in magazines for women. The scary man turns the woman into a helpless child. It happens so often that it has become "chic." It happens so often that it has become part of nature; Capote's nightmarish man is like a tree and then a rock. The looming "tree of night" *is* the nonverbal, wild, staring patriarchal threat now made completely normal, an everyday even lyrical thing.

The strain of female gothic that links *Ladies' Home Journal* to *Harper's Bazaar* can be admired for its reality or criticized for its escapism. From a certain angle, these stories quite properly work to expose the cruel tyranny of the patriarchal regime. With the terrorized college student as its focus, Capote's "A Tree of Night" certainly invites such a reading. From another angle, these stories are fantasies that have nothing to do with reality. Because the stories are often inverted fairy tales, no psychological explanation attends the violence. As this book comes full circle, we have landed once again in Diana Trilling's hell of subjectivity, where women's magazines, the sexual narcissism of their advertisements, and their self-enclosed fiction all work to cut women off from an objective relationship to the world.

White mainstream culture relegates female desire to an exotic elsewhere—to a film noir's underworld, to African American blues music, to the jumble of Shanghai. In contrast to this sexual elsewhere, culture for women often consigns female desire to an oppressive nowhere. The strain of gothic horror that passes from *Ladies' Home Journal* through confessional magazines and into the shiny pages of *Mademoiselle* leaves women oppressively enclosed, imprisoned, burnt to ash. In these women's magazine stories that are the opposite of women's magazine stories, desire is dried up and dead. When the female protagonist of "The Great Fire of 1945" stands in the ruins of her burning home, she can remember her husband's last words before he left: "You dirty, frustrated bitch, you dirty, frustrated bitch."[117] His mad curse names her as the origin of her own sexual destruction, and she agrees, "this is my atom bomb, conceived in me."[118] Hitchcock's *Rebecca* ends with Manderlay in flames, but these are liberating flames. Now that the gothic mansion is dust and ashes, hero and heroine can finally find their true heart's desire beyond its oppressive walls. But what if there is no place outside the house, beyond the flames? Then the woman's only home companion is anger and despair. "There was no longer any escaping from it; it was the last reality they shared—evil, life-sucking, all consuming" (Jane Cobb, "The Hot Day" [*McCall's*, September 1946]).[119]

Conclusion

Two Phantom Women

Ruth Herschberger and Elizabeth Hawes

> The unusual thing about her was the hat. It resembled a pumpkin, not only in shape and size but in color. . . . Not one woman in a thousand would have braved that color. She not only did, she got away with it. She looked startling, but good, not funny. The rest of her was toned-down, reticent in black, almost invisible against the beacon of a hat. Perhaps the thing was a symbol of some sort of liberation, to her. Perhaps the mood that went with it was, "When I have this on, watch out for me! The sky's the limit!"
>
> —William Irish (Cornell Woolrich), *Phantom Lady*[1]

In Woolrich's 1942 mystery *Phantom Lady*, the male hero spends an evening with this spectacularly attired woman. But later, when he needs her for an alibi, he completely forgets everything about her. As he explains from his prison cell, "I looked at her all night long; I didn't see her once."[2] This is also what happens in the 1940s, where numerous women present themselves as ambitious, unique, liberated persons. Men look at them, but do not see them. Women write thoughtful, liberating critiques of the decade's entrenched gender norms, but understanding readers seem to have gone missing. And to various degrees, later readers have also forgotten about them—these striking, confident phantom ladies.

We have met numerous phantom ladies over the course of this book. Diana Trilling is a name familiar to many—primarily thanks to her husband—but little effort has been made to rehabilitate her work.[3] In *The*

Waves (1943) and *Westward the Women* (1944), Nancy Wilson Ross writes about strong, capable women, and she ends each book with a polemical, feminist conclusion. Yet although these books were read, and the latter even made into a film (Wellman, 1951), their explicitly feminist character barely registered with readers. Jo Sinclair's *Wasteland* contains a remarkably rounded description of a lesbian character, but the novel remains relatively unstudied. And no one, herself included, suspected that Kathleen Winsor was working in a feminist mode; readers were busy ogling rather than seeing. So Elaine Showalter is alone when she looks past Winsor's giant orange hat to find a real sense of subversive female power in novels such as *Forever Amber* and *Star Money*.

In this concluding chapter, I briefly discuss the work of two of the decade's most important phantoms, Ruth Herschberger and Elizabeth Hawes. These writers looked at exactly the kinds of gender issues we have followed throughout this book. Herschberger in *Adam's Rib* (1948) and Hawes in *Anything but Love* (1948) take scathing and clear-eyed aim at the decade's misogynistic descriptions of female sexuality. Herschberger focuses her attacks on scientific schools, while Hawes targets mass culture. Yet despite their often witty approaches to a universally interesting topic—sex!—these books were almost invisible at the time. Sexual desire that was not merely wolfish or wolfish imitation turned out to be impossible to see.

It is worth noting that the one writer who can actually see both of these women—and who also has the potential for understanding them—proceeds to attack each in turn, one after the other. During the 1940s, there is no more thorough overview of sexuality in popular culture than Gershon Legman's *Love and Death: A Study in Censorship* (1949). In this still remarkably illuminating work, Legman argues that society censors the wrong things. That is, society nonsensically allows bloodthirsty violence in detective novels and comic books, while it simultaneously represses sex, although murder is illegal and sex is normal. His chapter, "The Bitch-Heroine," reads sexy heroines such as Amber and Duchess Hotspur as in reality powerful sadists who enjoy torturing men but "have no more sexual thrill in them than so many iced fish."[4] Legman asserts that these portrayals—these "onslaughts against a woman's self-respect"—should engender feminist ire. With an extraordinarily thorough grasp of a wide range of materials, and an unparalleled focus on sexuality, Legman is on the cusp of linking his critique of violence in mass culture to a political agenda.

But apparently this linkage cannot yet take place. Instead of seeing these female writers as allies, Legman proceeds to belittle the "latest and bitterest of the formal attacks on men that women are now writing, Ruth

Herschberger's *Adam's Rib* (1948)." Then, after citing Virginia Woolf, he attacks the emphases in Elizabeth Hawes, "who tabulates with bitter fairness in *Anything but Love* (1948) the pulverization of American women by all the suggestion-pressure of society."[5] Thanks to his fantastically erudite survey of sex in 1940s popular culture, Legman is about the only person on earth who can see and understand what these two women are up to. But he trivializes them both, attacking Herschberger for her attention to the pronunciation of "clitoris" and then Hawes for her supposed desire (in a 1939 book) to "put men into skirts." Just as these phantom women are about to come into the light, the very man who might see them plunges them back into darkness.

Ruth Herschberger's *Adam's Rib* (1948) was reprinted in 1970 as a "feminist classic," yet in the 1940s it seemed almost invisible. Quoting scientists, sex manuals, and polemicists, Herschberger brilliantly attacks the far-flung cultural repression of female sexual desire. Yet whereas openly misogynist books like *Modern Woman: The Lost Sex* (1947) were widely discussed, *Adam's Rib* was either mocked or ignored.

Edgar Brooke's book review in the *New York Times* essentially laughs at Herschberger: " 'Adam's Rib' is apparently the product of Ruth Herschberger's irritation after reading a number of 'popular' and scholarly works on the sex life of women. As the self-appointed champion of her sex, she attacks the scientists for their errors. The outcome of the conflict is clear: the battered figure pinned to the mat is that, alas, of Miss Herschberger."[6] Brooke not only treats the book with patronizing derision, he imagines his victory over her as one in which he beats her into the ground, a vanquished and "battered figure." After pointing out a few contradictions in Herschberger's book, Brooke ends his review in exasperation, "Would some maladjusted female like to take it from here?" This demeaning and violent review is designed to keep any reader from ever looking at *Adam's Rib*.

And for many years *Adam's Rib* remained, indeed, a phantom book. Feminists in the 1940s did not refer to it.[7] It was not until 1970, when the women's liberation movement had finally prepared the ground, that a book written more than twenty years earlier could find an audience. In 1970 Susan Brownmiller records a meeting of radical feminists that included not only many young women, but women from an earlier generation: " 'I almost wept after my first meeting. I went home and filled my diary,' says Ruth Herschberger, poet and author of *Adam's Rib*, a witty and unheeded expostulation of women's rights published in 1948. 'When I wrote *Adam's Rib*, I was writing for readers who wouldn't accept the first premise.' "[8] In the anatomizing, evaluating patriarchal culture of the 1940s, a misogynistic premise often made sense, while a contrary premise made no sense, was beaten down.

These books were hard for contemporary readers to process not so much because they were feminist, but because they were about female sexual desire. Strong, independent women were celebrated during the war, but female sexual desire remained opaque. In *Out of the Kitchen—Into the War* (1943), Susan B. Anthony II patriotically, but also politically, insists that woman workers be allowed into a predominantly male world.[9] The patriotic radio show, *Cavalcade of America*, produced numerous shows about heroic women (in 1940 alone they celebrated Mehitabel Wing, a strong Quaker woman; Anne Royall, who defended freedom of speech; Jane Addams of Hull House; Martha Berry, founder of a college; and Susan B. Anthony).[10] Almost without exception in the *Cavalcade of America* series, men who object to women's equality are regarded as fools. The 1947 *Life* magazine article "American Woman's Dilemma" states with perfect clarity the boring, laborious, contradictory nature of the American housewife ("John McWeeney looks at [his wife] Marjorie and sees her in seven different roles, laundress, cook, expert nurse-governess, seamstress, chauffeur, and housemaid; in addition to all the working roles she fills, Marjorie must also be John's glamour girl"), and even cites a passage from Elizabeth Hawes's *Why Women Cry* (1943).[11] 1940s culture is patriarchal, no doubt, through and through. But within that culture, feminists stake out recognizable positions.

But what is apparently unrecognizable is a straightforward treatment of female sexual desire. What kind of topic is this? As we have seen, the "frank" openness to sex and sexuality in the 1940s meant, above all, the recognition that male sexual desire needed to be satisfied. Female desire appears in novels, comics, confession magazines, and detective movies, but the time for official acknowledgement by the *New York Times* has not yet arrived. Popular culture and serious novels are more open to the possibility of female desire than the cultural administrators. Meanwhile ideological critiques by Hawes and Herschberger vanish into the murk of what passes for 1940s air.

Whereas Hawes aims her critique at the mass media, Herschberger, for the most part, takes on scientific authorities. We have seen how dangerously authoritative the scientists have become, so they are in need of some pointed demystification. One chapter title is "Society Writes Biology," and *Adam's Rib* continually reveals the gender bias inherent in supposedly objective disciplines such as biology and psychology.[12] These scientific authorities somehow always find that male sexuality is aggressive and that female sexuality is passive. In the chapter "Is Rape a Myth?" Herschberger shows how "man's natural sexual aggression" soon blurs into criminal assault. We should not be misled, she writes, "by the ease with which the forced and unwilling woman of the rape myth becomes transformed into the affectionate and grateful maiden."[13] Herschberger makes the same argument as the present book, namely that the wolfish man's "natural" desire for the beautiful woman is always about to turn into a horror story. By "objectively" describing male sexual desire as naturally aggressive and female sexual desire as naturally passive, the authorities accommodate male sexual coercion while they refuse to acknowledge the existence of female sexual desire.

Herschberger argues that everything in culture conspires toward an "education for frigidity." The way parents raise and reward their children leads to confident, aggressive boys and passive girls. Boys are congratulated for physical exertion and efficient, unsentimental activity. Girls are encouraged to be restrained, cautious, and above all, clean. Boys are likely to be proud of their bodies and even their secretions; girls are probably ashamed of their bodies and what comes out of them. If the sex act requires activity, "who acts?" When men and women finally come together in sexual embrace, society has made sure that men oversee this intimate space. As Herschberger writes, "In the invisible but nonetheless significant realm of sex an unchallenged patriarchy still holds."[14] In order to shed light on this invisible realm, Herschberger made one of the most articulate arguments of the decade, but alas her book for the most part remained a ghostly phantom.

Elizabeth Hawes was another 1940s phantom lady whom no one knew how to read. Unlike Herschberger, who was relatively unknown at the time, Hawes was a famous woman—a famous clothing designer and already a well-known writer. By the end of the 1930s Hawes was one of the nation's leading fashion designers. She then published several critiques of the fashion industry. The logic of the title, *Fashion Is Spinach* (1938), is that we buy our boring clothes uncomplainingly and obediently, just like we follow the command to "eat your spinach." She followed this with *Men Can Take It* (1939), which critiqued men's fashions. A description about the attractiveness of kilts seems to have made Legman decide that Hawes wants to put "men into skirts."[15] Her books throughout the 1940s would continue to focus provocatively on gender issues.

Gender concerns form the basis of her wartime tract, *Why Women Cry, or Wenches with Wrenches* (1943). Now Hawes has abandoned her fashion business and, as a kind of social experiment, taken a job in a factory alongside so many other women workers. The gender polemic, however, situates itself as more than wartime journalism; Hawes argues that the issues of women's work, career, and role in the family are ones that are central to the United States, whether at war or at peace. The middle part of the book details what it is like for men to work alongside women, considers whether women can do men's jobs, and explores possible "sex problems." The closing section of the book is given over in large part to the need for adequate childcare, which women need in order to allow themselves to explore employment opportunities beyond the drudgery of household chores.

The opening section of *Why Women Cry* categorizes women with politically aggressive and self-lacerating vigor. Many of these categories ("rich bitch," "clubwomen") are not too attractive since Hawes's point is that even the most privileged women live stunted lives. Almost all women are "wenches" because they are either "locked in their houses or tied to them by a strong rope, the other end of which rests in the hands of a child, husband, or servant":[16] "Ninety-nine percent of American females over twenty-one years of age cannot attain their full strength. There we are not adult. There we are not women. We are wenches."[17] Yet although twenty-first-century readers would identify her analysis as feminist, Hawes feels the need to distinguish herself from "feminists" and "equal-righters." She goes as far as to equate feminists who "stir up this kind of sex trouble" with "Ku Klux Klanners."[18] In contrast to feminists who only fight on behalf of women, Hawes sees her debate as one that benefits both sexes. It seems clear that Hawes feels the need to strategically sabotage herself from time to time in order to make her points appear less threatening.

One of the basic ways that Hawes critiques her own position is to define herself as a "she-wolf." Whereas 1940s culture typically took "she-wolves" for sexually aggressive women, Hawes uses the term to capture the ruthless independence of the successful businesswoman. While her book's positive goal is to give all women a chance to expand their vocational horizons, Hawes portrays her own ambitions in a less than positive light; "the She-Wolves," she writes, "are just as ruthless as the He-Wolves."[19] And soon enough the more typical associations of the "she-wolf" appear since the "She-Wolves trade on their femininity whenever it suits their purposes."[20] Hawes's idea is that these distorted forms of feminine character appear due to societal defects, but this large-scale point is easy to miss. An unusually perceptive *New York Times* review says that Hawes has written the book with "such wit that its true seriousness may not be visible to the naked eye."[21] And Hawes was still famous enough that *Why Women Cry* was, according to her biographer, "an instant success."[22]

Hawes's *Anything but Love* (1948) stands as the exemplary phantom critique of female sexuality in 1940s mass culture. The subtitle aims its withering satire at the gamut of popular culture: "A Complete Digest of the Rules of Feminine Behavior from Birth to Death, Given Out in Print, on Film, and Over the Air; Read, Seen, Listened to Monthly by Some 340,000,000 American Women."[23] This book serves as both the clearest and the most brilliant attack on the construction of femininity during the decade. Tonally and stylistically, it is a wild, violent, and repetitive performance as Hawes replicates the chain of contradictions that allows patriarchal culture to survive. Proffered advice for women turns around abruptly, from sentence to sentence, and it is sometimes hard to see where Hawes speaks in her own voice and where she ventriloquizes the "Authorities." From a contemporary vantage point, her message is poignantly and powerfully clear. But in its day the book entirely vanished and has managed to stay almost invisible ever since. *Anything but Love* could have been the decade's *Feminine Mystique*, but nobody paid attention. Indeed, years later, even Betty Friedan gives the impression of not knowing Hawes's work.[24]

Readers of course knew what to do with satire, and women's magazines had often been satirized. S. J. Perelman, one of America's most well-known playwrights and satirists, often lampooned women's magazines. In Perelman, however, there is no political or even personal edge; the lampoon is simply silliness. In a typical piece, "Bend Down, Sister," Perelman mocks feminine advertising and fashion talk, but on behalf of humor, not politics.[25] In the Broadway play *One Touch of Venus* (1944), coauthored by Perelman and Ogden Nash, the high romantic ambitions of the ancient love goddess become domesticated. At the end of the play she pathetically looks forward to a magazine consumer's paradise—a "fireplace that looks like a radio" and "a year's subscription to the *Reader's Digest*."[26] That end might seem desperately sad, but in its day it was just good comedy. A *New York Times* review says that the show provides the best entertainment since *Oklahoma*.[27]

In contrast to Perelman's very assimilable satire, then, is Hawes's *Anything but Love*, which apparently resisted assimilation. Since readers could understand attacks on women's magazines, comic or otherwise, and since they could also process identifiable feminism, one could again propose that what make Hawes so completely inscrutable is that at the heart of her polemic stands the hypothesis that female sexual desire actually exists.

The *New York Times* does manage to print a review, which performs the act of reading and then disposing of the book. Linking Hawes's *Why Women Cry* to *Anything but Love*, Thomas Sugrue says that "she fights with a bright and sometimes fierce pen for certain wayward and neglected causes, among them honesty of relationship between adult humans, male and female."[28] But Sugrue makes the problem seem as trivial as possible;

to attack the cultural construction of female sexuality is not—to twenty-first-century minds—to champion a "wayward cause." Sugrue acts out the reasonable male sense that he cannot see what the problem is. After all, the deluge of ads aimed at women is regarded by the "average husband and father, a realist," as "part of the general business of advertising." But Hawes reads this "normal routine" into something larger and more ominous; she argues that the cradle-to-grave advertising makes women into narcissists and megalomaniacs. For Hawes this is a "ghastly situation," but the reviewer cannot come close to taking the problem seriously.

At the end of the review, in a particularly useless gesture, Sugrue disqualifies himself from judging the book. Sugrue says that since this "psychological dilemma is female-made and female-inhabited, a man's opinion is of no interest or pertinence." A book reviewer's job is seemingly founded on an empathetic consciousness, but Sugrue reduces the problem to a "psychological dilemma" and declines further participation. Yet of course, hypocritically, he still wants to pass judgment, so he overhears some other opinions in his absence. He conjures up several female "goddesses" and asks them what they think. One says she liked it; others thought the book too long. But soon, Sugrue writes, "they had forgotten me and were discussing an article in the current *Woman's Home Companion*, something about a poll of goddesses on the subject of birth control." Even though we understand how patriarchal 1940s culture was, the obnoxious mockery that Hawes and Herschberger received in these *New York Times* reviews is still quite breathtaking.

Anything but Love is an ambitious book, complex in tonality and profound in its scope. On the first page, Hawes refers to two misogynistic bestsellers: "Is woman a lost sex? If so, is she the only lost sex? Has woman alone conceived all the vipers in our land?" Hawes thus places her book-length diatribe next to *Modern Woman: The Lost Sex* and Philip Wylie's *Generation of Vipers*. Wylie's books were also repetitive and generally "too long" (as one of the goddesses said of Hawes), but at least readers made an effort to reflect on his dark satirical reading of sexuality in contemporary culture. By invoking these books, Hawes implies that she would like the same generosity extended toward her own work. Like *Modern Woman* and *Generation of Vipers*, Hawes provides a full-scale interpretation of America in the midst of sexual crisis. The burden of female responsibility is envisioned not just as an individual, domestic problem, but also as a political patriotic problem: "The relief you are allowed to get from doing your duty is the sensation of being loved Nationally" (190). Hawes's argument thus connects ads for underwear and stockings to large-scale notions of American cultural identity. She wants readers to set her book next to the decade's other major pronouncements on these matters. But since her dark vision is dreamt on behalf of women, her book is dismissed as merely a bad dream—or as nothing at all.

Hawes agrees with Herschberger that American culture educates women into frigidity. Aphorisms and observations develop this point from various angles. Trapped by family responsibility and "labor-saving devices," women sublimate desire into commodities: "it is not so much through the husband as through the other goods that she must satisfy her sexual desires" (133). If women actually followed all the rules that society set down for them, all sexual desire would successfully be erased: "Statistics on frigidity among women vary, but they are always over 50 percent of the total adult female population. If They are ever totally successful in putting over the rules, frigidity among women will certainly rise to 100 percent" (192). These lines are delivered in Hawes's own voice; she also parodies the desire-crushing advice of authoritative counselors: "Women who are not passive in sex have something wrong with them. Man is born to give and woman is born to take and that is that. Should anyone try to change this, the entire sex pattern of our day would crash. (And if any reader thinks that would be a good thing, be quiet about it. It only shows you have a complex.)" (202). As part of numerous attacks on psychological authority, Hawes names these complexes the "masculinity complex" (if a woman is too career-oriented, 67) or the "vaginal complex" (if "you think the female is the whole race," 242). In general, women should be seen and not heard, stick to their prescribed roles, and not make trouble. And Hawes's readers followed the rules.

The tonality of the book is as striking as its content. It is defiantly not frivolous, not nonsensical in its comedy. On the contrary, there is a tearing desperation that comes through at numerous points. As a single woman, you are basically useless: "you may have to shoot yourself" (72). Middle-aged women are equally useless: "you begin to realize that after thirty-five you are as good as dead" (260). After a particularly exasperating section, Hawes writes, presumably in her own voice: "While writing this book, we have kept a sharp dagger at hand with which we have stabbed ourselves regularly every few hours. But we lived through it. Never really kill yourself. Just pretend" (223). "Just pretend" is the advice that patriarchal culture offers women—pretend to be a movie star, pretend to be the one your husband loves, pretend to be sexually satisfied. But here the book breaks through the superficial, made-up face of society's desire. This is real pain, real horror.

The *New York Times* reviewer uses this quote to pivot away from Hawes; exactly at this violent moment, he now loses interest in what she says. After Hawes says "just pretend," Sugrue wins a quick debate: "With regard to love, however, it isn't even necessary to pretend. Love is something all people feel for a modern American girl, and which she feels for herself. This, in the opinion of Miss Hawes, is a ghastly situation. The reason it is a ghastly situation is because it makes the women who become goddesses unhappy. Women should not be unhappy."[29]

Sugrue refutes Hawes by repeating her own ideas back to her, in simpler form. Concluding with a sentence so simple that even a lovable "American girl" can understand it ("Women should not be unhappy"), Sugrue exemplifies just what it means to be patronizing. Hawes is so exasperated with the Authorities that she is about to stab herself with a knife; meanwhile her authoritative reader teases her for female problems. He does not see what a horror show it is, that what this culture shows and does is truly ghastly. Although he created it, the self-wounding female body is not something he cares to contemplate. So ghastliness becomes ghostliness, and the body turns to air.

Notes

Chapter 1. Introduction: Sexual Visibility, or, The Duel in the Sun

1. For reasons primarily of space, I will not talk much about television. Two careful historians of television write that "protests over sex settled on more symbolic connections and issues because there was not any sex, per se, on television in 1950" (Harry Castleman and Walter J. Podrazik, *Watching TV: Four Decades of American Television* [New York: McGraw-Hill Book Company, 1982], 47). What follows, Arthur Godfrey's "few bawdy stories" and women's low necklines, apparently do not constitute "sex, per se." But television can concentrate the ribaldry of radio while also offering versions of Hollywood cheesecake. On an early episode of the *Ed Wynn Show* (1.3, October 6, 1949), Wynn says that his uncle cut pictures out of fashion magazines (he thought it was the Sears catalogue and he was trying to place an order); when Wynn shows up in Paris he asks to see their (French) postcards and remarks on French bathing suits; he then interacts with a lady named Belita who models her legs aggressively before performing a leggy can-can. None of this is "sex as such," perhaps, but it is certainly continuous with the male sexual humor and female sexual display found throughout 1940s culture.

2. John R. Whiting and George R. Clark, "The Picture Magazines," *Harper's* (July 1943), 159–60. In "One Every Minute, the Picture Magazines," Jackson Edwards gives an early overview of the thriving picture magazine scene (*Scribner's* [May 1938], 17–23).

3. In the November 1942 issue of *Coronet* there is "Your Enemy: The Jap," a "Picture Story" whose "purpose is to bring you face to face with your enemy so you may judge him for yourself" (27–42). Also in the "Features" section is "The Gallery of Photographs" (111–36), which sometimes puts humorous captions (a monkey is titled "sophomore") on various photos. Radio shows are visualized throughout the September 1947 issue of *Radio Mirror*. There is "Suspense! A Picture-Story" (38–41) in which the radio actors act out in thirteen panels a recent radio play; also "The Adventures of Frank Merriwell—in Pictures" (44–45); the regular column "In Living Portraits" provides full-color photographs of all the show's actors in character

("Pepper Young's Family," 50–53). With glamorous advertisements and a cover girl radio star on each issue, *Radio Mirror* attempts to turn imageless radio into a visual medium no different from the movies.

4. William Moulton Marston, "Why 100,000,000 Americans Read Comics," *American Scholar* 13 (1944): 37.

5. On the connection between visual culture and sexual culture at the turn of the twentieth century, see Sharon R. Ullman, *Sex Seen: The Emergence of Modern Sexuality in America* (Berkeley: U of California P, 1997). Critics who described the "picture magazines" inevitably noted that they offered not only "picture stories," but also sexy pictures. In his introduction to *The Great Pictures 1949* (New York: Greenberg, 1949), Clifton C. Edom claims that picture magazines are much less sensationalistic than they were ten years ago, when they were willing to run pictures of "human nakedness for its own sake" (14). But even in these less tabloid days, "what editor in his right mind," he asks, "will fully cover a leg or a bosom?" (14). Whiting and Clark point out that in parallel to the well-known picture magazines there emerges a whole gallery of cheesecake magazines, which are short-lived but dedicated straightforwardly to photographs of "underclad" women ("The Picture Magazines," 164).

6. Actually, the rules of canasta apparently packed plenty of oomph since three out of the top ten best-selling nonfiction books of 1949 were books on canasta by three different authors (Alice Payne Hickett, *60 Years of Best Sellers: 1895–1955* [New York: Bowker, 1956], 193). As Hickett observes in her comments on these lists, nonfiction bestsellers in the late 1940s were often picture books, such as Al Capp's *The Life and Times of the Shmoo* (1948), and the popular "zoo" series, where animal photographs are given humorous captions (Clare Barnes Jr., *White Collar Zoo* [1949], *Home Sweet Zoo* [1949], and *Campus Zoo* [1950]). Number one in nonfiction for 1950 is *Betty Crocker's Picture Cook Book* and number two is another picture-humor book: *The Baby: A Photographic Inquiry into Certain Private Opinions.*

7. Daniel D. Mich, ed. *The Technique of the Picture Story: A Practical Guide to the Production of Visual Articles* (New York: McGraw-Hill, 1945). The foreword is by Paul A. McGhee, Director, Division of General Education, at New York University. McGhee says that 1944 lectures in the NYU course "The Technique of the Picture Story" provided the "basis for this volume" (5).

8. *Technique of the Picture Story*, 64.

9. See Stephen King, *Danse Macabre* (New York: Everest House, 1981), 40–43.

10. John Dunning, despite his encyclopedic knowledge, calls old-time radio "curiously asexual" (*The Encyclopedia of Old-Time Radio* [New York: Oxford UP, 1998], 337). I have benefitted enormously from Dunning's old-time radio erudition, but 1940s radio is often both curious and sexual.

11. Robert Wilder, *Wait for Tomorrow* (New York: Putnam's Sons, 1950), 162.

12. "Love Crazy," *Lux Radio Theatre*, 10–5–42.

13. See the classified section of *Billboard*, February 12, 1949, 77–88, which includes ads for two sets of glamour girl photos, a pen whose stem comes in the

shape of a naked woman, and no less than seven kinds of "scopes" to look at pictures of women. In each case, cartoon men are shown wide-eyed with their tongues hanging out as they look through the scopes. "Scan-teez" is a homophone for "scanties" (i.e., female underwear).

14. Mary Ann Doane, *The Desire to Desire: The Woman's Film of the 1940s* (Bloomington: Indiana UP, 1987). Doane's book is full of terrific readings and I depend on it at various points in this study. Her book is more interested in the contemporary uses of psychoanalysis, however, than it is in the cultural context of the 1940s.

15. Scanlon's book covers *Ladies' Home Journal* from 1910 to 1930 (*Inarticulate Longings: The Ladies' Home Journal, Gender, and the Promises of Consumer Culture* [New York: Routledge, 1995]). "Inarticulate language" is the formulation of an advertising agency; they want to help women figure out what they want (to buy); by contrast Scanlon wants to keep track of "women's inarticulate longings for personal autonomy, economic independence, intimacy, sensuality, self-worth, and social recognition" that manage to be voiced through or around the magazine's prevalent "culture of consumption" (10).

16. Barbara Creed, *The Monstrous-Feminine: Film, Feminism, Psychoanalysis* (New York: Routledge, 1993), 7.

17. Fritz Leiber, "The Girl with the Hungry Eyes," *Night's Black Agents* (New York: Berkley Medallion, 1978), 241. Leiber's story first appeared in Avon paperback 184, *The Girl with the Hungry Eyes* (New York: Avon, 1949).

18. Walter Keating, *Sex Studies from Freud to Kinsey* (New York: Stravon, 1949), 81.

19. John Costello, *Virtue under Fire: How World War II Changed Our Social and Sexual Attitudes* (Boston: Little, Brown, 1985).

20. Leisa D. Meyer, *Creating G.I. Jane: Sexuality and Power in the Women's Army Corps during World War II* (New York: Columbia UP, 1998); Jane Mersky Leder, *Thanks for the Memories: Love, Sex, and World War II* (Westport, CT: Praeger, 2006); Marilyn E. Hegarty, *Victory Girls, Khaki-Wackies, and Patriotutes: The Regulation of Female Sexuality during World War II* (New York: New York UP, 2008); Meghan K. Winchell, *Good Girls, Good Food, Good Fun: The Story of USO Hostesses during World War II* (Chapel Hill: U of North Carolina P, 2008); Susan K. Kahn, *Sexual Reckonings: Southern Girls in a Troubling Age* (Cambridge, MA: Harvard UP, 2007).

21. The line of poetry is taken from a poem by Lisa Ben in *Vice Versa*, no. 3. Facsimile issues of *Vice Versa* are available online at www.queermusicheritage.us/viceversa.html (July 1, 2013).

22. Max Horkheimer and Theodor W. Adorno, "The Culture Industry: Enlightenment as Mass Deception," trans. John Cumming (New York: Continuum, 1989), 120–67.

23. In *The Communication of Ideas*, ed. Lyman Bryson (New York: Harper, 1948), Paul Lazarsfeld and Robert Merton argue that the mass media leads to social conformity and a degrading of aesthetic taste ("Mass Communications, Popular

Taste, and Organized Social Action," 95–118). In an article from the same time, "Role of Criticism in Management of Mass Media," Lazarsfeld gingerly defends his right to go beyond collecting data and criticize the mass media (*Communications in Modern Society*, ed. Wilbur Schramm [Urbana: U of Illinois P, 1948], 187–203). On the relationship between Lazarsfeld and Adorno, see David E. Morrison, "Kultur and Culture: The Case of Theodor W. Adorno and Paul F. Lazarsfeld," *Social Research* 45 (Summer 1978): 331–55.

24. Marshall McLuhan, *The Mechanical Bride: Folklore of Industrial Man* (Boston: Beacon Press, 1970). This edition reproduces the first edition of *The Mechanical Bride* published by Vanguard in 1951. Page numbers are cited parenthetically in text hereafter.

25. Thomas F. Brady, "Receipts of 'Duel in the Sun' Mount as Protests Grow," *New York Times*, January 26, 1947, X5.

26. Bosley Crowther, " 'Duel in the Sun,' Selznick's Lavish Western," *New York Times*, May 8, 1947, 30.

27. Whereas her famous essay "Visual Pleasure and Narrative Cinema" focuses on the male spectator, Laura Mulvey uses *Duel in the Sun* to reflect on the role of the female spectator. In Mulvey's argument, the female spectator follows Pearl Chavez in her unsuccessful masculine identification. See "Afterthoughts on 'Visual Pleasure and Narrative Cinema' Inspired by King Vidor's *Duel in the Sun* (1946)," in Laura Mulvey, *Visual and Other Pleasures* (Bloomington: Indiana UP, 1989), 29–38.

28. Middletown was the generically named site of a famous study of American culture in the late 1920s (Robert S. Lynd and Helen Merrell Lynd, *Middletown, A Study in Contemporary American Culture* [New York: Harcourt and Brace, 1929]). With a focus on teenagers, a 1940s descendent of this study was August B. Hollingshead, *Elmtown's Youth: The Impact of Social Classes on Adolescents* (New York: Wiley, 1949). The reading interests of young people is surveyed in "Recreation and Tabooed Pleasures," 288–325. For both boys and girls, "picture magazines such as *Life* and *Look* are the most popular items in the periodical field" (307). Without gendering the readers, the authors also write that "sex, screen, comic, western, and detective stories are read more widely than the above-mentioned magazines that are taken at the home on a subscription basis" (307). These latter magazines are purchased at the newsstand and "circulated clandestinely from student to student" (308).

29. In a history that emphasizes 1940 as a cut-off date, Dale M. Bauer argues that female "sex expression" is "exhausted" by 1940 (*Sex Expression and American Women Writers, 1860–1940* [Chapel Hill: U of North Carolina P, 2009], 16).

30. On the heightened interest in strip shows during the early 1940s, see Rachel Shteir, "Striptease during the War," *Striptease: The Untold History of the Girlie Show* (New York: Oxford UP, 2004), 215–33.

31. A photograph of the library display is reproduced in the "Letters to the Editor" section of the *Saturday Review of Literature*, January 8, 1949, 24. The other half of the library display reads "Adventurers/Great Men and Women/Inventors/Sportsmen!" As an accompanying letter explains, the display works against censorship since it hopes instead to use its argumentative display to cause prospective young readers to choose quality books over poisonous comics.

Chapter 2. Diana Trilling, Female Desire, and the Study of Popular Culture

1. Editorial, "The Inexhaustible Exuberance of Gilbert Seldes," *Esquire*, August 1943, 6.

2. Michael Kammen, *The Lively Arts: Gilbert Seldes and the Transformation of Cultural Criticism in the United States* (New York: Oxford UP, 1996), 13.

3. The "lively arts" are popular arts in contrast to the serious or high arts such as poetry or sculpture. Kammen shows that Seldes was not too concerned about the number seven in *Seven Lively Arts* or what these arts were (*The Lively Arts*, 86–93).

4. These Seldes columns appeared in the following issues of *Esquire*: ballet, March 1940; Abbott and Costello, April 1940; Chaplin, January 1941; slang, February 1942; parades, July 1942; vaudeville, September 1942, Superman, November 1942; war films, May 1943; faces, July 1943; Durante, August 1943; Fred Allen, September 1943; Bing Crosby, February 1944; night clubs, September 1944; Bergman, October 1944; television, May 1945.

5. In a study that repeatedly emphasizes negotiations between high and low culture, Kammen calls Seldes a "high lowbrow" (*The Lively Arts*, 12).

6. In a discussion of Archibald MacLeish's poems, Seldes writes, "There are moments in history when a jingle is required, and good prosody is not" ("MacLeish: Minister of Culture," *Esquire*, June 1945, 103).

7. Gilbert Seldes, "What Every Woman Hater Knows," *Esquire*, June 1942, 54ff.

8. Gilbert Seldes, "The Gibson Girl for Me," *Esquire*, February 1943, 49.

9. George Jean Nathan, "Of Ladies Who Trod the Boards," *Esquire*, September 1944, 76. Nathan begins his survey of the year's actresses with a description sure to please *Esquire*'s male clientele: "Ann Pennington, as the pert serving maid in *The Student Prince*, who saucily flirted her short skirt up over her fundament sixty-three times by actual count" (76).

10. Gilbert Seldes, "Guaranteed Innocent Praise," *Esquire*, April 1944, 73.

11. Seldes, "Guaranteed Innocent Praise," 73.

12. Gilbert Seldes, "The Great American Face," *Esquire*, July 1943, 80.

13. Gilbert Seldes, "Oh, Rare Miss Bergman," *Esquire*, October 1944, 84.

14. Gilbert Seldes, "S-E-X," *The Great Audience* (New York: Viking, 1950), 76.

15. Throughout *The Great Audience* Seldes returns to these "criteria of maturity" (87). His demolition of the Hays Code ("S-E-X," 68–81) has much in common with Manny Farber's critiques; in their view, Hays means that no adult sex can be shown in Hollywood films.

16. Otis Ferguson, *The Film Criticism of Otis Ferguson*, ed. Robert Wilson (Philadelphia: Temple UP, 1971), 304, 333; Ann Sheridan, 409, 416.

17. "If Agee's criticism reflects a passion for poetry, and Farber's a passion for painting, Ferguson's reflects a passion for music," writes Andrew Sarris, "Foreword," *Film Criticism of Otis Ferguson*, x.

18. Ferguson, *Film Criticism*, 302.
19. Ferguson, *Film Criticism*, 388.
20. Ferguson, *Film Criticism*, 414, 324.
21. Ferguson, *Film Criticism*, 320.
22. James Agee, *Agee on Film* (Boston: Beacon Press, 1964), 41. He is talking about *Stage Door Canteen* (1943) in this excerpt. Page numbers are cited parenthetically in text hereafter.
23. "Suffocating genteelism," *Agee on Film*, 137; "Screen lovers are seldom shown to be capable of love" (135).
24. Manny Farber, *Farber on Film: The Complete Film Writings of Manny Farber* (New York: Library of America, 2009), 269. Page numbers are cited parenthetically in text hereafter.
25. This is one of many praises on the back jacket of the Library of America edition; Susan Sontag says, "Manny Farber is the liveliest, smartest, most original film critic this country has ever produced."
26. In his book on Maya Deren's *Meshes of the Afternoon* (London: British Film Institute, 2011), John David Rhodes points out that Farber frames his dislike of Deren's film using derisively homosexual terms ("lesbianish," "pansyish," 103). Rhodes mentions this with the explicit intent of denting Farber's seemingly flawless reputation.
27. Wilbur Schramm, ed., *Communications in Modern Society: Fifteen Studies of the Mass Media prepared for the University of Illinois Institute of Communications Research* (Urbana: U of Illinois P, 1948).
28. Hadley Cantril, *The Invasion from Mars* (Princeton, NJ: Princeton UP, 1940). Robert K. Merton, *Mass Persuasion: The Social Psychology of a War Bond Drive* (New York: Harper, 1946).
29. Paul Lazarsfeld and Frank Stanton, ed., *Radio Research 1942–1943* (New York: Duell, Sloan, and Pearce, 1944).
30. Paul F. Lazarsfeld and Frank Stanton, eds., *Communications Research 1948–1949* (New York: Harper, 1949).
31. See J. Michael Sproule, *Propaganda and Democracy: The American Experience of Media and Mass Persuasion* (New York: Cambridge UP, 1997), who discusses the movement from research in propaganda to communications (chap. 7, "The New Communication—Or the Old Propaganda?" [224–61]), Lazarsfeld's conflict between data collecting and critique (237), and why Adorno did not make more of an impact on American studies of mass culture (254).
32. David Riesman, *The Lonely Crowd: A Study of the Changing American Character* (New Haven, CT: Yale UP, 1950), 51.
33. G. Balsley, "The Hot Rod Culture," *American Quarterly* 2 (1950), 353–58.
34. Geoffrey Gorer, *The American People: A Study in National Character* (New York: Norton, 1948), 85.
35. Gorer, *American People*, 125.
36. For example, Michael S. Kimmel, "Masculinity as Homophobia: Fear, Shame, and Silence," in *Toward a New Psychology of Gender*, ed. Mary M. Gergen

and Sara N. Davis (New York: Routledge, 1997), 223–42, which includes a citation of Gorer (230).

37. Hortense Powdermaker, rev. Gorer, *The American People*, in *American Anthropologist* 50, no. 4 (1948): 668. Powdermaker's film study *Hollywood, the Dream Factory: An Anthropologist Looks at the Movies* (1950) explicitly uses her South Seas anthropological methodology as a framework for an investigation of Hollywood.

38. Powdermaker, rev., *The American People*, 668.

39. The review in *Time* gives the topic one sentence ("Anthropological Provocateur," *Time*, March 29, 1948, 108). *Life* ran a 4,000–word digest version of Gorer's book in the August 18, 1947, issue (95ff), which leaves out most of Gorer's analysis of masculinity and homosexuality. This selection, however, includes the same sentence quoted in *Time*—"the concept of being a sissy is key to the understanding of American character" (104).

40. Martha Wolfenstein and Nathan Leites, "Note," *Movies: A Psychological Study* (Glencoe, Illinois: Free Press, 1950), 7.

41. In a later article Martha Wolfenstein provides a more explicitly theoretical approach to film; "Movie Analysis in the Study of Culture," *The Study of Culture at a Distance*, ed. Margaret Mead and Rhoda Metraux (Chicago: U of Chicago P, 1953), 267–80. This book provides the theoretical methodology for the Columbia Research in Contemporary Cultures project. Film analysis is an important focus as shown by the examples in part 6 (267–316).

42. Wolfenstein and Leites, *Movies: A Psychological Study*, 20.

43. Wolfenstein and Leites, *Movies: A Psychological Study*, 31. Without citing him, Wolfenstein and Leites here follow Gorer's analysis of American dating; what confused foreigners, according to Gorer, is that the "gestures and intimacies and language are identical with true love-making," but the goal is nonetheless "*not* sexual satisfaction" (Gorer, *American People*, 117).

44. Wolfenstein and Leites, *Movies: A Psychological Study*, 31.

45. Wolfenstein and Leites, *Movies: A Psychological Study*, 76.

46. Wolfenstein and Leites, *Movies: A Psychological Study*, 82.

47. Wolfenstein and Leites do take one sentence to make sure we know that the "masculine-feminine" woman is not a lesbian. "In her masculine aspect, she is free from the mannishness of women who wanted to be equal to men in a competitive way, felt solidarity with other women, and denied the importance of sex difference" (*Movies: A Psychological Study*, 76–77).

48. Louise M. Newman, "Coming of Age, but Not in Samoa: Reflections on Margaret Mead's Legacy for Western Liberal Feminism," in *Reading Benedict/Reading Mead: Feminism, Race, and Imperial Visions*, ed. Dolores Janiewski and Lois W. Banner (Baltimore, MD: Johns Hopkins UP, 2004), 56–57.

49. Ruth Benedict, "Anthropology and the Abnormal," *Journal of General Psychology* 19 (1934): 59–82.

50. Margaret Mead, "Sexual Behavior: An Anthropologist Looks at the Kinsey Report," in *Studying Contemporary Western Society: Method and Theory*, ed. William

O. Beeman (New York: Berghahn, 2004), 278–87. Gorer similarly attacks Kinsey for too much data and not enough interpretation in his review, "Justification by Numbers: A Commentary on the Kinsey Report," *American Scholar*, September 1948, 280–86.

51. Margaret Mead, *Male and Female: A Study of the Sexes in a Changing World* (New York: Morrow, 1949), 262–63.

52. Mead, *Male and Female*, 372.

53. Betty Friedan, *The Feminine Mystique* (New York: Norton, 2001), 208.

54. Friedan, *Feminine Mystique*, 209.

55. Friedan, *Feminine Mystique*, 212.

56. Diana Trilling, "Men, Women, and Sex," *Partisan Review* 17 (1950): 368.

57. Trilling, "Men, Women, and Sex," 373.

58. Trilling, "Men, Women, and Sex," 376.

59. Trilling, "Men, Women, and Sex," 378.

60. Diana Trilling, *Reviewing the Forties* (New York: Harcourt Brace Jovanovich, 1978). Page numbers are cited parenthetically in text hereafter.

61. Diana Trilling, *We Must March My Darlings* (New York: Harcourt Brace Jovanovich, 1977).

62. Paul Fussell, Introduction to *Reviewing the Forties*, by Diana Trilling (New York: Harcourt Brace Jovanovich, 1978), v.

63. Diana Trilling, *The Beginning of the Journey: The Marriage of Diana and Lionel Trilling* (New York: Harcourt Brace, 1993), 331.

64. See Stefan Collini's review of a new edition of *The Liberal Imagination*, "Trilling's Sandbags," *Nation*, December 22, 2008, 38–42.

65. Diana Trilling, *Beginning of the Journey*, 346.

66. Diana Trilling, *Beginning of the Journey*, 347.

67. Diana Trilling, *Beginning of the Journey*, 346.

68. Edmund Wilson, "Who Cares Who Killed Roger Ackroyd?" *Literary Reviews of the 1930s and 40s* (New York: Library of America, 2007), 677–84.

69. Wilson, *Literary Reviews*, 724.

70. Wilson, *Literary Reviews*, 715.

71. Diana Trilling, *Beginning of the Journey*, 326.

72. *The Portable D. H. Lawrence*, ed. with an introduction by Diana Trilling (New York: Viking Press, 1947), 2.

73. *Portable D. H. Lawrence*, 2, 10.

74. *Portable D. H. Lawrence*, 11.

75. Diana Trilling, *Beginning of the Journey*, 349.

76. Isabel Bolton, *Do I Wake or Sleep* in *New York Mosaic* (South Royalton, VT: Steerforth Press, 1998), 36, 37.

77. Bolton, *Do I Wake or Sleep*, 124.

78. Bolton, *Do I Wake or Sleep*, 73.

79. Isabel Bolton, *The Christmas Tree* in *New York Mosaic* (South Royalton, VT: Steerforth Press, 1998), 222.

80. In "Bergman Unseen" (1960), Trilling writes about a collection of Bergman's screenplays, while confessing not only that he has not seen one Bergman film,

but also that he has not seen any movies for quite some time. He claims that once he felt an "addiction" for cinema—one that "went on well into maturity"—but "there came a moment when the magic suddenly failed." Lionel Trilling, "Bergman Unseen," in *A Company of Readers: Uncollected Writings of W. H. Auden, Jacques Barzun, and Lionel Trilling from the Readers' Subscription and Mid-Century Book Clubs*, ed. Arthur Krystal (New York: Free Press, 2001), 206.

81. Christopher Lehmann-Haupt, "Books of the Times," *New York Times*, October 13, 1981, C11.

82. Diana Trilling, *Mrs. Harris: The Death of the Scarsdale Diet Doctor* (New York: Harcourt Brace Jovanovich, 1981), 315–16.

83. Trilling, *We Must March*, 208.

84. Germaine Greer, *The Female Eunuch* (New York: McGraw-Hill, 1971), 61.

85. Trilling, *We Must March*, 205.

86. Carolyn Heilbrun, *When Men Were the Only Models We Had: My Teachers Barzun, Fadiman, and Trilling* (Philadelphia: U of Pennsylvania P, 2002), 102.

87. Greer, *Female Eunuch*, 61.

Chapter 3. The Waiting Room: Female Desire in Women's Wartime Fiction

1. Susan M. Hartmann, "Prescriptions for Penelope: Literature on Women's Obligations to Returning World War II Veterans," *Women's Studies* 5, no. 3 (1978): 223–39.

2. Dorothy Thompson, "The Soldier's Wife," *Ladies' Home Journal*, February 1945, 6–8.

3. Kathleen Norris, "Short Story from Life," *Milwaukee Sentinel*, January 23, 1944, 14A.

4. "Playgirl Wife," *Real Story*, January 1945, 54–61.

5. Dorothy Dix, "Courting Taken Over by Women," *Pittsburgh Post-Gazette*, December 28, 1944, 22. As if to underscore the traditional direction of desire, a brief advice column right beneath Dix's tells a young woman not to pursue a young man. "Girls do not pursue boys by correspondence any more than they do for dates." Francine Markel, "Don't Chase Boy by Mail," *Pittsburgh Post-Gazette*, December 28, 1944, 22.

6. Author's name withheld, "Startling Collection of Misinformed Young Men," *Ladies' Home Journal*, February 1948, 8.

7. Ethel Gorham, *So Your Husband's Gone to War!* (Garden City, NY: Doubleday, Doran, 1942), 75.

8. Gorham, *So Your Husband's Gone to War!*, 123.

9. Anonymous, "When Your Soldier Comes Home," *Ladies' Home Journal*, October 1944, 204.

10. Trilling, *Reviewing the Forties*, 101.

11. Leslie B. Hohman, "How to Live without Your Husband," *Ladies' Home Journal*, March 1944, 148.

12. Thomas Doherty, "Women without Men," in *Projections of War: Hollywood, American Culture, and World War II* (New York: Columbia UP, 1993), 170. Similarly, Manny Farber calls *A Guy Named Joe* (1943) a "textbook movie," full of speechified advice for both soldiers and their relatives ("Earth on Heaven," *Farber on Film*, 137).

13. Margaret Buell Wilder, *Since You Went Away: Letters to a Soldier from His Wife* (New York: McGraw-Hill, 1943). Even more relentlessly chipper and cute than *Since You Went Away* is Margaret Shea's epistolary novel, *The Gals They Left Behind* (New York: Ives Washburn, 1944). Two wives, Taffy and Jo, move to Maine and chronicle for their husbands the charming rustic people and animals. Many magazine articles framed proper letter-writing etiquette, such as Helen Furnas, "Mail Means Morale," *Liberty*, April 3, 1943, 26–27, 54. "Make your letters cheerful and frequent," advises Furnas (26).

14. Beatrice Sherman, "How One War Family Kept Its Chin Up," *New York Times Book Review*, July 18, 1943, 5.

15. Wilder, *Since You Went Away*, 25, 137, 156.

16. Wilder, *Since You Went Away*, 50.

17. Trilling, *Reviewing the Forties*, 101.

18. Trilling, *Reviewing the Forties*, 102.

19. Trilling, *Reviewing the Forties*, 103.

20. Trilling, *Reviewing the Forties*, 101.

21. Sara Henderson Hay, "Crackup on the Home Front," *Saturday Review of Literature*, November 4, 1944, 25.

22. Sara Henderson Hay, "Crackup on the Home Front," 25.

23. "Prophylactic Pill," *Collier's*, June 5, 1943, 16; "So You Had a Virus," *Collier's*, November 19, 1949, 31ff; "What Men Can Learn about Women," *Argosy*, August 1953. Two of her scientific articles, "Fighting Blood" and "Brain Waves," appeared first in *Collier's* and were then reprinted in John D. Ratcliff, *Science Year Book of 1943* (New York: Doubleday, Doran, 1943), 54–61, 87–95.

24. Trilling, *Reviewing the Forties*, 103. *Till the Boys Come Home* can be seen in the tradition of progressive women's fiction outlined by Jaime Harker in *America the Middlebrow: Women's Novels, Progressivism, and Middlebrow Authorship between the Wars* (Amherst: U of Massachusetts P, 2007).

25. Hannah Lees, "The Word You Can't Say," *Hygeia* 22 (May 1944): 336–37. *Hygeia* is a medical journal, but one that aims at a mainstream, not academic, audience. As far as sex education goes, the ubiquitous marriage educator Ernest Groves wrote numerous articles about the sexuality of adolescents and adults; for example, Ernest R. Groves, "Plan Your Children's Sex Education," *Ladies' Home Journal*, April 1941, 92. Leslie Hohman's "The Twig Is Bent" column in *Ladies' Home Journal* touched sometimes on the sexual behavior of young children. For example, his "Escapades of the Years of Innocence" talks about children's "sex play" and advises parents not to make the child feel guilty (February 1941, 43).

26. "Some mothers are apt to say proudly that their children have never shown any interest in such matters. But the experts say that mothers like this are

either kidding themselves or being kidded by their children" (Lees, "The Word You Can't Say," 336).

27. Trilling, *Reviewing the Forties*, 103.

28. *Women in Wartime* (Chicago: Institute for Psychoanalysis, 1943), 10.

29. *Women in Wartime*, 19.

30. Evelyn Millis Duvall, "Loneliness and the Serviceman's Wife," *Marriage and Family Living* 7, no. 4 (1945): 77–81.

31. C. G. MacKenzie, "War and the Family," *Marriage and Family Living* 6, no. 3 (1944): 45–46.

32. Nadina R. Kavinocky, "Medical Aspects of War Time Marriages," *Marriage and Family Living* 6, no. 2 (1944): 27.

33. For example—using a photograph of an average, if cold-looking, housewife: "Wanted! For Murder. Her *careless talk* costs lives." This poster is reproduced in Emily Yellin, *Our Mothers' War: American Women at Home and at the Front during World War II* (New York: Free Press, 2004), in the photographs following page 242.

34. Trilling, *Reviewing the Forties*, 102.

35. Floyd Dell, "Sex in American Fiction," *American Mercury*, January 1948, 84.

36. Libbie Block, *Wild Calendar* (New York: Knopf, 1946), 349.

37. A hypersensationalistic scene of female masturbation ornaments Erskine Caldwell's *Trouble in July* (New York: Grosset and Dunlop, 1940). Caldwell's novels are well populated with nymphomaniacs; here a witness reports that "man crazy" Katy Barlow first masturbated in front of him ("she lay there carrying on with herself like I never saw before in my whole life") before biting him (89–91). Barlow is, without doubt, one of the most wolfish she-wolves of the decade.

38. "The advertising and publicity campaign which the publishers have lavished on *Forever Amber* would be a real asset to a Presidential candidate," Frances Woodward, rev. *Forever Amber*, *Atlantic Monthly*, December 1944, 137.

39. "Slings and Arrows," *Time*, November 21, 1949, 42.

40. John Bainbridge, "Significant Sig and the Funnies," *New Yorker*, January 8, 1944, 32.

41. For example, the "People" section in *Time* for April 8, 1946, shows pictures of both Marie McDonald ("The Body") and super-famous Chili Williams (42).

42. Niven Busch, *They Dream of Home* (New York: Appleton-Century, 1944), 107.

43. Cited in David Alexander Scott, *Behind the G-String: An Exploration of the Stripper's Image, Her Person, and Her Meaning* (Jefferson, NC: McFarland, 1996), 61.

44. Kathleen Winsor, *Forever Amber* (New York: Macmillan, 1944), 599.

45. Winsor, *Forever Amber*, 640.

46. Winsor, *Forever Amber*, 7.

47. Agnes E. Meyer, *Journey through Chaos* (New York: Harcourt, Brace, 1944), 250. "Ostentatious Sex Behavior," 246. A parallel cross-country trip through class and racial unrest is told in Selden Menefee, *Assignment: U.S.A.* (New York: Reynal and Hitchcock, 1943). John Marquand shows matter-of-factly the impulsive

nature of wartime love and sexual attraction in *Repent in Haste* (Boston: Little, Brown, 1945). At the very end, Boyden finds out that his brand new wife is cheating on him, but he is already in love with someone else. "She's really a cute trick. It's funny the way things happen, isn't it, when there's a war on?" (152).

48. Arthur D. Howden Smith, "Kathleen Winsor's Salty Dish," *Saturday Review of Literature*, October 14, 1944, 44.

49. Norman Cousins, "Reader Satisfaction," *Saturday Review of Literature*, April 15, 1950, 28.

50. "Forever Kathleen," *Time*, April 17, 1950, 119.

51. Rev. *Star Money*, *Atlantic Monthly*, June 1950, 88.

52. Richard H. Rovere, "Fever Chart for Novelists," *Harper's*, May 1950, 122.

53. Rovere, "Fever Chart for Novelists," 122.

54. Rovere, "Fever Chart for Novelists," 123.

55. Charles Poore, "Books of the Times," *New York Times*, April 13, 1950, 27.

56. The title story takes the form of a letter in reply to a woman who thanks Mr. Jackson for his "clean" stories with "no drinking, no sex, no murder" (Charles Jackson, *The Sunnier Side: Twelve Arcadian Tales* [New York: Farrar, Straus, 1950]), 3. The whole point of the title story is to disabuse the proper woman of her idealized aesthetics. Jackson substantiates his case by invoking Dostoevsky and, several times (45, 48, 66), D. H. Lawrence. To highlight his continued interest in "abnormal" sexuality, he writes: "A Hollywood wag recently said to me, 'Say, Jackson, I hear your next book is going to be about necrophilia' " (66).

57. Kathleen Winsor, *Star Money* (New York: Appleton-Century-Crofts, 1950), 21.

58. Winsor, *Star Money*, 168.

59. Rovere, "Fever Chart for Novelists," 122.

60. Winsor, *Star Money*, 5.

61. Mary Margaret McBride, *Out of the Air* (Garden City, NY: Doubleday, 1960), 311.

62. Elaine Showalter, *A Jury of Her Peers: American Women Writers from Anne Bradstreet to Annie Proulx* (New York: Knopf, 2009), 386.

63. Winsor, *Star Money*, 280.

64. Winsor, *Star Money*, 335. Shireen is "mysteriously pleased" when a man calls her "a whore at heart" (335).

65. Charles Poore, "Forever Shireen," *New York Times*, April 16, 1950, BR3.

66. Alice Beal Parsons, *I Know What I'd Do* (New York: Dutton, 1946). The book jacket's description begins, "A poignant and timely novel dealing with one of the major problems of the postwar world, *I Know What I'd Do* discloses the relationship between the returning veteran and his community—the community in which his wife has lived while awaiting his return—and sometimes has found the waiting hard."

67. Ann Petry, *Country Place* (Boston: Houghton Mifflin, 1947), 255.

68. Winsor, *Star Money*, 281.

69. Winsor, *Star Money*, 412.

70. Lees, *Till the Boys Come Home*, 61.

71. As told to Edith M. Stern, "Women without Men," *Pageant*, January 1949, 156–57.

72. Diana Frederics, *Diana: A Strange Autobiography* (New York: New York UP, [1939] 1995).

73. Earnest Hooton, "Is Your Man Normal?" *Ladies' Home Journal*, April 1946, 49.

74. Paul Popenoe, "What Makes a Successful Marriage?" *Ladies' Home Journal*, August 1943, 82.

75. After a brief meditation on normal and abnormal, the first chapter of *Adam's Rib* concludes with the provoking thought that man himself starts out as "abnormal" in his very existence ("Yet in his earliest emergence, a rib from the missing link, man was an aberrant and chance mutation, statistically uncommon and therefore abnormal," Ruth Herschberger, *Adam's Rib* [New York: Pellegrini and Cudahy, 1948], 3).

76. Philip Wylie, *Generation of Vipers* (New York: Farrar and Rinehart, 1942), 77 (true morality), 68 (insane).

77. Wylie, *Generation of Vipers*, 64.

78. Ferdinand Lundberg and Marynia F. Farnham, *Modern Woman: The Lost Sex* (New York: Harper, 1947), v.

79. Lundberg and Farnham, *Modern Woman*, v.

80. Lundberg and Farnham, *Modern Woman*, 265.

81. Marjorie Farber, "Freudian Nightmare," *New York Times Book Review*, August 22, 1943, 5.

82. Ethel Goldwater, "Woman's Place: The New Alliance of 'Science' and Anti-Feminism," *Commentary* 4 (1947): 584.

83. Therese Benedek, *Insight and Personality Adjustment: A Study of the Psychological Effects of the War* (New York: Ronald, 1946), 161.

84. Benedek, *Insight and Personality Adjustment*, 168.

85. Benedek, *Insight and Personality Adjustment*, 165.

86. Benedek, *Insight and Personality Adjustment*, 167–68.

87. Benedek, *Insight and Personality Adjustment*, 168.

88. Nancy Wilson Ross, *The Waves: The Story of the Girls in Blue* (New York: Holt, 1943). Ross provides a detailed exposition of training and duties, while keeping regular track of what it means for women to be doing jobs that are more often associated with men. The last chapter, "Threat or Promise?" (161–65), cites Virginia Woolf (whose *A Room of One's Own* has already been summarized [31–33]), discusses the prospects of women in postwar life, and quotes a female officer: " 'One thing I know,' said an officer solemnly, 'I'll leave the Navy a pacifist and a feminist' " (161).

89. Nancy Wilson Ross, *Westward the Women* (New York: Random House, 1944), 193. The last chapter, "Over the Top of the World," is a devastating attack on the constricting ideal of the domestic housewife; "society could organize the home very differently if it wished to; could take a lesson from industry in large-scale handling of the ever recurrent, boring, mind-dulling round of solitary household

tasks which accounts in large measure for the American woman's addiction to the dope of radio's soap operas" (194).

90. Ernest R. Groves, rev. of Nancy Wilson Ross, *Westward the Women*, and Amram Scheinfeld, *Women and Men* in *Social Forces* 23, no. 4 (1945): 471–72.

91. Ernest R. Groves, rev, of *Westward the Women*, 472.

92. Nancy Wilson Ross, *The Left Hand Is the Dreamer* (New York: William Sloane, 1947), 335.

93. *The Left Hand*, 378, (nature) 380.

94. *The Left Hand*, 68.

Chapter 4. He-Wolves and She-Wolves: From Tex Avery to Jackson Pollock

1. *The New Partridge Dictionary of Slang and Unconventional English*, ed. Tom Dalzell and Terry Victor (New York: Routledge, 2006), 2:2116. In their "Preface" the editors admit that Partridge's "dating was often problematic" (1: ix).

2. Jack Lait and Lee Mortimer, "White Way Wolves," *New York Confidential* (Chicago: Ziff-Davis, 1948), 201.

3. These phrases and definitions are drawn from *Dictionary of American Underworld Lingo*, ed. Hyman E. Goldin (New York: Twayne, 1950), and Dan Burley, *Original Handbook of Harlem Jive* (New York, 1944). According to Burley's *Handbook* a "wolf" is "a male who chases women" and a "wolverine" is a "woman who chases men" (150).

4. Gorham, *So Your Husband's Gone to War!*, 71.

5. Paul Ernst, "My Mother Told Me," *Saturday Evening Post*, September 11, 1945, 25.

6. Sol Zatt, "'Ork Wives' Is Almost a Killer, Mister Miller!" *Billboard*, October 3, 1942, 25.

7. "Golden Mould: Julie London, One of the Nebulae of Hollywood," *Esquire*, November 1943, 72.

8. "American Beauties, Eastern Style: The Face and Fortune of Betty Jane Hess," *Esquire*, March 1944, 54.

9. "Wolf! Wolf!," *Time*, October 9, 1944, 47.

10. John O' Hara and Lorenz Hart, *Pal Joey* (New York: Random House, 1952), 41.

11. With the intent of attracting "more attention than by driving a yellow Cadillac," a novelty distributor offers the "Woo Wee Auto Horn Wolf Whistle" for an amplified version. The advertisement shows a drawn female figure in a short dress looking lewdly receptive to the horn blast (*Popular Mechanics*, November 1947, 338).

12. "Cinema," *Time*, October 18, 1943, 94.

13. Nancy Ladd, "When War Came to New Jersey," *New York Times*, September 15, 1946, BR13.

14. Masculine and sexually aggressive women also wolf-whistle; teenage girls whistle at Cary Grant in *The Bachelor and the Bobby-Soxer* (1947); in *The More the Merrier* (1943) female factory workers whistle at the men; in *Dangerous Blondes* (1943) the confident wife/author/sleuth whistles at an attractive woman, just as her husband will a few minutes later.

15. Jo Stafford, "Good Wolfing, Girls," in Abner Silver, *All Women Are Wolves* (New York: Readers' Press, 1945), 32.

16. Bill Mauldin, foreword to *Male Call: The Complete War Time Strip: 1942–1946*, by Milton Caniff, ed. Peter Poplaski (Princeton, WI: Kitchen Sink Press, 1987), 7.

17. This animated short and other Private Snafu materials are available for viewing on the Internet Archive (www.archive.org).

18. "Charted Grable," *Life*, March 27, 1944, 38.

19. As noted in an earlier chapter, this interpretation of the military-sponsored pinup was made at the time by Geoffrey Gorer.

20. The discussion that follows refers to cartoons in Sgt. Leonard Sansone, *The Wolf* (New York: United Publishers, 1945). There is no pagination.

21. Cartoon, *New Yorker*, January 1, 1944, 20.

22. In "Sex and Violence," Joe Adamson enthusiastically collects the Avery cartoons that feature the most erotic mayhem (*Tex Avery: King of Cartoons* [New York: Da Capo, 1975, 1985], 94–106). Adamson's book includes a long interview in which Avery notes the challenge of passing some of his cartoons by the censor. "We had to watch bestiality, an animal against a human being—so they couldn't get close. Those were tough to keep clean!" (176).

23. With reference to *Little 'Tinker*, Floriane Place-Verghnes observes the rarity of female sexual desire in cartoons of this time (*Tex Avery: A Unique Legacy, 1942–1955* [Eastleigh, UK: John Libbey, 2006], 86). Place-Verghnes provides an excellent treatment of the old lady nymphomaniacs in Avery—such as the grandmother in *Red Hot Riding Hood*—which she puts in the category of "The Anti-Sex Symbol," 110–15.

24. The main complication of the pinup girl singer is that in *Swing Shift Cinderella* she is given the voice of Bette Davis. Avery cartoons like playing with language, and this might be a riff on Bette Davis/Betty Grable. Her very civilized voice also works to make clear that her real identity is not the same as the showgirl in the act. In *The Shooting of Dan McGoo*, however, she talks like Mae West, which makes the fantasy far simpler. The showgirl's Bette Davis voice is about the only thing that Jane Gaines does not account for in her still unsurpassed article on Avery's wolf series, "The Showgirl and the Wolf," *Cinema Journal* 20 (Autumn 1980): 53–67. Her idea that the singer is depicted as a "child-woman" (55), both "sexy and innocent," would be interestingly refined with the inclusion of the Bette Davis reference. The Mae West voice, in its turn, would seem to preclude all childishness.

25. "Die Monstersinger," *Time*, November 6, 1950, 78.

26. "Die Monstersinger," 72.

27. "Die Monstersinger, 72.

28. Rick Marschall, "Al Capp and *Li'l Abner* in 1946: Schoolbook Lessons in Producing a Comic Strip," *Li'l Abner: Dailies Volume 12: 1946*, ed. Dave Schreiner (Princeton, WI: Kitchen Sink Press, 1991), 7.

29. Al Capp, "The Comedy of Charlie Chaplin," *Atlantic Monthly*, February 1950, 29.

30. *Li'l Abner: Dailies: Vol. 12: 1946*, 33. Despite the title of the collection this strip appeared 12–27–45. In a smaller-scale example of wolfish female aggression, "Countess Wolfina" pants at Fearless Fosdick and begs him to "kiss me again and again and again until I go mad with ecstasy" (6–19–44, *Li'l Abner: Dailies, Vol. 10: 1944*, 96).

31. The quotation comes from the abstract for Trina Robbins's 2007 Comic Arts conference paper, "Wolf Gal and the Feral Women of 'Li'l Abner,'" retrieved July 26, 2013 (http://www.powerofcomics.com/id20.html).

32. *Li'l Abner: Dailies, Vol. 12: 1946*, 175.

33. An episode of Princess Pantha is reproduced in William W. Savage Jr., *Commies, Cowboys, and Jungle Queens: Comic Books and America, 1945–1954* (Hanover, NH: Wesleyan UP, 1990), 84–94.

34. Les Savage, "Señorita Scorpion," *Action Stories* (Spring 1944); "The Brand of Señorita Scorpion," *Action Stories* (Summer 1944); "Secret of Santiago," *Action Stories* (Fall 1944). These stories have since been republished as a continuous novel: Les Savage Jr., *The Legend of Señorita Scorpion* (Hampton Falls, NH: Thomas T. Beeler, 1996).

35. This is the opening motto of the famous radio adventure show, *Escape* (1947–1954).

36. Boris Karloff, introduction to William B. Seabrook, "The Caged White Werewolf of the Saraban," *And the Darkness Falls* (Cleveland, OH: World Publishing, 1946), 200. The story is drawn from William Seabrook, *Witchcraft: Its Power in the World Today* (New York: Harcourt, Brace, 1940).

37. "The Caged White Werewolf," 203.

38. Chris Fujiwara quotes this passage (*Jacques Tourneur: The Cinema of Nightfall* [Baltimore, MD: Johns Hopkins UP, 2000], 73), but without putting the language of normalcy into 1940s psychoanalytic context. Like many critics of Tourneur/Lewton, Fujiwara is excellent on stylistic points, but shows little interest in 1940s culture. The one treatment of Lewton that does work the films into cultural context is Alexander Nemerov, *Icons of Grief: Val Lewton's Homefront Pictures* (Baltimore, MD: Johns Hopkins UP, 2005). This study, which argues that Lewton's films often need to be read as emotional responses to the war, begins after *Cat People*.

39. Manny Farber calls Lewton's characters "insipidly normal"; they "reminded one of the actors used in small-town movie ads for the local grocery or shoe store" ("Val Lewton: Unorthodox Artistry at RKO," in *Kings of the Bs: Working within the Hollywood System*, ed. Todd McCarthy and Charles Flynn [New York: Dutton, 1975), 106). In *Cat People* I would again inflect this "normal" away from "average" and toward the psychoanalytical sense. Most acutely attuned to the psychoanalytically "normal" and "abnormal" in horror is Harry M. Benshoff, *Monsters*

in the Closet: Homosexuality and the Horror Film (New York: Manchester UP, 1997). His treatment of homosexuality in Lewton is superb (98–110).

40. Contemporary critics often cite screenwriter Dewitt Bodeen's comment on Irena at the wedding party ("she called me sister!"); when director Lewton received mail congratulating him "for his boldness in introducing Lesbiana to films in Hollywood," Bodeen first brushed aside the implication, but then admitted that he "rather liked the insinuation and thought it added a neat bit of interpretation to the scene" (Gregory William Mank, *Hollywood Cauldron: Thirteen Horror Films from the Genre's Golden Age* [Jefferson, NC: McFarland, 1994], 222).

41. In his book-length commentary, *Cat People* (London: British Film Institute, 1999), Kim Newman writes that Lewton "exposes the apparently benign analyst as a self-interested, shifty, unethical creep" (35).

42. William Paul, "What Does Dr. Judd Want? Transformation, Transference, and Divided Selves in *Cat People*," in *Horror Film and Psychoanalysis: Freud's Worst Nightmare*, ed. Steven Jay Schneider (New York: Cambridge UP, 2004), 161.

43. In a brief discussion of the animal-woman boundary in *Cat People* and *Phantom Lady*, Paula Rabinowitz writes, "The image of the woman turning into wild beast is a code for the impossible: to see the moment of female orgasm. Its terrifying ability to alter the woman's face is perhaps what these moments of vituperation are really about" (*Black and White and Noir: America's Pulp Modernism* [New York: Columbia UP, 2002], 27). If men actually wanted to see the female orgasm—after behaving so indifferently to it otherwise—then their visually compartmentalized catalogue of female sexuality would be complete. Rabinowitz's book goes far beyond the 1940s, but it stands nonetheless as the finest reading to date of 1940s sexual culture.

44. Mary Ann Doane writes of *Cat People*, "The film demonstrates that the woman, in becoming most like herself, that is, the embodiment of female sexuality, must become *other*" (*Desire to Desire*, 52). A high culture text that links female sexuality to feline animality, Jean Stafford's *The Mountain Lion* (New York: Farrar, Straus and Giroux, 1947) also ends in tragic disaster. Once her childhood concludes ("Ralph's childhood and his sister's expired at that moment," 159), Molly cannot survive her entrance into adolescent sexuality. In the final scene, she is mistakenly shot dead instead of the mountain lion.

45. Richard Hand, "Undead Radio: Zombies and the Living Dead on 1930s and 1940s Radio," in *Better Off Dead: The Evolution of the Zombie as Post-Human*, ed. Deborah Christie and Sarah Juliet Lauro (New York: Fordham UP, 2011), 42. Ironically, Hand names the episode's monster a werewolf in an essay otherwise about zombies. I call the monster a zombie.

46. Allison McCracken, "Scary Women and Scarred Men: Suspense, Gender Trouble, and Postwar Change, 1942–50," in *Radio Reader: Essays in the Cultural History of Radio*, ed. Michele Hilmes and Jason Loviglio (New York: Routledge, 2002), 201.

47. McCracken, "Scary Women and Scarred Men," 201.

48. Gerald Nachman, *Raised on Radio* (New York: Pantheon, 1998), 316.

49. Richard Hand, *Terror on the Air! Horror Radio in America, 1931–1952* (Jefferson, NC: McFarland, 2006), 141. Hand continues: "Perhaps the endless cycle in the play serves to expand and transform the violence and sexual deviancy of the story from an isolated incident (or 'legend') into a phenomenon that will recur and repeat in an ever-developing America."

50. In contrast to the lusty wolf, the hungry wolf makes his appearance in *How to Cook a Wolf* (New York: Duell, Sloan and Pearce, 1942), by M. F. K. Fisher. This is an inspirational, economizing cookbook designed to keep the wartime wolf of hunger at bay. While this wolf is not sexual desire, it is nonetheless, as Shakespeare said, "an appetite, a universal wolf" (83).

51. Jane Rice, "The Refugee," in *American Fantastic Tales: Terror and the Uncanny from the 1940s to Now*, ed. Peter Straub (New York: Library of America, 2009), 44. "The Refugee" originally appeared in *Unknown Worlds* (October 1943) and has been reprinted many times.

52. See Acquanetta's interview with Tom Weaver in *Science Fiction Stars and Horror Heroes* (Jefferson, NC: McFarland, 2006), 1–18.

53. Philip K. Scheuer, "Chaney Meets Lugosi and Reviewer Orders Aspirin," *Los Angeles Times*, July 23, 1943, 15.

54. On complaints about the racism in *Captive Wild Woman*, see Jessica Lauren Wagner, *"An Unpleasant Wartime Function": Race, Film Censorship, and the Office of War Information, 1942–45*, master's thesis, University of Maryland, 2007, 93–94.

55. A character sketch of Montez in *Photoplay* goes all out to emphasize her Latin hot-bloodedness. Her dialogue is rendered phonetically and focuses mostly on her desire. Thus: " 'White Savage,' her latest film, delights the Montez heart because 'I kees motch. . . . Eet ees loffly.' " Dennis Sprague, "Lush, Latin, and Lethal," *Photoplay*, June 1943, 41.

56. Bosley Crowther, "Snakebite Remedy," *New York Times*, May 18, 1944, 17. Crowther characterizes the film's staging of sexuality thus: "Cobra Island, we hasten to inform you, is ruled by a viperous doll who snake-dances in the sacred temple, surrounded by a bevy of night-gowned toots."

57. "Fiction House, which specialized in offering readers half-dressed heroines in exotic locations, found themselves put out of business by the code as well," writes Amy Kiste Nyberg, *Seal of Approval: The History of the Comics Code* (Jackson: UP of Mississippi, 1998), 124.

58. Numbers in parentheses refer to the issue of *Fight Comics*.

59. Without referring to *Tiger Girl*, William Savage gives basically the same description of the racism in 1940s jungle comics in *Commies, Cowboys, and Jungle Queens: Comic Books and America, 1945–1954* (Hanover, NH, Wesleyan UP, 1998), 76–77.

60. Quote is drawn from W. Savage, *Commies, Cowboys, and Jungle Queens*, 78.

61. W. Savage reads the jungle comics as "sexist" (*Commies, Cowboys, and Jungle Queens*, 77–78). By contrast, Trina Robbins reads the Fiction House jungle

heroines as strong and feminist (*The Great Women Superheroes* [Northampton, MA: Kitchen Sink Press, 1996], 86).

62. Philip Wylie, *Opus 21: Descriptive Music for the Lower Kinsey Epoch of the Atomic Age/A Concerto for a One-Man Band/Six Arias for Soap Operas/Fugues, Anthems, and a Barrelhouse* (New York: Rinehart, 1949), 17.

63. *Generation of Vipers* (New York: Farrar and Rinehart, 1942), which through the years would remain Wylie's most famous and controversial book, was listed on the *New York Time*'s nonfiction bestseller list from February 1943 through April 1943.

64. Philip Wylie, *An Essay on Morals* (New York: Rinehart, 1947), 156–57.

65. Wylie, *Essay on Morals*, 167.

66. Wylie, *Essay on Morals*, 167.

67. Hubert Creekmore, *The Welcome* (New York: Appleton-Century-Crofts, 1948), 29.

68. Creekmore, *Welcome*, 132.

69. Wylie, *Generation of Vipers*, 49.

70. Wylie, *Generation of Vipers*, 195.

71. James Thurber and Elliott Nugent, *The Male Animal* (New York: Random House, 1940), 129.

72. In his review of the play, Edwin Schallert spends a good deal of time worrying whether the inclusion of the Sacco and Vanzetti case makes an otherwise lighthearted play too serious. "Some will undoubtedly raise a question about bringing in so controversial an issue into an otherwise light play, although as I say it is pretty generally in the background" ("Kruger Regales Audience in 'Male Animal' Antics," *Los Angeles Times*, October 20, 1941, 22).

73. Lewis Mumford, *The Condition of Man* (New York: Harcourt, Brace, 1944), 417.

74. *The Jack Paar Show*, 7–13–1947.

75. "The Value of the College Woman to Society," *University Debaters' Annual*, ed. Edith M. Phelps (New York: Wilson, 1943), 48. In 1938 Dorothy Sayers gave an address to "a Woman's Society" called "Are Women Human?" in which she quotes D. H. Lawrence as saying, "Man is willing to accept woman as an equal, as a man in skirts, as an angel, a devil, a baby-face, a machine, an instrument, a bosom, a womb, a pair of legs, a servant, an encyclopedia, an ideal or an obscenity; the one thing he won't accept her as is a human being, a real human being of the feminine sex" (*Unpopular Opinions: Twenty-One Essays* [New York: Harcourt, Brace, 1947], 139).

76. William Ernest Hocking, *What Man Can Make of Man* (New York: Harper, 1942), virility: 61; "Surely here is the Eternal Pioneer, the self-made woman, the free, the individual, able to strike out for herself—only unable through a deficit of head and of feeling to see herself the poor imitator that she was!" (14–15).

77. Paul Weiss, *Nature and Man* (Carbondale: Southern Illinois UP, 1947), 267.

78. Weiss, *Nature and Man*, 266, 248.

79. For an overview of Fisher's monumental output, I have found helpful Joseph M. Flora, *Vardis Fisher* (New York: Twayne, 1965). Although Stone-Age fiction was a rarity, numerous other sequences of historical fiction sought to portray the emergence of civilization in America. Conrad Richter's "The Awakening Land" trilogy (*The Trees,* 1940; *The Fields*, 1946; *The Town*, 1950) portrays the transition from pioneers in the wilderness to urbanization.

80. Orville Prescott, "Books of the Times," *New York Times*, December 20, 1944, 21.

81. Vardis Fisher, *Darkness and the Deep* (New York: Vanguard, 1943), 259.

82. Fisher, *Darkness and the Deep*, 102.

83. Vardis Fisher, *Adam and the Serpent* (New York: Vanguard, 1947), 173.

84. "No Woman Born" appeared first in *Astounding Science Fiction*, December 1944. My page numbers refer to the republication in *The Best of C. L. Moore*, ed. Lester Del Rey (Garden City, NY: Doubleday, 1975), 200–42.

85. Raffaella Baccolini, "In Between Subjects: C. L. Moore's 'No Woman Born,' " *Science Fiction, Critical Frontiers*, ed. Karen Sayer and John Moore (New York: St. Martin's, 2000), 140–53.

86. Veronica Hollinger, "(Re)Reading Queerly: Science Fiction, Feminism and the Defamiliarization of Gender," *Reload: Rethinking Women + Cyberculture*, ed. Mary Flanagan and Austin Booth (Cambridge, MA: MIT Press, 2002), 301–20.

87. Prescott, "Books of the Times," 21.

88. Vardis Fisher, *The Golden Rooms* (New York: Vanguard, 1944), 324. In his *New York Times* review of *The Golden Rooms*, Gerald Heard objected to Fisher's idea that women were associated only with the practical and the domestic; on the contrary, Heard argued that it is more likely that women should be linked to the abstract and the unseen, as evidenced by characters such as the Sibyl ("Homo, Not Yet Sapiens," *New York Times*, December 3, 1944, 36). Heard also suggested that early man would be afraid of the day, not the night, as evidenced by the recently documented case of the Wolf-girl (J. A. L. Singh and Robert M. Zingg, *Wolf-Children and Feral Man* [New York: Harper and Row, 1942]). Heard himself speculated on the evolution of human consciousness in *Pain, Sex and Time: A New Outlook on Evolution and the Future of Man* (New York: Harper, 1939) and *Man the Master* (New York: Harper, 1941). Even though Heard's critique of gender stereotypes in Fisher hits the mark, in his own work he, like most other male writers, writes about human sexuality as equivalent to male sexuality ("The Present and Future Significance of Sex," *Pain, Sex and Time*, 42–54).

89. For a history of the she-wolf in literature, criticism, and art, see Cristina Mazzoni, *She-Wolf: The Story of a Roman Icon* (New York: Cambridge UP, 2010), which also treats Pollock's "She-Wolf" (237–40).

90. References to Wylie occur throughout Leja's book; "modern man discourse" is detailed in Michael Leja, "Narcissus in Chaos: Subjectivity, Ideology, Modern Man and Woman," in *Reframing Abstract Expressionism: Subjectivity and Painting in the 1940s* (New Haven, CT: Yale UP, 1993), 203–74.

Chapter 5. Phantom Ladies: On the Radio and Out of the Closet

1. Frances Walker, "FM Women Directors Pioneer in Pittsburgh at Radio Announcing," *Pittsburgh Post-Gazette*, May 20, 1944, 5.

2. Michele Hilmes, *Radio Voices: American Broadcasting, 1922–1952* (Minneapolis: U of Minnesota P, 1997), 142. In *The Psychology of Radio* (New York: Peter Smith, [1935] 1941), Hadley Cantril and Gordon W. Allport try to figure out "why is it that most people would rather hear a man than a woman speak over the radio" ("Sex Differences in Radio Voices," 127–38). They conclude that "prejudice is shown to be a large factor in the case" (127).

3. *Women in Radio: Illustrated by Biographical Sketches*, May 1947, Women's Bureau, U.S. Department of Labor, Bulletin No. 222, vi. This report names as the most successful woman in broadcasting, the "First Lady of Radio," Mary Margaret McBride (3). In her memoirs, McBride does not comment too much on her status as a female broadcaster, but she does quote for a chapter epigraph a complaint in a letter: "I can't stand a woman's voice on the air. Why don't you stay at home and take care of your family?" Mary Margaret McBride, *Out of the Air* (New York: Doubleday, 1960), 68. Susan Ware describes McBride's interviewing style in her terrific book, "Mary Margaret's Radio Technique," *It's One O'clock and Here Is Mary Margaret McBride: A Radio Biography* (New York: New York UP, 2005), 31–46.

4. In his radio-centered biography of Norman Corwin, R. LeRoy Bannerman cites both Max Wylie and Gilbert Seldes as critics of Corwin's abstract approach. "[Wylie] noted that Corwin, by the inclination of his style, wrote not of people but of Platonic individuals, disembodied, remote, symbolic" (*Norman Corwin and Radio: The Golden Years* [Tuscaloosa: U of Alabama P, 1986], 7). Without supplying a quotation, Bannerman says that Corwin "insisted that he *did* create full-dimensional characters for many of his plays" (7). In his notes to "The Oracle of Philadelphi," Corwin reports that he has done his best to support female radio narrators: "I had in mind when writing it the fact that there existed practically no material for women narrators, and I hoped I might be starting a shelf of such literature for the pretties. It turned out I wasn't, because none of radio's writers followed the lead" (*Thirteen by Corwin: Radio Dramas by Norman Corwin* [New York: Holt, 1942], 328).

5. Norman Corwin, "The Sovereign Word: Some Notes on Radio Drama," *Theatre Arts*, February 1940, 130.

6. Norman Corwin, "Daybreak," 115–36. Corwin, "We Hold These Truths," in *More by Corwin: Sixteen Radio Dramas by Norman Corwin* (New York: Holt, 1944), 55–96.

7. Norman Corwin, "Seems Radio Is Here to Stay," *Thirteen by Corwin*, 219–20.

8. Norman Corwin, notes to "Radio Primer," *Thirteen by Corwin*, 52.

9. Corwin, "Descent of the Gods," *More by Corwin*, 109.

10. Corwin, "Mary and the Fairy," *More by Corwin*, 19.

11. Corwin, "Mary and the Fairy," 23.

12. Corwin, "Appointment," *Thirteen by Corwin*, 307.

13. Corwin, "Samson," *More by Corwin*, 208.

14. Paul W. White, *News on the Air* (New York: Harcourt, Brace, 1947), 20.

15. Robert J. Landry, *This Fascinating Radio Business* (New York: Bobbs-Merrill Company, 1946), 91.

16. See John E. Semonche, *Censoring Sex: A Historical Journey through American Media* (Lanham, MD: Rowman and Littlefield, 2007), 185.

17. Sherwood Schwartz, "How to Write a Joke," in *Off Mike: Radio Writing by the Nation's Top Radio Writers*, ed. Jerome Lawrence (New York: Essential Books, 1944), 11.

18. As summarized in Edward M. Kirby and Jack W. Harris, *Star-Spangled Radio* (Chicago: Ziff-Davis, 1948), *Variety* in November 1942 ran an article called "Comics, Sex, and Casualties," which told how the Public Relations Bureau of the War Department had instructed radio comedians to present soldiers in "dignified terms only" and make certain that "sex jokes" and "allusions" not give "American parents the idea that Army life bears any resemblance to *What Price Glory* or *The Cockeyed World* of regretfully-too-recent memory" (14). Radio stations followed this form of voluntary self-censorship, and soldiers were treated with dignity by comedians. But the soldier's morale was also built up by a great many sexual allusions, which meant that sexual self-censorship was very strategic. *Star-Spangled Radio* contains an informative chapter on the morale building elements in *Command Performance*, including the requests for women's sighs (42–51).

19. In an otherwise all-male operation, Mary Livingstone regularly becomes the desirable, dateable girl when Jack Benny performs for soldiers. In the November 11, 1944, *Jack Benny Program* from Corona Naval Hospital, Mary compares herself humorously, but not ironically, to Betty Grable. After big applause for her entrance, Mary says, "These soldiers know a trim craft when they see one." Jack: "That's pretty egotistical; you'd think you were Betty Grable or someone." Mary: "As long as Betty Grable is in Hollywood, I'm somebody here."

20. "Lonesome Gal," John Dunning, *The Encyclopedia of Old-Time Radio*, 410. According to Dunning, *Lonesome Gal* is broadcast locally in 1947, then syndicated nationally starting in December 1949.

21. Gilbert Seldes, *The Public Arts* (New York: Simon and Schuster, 1956), 112. In a splendid article, Mary Desjardins and Mark Williams show how, through publicity photographs and contests, the producers of *The Lonesome Gal* sought to render her disembodied voice more concretely. "There is indication that the disembodied female voice was not entirely unthreatening and was best 'enjoyed' if contained within a sexually defined female body" ("'Are You Lonesome Tonight?': Gendered Address in *The Lonesome Gal* and *The Continental*," *Communities of the Air: Radio Century, Radio Culture*, ed. Susan Merrill Squier (Durham, NC: Duke UP, 2003), 260.

22. Jack Gould, "The Big Time: September Takes Away the Sustainers and Brings on the Tried Stars," *New York Times*, September 10, 1944, X5. Other "copies"

of Vera Vague include Brenda and Cobina, man-hungry socialites, who also work with Bob Hope. They appear on several programs of *Command Performance* (6–18–42, 7–14–42).

23. *Blue Ribbon Town*, 1–29–44.

24. *The Pepsodent Show Starring Bob Hope*, 5–6–41.

25. *The Pepsodent Show Starring Bob Hope*, 4–1–47.

26. Hyman Goldberg, " 'Our Miss Brooks': America's Favorite Schoolmarm," *Cosmopolitan*, June 1953, 73.

27. The best description of Eve Arden's character, Ida, in *Mildred Pierce* appears in Judith Roof, *All About Thelma and Eve: Sidekicks and Third Wheels* (Urbana: U of Illinois P, 2002); Roof refers to Ida's "hermaphroditism" (83).

28. Saul Carson, "Radio: Low Pressure," *New Republic*, August 2, 1948, 29.

29. Nachman, *Raised on Radio*, 218–19.

30. Jack Gould, "Programs in Review," *New York Times*, July 25, 1948, X7.

31. When Peggy Lee sings that she knows "a little bit about biology" in "I Don't Know Enough about You" (Capitol 236, 1945), the sexual insinuation is clear.

32. "The Working Girls," *Time*, February 8, 1954, 51.

33. The maternal strain in "Our Miss Brooks" is traced by Patrick A. Ryan, " 'Our Miss Brooks': Broadcasting Domestic Ideals for the Female Teacher in the Postwar United States," *NWSA Journal* 21, no. 1 (Spring 2009): 76–100. Miss Brooks does often play a maternal role, but Ryan's article does not relate this role to Miss Brooks' equally prevalent sexual and comic roles.

34. Kate Smith's maternal characteristics are described in these terms in Robert K. Merton, *Mass Persuasion: The Social Psychology of a War Bond Drive* (New York: Harper, 1946), 149.

35. There is a parallel moment of self-censorship in *The Big Sleep* (1946); aggressive dame Agnes says that Bogart's Marlowe "gives me a pain in my" at which point her boyfriend cuts in with "that goes for me too"; when Bogart asks "where does he give you a pain?" her reply is once again interrupted and cut off ("Get out!"). In this way the film gets to swear without swearing.

36. In this episode a photograph of Miss Brooks in a swimsuit circulates around the school. Eventually a picture of Principal Conklin's head is stuck on her swimsuited body for a gag. In "Heat Wave" (8–7–49) everyone wears a bathing suit underneath her or his clothes.

37. A. H. Maslow, "Self-Esteem (Dominance Feeling) and Sexuality in Women," *Journal of Social Psychology* 16 (1942): 259–94.

38. Maslow, "Self-Esteem (Dominance Feeling)," 261.

39. Maslow, "Self-Esteem (Dominance Feeling)," 276.

40. Biographical information on Lisa Ben is drawn from *Before Stonewall: Activists for Gay and Lesbian Rights in Historical Context*, ed. Vern L. Bullough (New York: Harrington Park, 2002), 64.

41. *Vice Versa*, September 1947, 3.

42. *Vice Versa*, August 1947, 14.

43. Terry Castle, *The Apparitional Lesbian: Female Homosexuality and Modern Culture* (New York: Columbia UP, 1993), 34.

44. The quotation and footnote (6) appear in Castle, *Apparitional Lesbian*, 34, 245.

45. Castle, *Apparitional Lesbian*, 19.

46. Donna B. Knaff, *Beyond Rosie the Riveter: Women of World War II in American Popular Graphic Art* (Lawrence: UP of Kansas, 2012).

47. Patricia White, *Uninvited: Classical Hollywood Cinema and Lesbian Representability* (Bloomington: Indiana UP, 1999).

48. Stacy Ellen Wolf, *A Problem Like Maria: Gender and Sexuality in the American Musical* (Ann Arbor: U of Michigan P, 2002).

49. Thomas Doherty, *Hollywood's Censor: Joseph I. Breen and the Production Code Administration* (New York: Columbia UP, 2009), 139. And *Turnabout* not only snuck past the Code once, but twice since Lisa Ben undoubtedly refers to the film's 1946 rerelease.

50. Although it omits *Turnabout*, the best list of cross-dressing women in 1940s Hollywood film is given by Rebecca Bell-Metereau, "Male Impersonation before 1960," *Hollywood Androgyny* (New York: Columbia UP, 1993), 63–115. Key examples from the 1940s include historical dramas (*Joan of Arc*, 1948, and Merle Oberon as George Sand in *A Song to Remember*, 1945) in addition to cowgirls in westerns (*Yellow Sky*, 1949, *Calamity Jane and Sam Bass*, 1949).

51. In its July 31, 1948, review of O'Brien's record, "Wrong Train," *Billboard* refers to her "familiar style" of "undersinging" (167).

52. The best reading of gender in the Broadway musical *Annie Get Your Gun* is by Raymond Knapp, "Gender and Sexuality," *The American Musical and the Performance of Personal Identity* (Princeton, NJ: Princeton UP, 2009), 209–15. Knapp's emphasis on the ethnic and racial othering of Annie is especially fine. "Oddly, the musical marker for Annie's 'true' identity is African American in derivation" (213).

53. Annie's song, "Doin' What Comes Natur'lly," is bowdlerized in the film version, but remains a clear expression of female sexual desire. According to theater critic Lewis Nichols, Ethel Merman gave Annie's voice "a leering note to even sedate lyrics" (Lewis Nichols, "The Play," *New York Times*, May 17, 1946, 14).

54. Frederick C. Othman, "The Huttontot," *Saturday Evening Post*, June 10, 1944, 27, 68, 70.

55. Bosley Crowther begins his *New York Times* review of *The Miracle of Morgan's Creek* by noting that "the watchmen for the usually prim Hays office certainly permitted themselves a Jovian nod" in the face of the film's "irrepressible impudence" (January 20, 1944, 15).

56. Quoted in Monica Bachmann, " 'Someone Like Debby': (De)Constructing a Lesbian Community of Readers," *GLQ: A Journal of Lesbian and Gay Studies* 6, no. 3 (2000): 378.

57. Elizabeth Hawes, *Anything but Love* (New York: Rinehart, 1948), 210.

58. Lisa Ben titles her list, "Other Fiction on the Same Subject," *Vice Versa*, 11.

59. Jeannette H. Foster, *Sex Variant Women in Literature* (Tallahassee, FL: Naiad Press, 1985), 326, 329.

60. Marion Zimmer Bradley, *Checklist: A Complete, Cumulative Checklist of Lesbian, Variant, and Homosexual Fiction, in English, or Available in English Translation* (Rochester, TX: Library of Alexandria, 1960), n.p.

61. Mary Speers, *We Are Fires Unquenchable* (Hollywood, CA: Murray and Gee, 1942).

62. Carney Landis and M. Marjorie Bolles, *Personality and Sexuality of the Physically Handicapped Woman* (New York: Paul B. Hoeber, 1942).

63. Speers, *We Are Fires Unquenchable*, 57, 219.

64. "Bookworms' Burrow," *Vice Versa*, February 1948, 5.

65. Bachmann, " 'Someone Like Debby,' " 377–88.

66. Grace Frank, "At the Boiling Point," *Saturday Review of Literature*, February 23, 1946, 8.

67. Nathan L. Rothman, "In Technicolor," *Saturday Review of Literature*, February 23, 1946, 38.

68. On Jewish themes in postwar 1940s fiction, see Gordon Hutner, *What America Read: Taste, Class, and the Novel: 1920–1960* (Chapel Hill: U of North Carolina P, 2009), 248–56.

69. Gertrude Springer, rev. *Wasteland* by Jo Sinclair, *Survey Graphic*, 35 (May 1946), 174.

70. Lee E. Cannon, "Wasteland and Reclamation," *Christian Century* 63 (June 5 1946), 721.

71. "The Steps of Brooklyn," *Time*, February 18, 1946, 108.

72. Edward A. Laycock, "Where There's Hope," *Boston Globe*, February 14, 1946, 15.

73. Chester Himes, "If He Hollers Let Him Go," *Saturday Review of Literature*, February 16, 1946, 13.

74. Harold Fields, "A Personal Conflict and Victory," *Saturday Review of Literature*, February 16, 1946, 18.

75. Bachmann, " 'Someone Like Debby,' " 386.

76. Chester Himes, *If He Hollers Let Him Go* (Cambridge, MA: Da Capo Press, [1945] 1986), 153.

77. Himes, "If He Hollers Let Him Go," *Saturday Review of Literature*, 13.

78. Jo Sinclair, *Wasteland* (New York: Harper, 1946), 123. Page numbers are cited parenthetically in text hereafter.

79. Lois Lenski spends some of her preface to *Texas Tomboy* (Philadelphia: Lippincott, 1950) defending the rights of tomboy girls to "attain the same freedom that ranch boys enjoyed" (ix).

80. Siegfried Kracauer, "Hollywood's Terror Films: Do They Reflect an American State of Mind?" *Commentary* 2 (1946): 135.

81. Kracauer, "Hollywood's Terror Films," 135.

82. Siegfried Kracauer, "Psychiatry for Everything and Everybody," *Commentary* 5 (1948): 222.

83. Steven Capsuto, "In the Beginning . . . Early Radio," in *Alternate Channels: The Uncensored Story of Gay and Lesbian Images on Radio and Television* (New York: Ballantine, 2000), 13–21. Matthew Murray, " 'The Tendency to Deprave and Corrupt Morals': Regulation and Irregular Sexuality in Golden Age Radio Comedy," in *Radio Reader: Essays in the Cultural History of Radio*, ed. Michele Hilmes and Jason Loviglio (New York: Routledge, 2002), 135–56.

84. *The Jack Benny Program*, 5–23–48.

85. In *The Psychology of Radio* (New York: Peter Smith, [1935] 1941) Harvey Cantril and Gordon W. Allport use several metaphors for radio ("Radio: A Psychological Novelty," 3–18). They compare radio's relationship to its listeners to an evangelist and his crowd, to a book and its reader, and to a movie and its audience. The authors emphasize that radio "intimacy" is more "personal" than the printed word; moreover, radio listeners form a "social unity" in ways unparalleled by a book's readership (18).

86. Jason Loviglio provides the definitive treatment of radio's "intimacy" in Roosevelt's broadcasts and elsewhere in *Radio's Intimate Public: Network Broadcasting and Mass-Mediated Democracy* (Minneapolis: U of Minnesota P, 2005).

87. George Sumner Albee's "The Next Voice You Hear" appeared in the August 1948 *Cosmopolitan* and is reprinted in Thomas Costain, *Read with Me* (Garden City, NY: Doubleday, 1965), 3–14. The producer of the 1950 film wrote a fascinatingly detailed description of the story's purchase, adaptation, and filming: Dore Schary, *Case History of a Movie* (New York: Garland, [1950] 1978).

88. John Cheever, "The Enormous Radio," *New Yorker*, May 17, 1947, 28–33.

89. See, for example, Rachel Adams, " 'A Mixture of Delicious and Freak': The Queer Fiction of Carson McCullers," *American Literature* 71, no. 3 (1999): 551–83.

90. Carson McCullers, *The Heart Is a Lonely Hunter* in *Complete Novels* (New York: Library of America, 2001), 87.

91. McCullers, *The Heart Is a Lonely Hunter*, 83, 179.

92. McCullers, *The Heart Is a Lonely Hunter*, 205. In McCullers's *The Member of the Wedding* (1946) the radio is replaced by more familiar images of a hopeful elsewhere—motorcycles and airplanes.

93. Speers, *We Are Fires Unquenchable*, 319.

94. Speers, *We Are Fires Unquenchable*, 347.

95. Speers, *We Are Fires Unquenchable*, 366.

Chapter 6. White Female Desire Wearing the Masks of Color

1. "Seductively bedecked" is the editorial self-description ("Life's Cover," *Life*, November 10, 1941, 30).

2. "Gene Tierney: She Makes Four Films a Year Climaxed by 'Shanghai Gesture,' " *Life*, November 10, 1941, 63.

3. On the Fox signings, see Thomas Schatz, *Boom and Bust: The American Cinema of the 1940s* (New York: Scribner, 1997), 53. Much the best book on

Twentieth Century-Fox as a production studio is Peter Lev, *Twentieth Century-Fox: The Zanuck-Skouras Years, 1935–1965* (Austin: U of Texas P, 2013).

4. On the role of sexuality in the musicals of Carmen Miranda, see Shari Roberts, "'The Lady in the Tutti-Frutti Hat': Carmen Miranda, a Spectacle of Ethnicity," *Cinema Journal* 32 (1993): 3–23. Eric Lawrence Gans details the sexualized promotion of another Fox actress from the same period in "'Sex Loaded': At Twentieth Century-Fox," *Carole Landis: A Most Beautiful Girl* (Jackson: UP of Mississippi, 2008), 64–93. Another Fox actress whose career runs parallel to Gene Tierney's is Linda Darnell, who rose to fame by playing Hispanic characters in *The Mark of Zorro* (1940) and *Blood and Sand* (1941). Darnell's cinematic biography is capably recounted by Ronald L. Davis, *Hollywood Beauty: Linda Darnell and the American Dream* (Norman: Oklahoma UP, 1991).

5. Bosley Crowther, "The Screen in Review," *New York Times*, April 24, 1942, L21.

6. "'Miss Pan-America' Chosen by South American Sculptor," *Los Angeles Times*, May 31, 1941, part 2, 3.

7. Paul Harrison, "Hollywood: New Rules Say Sarong Must Be Stretched if It Is to Be Seen," *San Jose News*, November 3, 1941, 40.

8. Patty O'Brien, *The Pacific Muse: Exotic Femininity and the Colonial Pacific* (Seattle: U of Washington P, 2006), 244, in a brief discussion of *Son of Fury* (243–44). The source novel (Edison Marshall, *Benjamin Blake* [New York: Literary Guild of America, 1941]) does in fact conclude in England with the marriage of Blake and the Englishwoman, Isabel. That the film is drawn back to the island can be attributed to the studio's desire to heighten the importance of Tierney's native character.

9. Thomas Brady, "Keeping the 'Gesture' Inoffensive," *New York Times*, September 28, 1941, X3.

10. Susan Courtney, *Hollywood Fantasies of Miscegenation: Spectacular Narratives of Gender and Race, 1903–1967* (Princeton, NJ: Princeton UP, 2005).

11. Courtney compares the way Hays treated different kinds of racial and ethnic miscegenation in *Hollywood Fantasies of Miscegenation*, 116–41.

12. Matthew Bernstein credibly argues that the coda of *Foreign Correspondent* is "unrelated to the rest of the film" (*Walter Wanger, Hollywood Independent* [Minneapolis: U of Minnesota Press, 2000], 162). Bernstein's book provides a top-notch overview of Wanger and his productions, although priorities allow for less than a page on *Sundown* (168).

13. Tom Pendergast, *Creating the Modern Man: American Magazines and Consumer Culture, 1900–1950* (Columbia: U of Missouri P, 2000), 51. The masculine emphasis of the *Saturday Evening Post* is shown when Ben Hibbs takes over as editor in 1942; in his "first declaration of policy" he writes: "We shall give the *Post* more woman interest—but that does not mean we shall become another woman's magazine" (Curtis Publishing, *A Short History of the Saturday Evening Post* [Philadelphia: Curtis Publishing, 1953], 41).

14. Barré Lyndon, "Sundown," *Saturday Evening Post*, January 18, 1941, 21.

15. Lyndon, "Sundown," 11.

16. Thomas Cripps, *Making Movies Black: The Hollywood Message Movie from World War II to the Civil Rights Era* (New York: Oxford UP, 1993), 38–41.

17. Hye Seung Chung, *Hollywood Asian: Philip Ahn and the Politics of Cross-Ethnic Performance* (Philadelphia: Temple UP, 2006), 174.

18. In her discussion of *Pinky* (1949), a later Fox feature, Susan Courtney shows how the visibly white actress, Jeanne Crain, is "inscribed" as black in various ways over the course of the film (*Hollywood Fantasies of Miscegenation*, 172–90). Pinky's visibly black grandmother (Ethel Waters) serves a similar purpose to Haoli Young's visibly Asian father.

19. Milton Caniff's comic strip *Terry and the Pirates* amounts to a full-scale negotiation of race and sexuality between white American and Chinese characters. In the early 1940s, the strip offers the possibility of a romance between Terry and a Chinese woman with the significant name of Hu-she. The educational radio series *Pacific Story* (1943–1947) demonstrates the need to distinguish between good and bad Asian voices in radio. For example, in the third episode, "The New China" (8–8–43), the bad Japanese are given much thicker accents than the good Chinese.

20. Ladd's previous Paramount feature, *Lucky Jordan* (1942), provides an analogous plotline for his hard-boiled character as he goes from hoodlum to patriot.

21. For a survey of typical studio publicity techniques, see Jeanine Basinger, *The Star Machine* (New York: Knopf, 2007), 45–72. A good popular account is Robert S. Sennett, *Hollywood Hoopla: Creating Stars and Selling Movies in the Golden Age of Hollywood* (New York: Billboard Books, 1998).

22. Leonard Hall, "Movies," *Mademoiselle*, March 1942, 181.

23. Henry F. Pringle, "Preview of a Star," *Collier's*, June 29, 1940, 49.

24. "Hedda Hopper's Hollywood," *Los Angeles Times*, July 5, 1942, part 3, 3.

25. Bob Thomas, "Gene Tierney," *Screen Guide*, July 1946, 60.

26. "Hedda Hopper's Hollywood," *Los Angeles Times*, February 24, 1943, part 2, 8.

27. "Hedda Hopper's Hollywood," February 24, 1943, part 2, 8.

28. Edwin Schallert, "Gene Tierney Cast as 'Ultimate' Sarong Girl," *Los Angeles Times*, April 1, 1942, part 1, 16.

29. George Frederick Custen, *Twentieth Century's Fox: Darryl F. Zanuck and the Culture of Hollywood* (New York: Basic Books, 1997), 290.

30. A memo from Zanuck to producer Otto Preminger, director Rouben Mamoulian, and writer Samuel Hoffenstein, dated March 20, 1944, quoted in *Memo from Darryl F. Zanuck*, selected, edited, and annotated by Rudy Behlmer (New York: Grove Press, 1993), 70.

31. Eliot Janeway, "Trials and Errors: A Christian Comes to Congress," *Fortune*, April 1943, 60.

32. In the novel Harland only thinks the words; in the film he says them out loud to her (Ben Ames Williams, *Leave Her to Heaven* [Boston: Houghton Mifflin, 1944], 25).

33. Advertisement for *Leave Her to Heaven* as a promotional book for the Doubleday One Dollar Book Club, *Radio Mirror*, February 1946, 11.

34. In its promotional magazine *The New Dynamo*, Fox promotes the not-yet-filmed *Leave Her to Heaven* by emphasizing Ellen's seductive, deadly desire. Floating over a picture of a woman initiating an embrace with a shirtless man are the words: "I will never let you go . . . I want all of you . . . nothing shall stand between us" (*The New Dynamo*, April 1945, 113). This issue also includes a big build up for *A Bell for Adano* (1945), where Tierney is masked once again, this time as a blonde Italian, Tina. According to the article, Tierney was perfect for the role; "Gene, long-called the screen's most international actress because of her multiple ancestry—French, Irish, Spanish, Italian, and Swedish—needed no makeup for her lovely olive skin, wore only lipstick" (74).

35. On the paucity of good roles for African Americans in 1940s Hollywood film, see Dalton Trumbo, "Blackface, Hollywood Style," *Crisis*, December 1943, 365–67, 378. Trumbo uses the term "blackface" to indicate the stereotypical roles offered to black actors.

36. For a good introduction to the origins of "race records," see Larry Starr and Christopher Waterman, " 'St. Louis Blues': Race Records and Hillbilly Music," *American Popular Music from Minstrelsy to MP3* (New York: Oxford UP, 2007), 86–108.

37. Quoted in Peter Townsend, *Pearl Harbor Jazz: Change in Popular Music in the Early 1940s* (Jackson: UP of Mississippi, 2007), 149.

38. "On the Records," *Billboard*, January 3, 1942, 66.

39. *Billboard*'s "Harlem Hit Parade" made its debut in the October 24, 1942, issue. On this first top ten list, eight of the entries are by African American performers; the Ella Mae Morse–Freddie Slack hit "Mr. Five by Five" (Capitol 115) stands at number three, while the Billie Holiday–Paul Whiteman record "Trav'lin Light" (Capitol 116) is ranked second (25). In the next "Harlem Hit Parade" (*Billboard*, October 31, 1942, 24), "Mr. Five by Five" is now ranked first, while the Slack-Morse hit, "Cow Cow Boogie" is ranked tenth.

40. "Popular Record Reviews," *Billboard*, August 5, 1944, 65.

41. Dick Carter, "On the Air," *Billboard*, January 24, 1942, 12.

42. "Night Clubs-Vaudeville," *Billboard*, October 17, 1942, 14; "Movie Machine Review," April 25, 1942, 67; "Night Club Reviews," November 11, 1944, 24. Soundies—short music films projected in their own jukebox cabinet—were produced by the Soundies Distributing Corporation of America from 1940 to 1946. An excellent survey of the field is provided by Scott MacGillivray and Ted Okuda, *The Soundies Book: A Revised and Expanded Guide* (New York: iUniverse, 2007).

43. "Night Clubs-Vaudeville," *Billboard*, October 14, 1944, 26; "Night Club Reviews," *Billboard*, January 17, 1942, 24; "Night Club Reviews," *Billboard*, April 24, 1943, 14.

44. "On the Records," *Billboard*, September 26, 1942, 63.

45. "Night Clubs-Vaudeville," *Billboard*, March 21, 1942, 13.

46. "Movie Machine Reviews," *Billboard*, March 23, 1946, 125.

47. "Billy ('Mr. B') Eckstine, a Stroke Victim, Dies of Cardiac Arrest at Age 78," *Jet*, March 22, 1993, 57.

48. Daniel Stein provides extraordinarily detailed context for a discussion of minstrelsy throughout *Music Is My Life: Louis Armstrong, Autobiography and American Jazz* (Ann Arbor: U of Michigan Press, 2012); see especially, " 'He didn't need black face—to be funny': The Double Resonance of Postcolonial Performance," 183–226. There are numerous debates about the role of minstrelsy in Louis Jordan. A good starting point is Guthrie P. Ramsay Jr., " 'Keep it Simple,' Louis Jordan, King of the Jukebox," *Race Music: Black Cultures from Bebop to Hip-Hop* (Berkeley: U of California P, 2004), 62–67.

49. See for example the two-page promotion for Jordan in the 1944 *Billboard* Music Year Book, 141–42. Jordan is promoted as the "King of the Bobby Sock Brigade" and must therefore be rendered even more nonthreatening. The smiling face with glasses derives from his pontificating character "Deacon Jones," who is featured in the film, *Meet Miss Bobby Socks* (1944). This promotion is linked to the 1944 film, but the smiling face "logo" appears also in the 1943 *Billboard* Music Year Book, 51. Teresa Reed links Jordan's "Deacon Jones" character to the minstrelsy tradition in *The Holy Profane: Religion in Black Popular Music* (Lexington: U of Kentucky P, 2003), 79.

50. Joseph F. Laredo, "Ella Mae Morse," liner notes, *Ella Mae Morse* (Hollywood, CA: Capitol Records, 1992), 3.

51. This anecdote appears in many places; for example, Roy R. Barkley, *The Handbook of Texas Music* (Austin: Texas State Historical Association, 2003), 218.

52. James Bacon, "Hollywood Highlights," *Spokane Daily Chronicle*, July 14, 1952, 14.

53. Frank Marshall Davis, "Rhythm and Blues" (1955) in *Writings of Frank Marshall Davis: A Voice of the Black Press*, ed. John Edgar Tidwell (Jackson: UP of Mississippi, 2007), 11.

54. "New Records Hit 17, 000 in Two Weeks," *Down Beat*, August 1, 1942, 8.

55. For comparable analyses of racism at the time, see the columns by Abe Hill in the *New York Amsterdam News* throughout the mid-1940s. He accepts the all-black musical play *Carmen Jones*; it "was colorful with the minimum disturbances to our acute racial sensitivity" (*New York Amsterdam News*, June 9, 1945, 6B). By contrast, he regrets the revival of *Porgy and Bess* as a "bias classic" (March 4, 1944, 10A). Hill is skeptical about black comedy that has its "roots in minstrel shows" since minstrelsy "was created by white showmen and designed to amuse a white clientele" [June 9, 1945, 6B].

56. For lists and descriptions of 1940s cartoons with black characters, see Henry T. Sampson, *That's Enough, Folks: Black Images in Animated Cartoons, 1900–1960* (Lanham, MD: Scarecrow, 1990).

57. "Cow Cow Boogie," *Ella Mae Morse: The Cow Cow Boogie Girl Sings* (New York: Leeds Music Corp., 1944), 2–4.

58. "Record Possibilities," *Billboard*, April 8, 1944, 18.

59. M. H. Orodenker, "Record Reviews," *Billboard*, December 15, 1945, 29.

60. I borrow the image of the speechless maid from Hazel V. Carby's foundational essay, "It Jus Be's Dat Way Sometime: The Sexual Politics of Women's

Blues," *The Jazz Cadence of American Culture*, ed. Robert G. O'Meally (New York: Columbia UP, 1998), 482.

61. "Record Reviews," *Billboard*, August 9, 1947, 138.

62. M. H. Orodenker, "Popular Record Reviews," *Billboard*, November 18, 1944, 21.

63. "Record Reviews," *Billboard*, June 21, 1947, 132.

64. "Record Reviews," *Down Beat*, February 15, 1944, 8.

65. "Boogie Woogie Conga," *Ella Mae Morse: The Cow Cow Boogie Girl Sings*, 6.

66. According to *A Century of American Popular Music: 2000 Best-Loved and Remembered Songs* (ed. David A. Jasen [New York: Routledge, 2002]), "Lonesome Mama Blues" was "introduced in vaudeville by Eddie Jackson and Dot Taylor" and "became a great favorite of jazz bands" (121).

67. Ted Gioia traces the history of "You Don't Know What Love Is" in *The Jazz Standards: A Guide to the Repertoire* (New York: Oxford UP, 2012), 467–68.

68. See Klaus Taubig, *Straighten Up and Fly Right: A Chronology and Discography of Nat "King" Cole* (Westport, CT: Greenwood, 1994), 80. This side was released on MacGregor.

69. In "The Patty Cake Man" (1944, Capitol 163) Morse sings about "a baker / Who is a solid love-maker." The singer and other ladies like to visit the baker at all hours ("midnight's just the time for love"), although sometimes they have to compete with his actual baking. The cover of the Capitol Songs sheet music for "The Patty Cake Man" shows a big-eyed woman visiting the grinning, wolfish-looking baker at work.

70. Lyrics quoted in Richard Goldstein, "Lunchtime Follies," *Helluva Town: New York City during World War II* (New York: Free Press, 2010), 146.

71. Lauren Rebecca Sklaroff provides the best description by far of *Jubilee*'s racial and political emphases ("Variety for the Servicemen," *Black Culture and the New Deal: The Quest for Civil Rights in the Roosevelt Era* [Chapel Hill: U of North Carolina P, 2009], 159–92). She properly highlights the "sexual candor" of the show (184–85). Sklaroff selects a 1947 show in which Ava Gardner introduces black musician Jack McVae as an example of *Jubilee*'s taboo-breaking progressive stance (189–90). I agree that the white female–black male boundary is crucial, but would say that the show went at that issue in 1945 by combining white female and black male musicians.

72. My overview of *Jubilee* programs relies mainly on three sources: (1) extant programs, many of which can be found on the Internet Archive; (2) Rainer Lotz and Ulrich Neuert, *The "AFRS" Jubilee Transcription Programs: An Exploratory Discography* (Frankfurt: Ruecker, 1985); and (3) an online supplement to Lotz and Neuert by Bo Scherman, Carl Hallstrom, and Michael Arié, *The AFRS Jubilee Transcription Series* (home.swipnet.se/dooji/jubilee.htm; accessed August 1, 2013).

73. Using the numbering system in the discography by Lotz and Neuert: Sweethearts (82 and 92), Hopper (87), Andrews Sisters (94), Pied Pipers (95).

74. Again following the Lotz and Neuert discography: King Sisters (97, 141), Anita O'Day (111b), Kitty Kallen (124), Ella Mae Morse (146), Peggy Lee (153),

June Christy (156), and Kay Starr (161, 162).

75. In *Lonesome Roads and Streets of Dreams: Place, Mobility and Race in Jazz of the 1930s and 40s* (Chicago: U of Chicago P, 2012), Andrew S. Berish provides context for the Krupa–O'Day–Eldridge number, "Let Me Off Uptown" ("Drop Me Off in Harlem," 105–10). As Berish writes, their dialogue ("blow, Roy, blow") "lends itself to a sexually charged reading, made all the more risqué by the interracialism of the speakers" (109). One could add that the energy and politics of "Let Me Off Uptown" is based on the irony that Anita O'Day knows more about Harlem than Roy Eldridge ("No, I haven't been uptown," he says. "What's uptown?"). In effect, O'Day talks Eldridge into his true black self, which he manifests in a trumpet solo. The other Krupa–O'Day–Eldridge Soundie, "Thanks for the Boogie Ride," comes with an equally interesting racial plot alongside the overt sexual insinuations.

76. The *Down Beat* review of Libby Holman's Decca album, *Blues Till Dawn*, says "This is the closest any white singer has come to colored blues" ("Record Reviews," *Down Beat,* June 1, 1942, 14).

77. The other most famous "black" white man of the era is "Mezz" Mezzrow, who peppers his autobiography *Really the Blues* (New York: Random House, 1946) with jive. Mezzrow's blackness amounts to a full-blown critique of white culture, which represents sexual repression ("a culture of masturbators" [205]), in contrast to Harlem, "where they didn't build any brick walls between wanting and doing, the urge and the act" (204). For a superb reading of *Really the Blues* in the context of racial passing, see Gayle Wald, "Mezz Mezzrow and the Voluntary Negro Blues," in *Crossing the Line: Racial Passing in Twentieth-Century U.S. Literature and Culture* (Durham, NC: Duke UP, 2000), 53–81.

78. The protests against *St. Louis Woman* were extensively reported in the *New York Amsterdam News*. An unsigned article reports that the Interracial Film and Radio Guild found the "atrocious dialect" highly offensive and recommends that Lena Horne not take the lead role ("it would cause irreparable harm to her reputation as one of the race's finest and most glamorous artists," September 8, 1945, 9B).

79. Philip Furia, *Skylark: The Life and Times of Johnny Mercer* (New York: St. Martins, 2003), 147. Jo Stafford is not a singer who sounded "black" to many ears, but in 1945 Dan Burley wrote the article "Song Stylist Jo Stafford Favorite with Harlemites," which observed that sales figures at Harlem's Rainbow Music Shop ranked female singers as follows: (1) Billie Holiday, (2) Jo Stafford, (3) Dinah Washington, (4) Ella Mae Morse, and (5) Ella Fitzgerald. Burley guessed that "the slight drawl in her voice may account for the kinship Negro listeners feel to the singer when they hear her on records" (*New York Amsterdam News*, March 17, 1945, 16).

80. The second season records have been published as *The Johnny Mercer Chesterfield Music Shop*, compiled by Harry Mackenzie (Zephyrhills, FL: Joyce Record Club, 1986).

81. According to John Dunning, Marlin Hurt played Beulah on *The Beulah Show* (1946–1947), was replaced by another white man when he died of a heart attack, and then Hattie McDaniel played Beulah from 1947 to 1952 (*The Encyclopedia of Old-Time Radio*, 83).

82. In contrast to the full records for the second season of *Johnny Mercer's Music Shop*, there are scarcely any records for the first season. The second season *Music Shop* was broadcast by Armed Forces Radio Service (AFRS) transcription, which means that both shows and playlists are extant. The AFRS did not rebroadcast the first season, however, which accounts for the almost complete lack of both shows and records. *Billboard* reviewed the first program of the first season and lists some of the songs ("Program Reviews," *Billboard*, July 17, 1943, 12).

83. *Mrs. Wiggs of the Cabbage Patch* is the title of a novel (1901), a 1930s soap opera, and a series of films, the latest produced in 1942. Mercer's comic novelty song makes Mrs. Wiggs into a restaurant owner whose food is worth the trip ("entertaining suburbanites").

84. Histories of blackface in the 1940s repeatedly turn to Bing Crosby, who not only does blackface numbers in *Holiday Inn* (1942), *Dixie* (1943), and *Here Come the Waves* (1944), but also turned his entire April 2, 1947, radio program into a minstrel show in honor of guest Al Jolson. Biographer Gary Giddins recounts a typical entertainment in the 1938 Crosby household; "The Midgie Minstrels" featured Joe Venuti and Johnny Mercer in blackface (*Bing Crosby: A Pocketful of Dreams, The Early Years 1903–1940* [Boston: Little, Brown], 2001, 460–61).

85. In his *Handbook of Harlem Jive* (1944), Dan Burley defines "homey" as "one newly arrived from the South, a person from one's hometown, one who isn't fully aware of what's going on" (140). Morse, then, uses the word in order to appear more authoritative than her male interlocutor.

86. The Capitol Records promotional magazine *Capitol News from Hollywood* makes a racially integrated impression with many articles about and many pictures of black artists. Like *Down Beat*, *Capitol News from Hollywood* runs short news stories about the where and what next of musicians who do not necessarily record for Capitol Records (i.e., "Basie without a Fem Singer" or "James Preparing New Tour in East"). The advertisements are all for Capitol artists, however, and here the whiteness comes through. The November 1947 issue includes ads for two African American women: Nellie Lutcher ("You Better Watch Yourself, Bub") and Julia Lee ("Snatch It and Grab It"). The May 1946 *Capitol News from Hollywood* includes ads for Mercer singing songs from *St. Louis Woman* ("Li'l Augie Is a Natural Man") and for the Morse-Slack "The House of Blue Lights," but no ads for recordings by black women.

87. Dave Dexter Jr., an important contributor to the success of Capitol Records, says that Nat King Cole was Capitol's single most important artist (*Playback: A Newsman/Record Producer's Hits and Misses from the Thirties to the Seventies* [New York: Billboard Publications, 1976], 88). In one of the more detailed descriptions of Capitol Records' early days (85–135), Dexter recalls an episode where Cole objected angrily to his likeness in a promotion: "'Looks like an old-fashioned pickaninny,' Cole snorted" (96). For some reason no one before Cole had noticed; Capitol then had the artwork changed.

88. On the May 22, 1943, broadcast of *Command Performance*, the King Cole Trio is introduced as "one of the hottest trios in the land of jive" and plays "Solid Potato Salad."

89. Daniel Mark Epstein credits Mercer with Capitol's focus on recording love ballads by Nat King Cole (*Nat King Cole* [New York: Farrar, Straus and Giroux, 1999], 112). By contrast, Cole himself—for the cultural reasons already noted—was hesitant to become a ballad singer (112).

90. In *Capitol News from Hollywood*, Kay Starr is promoted using the same kind of language that sprung up around Ella Mae Morse. If you listen to her "big, deep voice" on "Share Croppin' Blues," you will notice that Kay Starr does not "sound like the other girls on the radio" ("Singers' Stuff," *Capitol News from Hollywood*, November 1947, 13).

91. "Record Reviews," *Billboard*, January 18, 1947, 26; "Record Reviews," *Down Beat*, February 12, 1947, 21.

92. Lee's publicity could frame her as a femme fatale, however; the album cover for *Rendezvous with Peggy Lee* (Capitol, 1948) looks more like a sexy paperback cover than 1940s album art. Photographed lying on her back on a pillow, "it was all sex-bomb stuff" (Peter Richmond, *Fever: the Life and Music of Miss Peggy Lee* [New York: Holt, 2006], 151).

93. Mike Levin, "1942 Record Reviewed," *Down Beat*, January 1, 1943, 8.

94. "Reviews of New Records," *Billboard*, August 3, 1946, 33.

Chapter 7. What Young Women Want: From High School to College

1. Jon Savage, *Teenage: The Creation of Youth Culture* (New York: Viking Press, 2007), xv.

2. Savage, *Teenage*, 441–53. In her thoroughly researched survey of popular culture aimed at young women, *Some Wore Bobby Sox: The Emergence of Teenage Girls' Culture, 1920–1945* (New York: Palgrave Macmillan, 2004), Kelly Schrum also makes the point that "teenagers" emerge in the 1940s as females (19).

3. Sallie Belle Cox, "The Star that Fell in Ohio," *Ladies' Home Journal*, March 1946, 224.

4. Ben T. Logan, "Not Like in the Movies," *Calling All Girls*, June 1948, 52. Johnny copies George Sanders in *The Private Affairs of Bel Ami* (1947); Bel Ami's indifference to women paradoxically draws them to him. I refer often in these pages to *Calling All Girls*, which will be less familiar to most readers than *Seventeen*. *Calling All Girls* was published from 1941 to 1949. It was initially targeted to girls age twelve to thirteen, which can be gleaned not only from the numerous comics, but also as straightforwardly stated by Frances Ullmann, the editor of *Calling All Girls*, in her foreword to Alice Barr Grayson's collection of *Calling All Girls* columns, *Do You Know Your Daughter?* [(New York: Appleton-Century, 1944], ix). (In the *March of Time* newsreel on teenage girls, a befuddled father is seen reading Grayson's book.) After the war, no doubt under pressure from the appearance of *Seventeen* in 1944, the magazine aimed its material at high school aged girls.

5. Mary Brinker Post, "Web of Dreams," *Calling All Girls*, June 1946, 76.

6. *Movie Teen: The Movie Magazine for Miss Seventeen*, May 1947, 6.

7. "Dizzy Blonde," *Time*, October 20, 1947, 96.

8. My reading stresses patience and normalcy; for a contrasting reading of *The Bachelor and the Bobby-Soxer* that stresses conflict—Susan's real power over the adults and Grant's satire on teenage style—see Georganne Scheiner, *Signifying Female Adolescence: Film Representations and Fans, 1920–1950* (Westport, CT: Praeger, 2000), 108. Marynia Farnham, coauthor of *Modern Woman: The Lost Sex*, regarded the "crush" stage as homosexual; that is, a typical adolescent phase involved "hero worship" of an older person and a "crush" on "a person of the same age and sex" ("Homosexuality," *The Adolescent* [New York: Harper, 1951], 171). But if this phase is not soon outgrown, the "unfortunate" roots of homosexuality may set in. In this case, parents should remember that "homosexuality is not a disgrace," but "it is a sickness," and expert help must be sought as quickly as possible (178).

9. George Frazier, "Frank Sinatra," *Life*, May 3, 1943, 55.

10. Richard K. Bellamy, "Riding the Airwaves," *Milwaukee Journal*, December 27, 1943, 2.

11. Donald Laird's position was well known; see, for example, Margaret S. Wells, "Music in the News," *Billboard*, November 20, 1943, 67. The long parody of Sinatra and female swooning in *Li'l Abner* takes its premise from the idea that "all great crooner swooners have an emaciated, half-starved look that arouses the maternal instinct in females" (12–28–1943, Al Capp, *Li'l Abner: Dailies Volume 10: 1944* [Princeton, WI: Kitchen Sink Press, 1990], 21).

12. "Artur Rodzinski Condemns Boogie Woogie as 'Greatest Cause of Youth Delinquency,'" *New York Times*, January 22, 1944, 15.

13. Bruce Bliven, "The Voice and the Kids," *New Republic*, November 6, 1944, 593.

14. E. J. Kahn Jr., "Phenomenon: The Fave, the Fans, and the Fiends," *New Yorker*, November 21, 1946, 35.

15. Nancy Pepper, "Jabberwocky and Jive," *Calling All Girls*, June 1946, 41.

16. Manrey Jewelry, advertisement, *Calling All Girls*, June 1946, 81.

17. Joseley, advertisement, *Calling All Girls*, June 1948, 59.

18. "Tricks for Teens," *Calling All Girls*, June 1946, 48.

19. "Campus Capers on the Cover!" *Calling All Girls*, January 1946, 64.

20. Florida Fashions, advertisement, *Calling All Girls*, May 1947, 60.

21. "The Bashful Balloter," *Andy* (August 1948), n.p. The character Andy combines the looks of Archie Andrews with the personality of Li'l Abner. The cover shows Andy taking a picture of a flower while pretty girls primp themselves behind him, waiting for his attention.

22. Sally Togs, advertisement, *Calling All Girls*, May 1947, 56.

23. Sheila Daly published numerous teenage advice books during the 1940s; *Blondes Prefer Gentlemen* (New York: Dodd, Mead, 1949) puts her in the interesting position of giving advice to teenage boys. Since in this book female desire coincides

perfectly with male civility and restraint, Daly, not surprisingly, tells boys to avoid necking ("believe it or not, wolves are going out of style" [203]), while also warning boys away from aggressive women like "the wolfess—the gal who is out to conquer the heart of every boy she dates" (144).

24. Elizabeth Woodward, "We're Telling You," *Ladies' Home Journal*, December 1944, 20–21.

25. Elizabeth Woodward, "Alone Together," *Ladies' Home Journal*, July 1945, 8.

26. Maureen Daly, "No Parking Please," *Ladies' Home Journal*, May 1946, 8.

27. *Profile of Youth: By Members of the Staff of Ladies' Home Journal*, ed. Maureen Daly (Philadelphia: Lippincott, 1951), 147.

28. *Profile of Youth*, 152.

29. *Profile of Youth*, 152.

30. "What's the Do with Woo?," *Movie Teen*, May 1947, 49.

31. "What's the Do with Woo?," 79.

32. In this issue of *Seventeen* (October 1946), both "Political Quiz" (126–127) and "Mental Gymnasium" (55–56) treat their readers as capaciously intellectual. Page numbers are cited parenthetically in text hereafter.

33. For a detailed description of *Seventeen* in the 1940s, including good remarks on the sometimes contradictory relationship of articles to advertisements, see Kelley Massoni, *Fashioning Teenagers: A Cultural History of "Seventeen" Magazine* (Walnut Creek, CA: Left Coast Press, 2010).

34. Paul Popenoe, "Meet an Engaged Couple," *Ladies' Home Journal*, August 1943, 81.

35. Leslie B. Hohman, "Why Go to College," *Ladies' Home Journal*, February 1943, 103.

36. Dorothy Entwistle Swenson, "New Careers for College Girls," *Ladies' Home Journal*, May 1949, 109.

37. Beth L. Bailey, "Scientific Truth . . . and Love," in *From Front Porch to Back Seat: Courtship in Twentieth-Century America* (Baltimore, MD: Johns Hopkins UP, 1988), 119–40.

38. Betty Friedan, "The Sex-Directed Educators," *Feminine Mystique*, 227–67.

39. Friedan, *Feminine Mystique*, 235.

40. Friedan, *Feminine Mystique*, 236–37.

41. Frances C. Thurman, "College Courses in Preparation for Marriage," *Social Forces* 24, no. 3 (1946): 333.

42. Thurman, "College Courses," 333.

43. Thurman, "College Courses," 333.

44. Justin Landis, "The Teaching of Family and Marriage Courses by Sociologists and Home Economists," *Social Forces* 24, no. 3 (1946): 336–39.

45. Beth L. Bailey, "Scientific Truth . . . and Love," *From Front Porch to Back Seat*, 174.

46. James Wood authored "Should We Draft Mothers?" *Woman's Home Companion*, January 1944; "Let the Women In!," *Woman's Home Companion*, November 1946; "Unwanted Women," *Woman's Home Companion*, May 1948.

47. William F. McDermott, "Campus in the Sky," *Collier's*, July 8, 1944, 22–24.

48. Science and aviation journals also ran articles on Stephens College: "Marriage Goes to College," *Science Illustrated*, February 1948; "Cross-Country College Course," *Aviation Week and Space Technology*, May 17, 1948.

49. Bowman, "Are Girls becoming the Pursuers," *American*, April 1945, 32–33, 102–04.

50. Henry A. Bowman and Priscilla Scott, "Looks that Men Like," *American*, January 1948, 43.

51. Bowman and Scott, "Looks that Men Like," 42.

52. The Stephens College yearbook celebrates its busy Public Relations department, in 1947 headed by Robert J. Sailstad (*Stephensophia*, 1947, n.p.) With a pictured staff of four, the college's news bureau, in the words of the yearbook, "sends out newspaper releases to home-town newspapers and national magazines concerning both the work of the entire College as well as personal news stories about individual students." Judging from the sheer number of references to Stephens College in the general media, the publicity department did a terrific job.

53. S. J. Woolf, "Then and Now—Maude Adams," *New York Times*, October 17, 1948, Sunday Magazine, 17.

54. "Gives Full Time to Stephens Job," *New York Times*, August 9, 1942, D5.

55. "Changes Expected in Sex Problems: Family Relations Group Hears Effects of War," *New York Times*, January 1, 1942, 32.

56. [Henry Bowman,] "Education for Marriage," in *Explorations in General Education: The Experiences of Stephens College*, Roy Ivan Johnson, ed. (New York: Harper, 1947), 123. This collection of articles on Stephen College does not attribute authorship to each chapter, but a "foreword" does credit Bowman with providing a "first draft or suggestive outline" of material (ix). To my ears, the "Education for Marriage" chapter sounds like Bowman all the way. The book as a whole is a characteristic example of Stephens College self-promotion, as they present a full-scale version of their activities within a framework of deep research and scrupulously responsible pedagogy. Their teaching materials are typically presented in hyperrigorous and hyperorganized terms, in order to defend themselves against thought or unthought charges of frivolity. It does not say so in the book itself, but Roy Ivan Johnson is the director of Publications at Stephens College. The 1947 yearbook gives pride of place to this collection: "Outstanding among this year's publications is *Explorations in General Education*, edited by Dr. Johnson and published by Harper and Brothers" (*Stephensofia*, 1947, 27).

57. "Education for Marriage," 113.

58. "Education for Marriage," 115.

59. "Education for Marriage," 115.

60. "Education for Marriage," 115.

61. "Education for Marriage," 128.

62. "Education for Marriage," 116. I quote from the obituary of Bowman published in *Footnotes* (American Sociological Association), 6, no. 3 (May 1978): 7.

63. "Education for Marriage," 116.

64. Henry A. Bowman, *Marriage for Moderns* (New York: McGraw-Hill, 1948). This is the second edition of the textbook; the first appears in 1942. References will be cited parenthetically in the text. Jeffrey P. Moran, *Teaching Sex: The Shaping of Adolescence in the 20th Century* (Cambridge, MA: Harvard UP, 2000) provides a good, quickly moving history of sexual education in primary and secondary schools. It does move so quickly that it can say, without mentioning Stephens College, "the most thoroughgoing effort in marriage education appeared at an all-female institution, Russell Sage College, from the mid-1930s onward" (127). Moran quotes Bowman's statistics on the number of marriage courses offered across the country, but there is not time for the narrative to do more than mention Ernest Groves. And no college could possibly be more thoroughgoing in its marriage education than Stephens College, which draws a blank from this book.

65. *Explorations in General Education*, 109.

66. While noting that most sexual treatises "emphasize the disadvantages and general undesirability of pre-marital coitus," the second Kinsey report regards Bowman as presenting a "middle ground" interpretation of it—neither harshly judgmental nor entirely tolerant—because he "lists arguments pro and con" (*Sexual Behavior in the Human Female* [Philadelphia: Saunders, 1953], 307). I would suggest that Bowman's staged "pro and con" debate is a rhetorical gesture of reasonableness made along the way to an intolerant conclusion. The second Kinsey report also aligns Bowman with authors who "have stressed the unfavorable effects which pre-marital coitus might have on later marital adjustments" (*Sexual Behavior in the Human Female*, 388).

67. *Marriage for Moderns*, 215. In the fifth edition of his textbook (1965), Bowman removes the sentence about a man who has "probably had no direct sexual experience," since the 1948 Kinsey report put that to rest. Nonetheless he still tries to problematize the data of Kinsey and others as much as possible: "All studies of premarital intercourse up to date involve shortcomings of one sort or another, such as inadequate sampling, methodological errors, or time-relative validity" (Bowman, *Marriage for Moderns* [New York: McGraw-Hill, 1965], 129).

68. Ray E. Baber, *Marriage and the Family* (New York: McGraw-Hill, 1939), 564.

69. Amram Scheinfeld, *Women and Men* (New York: Harcourt, Brace, 1944), 228–29.

70. Scheinfeld, *Women and Men*, 231, 138.

71. Generalizing about all women—not just Dido—Mercury says these words to Aeneas in order to convince him to sail away from Carthage—"women are always changeable and unstable" (*Aeneid* 4:569).

72. As it so often did, Stephens College put itself on the leading edge of pedagogical advances; from 1949 to 1951 it hosted three conferences "On the Effective Utilization of Audio-Visual Materials in College Teaching." *General Education: A Report of Library-Instructional Activities at Stephens College*, ed. B. Lamar Johnson and Eloise Lindstrom (Chicago: American Library Association, 1948), gives

a detailed account of the college's "audio-visual" emphasis, including a copious list of instructional films ("Motion Pictures," 54–56). By the end of the decade, the educational film market is vast, as can be gleaned from the 1949 *Educational Film Guide* (compiled by Dorothy E. Cook and Katherine M. Holden [New York: Wilson, 1949]), which lists 7,030 titles.

73. "Protestants Show Films on Marriage," *New York Times*, May 3, 1950, 31.

74. "Protestants Show Films on Marriage," 31.

75. A brief paragraph in the *New York Times* announces that "well known documentary-film makers" have formed a "new film producing company known as Affiliated Film Producers." "Film Producing Concern Formed," *New York Times*, March 18, 1946, 25.

76. The significant documentary films of Hammid, Jacoby, and Van Dyke are described in Richard Meran Barsam, *Nonfiction Film: A Critical History* (New York: Dutton, 1973), 216–20. In James L. Enyeart's biography of Van Dyke, these marriage films go unmentioned, vanished into what Enyeart calls the "lost years" of assignments that lacked any creative component. "Lost Years," *Willard Van Dyke: Changing the World through Photography and Film* (Albuquerque: U of New Mexico P, 2008, 239–69). Gloria Waldron's overview, *The Information Film* (New York: Columbia UP, 1949), chooses Van Dyke's *The City* (1939) as a "noteworthy" example of a "successful" film (28–30).

77. For descriptions of numerous Coronet films (many of which can be watched on YouTube or at the Prelinger archives [http://archive.org/details/prelinger]), see Ken Smith, *Mental Hygiene: Classroom Films 1945–1970* (New York: Blast Books, 1999). Smith includes an overview of Coronet as a production company ("Coronet Films: Social Guidance Gothic," 89–98). A Coronet marriage film comparable to the five under discussion would be "Marriage Is a Partnership" (1951).

78. Cecile Starr, "The Film Forum," *Saturday Review of Literature*, October 21, 1950, 49.

79. Starr, "Film Forum," 49.

80. Starr, "Film Forum," 49.

81. "This Charming Couple: Film Discussion Guide," *Coordinator*, 4:1 (September 1955), 65–66.

82. Willard Van Dyke, "The Director on Location," in *Ideas on Film*, ed. Cecile Starr (New York: Funk and Wagnalls, 1951), 26.

83. Van Dyke, "Director on Location," 27.

84. Van Dyke, "Director on Location," 28.

Chapter 8. The Power and the Horror: Male and Female Cultural Spaces

1. The most illuminating history of U.S. "women's culture" is Lauren Berlant's *The Female Complaint: The Unfinished Business of Sentimentality in American*

Culture (Durham, NC: Duke UP, 2008). Her treatment of female desire in Olive Higgins Prouty's *Now, Voyager* (Boston: Houghton Mifflin, 1941) and in the film adaptation (Rapper, 1942) is unsurpassed (169–205).

2. Items in this sentence and the next refer to *Photoplay*, June 1942.

3. Despite the fact that departments and ads in these film magazines are entirely geared toward women, men may still wish to cross the gendered line to read the latest movie gossip and look at pictures of the stars. One can see this impulse in the first set of magazines sent as a unit to soldiers overseas; in addition to titles such as *Baseball, Detective Story, Popular Mechanics, Superman*, and *Western Trails*, the set also contains *Modern Screen*, which, like *Photoplay*, is arranged as a woman's magazine (John Jamieson, "The Overseas Magazine Set," *Books for the Army: The Army Library Service in the Second World War* [New York: Columbia UP, 1950], 130). The October 1943 issue of *Modern Screen* has two "beauty columns," recipes for the "Modern Hostess," and *Modern Screen* coupons for brochures on making jewelry, mending clothes, and learning to crochet. It also has Betty Grable on the cover. The 1944 set of magazines sent to soldiers continues to include *Modern Screen*, although now all magazines have had advertisements removed; the 1944 set even includes *Cosmopolitan*, but with "serials and feminine features omitted" (Jamieson, "The Overseas Magazine Set," 134–35).

4. The reference guide *American Humor Magazines and Comic Periodicals* (ed. David E. E. Sloane [New York: Greenwood Press, 1987]) contains dozens of titles for 1940s ribald humor magazines that often contain cheesecake drawings or photographs in addition to jokes. See the chronological listing from 581–85. A typical description runs: "*Smiles*, number 1 (May 1942), was a digest-sized quarterly featuring 132 pages of cartoons and jokes. After the war, it continued at 25 cents an issue, featuring more girlie and dating humor, with covers by Bill Wenzel and other drawers of lush cuties" (465).

5. In *The Magazine World: An Introduction to Magazine Journalism* (New York: Prentice-Hall, 1951), Roland E. Wolseley juxtaposes "Fan Magazines" to "Cheesecake Magazines" (36–37). Wolseley notes that "fan magazines often come from the same editorial offices as the confessions" (36). But where he notes that advertising in confessions magazines is "distinctly feminine," he attaches no gender to fan magazines. Similarly, while he says that "cheesecake or 'girly' magazines" are aimed at readers who feel "sex frustration or loneliness," he oddly declines to gender these readers as male.

6. Anthony Slide's *Inside the Hollywood Fan Magazine: A History of Star Makers, Fabricators, and Gossip Mongers* (Jackson: UP of Mississippi, 2010) contains an unparalleled list of movie fan magazines and their run dates. According to Slide, *Film Fun* runs from 1915 to 1942 (234). Slide's descriptions of the magazines are beautifully detailed, although he does not divide them into "male" and "female" audiences.

7. "3 Dears for Love," *Film Fun*, March 1941, 42–43.

8. "A Man's World," *Time*, February 6, 1950, 38–40.

9. Theodore Peterson, *Magazines in the Twentieth Century* (Urbana: U of Illinois P, 1956), 286.

10. Carle Hodge, "For Men Only," *Magazine Industry*, Winter 1950, 13.

11. Kenon Breazeale shows how *Fortune*'s success in the 1930s inspired the creation of *Esquire* as a "male-identified magazine" ("'In Spite of Women': *Esquire* Magazine and the Construction of the Male Consumer," *Signs* 20, no. 1 [1994]: 5).

12. James Playsted Wood, *Magazines in the United States: Their Social and Economic Influence* (New York: Ronald Press, 1949), 194.

13. *Life*, August 12, 1946, Weegee (8–9), "hand of dead victim" (23), and Dictator hangs from a lamp post (29).

14. Richard Rovere, "American Magazines in Wartime," *New Republic*, March 6, 1944, 311.

15. See Hugh Merrill, "Vargas, World War II, and All that Jazz," and "Esky Goes to Court" in *Esky: The Early Years at "Esquire"* (New Brunswick, NJ: Rutgers UP, 1995), 81–123.

16. After the death of William Lyon Phelps in August 1943, Bennett Cerf takes over with the December 1943 issue of *Esquire*. Both he and his successor, Sinclair Lewis, write in a much more approachable style.

17. In her splendid history of female cartoonists at the *New Yorker*, Liza Donnelly describes numerous overlaps between *Esquire* and the *New Yorker*; in addition to *Esquire*'s emphasis on literary big shots, the magazine "also published a large number of cartoonists, many of whom came from the *New Yorker*" (*Funny Ladies: The New Yorker's Greatest Women Cartoonists and Their Cartoons* [New York: Prometheus Books], 2005, 82). One of their most notable "shared" cartoonists is Barbara Shermund, who in the 1930s often drew "feminist" cartoons at the *New Yorker* (59), but who in the 1940s produced some of the most recognizably silly, buxom women at *Esquire*. The shift in Barbara Shermund's work is partly due to the fact that cartoonists rarely wrote their own captions, so a magazine's idea of humor took precedence over individual artists. In a "feminine" gesture, which I have not seen replicated by any male cartoonist, Helen Hokinson, whose cartoons of matronly society women graced the *New Yorker* for many years, shares the credit with her writer, and so dedicates her collection, *When Were You Built* (New York: Dutton, 1948), to "James Reid Parker, whose captions inspired most of these drawings."

18. Ad for December "Varga Girl" calendar in *Esquire*, November 1940, 14.

19. After Arnold Gingrich departs as editor in 1945, the approach clearly changes, and more female writers appear in the magazine from 1946–1950.

20. Mark Schorer, "The Long Embrace," *Esquire*, June 1941, 145.

21. "American Beauties, Eastern Style: The Face and Fortune of Pat Boyd," *Esquire*, March 1943, 80.

22. "American Beauties, Eastern Style: Chili Williams," *Esquire*, August 1944, 46.

23. Himself, "Credo of an American Husband," *Esquire*, April 1942, 42.

24. J. George Frederick, "From Babe to Battle-Axe," *Esquire*, June 1944, 38.

25. "Little Sister Pin-Up," *Esquire,* July 1944, 59.

26. Parke Cummings, "Specifications for Superwife," *Esquire,* July 1942, 108.

27. On the evolution of *Argosy* and *True,* see Max Allan Collins and George Hagenauer, "Blood, Sweat, and Tits: A History of Men's Adventure Magazines," in *Men's Adventure Magazines in Postwar America* (Los Angeles: Taschen, 2004), 13.

28. Clee Woods, "Señor Americano," and Alex Crawford, "I Was a Young Trail Boss," *True: The Man's Magazine* (February 1946), 60, 45.

29. Count Byron de Prorok, "World's Greatest He-Man," *True: The Man's Magazine* (February 1946), 24.

30. In some men's magazines blatant class warfare is present. In part this is a way to distinguish those magazines from *Esquire* (which often has a strong anti-intellectual element itself); more generally, this makes their men more masculine at the expense of effete intellectuals. A 1950 incarnation of the magazine *Stag* promotes a story about "Why College Men Are Sexually Inferior"; the article uses Kinsey to describe college students as thinking about sex a great deal, but mostly—in contrast to less-educated men—masturbating or using prostitutes (Milton Leekoff, "Why College Men Are Sexually Inferior," *Stag,* July 1950, 14–15).

31. As quoted in Hugh Merrill, "Vargas, World War II," *Esky,* 89.

32. In his useful but also very opinionated survey of Petty's work, Reid Stewart Austin calls Marston's psychological texts "often risible." Since he finds these texts ridiculous, he speculates that contemporary readers did too: "This psychiatric hash apparently bored the average *True* reader right off his shiny new suburban lawnchair. After eighteen months it was canned in favor of the familiar gag caption, sometimes in rhyme" (*Petty: The Classic Pin-Up Art of George Petty* [New York: Gramercy Books, 1997], 107). Since Marston dies of lung cancer in May 1947, it seems possible that ill health, in addition to bored readers, may have helped end Marston's contributions to *True* in June 1946.

33. *Esquire* provides a procedural analogue for Marston's psychological readings of the pinup women. Throughout 1940 *Esquire* ran a series called "The Types of American Beauty." This feature showed a sculpture by Frank Nagy—always a female nude—along with commentary by "Nostradamus, M.D." Like Marston's comments, these comments were validated by science and learning. Nostradamus would describe the sculpture in anatomical detail, "breasts full, firm, glandular, pointing sidewise. Nipples inconspicuous. Hips full but not fleshy, denoting the broad feminine pelvis." Then he would read the body in terms of its potential for sex and marriage: "Born, probably, on the wrong side of the railroad tracks, in which case her attractiveness and crude sex appeal are her ruin from the sixth grade up." Nostradamus would conclude his interpretation with a final bit of learning, as he named her in Latin, "mulier erotica vulgaris." His interpretation would be followed by the magazine's explanation of his authority: " 'Nostradamus' is the pseudonym of a prominent New York specialist, author of many medical texts and treatises, who has never before written for non-scientific publications." (All quotations above taken from "The Types of American Beauty: Number 1. Perdita," *Esquire,* April 1940, 129.) The "science" Dr. Nostradamus practiced is, in actuality, a contemporary science—the science

of somatotyping, as put forward by W. H. Sheldon of Harvard University in *The Varieties of Human Physique: An Introduction to Constitutional Psychology* (New York: Harper, 1940) and *The Varieties of Temperament: A Psychology of Constitutional Differences* (New York: Harper, 1942). In these texts, Sheldon argued that one could link aspects of psychology and personality to certain body types.

34. Les Daniels provides an excellent overview of many of Marston's various projects in *Wonder Woman: The Life and Times of the Amazon Princess* (San Francisco, CA: Chronicle Books, 2000), 10–31.

35. A. P. Sperling, "America Bares Its Body and Soul," *Psychology for the Millions* (New York: Frederick Fell, 1946), 4.

36. William Moulton Marston, "Miss Bewitching," *True: The Man's Magazine*, November 1945, 54.

37. Marston, "Why 100,000,000 Americans Read Comics," 43.

38. Tom Pendergast, *Creating the Modern Man; American Magazines and Consumer Culture* (Columbia: U of Missouri P, 2000), 236.

39. Pendergast, *Creating the Modern Man*, 240.

40. *Argosy*, November 1947: November pin-up (25), Myra Keck (112), December's issue (2).

41. Count Byron de Prorok, "Sahara She-Wolves," *Argosy*, November 1947, 40, 41, 110.

42. For a brief account of the government's offensive against the magazines, see James C. N. Paul and Murray L. Schwartz, "Federal Censorship from 1930 to 1945: The Divergent Responses to New Court Standards; The Postal Fight to Clean Up the Magazine Industry," in *Federal Censorship: Obscenity in the Mail* (New York: Free Press, 1961), 68–77. In terms of sexual vocabulary, "spicy" is used as a more intense version of "sexy" beyond the "spicy" pulps. Soldier Franc Shor, for example, says he enjoys the "good advice" in *Esquire* sandwiched "between its spicy cartoons" ("Shor Nuff!," *Esquire*, January 1943, 6). In a 1950 *Dragnet* episode, a sleaze peddler defends himself against the charges of distributing obscene literature: "Just candid shots, you know, spicy, for my private collection, there's nothing wrong in that, I figured I'd give the girls a break, let 'em earn a few bucks" ("The Big Picture," *Dragnet*, 12–7–50).

43. Peter Haining, "The Spice of Life and Lust: The Spicy Pulps," in *The Classic Era of American Pulp Magazines* (Chicago: Chicago Review Press, 2000), 79.

44. Page numbers that follow refer to *Spicy Detective Stories*, January 1942. Adventure House (Silver Spring, MD) has published facsimile reprints of many pulps from the 1930s and 1940s.

45. Gershon Legman, *Love and Death: A Study in Censorship* (New York: Breaking Point, 1949).

46. Clarence Peterson, *The Bantam Story: Thirty Years of Paperback Publishing* (New York: Bantam Books, 1975), 13–14.

47. " 'Filth' in Books Scored," *New York Times*, April 14, 1950, 15.

48. "Dial Press Gift Books" (advertisement), *New York Times*, December 5, 1948, BR23.

49. In one of his *New Yorker* cartoons, Peter Arno points up the regularly sexy nature of historical fiction; a pretty model, bosom bursting out of her costume, asks her bald portraitist, "Don't you ever do anything but covers for historical novels, Mr. Carmichael?" (*Sizzling Platter* [New York: Simon and Schuster, 1949], 60.)

50. James MacBride, "Trigger Man's Genesis," *New York Times*, January 19, 1947, BR12.

51. Charles Gorham, *The Future Mister Dolan* (New York: Signet, 1948 [Signet, no. 752]). Paula Rabinowitz provides a terrific reading of the relationship between pulps, noirs, paperbacks, and fiction in "Pulping Ann Petry: The Case of *Country Place*," in *Revising the Blueprint: Ann Petry and the Literary Left*, ed. Alex Lubin (Jackson: UP of Mississippi, 2007), 49–71. Petry's *Country Place* (1947) is issued as Signet paperback, no. 761 in 1950.

52. David T. Bazelon, "The Dream Life of the New Woman: As Mirrored in Current 'Historical' Heroines," *Commentary* 8 (1949), 255.

53. Jack Woodford, *The Autobiography of Jack Woodford* (Garden City, NY: Doubleday, 1962), 323.

54. Felice Swados, "Two Types of Materialism: The Mechanical Materialism of Holbach and the Dialectical Materialism of Marx and Engels," master's thesis, Smith College, 1936. Felice Swados, "Negro Health on the Ante Bellum Plantations," *Bulletin of the History of Medicine* 10, no. 3 (1941): 460–72.

55. Felice Swados, *House of Fury* (New York: Avon, 1950), 47.

56. "Zonite for Newer Feminine Hygiene" (advertisement), *Modern Romances*, October 1946, 95. Different versions—for different brands—of this nightmarish ad appeared in many women's magazines throughout the decade. In *American Story* (New York: Harper and Row, 1968), the 1940s editors of *Ladies' Home Journal*, Bruce Gould and Beatrice Blackmar Gould, reveal that they refused to run this "repugnant" ad campaign in their magazine, which cost their publishers more than $250,000 (179–81).

57. Max Wylie, "Washboard Weepies," *Harper's*, November 1942, 635.

58. Jeanine Basinger, *A Woman's View: How Hollywood Spoke to Women, 1930–1960* (New York: Knopf, 1993); Christine Gledhill, ed., *Home Is Where the Heart Is: Studies in Melodrama and the Woman's Film* (London: British Film Institute, 1987); Helen Hanson, *Hollywood Heroines: Women in Film Noir and the Female Gothic Film* (New York: Tauris, 2007).

59. Hanson, *Hollywood Heroines*, 225–28.

60. On *China* as a woman's film, with Loretta Young's character as the center of interest, see Basinger, *A Woman's View*, 26–30. Basinger's reading is, as always, resourceful and persuasive. It also flies in the face of a full-page ad in *Photoplay* (June 1943, 5) that focuses entirely on Ladd. "Alan Ladd and Twenty Girls . . . Trapped by the Rapacious Japs!" screams the ad, which also provides two panels starring Ladd ("Alan Ladd dynamites a mountain") and promotes both director and William Bendix in their association with their earlier film, *Wake Island*. If this ad is meant to appeal to women (who supposedly did not want to see war movies during the war), it is not through an identification with Loretta Young, but through an idolization of hunky, shirtless, heroic Ladd.

61. "The Reviewer's Box," *Movieland,* August 1949, 88. And women will need to see some westerns if they want to ogle "John Wayne—Handsome Hunk of Sex Appeal!" as a cover caption exclaims.

62. du Maurier's *Frenchman's Creek* is serialized in five parts in *Ladies' Home Journal,* from October 1941 to February 1942.

63. Margaret Carpenter's *Experiment Perilous* and Anya Seton's *Dragonwyck* are condensed in the July 1943 and August 1943 issues of *Ladies' Home Journal.*

64. Mignon Eberhart, "Speak No Evil," *Ladies' Home Journal,* September 1940, 18.

65. *Ladies' Home Journal,* September 1943, 62. For an overview of Eberhart's many novels, see Rick Cypert, *America's Agatha Christie: Mignon Good Eberhart* (Selinsgrove, PA: Susquehanna UP, 2005).

66. John Crosby, "Murder Is Now Fashionable in the World of Soap Opera," *Boston Globe,* February 8, 1951, 20.

67. Herta Herzog, "What Do We Really Know about Daytime Serial Listeners?," in *Radio Research 1942–1943,* ed. Paul F. Lazarsfeld and Frank N. Stanton (New York: Arno, [1944] 1979), 10.

68. The descriptions of Mike Malone and Doria Van Dorn are taken from "In Living Portraits: Joyce Jordan, M.D," *Radio Mirror,* July 1947, 53.

69. "The Romance of Helen Trent," *Radio Mirror,* May 1940, 26, 27.

70. "Through the Years with Young Widder Brown," *Radio Mirror,* November 1948, 38.

71. "Through the Years with Young Widder Brown," 38.

72. "Big Sister: In Living Portraits," *Radio Mirror,* October 1947, 27.

73. "Joyce Jordan, Girl Interne," *Radio Mirror,* June 1940, 18.

74. "Bitter Marriage," *Radio Mirror,* January 1943, 9. A note says that this story was adapted from a program heard on "True Story Theater."

75. "Second Husband," *Radio Mirror,* Jan 1940, 12.

76. *Backstage Wife* episodes 3949 and 3928. In the following pages I refer to several episodes of *Backstage Wife* and *Big Sister* using episode numbers. The *Backstage Wife* episodes are from 1950, while the *Big Sister* episodes are from 1944; however, exact broadcast dates are unknown. If the interested reader wants to track them down using the numbers, these episodes are available on the Internet Archive (archive.org).

77. Crosby, "Murder Is Now Fashionable," 20.

78. Rudolf Arnheim, "The World of the Daytime Serial," in *Radio Research 1942–1943,* ed. Paul F. Lazarsfeld and Frank N. Stanton (New York: Arno, [1944] 1979), 49–55.

79. Arnheim, "World of the Daytime Serial," 59–60.

80. Arnheim, "World of the Daytime Serial," 44.

81. Postum is advertised on *Joyce Jordan* (6–7–44), and Bisodol on *Front Page Farrell* (8–10–45).

82. *Big Sister,* no. 8.

83. *Big Sister,* no. 15.

84. *Backstage Wife,* no. 3923.

85. *Big Sister,* no. 15.

86. *Backstage Wife*, no. 3916.

87. "Heroes and heroines of Hummert serials were subject to the usual string of half-crazed suitors who would stop at nothing to marry one or the other of the principals," writes Jim Cox, *The Great Radio Soap Operas* (Jefferson, NC: McFarland, 1999), 101.

88. James Thurber, "Soapland," *The Beast in Me and Other Animals* (New York: Harcourt, Brace, 1948), 218, 219.

89. Raymond William Stedman, *The Serials: Suspense and Drama by Installment* (Norman: U of Oklahoma P, 1971), 317.

90. Quoted by Stedman, *The Serials*, 345.

91. After warding off sexually aggressively Diane, John has, in the words of Jim Cox, a "torrid affair" with Ned's wife, Hope (*Big Sister*, *The Great Radio Soap Operas*, 33).

92. According to the genre distinctions of the day, "love pulps" are distinguished from "confession magazines." For example, we can compare two articles from a series of articles run on magazine genres: Thomas H. Uzzell, "The Love Pulps," *Scribner's*, April 1938, 36–41, and Harland Manchester, "True Stories: The Confession Magazines," *Scribner's*, August 1938, 25–29. All the magazines I discuss in this section have been identified as confession magazines in T. Peterson, *Magazines in the Twentieth Century*, 278–80.

93. Kathleen L. Endres, "True Story," in *Women's Periodicals in the United States: Consumer Magazines*, ed. Kathleen L. Endres and Therese L. Lueck (Westport, CT: Greenwood Press, 1995), 366.

94. Vera Stretz, "She Killed Own Fifth Column Nazi Lover," *True Story*, October 1940, 26ff. "His 10,000 Women Victims" ("a doctor's secretary-nurse tells all"), 34ff.

95. Maureen Honey provides a detailed analysis of how class, morality, and World War II propaganda fold together in *True Story* from 1941 to 1943 in "The Working-Class Woman and the Recruitment Campaign," in *Creating Rosie the Riveter: Class, Gender and Propaganda during World War II* (Amherst: U of Massachusetts P, 1984), 139–81.

96. "In My Wildest Dreams," *True Experiences*, June 1942, 21. After the husband attempts suicide, the couple eventually "slave and starve" their way back to financial solvency. The woman's moral conclusion justifies the horrors that they have experienced: "We love each other now, not just for the emotion that we feel when we are in each other's arms, but because we have suffered together" (71).

97. "Conventionally Yours," *True Experiences*, 38.

98. "Let the Past Alone," *Modern Romances*, October 1946, 25. The story's blurb says: "A strange and haunting story of a woman who was jealous of the dead" (23).

99. Adeline Bullock, "Masher Menace," *Modern Romances*, December 1947, 57ff; "Murder in My Mind," 40ff.

100. "My Free Lance Date," *Modern Romances*, October 1946, 62.

101. "He Took My Love—and Told," *True Confessions*, June 1942, 77.

102. "He Took My Love—and Told," 78.

103. Friedan, *Feminine Mystique*, 85–93.

104. Nancy A. Walker, *Shaping Our Mothers' World: American Women's Magazines* (Jackson: UP of Mississippi, 2000), 11.

105. Martha Foley, "Foreword," *The Best American Short Stories 1949* (Boston: Houghton Mifflin, 1949), x.

106. Mary McCarthy, "Up the Ladder from *Charm* to *Vogue*," *The Reporter*, August 1, 1950, 32.

107. Leslie Fiedler, *Love and Death in the American Novel* (New York: Stein and Day, 1966), 476.

108. Marianne Hauser, "The Other Side of the River," in *Prize Stories of 1948*, ed. Herschel Brickell (Garden City, NY: Doubleday, 1948), 124. Hauser's "Dark Dominion" was condensed in the December 1946 issue of *Harper's Bazaar*.

109. Gladys Schmitt, "The Mourners," *The Best American Short Stories 1945* (Boston: Houghton Mifflin, 1945), 237.

110. Bessie Breuer, "The Skeleton and the Easter Lily," in *Prize Stories of 1947*, ed. Herschel Brickell (Garden City, NY: Doubleday, 1947), 92.

111. In his "Introduction" to *Prize Stories of 1947*, Herschel Brickell says Bradbury's "Homecoming" (published in *Mademoiselle*) "invokes the shades of Irving, Poe, and Hawthorne," while a reader on the jury calls the story, admiringly, "outlandish, ghoulish, horrible" (xiii).

112. Trilling, *Reviewing the Forties*, 231.

113. Truman Capote, "Miriam," *A Tree of Night and Other Stories* (New York: Random House, 1949), 132.

114. Shirley Jackson, who would become one of the most celebrated writers of gothic fiction, published her early work most often in the *New Yorker* (including "The Lottery"), but many stories also appeared in women's magazines. Jackson's scary "The Daemon Lover" (*The Lottery and Other Stories* [New York: Farrar, Straus and Giroux, 1949], 9–28), appeared in an only slightly less disturbing version as "The Phantom Lover" in *Woman's Home Companion*, February 1949, 24ff. That magazine's cover shows two cute kids reading the Sunday comics, but Jackson's story punches a hole through their domestic tranquility.

115. Capote, "A Tree of Night," *A Tree of Night and Other Stories* (New York: Random House, 1949), 191–209. Page numbers are cited parenthetically in text hereafter.

116. Margaret Carpenter, "Experiment Perilous," *Ladies' Home Journal*, July 1943, 25.

117. Margaret Shedd, "The Great Fire of 1945," in *Prize Stories of 1947*, ed. Herschell Brickell (Garden City, NY: Doubleday, 1947), 223.

118. Shedd, "The Great Fire of 1945," 225.

119. Jane Cobb, "The Hot Day," *McCall's*, September 1946, 21. What is remarkable about this portrait of ferociously angry domesticity is that the anger never lets up. And even the story's blurb says so: "Yesterday's love was today's hatred—a hatred that held them captive and would not die with the setting sun" (20).

Conclusion. Two Phantom Women: Ruth Herschberger and Elizabeth Hawes

1. William Irish, *Phantom Lady* (New York: Norton, [1942] 1967), 12.

2. Irish, *Phantom Lady*, 104.

3. The most substantial discussion of Diana Trilling recently is by Gordon Hutner, "The 1940s," 194–268. Hutner uses comments by Trilling to annotate his extraordinarily useful survey of 1940s literature.

4. Legman, *Love and Death*, 74.

5. Quotations about Herschberger and Hawes both from *Love and Death*, 76.

6. Edgar Brooke, "Female of the Species," *New York Times*, August 1, 1948, BR20.

7. "For some inexplicable reason, one of the most feminist books, Ruth Herschberger's *Adam's Rib*, received no attention in the correspondence of women's rights supporters," write Leila J. Rupp and Verta Taylor, *Survival in the Doldrums: The American Women's Rights Movement, 1945 to the 1960s* (New York: Oxford UP, 1987), 21.

8. Susan Brownmiller, "Sisterhood Is Powerful," *New York Times*, March 15, 1970, 232.

9. Susan B. Anthony II, *Out of the Kitchen—Into the War: Woman's Winning Role in the Nation's Drama* (New York: Stephen Daye, 1943). Susan B. Anthony II is the great-niece of Susan B. Anthony; in *Out of the Kitchen*, Anthony focuses on women's qualifications to do work ordinarily done by men. But she does pause to critique society's expectations for female sexuality: "From the cradle to the grave women are adjured to chastity, though constantly urged to make themselves alluring" (18).

10. Dates for these *Cavalcade of America* episodes are: "Mehitabel Wing" (1–16–40), "Anne Royall" (2–20–40), "Jane Addams of Hull House" (5–21–40), "Susan B. Anthony" (6–18–40), and "Light in the Hills" (about Martha Berry, 11–27–40).

11. "American Woman's Dilemma," *Life*, June 16, 1947, 101–16. The wife's different roles are both pictured and captioned on page 106.

12. The best (and nearly only) treatment of Herschberger to date is Shira Tarrant, "No Woman Is an Island: Ruth Herschberger and Postwar Pollination," in *When Sex became Gender* (New York: Routledge, 2006), 195–212. Tarrant situates Herschberger's work within a feminist tradition and notes compelling parallels with Simone de Beauvoir's *The Second Sex* (1949).

13. *Adam's Rib*, 17.

14. *Adam's Rib*, 135.

15. "There are innumerable gentlemen who suggest that Scotch kilts are cool, practical and comfortable and, having worn skirts all my life, I am on their side." Elizabeth Hawes, *Men Can Take It* (New York: World Publishing, 1939), 252.

16. Elizabeth Hawes, *Why Women Cry: or, Wenches with Wrenches* (New York: Reynal and Hitchcock, 1943), 48.

17. Hawes, *Why Women Cry*, 50.

18. Hawes, *Why Women Cry*, 22.

19. Hawes, *Why Women Cry*, 32.

20. Hawes, *Why Women Cry*, 33.

21. Jane Cobb, "From Gusseting to Riveting," *New York Times*, December 5, 1943, BR5. For once the *New York Times* reviewer is up to the task. Jane Cobb occasionally wrote fiction, including the O. Henry prize-winning story "The Hot Day" (*McCall's* [September 1946]), which we met at the end of the previous chapter.

22. Bettina Berch, *Radical by Design: The Life and Style of Elizabeth Hawes* (New York: Dutton, 1988), 103.

23. Hawes, *Anything but Love*. Page numbers are cited parenthetically in text hereafter.

24. Friedan knew about Hawes and even wrote about her in the early 1940s, but as Daniel Horowitz has shown, the Friedan of *The Feminine Mystique* reinvented herself as a woman who had no political awareness in the 1940s. Hence Hawes was, for the sake of this myth of political awakening, retrospectively erased. For analysis of an article Friedan wrote on Hawes's *Why Women Cry*, see Daniel Horowitz, *Betty Friedan and the Making of the Feminine Mystique: The American Left, the Cold War, and Modern Feminism* (Amherst: U of Massachusetts P, 1998), 107–09.

25. S. J. Perelman, "Bend Down, Sister," in *The Dream Department* (New York: Random House, 1943), 71–78.

26. S. J. Perelman and Ogden Nash, *One Touch of Venus* (Boston: Little, Brown, 1944), 94.

27. Lewis Nichols, "One Touch of Venus," *New York Times*, October 17, 1943, X1.

28. Thomas Sugrue, "Goddesses or Women," *New York Times*, September 26, 1948, BR18.

29. Sugrue, "Goddesses or Women," BR18.

Selected Bibliography

What follows is a listing of most of the secondary criticism that I have found helpful. I also collect here many of the 1940s books that feature in my discussion, in addition to titles of cartoons, comics, films, radio programs, magazines, and songs.

Secondary Criticism

Adams, Rachel. " 'A Mixture of Delicious and Freak': The Queer Fiction of Carson McCullers." *American Literature* 71, no. 3 (1999): 551–83.

Adamson, Joe. *Tex Avery: King of Cartoons*. New York: Da Capo, 1985, 1975.

Austin, Reid Stewart. *Petty: The Classic Pin-Up Art of George Petty*. New York: Gramercy Books, 1997.

Bachmann, Monica. " 'Someone Like Debby': (De)Constructing a Lesbian Community of Readers." *GLQ: A Journal of Lesbian and Gay Studies* 6, no. 3 (2000): 377–88.

Bailey, Beth L. *From Front Porch to Back Seat: Courtship in Twentieth-Century America*. Baltimore, MD: Johns Hopkins UP, 1988.

Bannerman, R. LeRoy. *Norman Corwin and Radio: The Golden Years*. Tuscaloosa: U of Alabama P, 1986.

Barsam, Richard Meran. *Nonfiction Film: A Critical History*. New York: Dutton, 1973.

Basinger, Jeanine. *A Woman's View: How Hollywood Spoke to Women, 1930–1960*. New York: Knopf, 1993.

———. *The Star Machine*. New York: Knopf, 2007.

Bell-Metereau, Rebecca. "Male Impersonation before 1960." In *Hollywood Androgyny*, 63–115. New York: Columbia UP, 1993.

Benshoff, Harry M. *Monsters in the Closet: Homosexuality and the Horror Film*. New York: Manchester UP, 1997.

Berch, Bettina. *Radical by Design: The Life and Style of Elizabeth Hawes*. New York: Dutton, 1988.

Berish, Andrew S. *Lonesome Roads and Streets of Dreams: Place, Mobility and Race in Jazz of the 1930s and 40s*. Chicago: U of Chicago P, 2012.

Bernstein, Matthew. *Walter Wanger, Hollywood Independent*. Minneapolis: U of Minnesota P, 2000.

Berlant, Lauren. *The Female Complaint: The Unfinished Business of Sentimentality in American Culture*. Durham, NC: Duke UP, 2008.

Bradley, Marion Zimmer. *Checklist: A Complete, Cumulative Checklist of Lesbian, Variant, and Homosexual Fiction, in English, or Available in English Translation*. Rochester, TX: Library of Alexandria, 1960.

Breazeale, Kenon. "'In Spite of Women': *Esquire* Magazine and the Construction of the Male Consumer." *Signs* 20, no. 1 (1994): 1–22.

Bullough, Vern L., ed. *Before Stonewall: Activists for Gay and Lesbian Rights in Historical Context*. New York: Harrington Park, 2002.

Capsuto, Steven. "In the Beginning . . . Early Radio." In *Alternate Channels: The Uncensored Story of Gay and Lesbian Images on Radio and Television*, 13–21. New York: Ballantine, 2000.

Carby, Hazel V. "It Jus Be's Dat Way Sometime: The Sexual Politics of Women's Blues." In *The Jazz Cadence of American Culture*, ed. Robert G. O'Meally, 471–83. New York: Columbia UP, 1998.

Castle, Terry. *The Apparitional Lesbian: Female Homosexuality and Modern Culture*. New York: Columbia UP, 1993.

Castleman, Harry, and Walter J. Podrazik. *Watching TV: Four Decades of American Television*. New York: McGraw-Hill, 1982.

Chung, Hye Seung, *Hollywood Asian: Philip Ahn and the Politics of Cross-Ethnic Performance*. Philadelphia: Temple UP, 2006.

Collins, Max Allan, and George Hagenauer. *Men's Adventure Magazines in Postwar America*. Los Angeles: Taschen, 2004.

Courtney, Susan. *Hollywood Fantasies of Miscegenation: Spectacular Narratives of Gender and Race, 1903–1967*. Princeton, NJ: Princeton UP, 2005.

Cox, Jim. *The Great Radio Soap Operas*. Jefferson, NC: McFarland, 1999.

Creed, Barbara. *The Monstrous-Feminine: Film, Feminism, Psychoanalysis*. New York: Routledge, 1993.

Cripps, Thomas. *Making Movies Black: The Hollywood Message Movie from World War II to the Civil Rights Era*. New York: Oxford UP, 1993.

Custen, George Frederick. *Twentieth Century's Fox: Darryl F. Zanuck and the Culture of Hollywood*. New York: Basic Books, 1997.

Cypert, Rick. *America's Agatha Christie: Mignon Good Eberhart*. Selinsgrove, PA: Susquehanna UP, 2005.

Daly, Maureen, ed. *Profile of Youth: By Members of the Staff of Ladies' Home Journal*. Philadelphia: Lippincott, 1951.

Daniels, Les. *Wonder Woman: The Life and Times of the Amazon Princess*. San Francisco, CA: Chronicle Books, 2000.

Davis, Frank Marshall. *Writings of Frank Marshall Davis: A Voice of the Black Press*, ed. John Edgar Tidwell. Jackson: UP of Mississippi, 2007.

Desjardins, Mary, and Mark Williams. "'Are You Lonesome Tonight?': Gendered Address in *The Lonesome Gal* and *The Continental*." In *Communities of the*

Air: Radio Century, Radio Culture, ed. Susan Merrill Squier, 251–74. Durham, NC: Duke UP, 2003.

Dexter, Dave, Jr. *Playback: A Newsman/Record Producer's Hits and Misses from the Thirties to the Seventies*. New York: Billboard Publications, 1976.

Doane, Mary Ann. *The Desire to Desire: The Woman's Film of the 1940s*. Bloomington: Indiana UP, 1987.

Doherty, Thomas. *Hollywood's Censor: Joseph I. Breen and the Production Code Administration*. New York: Columbia UP, 2009.

———. *Projections of War: Hollywood, American Culture, and World War II*. New York: Columbia UP, 1993.

Donnelly, Liza. *Funny Ladies: The New Yorker's Greatest Women Cartoonists and Their Cartoons*. New York: Prometheus Books, 2005.

Dunning, John. *The Encyclopedia of Old-Time Radio*. New York: Oxford UP, 1998.

Endres, Kathleen L., and Therese L. Lueck, ed. *Women's Periodicals in the United States: Consumer Magazines*. Westport, CT: Greenwood Press, 1995.

Enyeart, James L. *Willard Van Dyke: Changing the World through Photography and Film*. Albuquerque: U of New Mexico P, 2008.

Epstein, Daniel Mark. *Nat King Cole*. New York: Farrar, Straus and Giroux, 1999.

Fiedler, Leslie. *Love and Death in the American Novel*. New York: Stein and Day, 1966.

Flora, Joseph M. *Vardis Fisher*. New York: Twayne, 1965.

Foster, Jeannette H. *Sex Variant Women in Literature*. Tallahassee, FL: Naiad Press, 1985.

Friedan, Betty. *The Feminine Mystique*. New York: Norton, 2001.

Fujiwara, Chris. *Jacques Tourneur: The Cinema of Nightfall*. Baltimore, MD: Johns Hopkins UP, 2000.

Furia, Philip. *Skylark: The Life and Times of Johnny Mercer*. New York: St. Martins, 2003.

Gaines, Jane. "The Showgirl and the Wolf." *Cinema Journal* 20 (Autumn 1980): 53–67.

Giddins, Gary. *Bing Crosby: A Pocketful of Dreams, The Early Years 1903–1940*. Boston: Little, Brown, 2001.

Greer, Germaine. *The Female Eunuch*. New York: McGraw-Hill, 1971.

Haining, Peter. *The Classic Era of American Pulp Magazines*. Chicago: Chicago Review Press, 2000.

Hand, Richard. *Terror on the Air! Horror Radio in America, 1931–1952*. Jefferson, NC: McFarland, 2006.

———. "Undead Radio: Zombies and the Living Dead on 1930s and 1940s Radio." In *Better Off Dead: The Evolution of the Zombie as Post-Human*, ed. Deborah Christie and Sarah Juliet Lauro, 39–49. New York: Fordham UP, 2011.

Hanson, Helen. *Hollywood Heroines: Women in Film Noir and the Female Gothic Film*. New York: Tauris, 2007.

Harker, Jaime. *America the Middlebrow: Women's Novels, Progressivism, and Middlebrow Authorship between the Wars*. Amherst: U of Massachusetts P, 2007.

Hartmann, Susan M. "Prescriptions for Penelope: Literature on Women's Obligations to Returning World War II Veterans." *Women's Studies* 5, no. 3 (1978): 223–39.

Heilbrun, Carolyn. *When Men Were the Only Models We Had: My Teachers Barzun, Fadiman, and Trilling*. Philadelphia: U of Pennsylvania P, 2002.

Hickett, Alice Payne. *60 Years of Best Sellers: 1895–1955*. New York: Bowker, 1956.

Hilmes, Michele. *Radio Voices: American Broadcasting, 1922–1952*. Minneapolis: U of Minnesota P, 1997.

Honey, Maureen. "The Working-Class Woman and the Recruitment Campaign." In *Creating Rosie the Riveter: Class, Gender and Propaganda during World War II*, 139–81. Amherst: U of Massachusetts P, 1984.

Horowitz, Daniel. *Betty Friedan and the Making of the Feminine Mystique: The American Left, the Cold War, and Modern Feminism*. Amherst: U of Massachusetts P, 1998.

Hutner, Gordon. *What America Read: Taste, Class, and the Novel: 1920–1960*. Chapel Hill: U of North Carolina P, 2009.

Jamieson, John. *Books for the Army: The Army Library Service in the Second World War*. New York: Columbia UP, 1950.

Kammen, Michael. *The Lively Arts: Gilbert Seldes and the Transformation of Cultural Criticism in the United States*. New York: Oxford UP, 1996.

Kimmel, Michael S. "Masculinity as Homophobia: Fear, Shame, and Silence." In *Toward a New Psychology of Gender*, ed. Mary M. Gergen and Sara N. Davis, 223–42. New York: Routledge, 1997.

King, Stephen. *Danse Macabre*. New York: Everest House, 1981.

Knaff, Donna B. *Beyond Rosie the Riveter: Women of World War II in American Popular Graphic Art*. Lawrence: UP of Kansas, 2012.

Knapp, Raymond. "Gender and Sexuality." In *The American Musical and the Performance of Personal Identity*, 209–15. Princeton, NJ: Princeton UP, 2009.

Leja, Michael. *Reframing Abstract Expressionism: Subjectivity and Painting in the 1940s*. New Haven, CT: Yale UP, 1993.

Lev, Peter. *Twentieth Century-Fox: The Zanuck-Skouras Years, 1935–1965*. Austin: U of Texas P, 2013.

Lotz, Rainer, and Ulrich Neuert. *The "AFRS" Jubilee Transcription Programs: An Exploratory Discography*. Frankfurt: Ruecker, 1985.

Loviglio, Jason. *Radio's Intimate Public: Network Broadcasting and Mass-Mediated Democracy*. Minneapolis: U of Minnesota P, 2005.

Mank, Gregory William. *Hollywood Cauldron: Thirteen Horror Films from the Genre's Golden Age*. Jefferson, NC: McFarland, 1994.

Massoni, Kelley. *Fashioning Teenagers: A Cultural History of "Seventeen" Magazine*. Walnut Creek, CA: Left Coast Press, 2010.

Mazzoni, Cristina. *She-Wolf: The Story of a Roman Icon*. New York: Cambridge UP, 2010.

McCracken, Allison. "Scary Women and Scarred Men: Suspense, Gender Trouble, and Postwar Change, 1942–50." In *Radio Reader: Essays in the Cultural His-*

tory of Radio, ed. Michele Hilmes and Jason Loviglio, 183–208. New York: Routledge, 2002.

McLuhan, Marshall. *The Mechanical Bride: Folklore of Industrial Man*. Boston: Beacon Press, [1951] 1970.

Merrill, Hugh. *Esky: The Early Years at "Esquire."* New Brunswick, NJ: Rutgers UP, 1995.

Moran, Jeffrey P. *Teaching Sex: The Shaping of Adolescence in the 20th Century*. Cambridge, MA: Harvard UP, 2000.

Mulvey, Laura. *Visual and Other Pleasures*. Bloomington: Indiana UP, 1989.

Murray, Matthew. " 'The Tendency to Deprave and Corrupt Morals': Regulation and Irregular Sexuality in Golden Age Radio Comedy." In *Radio Reader: Essays in the Cultural History of Radio*, ed. Michele Hilmes and Jason Loviglio, 135–56. New York: Routledge, 2002.

Nachman, Gerald. *Raised on Radio*. New York: Pantheon, 1998.

Newman, Kim. *Cat People*. London: British Film Institute, 1999.

Newman, Louise M. "Coming of Age, but Not in Samoa: Reflections on Margaret Mead's Legacy for Western Liberal Feminism." In *Reading Benedict/Reading Mead: Feminism, Race, and Imperial Visions*, ed. Dolores Janiewski and Lois W. Banner, 51–69. Baltimore, MD: Johns Hopkins UP, 2004.

Nyberg, Amy Kiste. *Seal of Approval: The History of the Comics Code*. Jackson: UP of Mississippi, 1998.

O'Brien, Patty. *The Pacific Muse: Exotic Femininity and the Colonial Pacific*. Seattle: U of Washington P, 2006.

Paul, William. "What Does Dr. Judd Want? Transformation, Transference, and Divided Selves in *Cat People*." In *Horror Film and Psychoanalysis: Freud's Worst Nightmare*, ed. Steven Jay Schneider, 159–176. New York: Cambridge UP, 2004.

Pendergast, Tom. *Creating the Modern Man: American Magazines and Consumer Culture, 1900–1950*. Columbia: U of Missouri P, 2000.

Peterson, Theodore. *Magazines in the Twentieth Century*. Urbana: U of Illinois P, 1956.

Place-Verghnes, Floriane. *Tex Avery: A Unique Legacy, 1942–1955*. Eastleigh, UK: John Libbey, 2006.

Rabinowitz, Paula. *Black and White and Noir: America's Pulp Modernism*. New York: Columbia UP, 2002.

———. "Pulping Ann Petry: The Case of *Country Place*." In *Revising the Blueprint: Ann Petry and the Literary Left*, ed. Alex Lubin, 49–71. Jackson: UP of Mississippi, 2007.

Ramsay, Guthrie P., Jr. *Race Music: Black Cultures from Bebop to Hip-Hop*. Berkeley: U of California P, 2004.

Reed, Teresa. *The Holy Profane: Religion in Black Popular Music*. Lexington: U of Kentucky P, 2003.

Richmond, Peter. *Fever: The Life and Music of Miss Peggy Lee*. New York: Holt, 2006.

Robbins, Trina. *The Great Women Superheroes.* Northampton, MA: Kitchen Sink Press, 1996.

Roberts, Shari. "'The Lady in the Tutti-Frutti Hat': Carmen Miranda, a Spectacle of Ethnicity." *Cinema Journal* 32 (1993): 3–23.

Roof, Judith. *All about Thelma and Eve: Sidekicks and Third Wheels.* Urbana: U of Illinois P, 2002.

Rupp, Leila J., and Verta Taylor. *Survival in the Doldrums: The American Women's Rights Movement, 1945 to the 1960s.* New York: Oxford UP, 1987.

Ryan, Patrick A. "'Our Miss Brooks': Broadcasting Domestic Ideals for the Female Teacher in the Postwar United States." *NWSA Journal* 21, no. 1 (Spring 2009): 76–100.

Sampson, Henry T. *That's Enough, Folks: Black Images in Animated Cartoons, 1900–1960.* Lanham, MD: Scarecrow, 1990.

Savage, Jon. *Teenage: The Creation of Youth Culture.* New York: Viking Press, 2007.

Savage, William W., Jr. *Commies, Cowboys, and Jungle Queens: Comic Books and America, 1945–1954.* Hanover, NH: Wesleyan UP, 1998.

Scanlon, Jennifer. *Inarticulate Longings: The Ladies' Home Journal, Gender, and the Promises of Consumer Culture.* New York: Routledge, 1995.

Schatz, Thomas. *Boom and Bust: The American Cinema of the 1940s.* New York: Scribner, 1997.

Scheiner, Georganne. *Signifying Female Adolescence: Film Representations and Fans, 1920–1950.* Westport, CT: Praeger, 2000.

Schrum, Kelly. *Some Wore Bobby Sox: The Emergence of Teenage Girls' Culture, 1920–1945.* New York: Palgrave Macmillan, 2004.

Seldes, Gilbert. *The Public Arts.* New York: Simon and Schuster, 1956.

Semonche, John E. *Censoring Sex: A Historical Journey through American Media.* Lanham, MD: Rowman and Littlefield, 2007.

Showalter, Elaine. *A Jury of Her Peers: American Women Writers from Anne Bradstreet to Annie Proulx.* New York: Knopf, 2009.

Shteir, Rachel. "Striptease during the War." In *Striptease: The Untold History of the Girlie Show,* 215–33. New York: Oxford UP, 2004.

Sklaroff, Lauren Rebecca. *Black Culture and the New Deal: The Quest for Civil Rights in the Roosevelt Era.* Chapel Hill: U of North Carolina P, 2009.

Slide, Anthony. *Inside the Hollywood Fan Magazine: A History of Star Makers, Fabricators, and Gossip Mongers.* Jackson: UP of Mississippi, 2010.

Sloane, David E. ed. *American Humor Magazines and Comic Periodicals.* New York: Greenwood Press, 1987.

Smith, Ken. *Mental Hygiene: Classroom Films 1945–1970.* New York: Blast Books, 1999.

Starr, Cecile, ed. *Ideas on Film.* New York: Funk and Wagnalls, 1951.

Starr, Larry, and Christopher Waterman. *American Popular Music from Minstrelsy to MP3.* New York: Oxford UP, 2007.

Stedman, Raymond William. *The Serials: Suspense and Drama by Installment.* Norman: U of Oklahoma P, 1971.

Stein, Daniel. *Music Is My Life: Louis Armstrong, Autobiography and American Jazz.* Ann Arbor: U of Michigan P, 2012.

Tarrant, Shira. "No Woman Is an Island: Ruth Herschberger and Postwar Pollination." *When Sex became Gender*, 195–212. New York: Routledge, 2006.

Taubig, Klaus. *Straighten Up and Fly Right: A Chronology and Discography of Nat "King" Cole.* Westport, CT: Greenwood, 1994.

Townsend, Peter. *Pearl Harbor Jazz: Change in Popular Music in the Early 1940s.* Jackson: UP of Mississippi, 2007.

Trilling, Diana. *The Beginning of the Journey: The Marriage of Diana and Lionel Trilling.* New York: Harcourt Brace, 1993.

———. *Mrs. Harris: The Death of the Scarsdale Diet Doctor.* New York: Harcourt Brace Jovanovich, 1981.

———. *Reviewing the Forties.* New York: Harcourt Brace Jovanovich, 1978.

———. *We Must March My Darlings.* New York: Harcourt Brace Jovanovich, 1977.

Wagner, Jessica Lauren. *"An Unpleasant Wartime Function": Race, Film Censorship, and the Office of War Information, 1942–45.* Master's thesis, University of Maryland–College Park, 2007.

Wald, Gayle. "Mezz Mezzrow and the Voluntary Negro Blues." In *Crossing the Line: Racial Passing in Twentieth-Century U.S. Literature and Culture*, 53–81. Durham, NC: Duke UP, 2000.

Walker, Nancy A. *Shaping Our Mothers' World: American Women's Magazines.* Jackson: UP of Mississippi, 2000.

Ware, Susan. *It's One O'clock and Here Is Mary Margaret McBride: A Radio Biography.* New York: New York UP, 2005.

Weaver, Tom. *Science Fiction Stars and Horror Heroes.* Jefferson, NC: McFarland, 2006.

White, Patricia. *Uninvited: Classical Hollywood Cinema and Lesbian Representability.* Bloomington: Indiana UP, 1999.

Wolf, Stacy Ellen. *A Problem Like Maria: Gender and Sexuality in the American Musical.* Ann Arbor: U of Michigan P, 2002.

Wolseley, Roland E. *The Magazine World: An Introduction to Magazine Journalism.* New York: Prentice-Hall, 1951.

Woodford, Jack. *The Autobiography of Jack Woodford.* Garden City, NY: Doubleday, 1962.

1940s Fiction

Block, Libbie. *Wild Calendar.* New York: Knopf, 1946.

Bolton, Isabel. "The Christmas Tree." In *New York Mosaic*, 131–266. South Royalton, VT: Steerforth Press, 1998.

———. "Do I Wake or Sleep." In *New York Mosaic*, 3–124. South Royalton, VT: Steerforth Press, 1998.

Caldwell, Erskine. *Trouble in July.* New York: Grosset and Dunlop, 1940.

Capote, Truman. *A Tree of Night and Other Stories*. New York: Random House, 1949.
Cheever, John. "The Enormous Radio." *New Yorker*, May 17, 1947, 28–33.
Cobb, Jane. "The Hot Day." *McCall's*, September 1946.
Creekmore, Hubert. *The Welcome*. New York: Appleton-Century-Crofts, 1948.
du Maurier, Daphne. *Frenchman's Creek*. Garden City, NY: Doubleday, Doran, 1942.
Fisher, Vardis. *Adam and the Serpent*. New York: Vanguard, 1947.
———. *Darkness and the Deep*. New York: Vanguard, 1943.
———. *The Golden Rooms*. New York: Vanguard, 1944.
"He Took My Love—and Told." *True Confessions*, June 1942.
Himes, Chester. *If He Hollers Let Him Go*. Cambridge, MA: Da Capo, [1945] 2002.
Irish, William. *Phantom Lady*. New York: Norton, [1942] 1967.
Jackson, Charles. *The Sunnier Side: Twelve Arcadian Tales*. New York: Farrar, Straus, 1950.
Jackson, Shirley. *The Lottery and Other Stories*. New York: Farrar, Straus and Giroux, 1949.
Karloff, Boris, ed. *And the Darkness Falls*. Cleveland, OH: World Publishing, 1946.
Lees, Hannah. *Till the Boys Come Home*. New York: Harper, 1944.
Marquand, John. *Repent in Haste*. Boston: Little, Brown, 1945.
McCullers, Carson. *Complete Novels*. New York: Library of America, 2001.
Moore, C. L. "No Woman Born." *Astounding Science Fiction*, December 1944.
Morley, Susan. *Mistress Glory*. New York: Signet, 1948.
Parsons, Alice Beal. *I Know What I'd Do*. New York: Dutton, 1946.
Petry, Ann. *Country Place*. Boston: Houghton Mifflin, 1947.
Schorer, Mark. "The Long Embrace." *Esquire*, June 1941.
Shedd, Margaret. "The Great Fire of 1945." *Harper's Bazaar*, July 1946.
Rice, Jane. "The Refugee." *Unknown Worlds*, October 1943.
Ross, Nancy Wilson. *The Left Hand Is the Dreamer*. New York: Sloane, 1947.
Sinclair, Jo. *Wasteland*. New York: Harper, 1946.
Speers, Mary. *We Are Fires Unquenchable*. Hollywood, CA: Murray and Gee, 1942.
Stafford, Jean. *The Mountain Lion*. New York: Farrar, Straus and Giroux, 1947.
Swados, Felice. *House of Fury*. New York: Avon, [1941] 1950.
Williams, Ben Ames. *Leave Her to Heaven*. Boston: Houghton Mifflin, 1944.
Winsor, Kathleen. *Forever Amber*. New York: Macmillan, 1944.
———. *Star Money*. New York: Appleton-Century-Crofts, 1950.

1940s Nonfiction and Miscellaneous Books

Burley, Dan. *Original Handbook of Harlem Jive*. New York: Dan Burley, 1944.
Corwin, Norman. *More by Corwin: Sixteen Radio Dramas by Norman Corwin*. New York: Holt, 1944.
———. *Thirteen by Corwin: Radio Dramas by Norman Corwin*. New York: Holt, 1942.

Gorham, Ethel. *So Your Husband's Gone to War!* Garden City, NY: Doubleday, Doran, 1942.

Johnson, B. Lamar, and Eloise Lindstrom, ed. *General Education: A Report of Library-Instructional Activities at Stephens College*. Chicago: American Library Association, 1948.

Johnson, Roy Ivan. *Explorations in General Education: The Experiences of Stephens College*. New York: Harper, 1947.

Lait, Jack, and Lee Mortimer. *New York Confidential*. Chicago: Ziff-Davis, 1948.

Meyer, Agnes E. *Journey through Chaos*. New York: Harcourt, Brace, 1944.

Mich, Daniel D., ed. *The Technique of the Picture Story: A Practical Guide to the Production of Visual Articles*. New York: McGraw-Hill, 1945.

Ross, Nancy Wilson. *The Waves: The Story of the Girls in Blue*. New York: Holt, 1943.

———. *Westward the Women*. New York: Random House, 1944.

Thurber, James, and Elliott Nugent. *The Male Animal*. New York: Random House, 1940.

Waldron, Gloria. *The Information Film*. New York: Columbia UP, 1949.

Wilder, Margaret Buell. *Since You Went Away: Letters to a Soldier from His Wife*. New York: McGraw-Hill, 1943.

Wilson, Edmund. *Literary Reviews of the 1930s and 40s*. New York: Library of America, 2007.

1940s Studies of Popular Culture

Agee, James. *Agee on Film*. Boston: Beacon Press, 1964.

Arnheim, Rudolf. "The World of the Daytime Serial." In *Radio Research 1942–1943*, ed. Paul F. Lazarsfeld and Frank N. Stanton, 34–85. New York: Arno, [1944] 1979.

Bazelon, David T. "The Dream Life of the New Woman: As Mirrored in Current 'Historical' Heroines." *Commentary* 8 (1949): 252–57.

Cantril, Hadley. *The Invasion from Mars*. Princeton, NJ: Princeton UP, 1940.

Farber, Manny. *Farber on Film: The Complete Film Writings of Manny Farber*. New York: Library of America, 2009.

Ferguson, Otis. *The Film Criticism of Otis Ferguson*, ed. Robert Wilson. Philadelphia: Temple UP, 1971.

Gorer, Geoffrey. *The American People: A Study in National Character*. New York: Norton, 1948.

Hawes, Elizabeth. *Anything but Love*. New York: Rinehart, 1948.

Horkheimer, Max, and Theodor W. Adorno. "The Culture Industry: Enlightenment as Mass Deception," trans. John Cumming. In *Dialectic of Enlightenment*, 120–67. New York: Continuum, 1989.

Kirby, Edward M., and Jack W. Harris. *Star-Spangled Radio*. Chicago: Ziff-Davis, 1948.

Kracauer, Siegfried. "Hollywood's Terror Films: Do They Reflect an American State of Mind?" *Commentary* 2 (1946): 132–36.

Lazarsfeld, Paul F., and Frank Stanton, ed. *Communications Research 1948–49*. New York: Harper, 1949.

———. *Radio Research 1942–1943*. New York: Arno, [1944] 1979.

Legman, Gershon. *Love and Death: A Study in Censorship*. New York: Breaking Point, 1949.

Marston, William Moulton. "Why 100,000,000 Americans Read Comics." *American Scholar* 13 (1944): 35–44.

McCarthy, Mary. "Up the Ladder from *Charm* to *Vogue*." *Reporter*, August 1, 1950, 32–35.

Merton, Robert K. *Mass Persuasion: The Social Psychology of a War Bond Drive*. New York: Harper, 1946.

Riesman, David. *The Lonely Crowd: A Study of the Changing American Character*. New Haven, CT: Yale UP, 1950.

Rovere, Richard. "American Magazines in Wartime." *New Republic*, March 6, 1944, 308–12.

Schramm, Wilbur, ed. *Communications in Modern Society: Fifteen Studies of the Mass Media Prepared for the University of Illinois Institute of Communications Research*. Urbana: U of Illinois P, 1948.

Seldes, Gilbert. *The Great Audience*. New York: Viking, 1950.

Thurber, James. "Soapland." In *The Beast in Me and Other Animals*, 189–260. New York: Harcourt, Brace, 1948.

Whiting, John R., and George R. Clark. "The Picture Magazines." *Harper's*, July 1943, 159–69.

Wolfenstein, Martha, and Nathan Leites. *Movies: A Psychological Study*. Glencoe, IL: Free Press, 1950.

Wood, James Playsted. *Magazines in the United States: Their Social and Economic Influence*. New York: Ronald Press, 1949.

Wylie, Max. "Washboard Weepies." *Harper's*, November 1942, 633–38.

1940s Gender and Sexuality

"American Woman's Dilemma." *Life*, June 16, 1947, 101–16.

Anthony, Susan B., II. *Out of the Kitchen—Into the War: Woman's Winning Role in the Nation's Drama*. New York: Stephen Daye, 1943.

Ben, Lisa. *Vice Versa*. 1947–1948. Facsimile issues of *Vice Versa* are available online at www.queermusicheritage.us/viceversa.html (July 1, 2013).

Benedek, Therese. *Insight and Personality Adjustment: A Study of the Psychological Effects of the War*. New York: Ronald Press, 1946.

Bowman, Henry A. "Are Girls becoming the Pursuers?" *American*, April 1945, 32–33, 102–04.

———. *Marriage for Moderns*. New York: McGraw-Hill, 1948.

Bowman, Henry A., and Priscilla Scott, "Looks that Men Like." *American*, January 1948, 42–43, 125.

Cummings, Parke. "Specifications for Superwife." *Esquire*, July 1942, 108.
De Prorok, Count Bryon. "Sahara She-Wolves." *Argosy*, November 1947, 40–41, 110.
Frederick, J. George. "From Babe to Battle-Axe." *Esquire*, June 1944, 38–39.
Goldwater, Ethel. "Woman's Place: The New Alliance of 'Science' and Anti-Feminism." *Commentary* 4 (1947), 578–85.
Hawes, Elizabeth. *Why Women Cry: or, Wenches with Wrenches*. New York: Reynal and Hitchcock, 1943.
Herschberger, Ruth. *Adam's Rib*. New York: Pellegrini and Cudahy, 1948.
Keating, Walter. *Sex Studies from Freud to Kinsey*. New York: Stravon, 1949.
Kinsey, Alfred C., Wardell B. Pomeroy, and Clyde E. Martin. *Sexual Behavior in the Human Male*. Philadelphia: Saunders, 1948.
Landis, Carney, and M. Marjorie Bolles. *Personality and Sexuality of the Physically Handicapped Woman*. New York: Hoeber, 1942.
Leekoff, Milton. "Why College Men Are Sexually Inferior." *Stag*, July 1950, 14–15, 50.
Lees, Hannah. "The Word You Can't Say." *Hygeia* 22 (May 1944): 336–37.
Lundberg, Ferdinand, and Marynia F. Farnham. *Modern Woman: The Lost Sex*. New York: Harper, 1947.
Maslow, A. H. "Self-Esteem (Dominance Feeling) and Sexuality in Women." *Journal of Social Psychology* 16 (1942): 259–94.
Mead, Margaret. *Male and Female: A Study of the Sexes in a Changing World*. New York: Morrow, 1949.
Perelman, S. J. "Bend Down, Sister." In *The Dream Department*, 71–78. New York: Random House, 1943.
Scheinfeld, Amram. *Women and Men*. New York: Harcourt, Brace, 1944.
Silver, Abner. *All Women Are Wolves*. New York: Readers' Press, 1945.
Trilling, Diana. "Men, Women, and Sex." *Partisan Review* 17 (1950): 365–78.
Women in Radio: Illustrated by Biographical Sketches. May 1947, Women's Bureau, U.S. Department of Labor, Bulletin No. 222.
Women in Wartime. Chicago: Institute for Psychoanalysis, 1943.
Wylie, Philip. *Generation of Vipers*. New York: Farrar and Rinehart, 1942.
Wylie, Philip. *Opus 21: Descriptive Music for the Lower Kinsey Epoch of the Atomic Age/A Concerto for a One-Man Band/Six Arias for Soap Operas/Fugues, Anthems, and a Barrelhouse*. New York: Rinehart, 1949.

Cartoons and Comics

Arno, Peter. *Sizzling Platter*. New York: Simon and Schuster, 1949.
Caniff, Milton. *Male Call: The Complete War Time Strip: 1942–1946*, ed. Peter Poplaski. Princeton, WI: Kitchen Sink Press, 1987.
Capp, Al. *Li'l Abner: Dailies Volume 10: 1944*, ed. Dave Schreiner. Princeton, WI: Kitchen Sink Press, 1990.

Capp, Al. *Li'l Abner: Dailies Volume 12: 1946*, ed. Dave Schreiner. Princeton, WI: Kitchen Sink Press, 1991.
Cow Cow Boogie. Directed by Alex Lovey. 1943. Walter Lantz Productions.
Little 'Tinker. Directed by Tex Avery. 1949. MGM.
Private Snafu: Booby Traps. 1944. Warner Brothers.
Red Hot Riding Hood. Directed by Tex Avery. 1943. MGM.
Sansone, Sgt. Leonard. *The Wolf.* New York: United Publishers, 1945.
Swing Shift Cinderella. Directed by Tex Avery. 1945. MGM.
Tiger Girl in *Fight Comics*, 1944–1950. Fiction House.

Films

Annie Get Your Gun. Directed by George Sidney. 1950. MGM.
Bachelor and the Bobby-Soxer, The. Directed by Irving Reis. 1947. RKO.
Bedlam. Directed by Mark Robson. 1946. RKO.
Bombs over Burma. Directed by Joseph H. Lewis. 1942. PRC.
Captive Wild Woman. Directed by Edward Dmytryk. 1943. Universal.
Cat People. Directed by Jacques Tourneur. 1942. RKO.
China. Directed by John Farrow. 1943. Paramount.
China Girl. Directed by Henry Hathaway. 1942. Twentieth Century-Fox.
Choosing for Happiness. Directed by Willard Van Dyke. 1950. Affiliated Film Producers.
Cobra Woman. Directed by Robert Siodmak. 1944. Universal.
Duel in the Sun. Directed by King Vidor. 1946. Vanguard Films.
Frenchman's Creek. Directed by Mitchell Leisen. 1944. Paramount.
Here Come the Waves. Directed by Mark Sandrich. 1944. Paramount.
How Doooo You Do? Directed by Ralph Murphy. 1945. PRC.
It Takes All Kinds. Directed by Alexander Hammid. 1950. Affiliated Film Producers.
Laura. Directed by Otto Preminger. 1944. Twentieth Century-Fox.
Leave Her to Heaven. Directed by John M. Stahl. 1945. Twentieth Century-Fox.
Marriage Today. Directed by Alexander Hammid. 1950. Affiliated Film Producers.
Miracle of Morgan's Creek, The. Directed by Preston Sturges. 1944. Paramount.
Next Voice You Hear, The. Directed by William Wellman. 1950. MGM.
Perils of Pauline, The. Directed by George Marshall. 1947. Paramount.
Rebecca. Directed by Alfred Hitchcock. 1940. Selznick International Pictures.
Red, Hot, and Blue. Directed by John Farrow. 1949. Paramount.
Shanghai Gesture, The. Directed by Josef von Sternberg. 1941. Arnold Productions.
Since You Went Away. Directed by John Cromwell. 1944. Selznick International Pictures.
Son of Fury. Directed by John Cromwell. 1942. Twentieth Century-Fox.
Sundown. Directed by Henry Hathaway. 1941. Walter Wanger Pictures.
Swing Shift Maisie. Directed by Norman McLeod. 1943. MGM.

Tarzan and the Leopard Woman. Directed by Kurt Neumann. 1946. Sol Lesser Productions.

Tender Comrade. Directed by Edward Dmytryk. 1943. RKO.

This Charming Couple. Directed by Willard Van Dyke. 1950. Affiliated Film Producers.

Thunder Birds. William Wellman. 1942. Twentieth Century-Fox.

Turnabout. Directed by Hal Roach, 1940. Hal Roach Studios.

Very Thought of You, The. Directed by Delmer Daves. 1944. Warner Brothers.

Who's Boss. Directed by Alexander Hammid. 1950. Affiliated Film Producers.

Magazines

Argosy.
Billboard.
Calling All Girls.
Capitol News from Hollywood.
Down Beat.
Esquire.
Film Fun.
Harper's Bazaar.
Ladies' Home Journal.
Life.
Mademoiselle.
Modern Romances.
Movie Teen.
Photoplay.
Radio Mirror.
Saturday Evening Post.
Seventeen.
Spicy Detective Stories.
Time.
True Confessions.
True Story.
True: The Man's Magazine.

Records Released by Capitol

Ella Mae Morse. "Cow Cow Boogie." Capitol 102, 1942.
Johnny Mercer. "Strip Polka." Capitol 103, 1942.
Nat King Cole. "All for You." Capitol 139, 1942.
Nat King Cole. "Vom Vim Veedle." Capitol 139, 1942.

Johnny Mercer. "G.I. Jive." Capitol 141, 1943.
Ella Mae Morse. "No Love, No Nothin'." Capitol 143, 1943.
Ella Mae Morse. "Milkman, Keep Those Bottles Quiet." Capitol 151, 1944.
Ella Mae Morse. "The Patty Cake Man." Capitol 163, 1944.
Nat King Cole. "I Realize Now." Capitol 169, 1944.
Ella Mae Morse. "Hello Suzanne." Capitol 176, 1944.
Johnny Mercer. "Accentuate the Positive." Capitol 180, 1944.
Betty Hutton. "Stuff Like That There." Capitol 188, 1945.
Nat King Cole. "Bring Another Drink." Capitol 192, 1945.
Johnny Mercer. "De Camptown Races." Capitol 217, 1945.
Nat King Cole. "Frim Fram Sauce." Capitol 224, 1945.
Ella Mae Morse. "Buzz Me." Capitol 226, 1945.
Peggy Lee. "I Don't Know Enough about You." Capitol 236, 1946.
Ella Mae Morse. "The House of Blue Lights." Capitol 251, 1946.
Johnny Mercer. "Ugly Chile." Capitol 268, 1946.
Nat King Cole. "You Call It Madness but I Call It Love." Capitol 274, 1946.
Peggy Lee. "Aren't You Kind of Glad We Did?" Capitol 292, 1946.
Peggy Lee. "It's Lovin' Time." Capitol 343, 1946.
Ella Mae Morse. "Get Off It and Go." Capitol 424, 1947.
Peggy Lee. "It Takes a Long, Long Train (with a Red Caboose)." Capitol 445, 1947.
Kay Starr. "You've Got to See Mama Every Night." Capitol 497, 1947.

Radio Programs

Backstage Wife.
Big Sister.
Cavalcade of America.
Columbia Workshop.
Command Performance.
Date with Judy, A.
Great Gildersleeve. The.
Jack Benny Program, The.
Johnny Mercer's Music Shop.
Jubilee.
Lux Radio Theatre.
Maisie.
Our Miss Brooks.
Pat Novak for Hire.
Pepsodent Show Starring Bob Hope, The.
Suspense.

Index

Note: Titles with dates refer to films